The Meanings of Social Interaction:
An Introduction to Social Psychology

THE REYNOLDS SERIES IN SOCIOLOGY

Larry T. Reynolds, *Editor*

by **GENERAL HALL, INC.**

The Meanings of Social Interaction: An Introduction to Social Psychology

Jeffrey E. Nash
Southwest Missouri State University
and
James M. Calonico
Social Work Consultant
San Francisco, California

GENERAL HALL, INC.
Publishers
5 Talon Way
Dix Hills, New York 11746

The Meanings of Social Interaction:
An Introduction to Social Psychology

GENERAL HALL, INC.
5 Talon Way
Dix Hills, New York 11746

Publisher: Ravi Mehra
Composition: *Graphics Division,* General Hall, Inc.

LIBRARY OF CONGRESS CATALOG CARD NUMBER: **96–75605**

ISBN: 1–882289–29–3 [paper]
      1–882289–30–7 [cloth]

Manufactured in the United States of America

Contents

Preface

To us as ordinary, everyday citizens of the world, perhaps the least obvious fact of society (of social life) is that we are in it. Most of us go about our daily lives without ever thinking about where we live, how we came to be who we are, or just what makes up the mechanics and dynamics of our lives. And this is a good thing; for although we might find some agreement with Socrates, that life without reflection is not worth living, we must also admit that a society of individuals continuously caught up in self-reflection might well accomplish very little of what must be done to carry on with life. So it is, then, rather natural that most persons are born into worlds about which they are taught and in which they learn to play roles and act out parts without ever paying much attention to the hows and whys of it all. Peoples' societies and the roles they play become, as it were, "second nature" to them, so seldom do they notice even their own presence.

On the other hand, it is the "job" of social psychology to analyze and discuss social life, the relationship between society and the individual, and the mechanisms by which new members of a society come to learn about who and where they are and how they can sustain membership in the groups of which they are a part. These and the many other related issues of social psychology make up the basis of this text. And an Appendix is included to present briefly the methods used to study them.

Now ours is but one version of how to study social interaction. But there is no need to detail here the various approaches to social psychology. Suffice it to say that many are more psychologically oriented, perhaps placing great importance on instinct as a motivator for human behavior. Others are more sociological, emphasizing the role of institutions, like school and the family, in shaping development.

In the present work we place ourselves firmly within the perspective of what is known as "symbolic interactionism." Here we detail some of the intricacies of this school of thought; and while we do not wish to debate its relative merits over other versions of social psychology, we can note that it seems the most natural to us. We demonstrate this by calling up its major tenet, namely, that human beings interact through the use of symbols. The fact that you are reading this text itself embodies this principle, for written language is perhaps the most sophisticated system of symbolic communication. But reading-and-writing is only one form of symbolic interaction. Rather, it is the spoken language which plays a greater role in most of our lives, whether this involves making our way into

ix

selfhood as children or becoming members of groups once we have already learned to interact.

It is by introducing our readers to symbolic interactionism, then, that we hope also to equip them with the tools to reflect upon themselves, their worlds, and the ways they use to negotiate their way through everyday life. To be sure, the world in which we now live seems to be changing more rapidly than ever. Today, to be able to understand one's world from a well-founded social psychological perspective is a critical skill, for it is only from such a foundation that the reasonable decisions which will affect one's future can be made.

All of us know best that which is most familiar to us, but we know that we understand what we have learned only when we can successfully apply it to the unfamiliar. The following pages result from the application of a set of principles to the ordinary, everyday behavior of people mostly outside our readers' lives. If our readers can learn from this how to apply those principles in such a way as to better understand the meaningfulness of their own lives, we will have been successful at our task.

In conclusion, we would like to acknowledge those who helped us get started. First, Larry Reynolds interested us in beginning with *Social Psychology: Self and Society* and working toward a new text more interactionist in perspective; and Clark Baxter, of West Publishing Company, allowed us to do this. Finally, of course, we are indebted to Euphemia and Patti, who provide perspectives of a different kind.

Chapter 1

Sociological Social Psychology

"What is the relationship between the 'individual' and 'society'?" This is perhaps the primary question of social psychology. We answer it from our conviction that societies and the individuals who constitute them are inseparable phenomena. One implies the other; so when we explore deeply the experiences of individuals, whether those experiences are attitudes they espouse, political protests they participate in, or simply their conduct in everyday life, we discover collective or social phenomena. Likewise, when we investigate collective phenomena, say, the pro-life movement, we come face to face with individuals, their emotions, motives and skills in dealing with other people. As Charles H. Cooley expressed it, individual and society are "twin born," two sides of the same coin. We want to discover what the coin itself is like.

The rich and far-reaching literature we rely on teaches that the best approach to appreciating the nature of the "coin" involves viewing the lives of individuals in a pragmatic way, starting with what we find when we consciously attend to the world immediately around us. In describing how people do things with one another, how they interact and learn to accomplish tasks as simple as greeting one another or as complex as falling in love, we engage the social world. In that world, people are agents; they learn to do and re-do social things. Moreover, they understand that what they are doing *means* something; and it is in the complex matrix of what we commonly call "meanings" that we discover the relationship between individual and society, between agents and the products of their agency. The "coin" we are after, then, is social meanings.

How many times have you heard or used some form of the expression "Do you know what I mean?"

"The dude come up on me, so I jus' dipped 'im right there. Y' unnerstan' what I'm sayin'."

"So I said, like, 'Why don't we go to the mall now, and then go to the beach.' Y'know."

"I said 11 o'clock at night, not one o'clock in the morning. Do you know what I mean, young lady?"

"O.K. listen up! We're gonna run a two-one-two zone and we're gonna sag on the big man in the paint. Y'got that?"

"Just let me say one thing. I am the President, and I am not a crook. Do I make myself perfectly clear?"

1

"Now, I got to admit it. The man played a mean piano. But when it come to the composition, he couldn't polish the keys for the Monk. You dig?"

Each of these six expressions comes from a different world of social meaning and seeks to establish a different kind of understanding, for to know what is meant by each requires a unique knowledge. In the first expression, the speaker might be describing a killing or at least some act of violence and is evoking what he believes are commonly accepted grounds that justify such acts. The "dude come up" or threatened or somehow encroached on the speaker's sense of territory and was therefore "dipped" or repelled, shot or struck down with a fist or weapon. While the details of the occurrence might be pertinent to a trial, they are not so for the speaker's appeal for understanding. In this expression, the speaker wants his listener to know that the action he took was perfectly normal as "street life." To "unnerstan'" him is to think like he does, to know that "comin' up" on someone is a threat and "dippin'" is retaliation.

The frequent use of "y'know" so parodied as Valley Girl talk is a plea for mutuality of values, for affirmation of action, and most important for validation of one's own thinking. For the young lady to understand what her parents mean by "eleven o'clock" forces her to recognize their authority over her; and the coded talk about a basketball play depicts the specific movements of players of the game. A public figure under extreme criticism, as was former President Richard Nixon when he reaffirmed who he was, may attempt to impart truth to his statements by simple association with his social position. Finally, in the argot of the jazz musician, "you dig" elicits agreement with a stated opinion.

Even proficient English speakers might not fully understand what all these expressions mean, since each is dependent on an at least slightly different context. Even within different social contexts in the same society, meanings are not always clear. With an increasingly diverse, multiethnic nation such as the United States, and especially given the now tumultuous international changes affecting all of us, understanding just what people mean has become critical.

Regardless of the social setting, then, people are not always sure about each other's intentions. All of us spend time trying to understand one another and just what is happening as we and those around us build and maintain our social worlds. And even though making sense of each other's words and actions may be problematic, we all eventually learn to guess what other people mean. What is most important, we come to know how to act on the basis of those guesses. The conditions under which we act, think, and feel are therefore social. Thus the subject matter of this book is what everybody knows, the commonsense world of everyday experiences, and so our task is to understand the complex and profound process of being social.

Social Psychology As Perspective

From the moment of birth, human beings live out their lives under social influences. Society pervades our lives, affecting even those parts not ordinarily thought of as social. For example, how we sleep, the decor of our bedroom, and even the content of our dreams may be influenced by a magazine we have read, a relationship just ended, or the last interactive video game we played. In whatever we do, it is impossible to escape our bonds with others. The uninformed Japanese soldier who hid in the Philippine jungles for twenty-five years waiting for the end of World War II long after it was over, still lived under the constraint of the distant society to which he belonged. His refusal to surrender made perfect sense to him in terms of his understanding of the social values of the Japanese society.

Sometimes the other people who affect our interaction may not even exist, as was true with this solider and is the case when we think about what our deceased parents might think about our actions or decisions. Inevitably, ours is a social existence, one created and shared through interaction with other people. Hence, to understand a person is to understand people, to know the individual is to know society. We reiterate, in our work, social and psychological meanings are inseparable in the task of human understanding.

Social psychologists seek to understand human experiences through the web of social influences surrounding every human being. In doing so, they ask many questions: Who are we? What is it about the species that people everywhere, in normal conditions, seem to need their own kind? What is society? Of what is it composed? What are social pressures and how do individuals deal with them? What are the differences between the social lives of males and females? How do children learn the ways of their social worlds? Why are people so interested in communicating with one another? What are the purposes and forms of aggression, submission and passion? These and a host of other questions guide social psychologists in their study of social and psychological phenomena.

Another fundamental question in social psychology asks about method: "How shall we study human social experience?" The answer to this question has been debated throughout the history of the discipline, and differences of opinion continue today. Among the diverse answers, two are especially important for our purposes.

On the one hand, many investigators insist that social psychological investigations follow as closely as possible the canons of rigorous scientific analysis. They seek to make objective, detached observations about social life. Their ideal is to gather data under carefully controlled laboratory or field conditions. For the purposes of research, human beings and their social situations are treated as equivalent to the objects and creatures studied by the natural sciences. The goal of this kind of social psychology is to identify the causes of social interaction and, ultimately, to make accurate predictions of the behaviors of individuals in groups.

Other students of human behavior maintain that although the techniques of the natural sciences provide significant information about some aspects of people living with people, these techniques taken alone fall short of providing an adequate understanding of the social dimensions of human existence. This is the course we choose to follow, for we believe the experimental approach may miss some essential social phenomena, namely, the intersubjective intentions and motives of individuals. Humans have intentions, wishes, reasons, motives, and meanings that affect social interaction or make up the social context of practical action. Social phenomena, and individuals themselves, are not mere objective entities. Instead, they also represent the results of relationships made from subjective meanings. The essence of any human group is the set of realities created by group members themselves, including people whose primary preoccupation seems to be figuring out what everybody else thinks is real.

For our purposes, then, social psychology is the understanding of the complicated ways in which social life is accomplished. Like many aspects of life, the principles that underlie a phenomenon may seem simple. Indeed, as we shall learn, often a simple rule will underlie the organization of a conversation, such as the understanding that one person speaks at a time. The practice of that rule, however, gives us an appreciation of the sophisticated skills of our species.

For the most part, we do not give the rules and regulations we follow in our daily lives much thought. They have become "second nature" to us, and we behave according to them without realizing it. But, of course, we were not born knowing the rules. We adopted them as our own, and now they act as guides to what we do with other people. Finally, and this is important, the rules are social, that is, shared with others around us, so when we want to initiate interaction, we know how to do it.

That people act purposefully, with initiative, is a chief assumption of sociological social psychology, one that suggests humans have a unique quality distinguishing them from other animals and from the physical world. As we have intimated, people do not merely respond, they initiate action, and they react in different ways depending on how they interpret their environments. People have purposes to carry out, plans to organize their actions, and methods they employ to join in the building and even the destruction of social worlds. Although most people never think about it, in a very real sense all persons act as if they were scientists planning and carrying out experiments. Thus, everyday life is purposeful, full of thoughtful intention, actions, results and reactions; as such, it is "accomplished."

To understand social life in a way that fully accepts a "human coefficient," we begin with the conviction that our society is composed of subjective meanings, the socially constructed realities people live by. This belief requires that we preserve the points of view of the people we study both in terms of their beliefs, feelings and actions and in the idioms we select to communicate our findings. In this, we will learn how to use experimental observations, survey data, and information gathered in a variety of sometimes ingenious ways. Throughout, our target is to comprehend the relativity of social life while searching for the principles that make such relativity possible.

Basic Elements of Social Phenomena

Social Phenomena Involve Subjective Meanings In order to understand the six expressions at the start of this chapter (the "dude on the street," the "Valley Girl," the "parent," the "president," the "basketball player," and the "musician"), we must recognize that all are built out of the subjective experiences of those involved in each setting. Another way of stating this is to say that each expression has a location in some context within a social world; and for us to understand an expression, we must know its location, who speaks, who knows what, who is trying to get something done, what that something is, and so forth.

The observable events in our examples, the six expressions given earlier, are the starting points for an interpretation of meanings. We can view the utterances from the outside or the inside. Objectively, we can depict the speakers as belonging to categories of people we take as making up the social world—street gang members, teenagers, parents, basketball players, public officials, and jazz musicians. But knowing the speakers as types of people in society tells only part of their meanings. We must also examine the ways they construct utterances, the ways they form their talk so that it is received or understood by their audiences as they intended to be understood. To take up this task as social psychology, we need to know just what subjective meanings are.

Subjective Meanings are Arbitrary By "arbitrary" we do not mean you can call what someone does or says anything you like and still understand their motives. No, when we say meanings are arbitrary, we do so in full awareness that human beings are restricted, in the same way that all life forms are, by laws of biology and psychology. For example, all people must eat, all persons must perceive and recognize food, but the matter and customs of eating are arbitrarily defined by the culture to which one belongs. We can be specific about what we mean by arbitrary: the meaning of a social action is said to be arbitrary whenever that action has a significance that, in some sense, was put there by people. By implication, arbitrary meanings vary from person to person and group to group.

On this point, social psychology aligns its perspective with those of many other disciplines. Anthropologists regard culture as arbitrary. Linguists write of languages, with their rules and content, as arbitrary. The great sociologist Emile Durkheim wrote that there is nothing intrinsic in any act that makes it have one meaning over another. For example, nothing in the nature of a person striking another human being demands that we understand it as a hostile or even an aggressive act. A football player strikes a teammate on the buttocks with a resounding blow as they start to run on the field together. What does this act mean? A young man strikes his friend on the shoulder with his fist. A father asks his young son to hit him in the stomach as hard as he can, as the father flexes his abdominal muscles. Two youths attack an old man, hitting on his chest with their fists. A policeman strikes a woman repeatedly on the chest as she lies on the ground. Do all these similar actions mean the same thing? All are social acts, but their meanings vary. More important, each of these actions can have numerous meanings depending on the circumstances in which they occur. In the language of social psychology, we say that meanings are situated; they can be understood only by knowing the situation in which they occur.

In human societies anything imaginable can take on subjective meanings and become part of the social process. A slight movement of one eyelid or a tiny movement of the head may be assigned an arbitrary meaning. A person stands among a group of friends motionlessly and in silence; the absence of action in this instance may be quite meaningful. A young man runs along a city street, and the meaning of his behavior changes with the time of day, whether late afternoon, early evening, or three in the morning. And what his behavior means varies from the observer to the actor and from one observer to another.

The arbitrary meanings that make up social life take on even greater importance when we look at societies other than our own. It is easy to see that the sounds of languages have different meanings, but we might overlook such subtlety of behavior as how close people stand when they talk. In Latin American societies the physical distance between people in normal conversations is much less than in our own society. This subjective meaning assigned to "talking distance," so called by the anthropologist Edward Hall (1966), is largely outside awareness; still we "know" when someone is standing too close. Hall observed two businessmen, a Latin and a North American, talking. The former would move a bit closer to feel comfortable with the conversation. The subjective meanings assigned by the American businessman to this new proximity raised feelings in him that the other man was pushy, and he began to feel ill at ease. He stepped back. In a few moments, as the conversation continued at full clip, the Latin businessman stepped forward; the American retreated. And so the pair marched down a long corridor, unaware of their own rules, but acting on them nonetheless. Each had learned an arbitrary meaning for how close to stand when talking. Social psychology takes as its first task the understanding of such subjective meanings as they function to make up the very fabric of social life.

Social Phenomena are Intersubjective In some of the examples we have given, individuals do not share the same meanings for a particular event. A policeman pounding on a woman's chest might be attempting to restart her heart after an accident or might be engaged in some heinous act of brutality. Obviously, since acts are open to many interpretations and people bring to any social encounter their histories of what they think people are like and what they might do, misunderstanding is always possible. Indeed, in today's complex societies, those in which many, if not most, of the people we deal with in our everyday lives are strangers, the misreading of intentions and purposes is a very real occurrence and may lead to the disruption of social interaction. But in all societies, the subjective meanings that constitute social phenomena are, to some extent, shared, or intersubjective.

Let us add detail here to an earlier example, with two white police officers speeding in their squad car toward a neighborhood in which mostly Hispanic people live. As the driver of the car increases speed, the other interprets his action as reasonable, given the urgency of a citizen's report. They share similar definitions of "appropriate speed." One says, "It's a cardiac arrest"; the other nods his head. Somehow they share in the subjective meanings of a complex condition they have not actually seen. "Let's go," says one officer as the car comes to a screeching halt and he opens the door. Both know what is meant by this short utterance. Both view the woman lying on the ground in much the same way and begin their joint efforts to administer firstaid. In some strange way that we try to uncover and analyze in this book, these two officers have achieved a form of mutual consciousness. They have come to share the subjective meanings of the situation, or at least they think they share them. In like manner, the crowd of mostly Hispanics that gathers to witness the event also shares meanings of it intersubjectively. But given previous experiences with the police in their neighborhood, to them the officers appear to be assaulting the woman.

If we merely assume the stance of an outsider, it is easy to miss the significance of the intersubjective element in social life. The police officers, for example appear to share the same physical space, the squad car; they have similar clothes; they look about the same age and size; both are white. But these are external characteristics the observer thinks they share. From the participants' vantage these commonalties may be totally irrelevant to this specific happening. They select, as it were, from a host of characteristics the ones they can use in order to accomplish a practical act. The sense of sharing they achieve for the moment is a relative thing. Many subjective meanings function as a sufficient reason to act, with some so thoroughly shared by members of a society that they are rarely talked about.

These are the hidden assumptions we all have learned about the nature of life and the grand purposes of existence. Other meanings are quite specific to a certain setting, like the idea of "this is a woman who has just had a heart attack." Some meanings are easily accomplished and rarely result in problems for those who seek to use them. Greetings are good examples of these. Other meanings may be elusive but still are regarded with such importance that interactions based on them are almost always highly problematic. In our society, love is a good example of this.

Social Phenomena Consist of Socially Constructed Realities For some social psychologists, human beings are like complex computers, carefully programmed with social attributes and knowledge, reacting to situations as they were programmed to act. Although few would defend this analogy to the last detail, whole schools of thought, depending on where they start, argue that people are not especially distinctive among forms of life or that it is not a wild pipe dream to envision computers with human capabilities. This analogy seriously distorts both the nature of computers and the character of human social life.

When people interact, they do so on the basis of their intersubjective understandings of a particular situation. To be sure, they do follow rules somewhat like computers do, but the understandings on which the social world is built are never static. Each situation requires a creative solution, a working-out process, or, in the idiom of social psychology, a negotiation or definition of the situation. We can imagine that the Hispanics who saw the police officers hammering on the chest of a woman lying on the street did not automatically react to the policemen, nor did they merely follow a rule about how to act around white cops. Instead, they made judgments about what was happening. They weighed possible interpretations of the event taking place before them. Communications flitted back and forth among the people watching, by gesture, word of mouth, posture, facial expressions, and bodily movement. A social context was constructed, shared by some but not all, and action flowed out of this subjective assessment of the situation. To the police officers, a life was being saved. But to the spectators, those who happened to see the squad car skid to a stop and the officers rush the woman and begin pounding on her chest, an act of police brutality could have been taking place. In such situations, versions of what is happening quickly spread among the spectators and they arrive at a version of the occurrence that results in their praise or condemnation of the actors they are observing. Obviously, the simple acts of watching the police officers or intervening to stop them depend at least in part on the meanings given to "what is happening." But this example represents one small instance of human social life, all of which consists of constructing meanings that people find sufficient for taking action, that is, for doing something or doing nothing. Our approach to sociological social psychology takes as its primary task the careful description and analysis of these meanings and the contexts that derive from them.

While we shall eventually drop the cumbersome phrase sociological social psychology, we use it to distinguish our approach from others. Psychological social psychology is typically a specialization within the discipline of scientific psychology and generally follows the model of experimentation to test theories about the behavior of individuals in groups. From this perspective, the social world is seen as sets of measurable constraints on individuals or an environment within which individuals behave. While we have learned a great deal about the behavior, thought, and feelings of individuals in the presence of others from such studies, our perspective stresses the unitary nature of individual and group, the symbolic links among people and how these links form the subject matter of our inquiry.

As we mentioned earlier, an important question of social psychology regards how we know about social phenomena; that is, "How do we go about understanding the lives of people?" In our example of the police officers, how do we know what is really happening? We can, of course, simply ask the police officers what they are doing and ask the spectators what they think is happening. But this approach will give us only the subjective, not the intersubjective, side of the meanings of this particular "context." As we later learn, the preferred methods are ones that provide us with both the subjective and intersubjective senses of practical action. This means that we want to know what people think is happening, what they think others think is happening, and the interaction that results from these processes. Generally, we must preserve the actor's viewpoint to do this, but we also go beyond the "subjective" aspect when we look for the resultant interaction or the context of social meaning. To do this we must have an analytic stance, a conceptual framework that makes it possible for us to reconstruct what happens in social life.

Knowing Social Phenomena

Simply from living in a conscious state, each of us has learned a great deal about social phenomena. In our ordinary states of mind, however, we rarely question seriously how we learned what we know and do. It is enough for the practical purposes of everyday life to know how to do something.

The social psychologist follows a different path, one requiring a continuous inquiry about how we know what to do. The act of doing social psychology is, then, extraordinary. A goal of this inquiry is to be able to make the grounds of social interaction explicit so that others, including the actors themselves, may understand precisely how social life is carried on.

The social psychologist must be a regular run-of-the-mill participant in the ordinary, everyday social world and at the same time must view that world in such a way as to reframe it and present to others a version of how it "really" works. This difficult job demands not only a thorough awareness of living in society but also a mastery of devices for distancing oneself from one's experiences. Obviously, no single social psychologist can have all, or even a significant portion, of the array of experiences of all members of society. In the complex modern world, the prospect of appreciating all the various ways in which people make sense out of their social lives is overwhelming. But concentrating on an understanding of only our own accomplishments, our little corner of the world, is equally undesirable. So we can easily see that the social psychologist must have help to escape the dilemma of too much experience versus not enough of it. The escape comes in the form of methods allowing us vicarious and indirect experience. Thus, a major part of social psychology is concerned with discovering the nature and range of human experience.

Essentially, in our work we want to depict accurately two types of people: those who have had experiences and those who wish to understand them. And we utilize two general techniques used to reach this goal. The first is a cumulative and indirect approach and the second is creative and direct. The first type of inquiry we call *understanding through deductive observation* and the second *understanding through inductive observation*. The reader should note that we use the terms deduction and induction in ways subtly different from the traditional ones. We use deduction to refer to the act of understanding specific experiences from the application of more general ideas, or concepts, while induction for us is an understanding that emerges in its general expression from specific and context-bound experiences. Both processes of understanding are part of the encompassing effort of the social psychologist to understand social phenomena. Hence the separation of the two observational methods is admittedly arbitrary, but it is necessary for our purpose of distinguishing ways to know about social realities.

Deductive Observation

Whenever we gather data, our observations—remarks about, comments on and interpretations of the experiences of others—must be guided by a systematically organized way of thinking. In deductive observation, we judge actions to have meaning by relying on (deducing from) a body of knowledge already in existence, usually in books, lectures, or conversations among those who have read the books and heard the lectures. At the level of common sense (which can be both an ordinary concept and a scientific one) we can say in our earlier example that the Hispanic crowd did not understand the actions of the policemen. When we say this, we go beyond the description of the events in terms of their subjective meanings. We are also evaluating these meanings (of the police and the crowd) by comparing them and finding them dissimilar.

One of the differences between knowing what happened in commonsense terms and offering a social psychological account of it is that in social psychology we are required to be explicit about how we make our evaluations. We follow this requirement in order to meet expectations shared with our colleagues about the scientific status of our inquiry. By being explicit, we make public our techniques for acquiring knowledge about experience, and thus we allow others the opportunity to replicate our work and make alternative evaluations. This process is essentially deductive because it discovers meaning through the application of ideas, typically the ideas of others who themselves have attempted to understand social experiences and then relate their understanding to an audience.

In general, discovering meaning through the application of ideas may be depicted according to four stepwise phases: (1) developing concepts; (2) having experiences (making observations); (3) the intellectual act of matching concepts with experiences; and (4) the formulation of a theme or hypothesis to evaluate our experiences in terms of the concepts developed.

Phase 1, in which we develop concepts, requires the social psychologist to be conversant with the ideas of the discipline. Social psychology is available to us mostly in the form of written texts. To carry out a deductively organized study, one first must have an understanding of conceptualization in social psychology. This understanding is acquired by communicating with others who already have it. In practice, this is done by reading the books and journal articles agreed upon by those in the field as conveying the perspective, as well as by talking with those who use the perspective both to do their professional work (as teachers, researchers, and students) and to understand their personal lives.

Concepts are arranged in the textual materials of social psychology according to plans and schemes. Some of these ideas have been developed by the many scholars and researchers who have organized them into tightly woven systems of sentences called *theories*. In sociological social psychology, there are theories of attitude formation and change, of self-concept development, and even of turn taking in conversations. Theories may be grand, in the sense that they pertain to experiences that are general, shared by all or large portions of a population of people, or they may be delimited to a specific subpopulation, such as people who practice certain acts regarded by others as perverse or deviant.

Not all concepts are so well organized. New concepts, just articulated in the latest journal or recently conceived, that seem to have the potential to become more fully developed, we call *theory sketches*. As we later learn, social psychology has many of these. Lastly, there are ideas that have a profound impact on our understanding of some aspects of social experience, but that consist of a single idea, a major insight, as it were. These are referred to as *isolated concepts* (Dumont and Wilson 1967; Ogles 1980).

One may utilize a concept, then, by drawing it from any one of these three sources: theory, theory sketch, or isolated concept. Of course, the degree to which a particular study contributes to our understanding depends on the relationship between the study and the concept. A study may seem to disprove a whole theory, or suggest a possible new theory, or simply be provocative.

Observations (phase 2) constitute sets of awareness we associate with our experience. They can be treated as information in social psychology by being packaged into data. We do this by recalling what we know in the form of strings of happenings, by telling stories, for example, about our past or about the actions of others. Or, as social psychologists, we may simply watch other people. But, we must always be on the scene, be there firsthand.

There are many strategies for watching people. These range from becoming full participants in the social phenomenon (being an actual member of the group, for instance) to merely standing by, watching and wondering about the goings-on before one. No matter which strategy proves to be most useful to a particular study, the sense of being there must be conveyed in the report. Being in the presence of the social reality forces the observer to figure out what is happening, to use vicarious or newly acquired experiences to capture the essence of what is seen.

Among the many ways experiences may be readied for analysis are talking with people (the interview), writing up the totality of a person's experiences (the life history), or asking people to write or tell you about their experiences (the autobiography). Some of these methods of social psychological research are introduced in more detail throughout the text. Now, we want to review the organization of deductive observations and provide an example.

Observations guided by concepts are deductive because they move from abstract generalizations to specific instances of experiences (phase 3). In traditional logic, deduction has a stricter definition; it refers to following steps of reasoning to draw conclusions about events from lawlike sentences—the syllogism is the classic example. Our use of the term captures the procedure of analysis that allows us to use already existing knowledge to interpret sets of actual social happenings.

For example, often conversations among students in today's universities and colleges include some reference to feminism. What students actually say, of course, will have a great deal to do with the meanings they attribute to the concept "feminism." But that such a concept exists is beyond dispute. It is a part of the way students make sense out of their personal lives, and it affects how they interpret the world outside the scope of their primary experience. It influences their selection of reading materials and research topics for term papers, as it does the judgments and meanings they give to newspaper articles, controversial occurrences on their campus, and so forth.

Now a social psychologist might notice, either as an expert observer or as a participant, how the concept seems to be used differentially; that is, some people appear to use it relatively infrequently, while others apply it to arrive at distinctive and identifiable meanings for themselves. Further, the researcher may notice that women who have a commitment to a particular lifestyle also have unique attitudes toward issues defined and highlighted by "feminism."

In order to become deductively arranged, all the research-oriented thinking our social psychologist does about feminism must be organized. This organization itself follows the form of relating ideas within a system to suggest patterns among the ways people think, feel and act (phase 4). In her study of pro-life and pro-choice activists in California, Luker (1984) explained women's adherence to pro-choice or pro-life politics in terms of the degrees to which their lifestyles were traditional. Pro-life activists tended to have and value large traditional (patriarchal, heterosexual) families. Pro-choice women, in contrast were far more likely to be single or divorced or to have small nuclear families; and they were more apt to have careers and view unplanned pregnancies as interfering with their life commitments.

Luker interpreted the meanings attributed by activists to the issue of abortion in terms of concepts of social science. To her, the ways her subjects talked and the conclusions and judgments they rendered reflected their involvement with others, the general ways they participated in society. A woman who supported feminist goals, that is, those positions associated with being a feminist, such as pro-choice opinions about abortion, approval of situational sexual ethics, support of equality in the workplace, and individually defined family responsibility, would be likely to participate in society quite differently from one whose life was bound up in the details of family life. Indeed, this kind of deductive reasoning has led several researchers to suggest that a good way to think about feminists is to describe them in terms of their commitment toward their lifestyle. Hence, drawing on Luker's work, Plutzer (1988, 641–42) tested these hypotheses about women who support feminist goals:

1. Women's family lifestyles are related to their support of feminist goals such that

a. Divorced and never-married women are more feminist than those who are married or widowed.

b. The number of children a woman has is negatively associated with her feminists attitudes.

2. Women's employment status and experience is related to support of feminist goals such that

a. Women in the labor force are more feminist than all others,

b. Women who have never worked are more traditional,

c. The number of hours worked is positively associated with feminism.

d. The proportion of the family's income earned by the woman is positively associated with support of feminist goals.

3. A woman's expressed commitment to work is positively related to her support of feminist goals.

Using data from interviews once conducted with a representative sample of the adult American population (the General Social Survey), Plutzer tested his own deductively arranged hypotheses. He found, as he suspected he would, that various aspects of a woman's family and work life have effects on her support of feminist goals. So we can expect that if we know how a woman lives, with whom she interacts in the course of her daily life, and how those people think and act respecting feminist goals, we will know a great deal about what that woman thinks. We can say that feminist attitudes seem to be a function of the kind of participation a woman has in society.

Studies such as Plutzer's can be criticized for using data far removed from the phenomenon under investigation, in this case approving of feminist goals; and perhaps the statistical associations taken as evidence for the validity of the theory only gloss over some of the complicated and dynamic ways people make decisions. Nevertheless, research like this illustrates what we call deductive studies. For example, this work derives from concepts the researcher knew before he conducted his study. And it was the logical arrangement of the concepts prior to conducting the research that guided the inquiry. Even if a different method of gathering data had been employed, say, Plutzer had selected a smaller number of women and interviewed them over a long period of time, he would still be interested in how social scientific ways of thinking (concepts) transform the way we understand mundane experience. So the category "feminist," which is part of what everybody knows about the range of attitudes a person may have, becomes part of a formulation for understanding social life. In this instance, we formulate our understanding thus: attitudes are framed or found in contexts of social life, of real relationships with feelings and consequences, and these attitudes are shaped through their expression and by what they accomplish within a particular way of conducting social life.

Inductive Observation

Inductively organized observations are ones made through a process that discovers meaning by interpreting personal experience. Some inductive studies seem exotic in comparison with deductive ones, such as those relying on the narrative abilities of the very people being studied; others may seem merely descriptive. In either instance, the inductive approach requires some mental gymnastics. Here, the inquirer starts with an idealization, namely, pure experience. Obviously, no such thing exists as pure, uninterpreted experience; however, it can be imagined. The researcher proceeds from a mental state in which he or she assumes nothing whatsoever is known about the phenomenon in question. Starting with this assumption of naiveté allows the social psychologist, at least figuratively, to become the phenomenon. Social psychologists say that whenever this state is achieved, the researcher has accomplished a membership stance, meaning that he or she can think, act, and feel like the people being studied.

Having arrived at this level of knowing, the researcher can draw on another set of rules to decide what is happening; now his or her expertise as a social psychologist comes into play. In fact, the analytic task of discovering meaning is identical to that in deductive observation. Concepts, theories, and ideas from the literature of social psychology are applied in order to gain a fresh perspective on the experience. Nevertheless, the researcher must not miss the significant differences between deduction and induction. In the deductive approach, the analyst's consciousness builds on already existing knowledge of the social world. In the inductive approach, it builds on "new" knowledge, that is, the researcher's own experience.

Often the acquisition of membership knowledge is a dramatic occurrence. Since the researcher is purposely naive, when the point of view of the population under study is actually seen, the consequences may be quite shocking. For example, one researcher reports precisely how a hit man learned to control his emotions during the commission of a murder. After several months of visiting the hit man and listening to his stories, the researcher was able at least to empathize with him. In this case, we are allowed to understand and appreciate how one person coolly and deliberately kills another—it seems that part of the secret is in not looking into the victim's eyes, an interesting comment on the power of nonverbal communication.

More generally, this research (Levi 1981) shows how hit men learn to dissociate the ordinary meanings of human interaction. Levi interviewed one hit man, "Pete," who described the ability to dissociate as "heart," which he defined as "coldness." As Levi learned, the hit man just "blanks out" when he kills. He learns a negative routine that helps him transform his victims into targets. Hit men reframe their experiences so that features of their victims are attended in a negative way: "[The victim was] a nice looking woman ... She started weeping, and [she cried] 'I ain't did this, I ain't did that' ... and [Pete] said that he shot her. Like it was nothing ... he didn't feel nothing. It was just money" (Levi 1981, 59).

Acquiring the assumptions of membership stances can be hastened through the use of certain techniques, devices, and equipment. For example, the researcher may attempt to draw maps of the occasion of an experience as if he or she were leading a stranger through his or her house. This is a task much like playing a fantasy game where someone must find a way out of a dungeon by giving instructions to a stranger in a limited language (Fine 1983). Or the researcher may actually wear special glasses that invert one's usual perception of the world and thereby force the wearer to become conscious of his or her usual ways of knowing the ordinary world (Mehan and Wood 1974).

The occasion of having one's experiences disordered is called a *breach*. Breaches may occur naturally, as when you begin talking to someone whom you mistake for a close friend, only to discover that the person is a stranger; or when you believe you are alone and act accordingly, only to look up and find yourself being observed. Breaches may also be contrived; they may be the result of a carefully designed manipulation of behavior. A well-know illustration of this is the assignment Garfinkel (1962) gave his students to behave as if they were out-of-town visitors in their own homes over a Christmas vacation.

Garfinkel also devised a laboratory experiment to show the extent to which people go to give subjective meaning to their experiences. He used a breaching procedure, after requesting that students participate in what he called "an exercise." The students who agreed were informed that they were a part of an experiment to explore alternative means to psychotherapy as a way of giving people advice about their personal problems. The students were to discuss any problem they wished into a tape recorder microphone as they sat at a desk in front of a one-way mirror. They were to phrase their questions in such a fashion that the questions could be answered with a simple yes or no by the "counselor" on the other side of the mirror.

Actually, on the other side of the mirror was an experimenter who responded with random yes and no answers to the questions submitted. The students, undaunted by these meaningless responses, searched out patterns of meaning. They presumed the existence of a qualified counselor and made sense out of apparently contradictory advice, this advice being the breach. When asked his opinion of the advice he received after the experiment was concluded, one student replied:

> The answers I received, I must say that the majority of them were answered the same way that I would answer them to myself knowing the differences in types of people. One or two did come as a surprise to me and I felt the reason perhaps he answered these questions the way he did is ... that he is not aware of the personalities involved and how they are reacting or would react to a certain situation. (Garfinkel 1962, 696)

A final method to arrive at understanding inductively is imaginative reconstruction, or the use of fictive devices. Frequently, it is impossible to observe, talk with, or elicit information from those we wish to understand. For many reasons, face-to-face contact may not be feasible. In such an instance, the social psychologist does not forego research and analysis. Instead, he or she exercises imagination to reconstruct what the phenomena of interest may be like or used to be like. The researcher relies on all the materials he or she can get: historical accounts, diaries, case and life studies, court opinions, newspaper stories, or photographs, and then interprets the phenomena in appropriate and plausible ways. The researcher tries to imagine the phenomena as if he or she were there.

Sometimes imaginative exercises employ another device, called the *ideal type*, a concept we discuss more fully later. For now, the ideal type can be defined as a fictitious construction invented by the social psychologist for the purposes of finding out what a given social phenomenon is like. For example, in order to suggest what the hearing parents of a deaf child might experience, we, as social psychologists who have had some experience with the deaf community, can imagine a parent we will call the "sign changer." Such parents, our experience indicates, believe that some manual communication, using the hands as the primary instrument of communication, is necessary for their child to learn normal communicative competency. But, they do not wish their child to master sign language, the natural language of deaf people, because they believe that language is less desirable than English. And while it can have some utility, its use identifies their child as deaf ("disabled") and them as parents of a deaf child. In sum, they have a positive attitude toward manual communication and a negative one toward deafness. This predisposes them to look for a means of communication other than that used by deaf people. They proffer their own language to their child and allow only a certain number of signs, changing some to fit English, inventing articles (sign language has none), and reordering sign sequences to conform to the word order of English.

Our "ideal type" parent may not exist as a real person at all. He or she is someone we induce through our imagination after having had some experience with deaf parents in general. We admittedly exaggerate to create a fictitious character. But our imagining of a plausible person allows us to discover trends, interrelationships, and overall patterns in social phenomena.

Symbolic Interaction

Regardless of whether they are based on deductive or inductive observations, all the ways to know about social phenomena rest on a single supposition: human interaction is symbolic. Although we learn throughout this book that sociologists differ in their approaches to inquiry and in their interpretations of their work, a particular version of sociological social psychology, first put forth in the early part of the twentieth century, does provide a consistent organizing theme for a great deal of work being carried out today.

We want to place this text squarely within that tradition. Most sociologists would readily agree with the principles we have identified about the nature of the social world. And we need to recognize that these principles have been developed mostly through the writings of a group of scholars known as *symbolic interactionists*, that is, scholars who operate under the above supposition. And while the musings and studies of these women and men range over an amazingly broad array of topics and concerns, they are anchored in common premises that account for the process through which humans attribute to each other qualities of character, states of mind, motivations and intentions.

Perhaps the most parsimonious description of symbolic interaction is Herbert Blumer's (1969). Blumer studied with other scholars who formulated the perspective, but he was most effective in systematically identifying its core components, as well as in suggesting the term "symbolic interactionism." We have already presented an elementary description of what social phenomena are and how they are maintained and sustained. Blumer, however, emphasized the interactive character of these phenomena. He suggested that three premises capture the importance of meanings in human action.

1. Human beings act toward things on the basis of the meanings that the things have for them.

2. The meanings of things arise out of the social interaction one has with one's fellows.

3. The meanings of things are handled in and modified through an interpretative process used by the person in dealing with the things he or she encounters.

While these premises cover many complicated and interdependent processes of human interaction, they serve to remind us that the work we set out to do in this book is concerned with symbolic interaction and that the type of social psychological analysis we intend to introduce to you is grounded in a rich, growing and increasingly influential way of thinking about ourselves and others. We turn in the next chapter to a brief and selective survey of the roots of symbolic interactionism.

Summary

Social psychology seeks to understand social life by recognizing the importance of subjective meanings. It must attend to the distinctive qualities of these experiences—their arbitrary, intersubjective, and constructed nature. The goal of understanding can be realized by following procedures and rules that researchers have devised for conducting inquiry. These procedures and rules can be summarized according to how observations are organized, either deductively or inductively. Deduction begins with established understanding in the form of theories and various kinds of concepts. These are applied to sets of experiences that the researcher acquires directly or indirectly. The theories or concepts turn out to be valid, or they are modified or discarded.

The inductive approach moves the researcher from naive or unanalyzed experience to social psychological understanding by way of processing or reorganizing ordinary happenings. In the task of analysis, special attention is given to capturing the sense of the experience in the description and in the higher-order understandings of observations.

Exercises in Observations and Analysis

1. Next time you are at a public restaurant, take notes on the activities of the people around you. Notice how they are eating, what they are doing with their hands, and their general posture and overall appearance. Do not eavesdrop and do not be concerned with finding out what they are actually talking about. After you have about three pages of detailed observation, think of three different versions of what they may be doing. Match the details of your versions to the details from your observations.

This exercise will increase your conscious awareness of how we impute meanings to the actions of others in everyday life. Since you will probably be able to support all three versions with your observations, it will also help you appreciate the nature of social phenomena. It is a good idea to show how each version you have of what is going on addresses the features of social phenomena (subjectivity, arbitrary definitions, intersubjectivity, and constructed realities).

2. When you are out about town, pay attention to people who exercise in public. A city park is an excellent site for doing this work. See if you can classify them into different groups—joggers, bicyclists, walkers, etc. Try to come up with at least four groupings. Describe the range of appearances within each grouping, with at least two words or phrases for the variation within the type. You should be able to draw a simple table with labels and sublabels from your observations. This exercise should help you understand how to induce concepts from observations.

Suggested Readings

Perhaps the only time-tested way to become familiar with the form of inquiry we introduce is to read examples of it. The literature of symbolic interactionism consists of both very abstract and dense books and articles, and more descriptive accounts of everyday life. Beginning students may profit from starting with the slices of life studies, but these must be cast within the larger goal of developing a stance toward understanding social phenomena in a programmatic way. So we suggest that a book such as Kristen Luker's, *Abortion and the Politics of Motherhood* (Berkeley: University of California Press, 1984) is good place to start. Abortion is a contemporary issue people often have strong opinions about. Luker's book is a study of a group of pro-life activists in California. She captures who these people are and the passions they bring to the issue, and offers an interpretation of their lives that identifies the social contexts for their beliefs. Mary Jo Deegan, in her *American Ritual Dramas: Social Rules and Cultural Meanings* (New York: Greenwood Press, 1989), offers the reader an entertaining and thoughtful collection of her essays on a variety of aspects of life in America. She writes from a feminist perspective about the "meet/meat" market rituals of singles bars and the cultural meanings of American football and Star Trek. Finally, for the serious methodologically minded reader, Richard H. Ogles' "Concept Formation in Sociology: The Ordering of Observational Data by Observational Concepts," in *Theoretical Methods in Sociology*, ed. Lee Freese (Pittsburgh: University of Pittsburgh Press, 1980) introduces both the types of observational research done and a novel idea about how to come up with valid concepts.

Chapter 2

The Roots of Sociological Social Psychology

The adage "there's nothing new under the sun" is particularly appropriate for our history of social psychology, for much of the basis of today's sociological social psychology comes from thinkers born well over a century ago. Nevertheless, in rethinking ideas and newly applying old theories each generation, each class of readers, learns and interprets them anew in ways relevant to contemporary life. Our historical analysis involves establishing biographical identities or personages on which certain historical concepts can be "hung." As we read about how particular people thought about society and the social self, we reconstruct their ideas for the purposes of our own understanding. In the process, these people become abstractions or, as Goffman (1959) called them, "identity pegs."

Since all history is subject to human interpretation, it is always biased; so also is ours, from a sociological perspective. In our study of persons whose writing and ideas still appear in contemporary literature we agree with Gordon Allport (1968) that social psychology is "an attempt to understand and explain how the thought, feeling, and behavior of individuals are influenced by the actual, imagined, or implied presence of others" (p. 3). But we place particular importance, our bias, on that "presence."

Traditionally, the "presence of others" has been understood from various perspectives, each of which persists in modern social psychology. The first involves the question of how to define social reality itself; second, there are inquiries into the nature of the individual; and finally, efforts are made to explain the links between individual existence and social reality.

Now, although there are many exceptions, European scholars generally have been preoccupied with the nature and power of social forces, while American scholars have worked hard to preserve a place for the dignity of the individual in the face of strong and overpowering social influences. We work our way through these two tendencies and in the following two chapters appreciate their reconciliation.

Our discussion of the founders of social psychology differs from most presentations of this sort, even those of others with a sociological persuasion. The difference is that we begin with the work of two authors not usually considered to be social psychologists; and, second, we do not address in detail the work of other authors, such as William James, who are almost always included in texts such as ours. In the former instance, we include Emile

Durkheim and Max Weber because they encapsulate the European tradition from which all sociology emerged, with its respect for the importance of social reality and the forces of society that affect us. We make only brief mention of such a giant as James because his work, and that of others often recognized as founders of social psychology, is amply represented in the writings of Georg Simmel, Charles Horton Cooley, George Herbert Mead, and William Isaac Thomas, whom we do include. We also devote the entire following chapter to Mead. Finally, throughout the text we introduce more contemporary writers to complement the work of those we recognize as founders, thus completing, however broadly, the basis of our social psychology.

Emile Durkheim (1859–1917): The Search For Social Existence

The great French sociologist Emile Durkheim wrote at the turn of the century, a time, like ours, of great social changes, ones that at the end of his life would culminate in "the Great War" (World War I). Like many sociologists, Durkheim understood the powerful forces that created such events, and he dreamed of the important role sociology and sociologists could play in fashioning a better world. We want to give Durkheim ample appreciation because, as did his work, our social psychology depends on a strong sense of social reality, supplemented by an equally persuasive concept of the individual.

We begin with the understanding that people's ideas of what is socially right and wrong depend upon two interrelated processes: the existence of an ongoing external social reality; and from that reality, the development of individual selves.

We can illustrate these two points with a simple example. Dating in our society has enough history and tradition that we could with some justification call it a social institution; yet, because there are no universally accepted formal "rules of the game," dating is usually both novel and challenging for those just beginning the experience. For the most part, these are young people, whose emotions, and therefore imaginations, often run wild. In addition they are substantially affected by peer pressure, and this at a time when they are attempting to break away from the parental restrictions of childhood, to establish themselves as independent actors. All these factors, especially when accompanied by self-consciousness over the physiological changes of adolescence, contribute to the fact that for many of us our earliest dating experiences are ones we would just as soon forget.

Although, as we have said, there are no formal rules for dating, there are some generally accepted standards we all might agree exist. For example, if two persons are to "have a date," someone has to ask someone else "out," and the person who does the asking is usually responsible for providing the transportation and paying for the date; he or she also usually gets to choose what the date will be, such as a movie, dance, or party. In addition, and especially if we can assume there is some mutual attraction between the couple, important to any date are the standards of conduct that will be observed; that is, ultimately they must answer the question so often raised in teen magazines: "How far do you go?" Other important questions, which are often tacit but are well understood, include Who else is going, and with whom? For youth, Will there be any adult supervision? Will alcohol or drug use be an issue? and What will I wear?

> Derick, 16, had just gotten a part-time job as a stocker-and-bagger at the Food Mart, one of the largest grocery stores in Minneapolis, but it was not long before he noticed Kim, also 16, a part-time checker who sometimes worked the same shift as he. He wanted to ask her out, but he was shy, and she had a more important job than his, which made things worse; and since they went to different high schools, he didn't even know someone who knew her and could introduce them. Besides, he once saw another guy pick her up after work, and in a new five-point-oh, to which he felt his '79 Rabbit didn't compare.
>
> Just when Derick was about to give up all hope, another stocker-bagger told him he heard Kim telling her supervisor she thought Derick was "really cute; I'd like to go out with him." He had talked to a couple of his friends about her, and they were full of encouragement, even to the point of suggesting he could probably "kick that other guy in the 5.0's butt," if it came to that. In the meantime, he said nothing to his parents; that would be embarrassing enough, to say nothing of the flak he would take from his 13-year-old sister if she found out about it. Finally, after establishing a nodding acquaintance with her, Derick struck up a conversation with Kim during a break, but just safe conversation: How long have you been working here? Where do you go to school? Things like that. After this, he found he liked her even more, and by the following week he had mustered enough courage to ask her for a date. But before he had the chance, she said a friend had given her two tickets and asked if he'd like to go to the Prince concert with her in two weeks. Although not at all a Prince fan, he of course said, "Yes!"

A Durkheimian view of this example would portray the emergence of a single social relationship from two independent lives. Although Kim and Derick are separate individuals, they have started to build a relationship that belongs to both of them, and more. In fact, their friendship itself, and even whether and how it would begin, had already been influenced by certain social forces before each knew the other even existed. For what we find attractive in another and how we react to our attractions (and repulsions) depend heavily on what we learn from social influences experienced while growing up. Beyond this, Durkheim's position helps us understand the more obvious social processes operating to affect a relationship once it has begun. Kim and Derick both are aware of their feelings and of.the inevitable involvement of others—co-workers, family, and friends—if anything "serious" is to "happen" between them. And both will be affected by various forces as things develop. Given this, we now continue our illustration:

> Not surprisingly, Derick offers to drive (he would be embarrassed to have Kim pick him up). When he arrives at her house, he is relieved when he meets her brother, whom he recognizes as the driver of the enviable 5.0. During their date, they talk freely with one another, a plus; but Derick also finds out Kim is almost 17, in fact, she's ten months older than he, a minus; and what's worse, she's a year ahead of him in school. Each runs into other friends at the concert, and each is drawn aside to be asked, "How's it going?" by those who know it's their first date. But through all the anxiety, they have a lot of fun, enough that, as the evening draws to a close, both begin to wonder if it and when and how they'll face the ultimate question—the Good-Night Kiss. Finally, as they walk from his car to her front door, Derick and Kim become quieter than they've been all evening.

Whether this date was ever consummated in that potential kiss need not concern us here. Following Durkheim, we already have more than enough information to imagine the processual development of and the subtle social forces affecting this new relationship. Through their conversation, Kim and Derick came to certain agreements about whether, when and how they would go out, and of what their date actually would be like as it progressed. But none of their interaction was unaffected by the influence of others. Especially for teenagers, going to the "right" places, doing the "right" things, listening to the "right" music and wearing the "right" clothes—with what is "right" often being defined by one's peers—can be very important. And all of this must be done either within the boundaries set by parents or guardians or, if the boundaries are to be broken, by keeping secrets and living with a certain amount of guilt and fear that one might eventually get caught.

For Durkheim, the action of such forces as these, developing according to various group processes, was, in fact, social reality. He insisted that the group, with its larger manifestations and complex connections to institutions and to society itself, could be thought of as existing in and of itself. To him the behavior of individuals, sometimes to a surprising degree, could be accounted for in terms of these group-level phenomena. For example, that we can see a pattern in our illustration, or recognize experiences we ourselves once might have had, suggests that we could plug many, perhaps most American teenagers into the situation with approximately the same results.

Our illustration of Kim's and Derick's developing relationship demonstrates two facts that, for Durkheim, are fundamental to all groups: constraint and integration. Constraint refers to the capacity of groups to establish boundaries and compel persons to think and act in particular ways. The Good-Night Kiss is a good example of the interplay of various constraining forces. Individually, Kim and Derick may have thought they heard their hormones shouting, "Go for it!" and they likely could have assumed correctly the encouragement of their respective peer groups to do so; but perhaps both also imagined parental pressures against kissing on the first date. And there's always the possibility of one wanting to go farther than the other or of, say, parking out by the lake and suddenly finding themselves more involved than either had anticipated. At such times, it is reactions to one's imagination of what one's parents or people in general might say that would cause one or the other of them to "put on the brakes." Regardless of whatever individual desires might be involved in such situations, what decisions will be made and how they will be played out are not accomplished without reference to deeper social phenomena, called social constraints.

Durkheim's second fact, integration, is defined as the degree of personal involvement a group requires of its members. Our example of a couple dating suggests a highly integrated, two-person group, where the participants are held together by a commitment to each other rather than to some external goal. At the other end of the spectrum of integration might be a group of two or three students, selected at random, attempting to complete a classroom assignment. In the latter case, there is usually a preexisting formal structure outlining project goals and the process to be used in achieving it. In such a situation, integration could be considered formalized and commitment to the group fairly weak, with each student contributing, and sometimes compromising, for the sake of achieving the goal, and a grade, rather than in the interest of keeping the group itself together. Whereas a highly integrated personal group such as the one formed by Kim and Derick is primarily an end in itself, a formally integrated one like the classroom project group is for its members a means to an end.

Durkheim argued that once they come into being and establish customs, traditions, and codes of behavior, all groups shape and educate individuals who subsequently become members, and these in turn shape others, and so on throughout the life of the group. But though he recognized the importance of the individual, Durkheim still placed his greatest emphasis on the group. For without a strong sense of group life, any collection of people would lose its capability to engender moral commitment in its members.

Durkheim also held that we cannot fully understand any social phenomenon, like the small group represented by Kim and Derick, without seeing its relationship to many others. As we have already suggested, the roles of families and friends must be considered by any dating couple. We have noted further that age differences can be important, and if we add in additional variables, such as race, religion, class, and ethnicity, the complexity of the situation becomes even more apparent. If Kim were white and from a traditional Irish Catholic family, and Derick African American and a Baptist, but their attraction for each other was the same, we can begin to imagine the various social forces that might come into play. Or we might imagine an even more powerful situation, one of a gay teen, still "in the closet," whose family and friends "don't know." How does such a teen even consider striking up a conversation with an attractive other who may or may not also be gay? The social forces in this case are sometimes overwhelming.

The greatest contribution Durkheim gives us, then, is his emphasis on the importance of social realities. In the relationship between society and the individual, society defines the parameters of individual performances. As Erving Goffman (1974), a modern social psychologist and leading proponent of the study of the details of everyday life, put it: "I personally hold society to be first in every way and any individual's current involvement to be second (p 13).

Following Goffman, the sociological social psychologist is concerned with what individuals do within social parameters, with how the latitude a person finds there is put to use. Given the social facts of a situation, what kinds of relationships exist among individuals, and how might the actions of individuals alter the social boundaries of their existence?

Max Weber (1864–1920)

The German scholar and intense thinker Max Weber lived during the same tumultuous era as did Durkheim. Not surprisingly, he dreamed some of the same dreams; but for Weber some of these came true, for he personally played an important role in the development of the German legal code after World War I. In addition, Weber did more than any other thinker to show how the concerted actions of individuals can have a profound influence on the parameters of society itself. In this sense, he is a major figure in the history of social psychology.

The task of inquiry, as Weber saw it, is to discover how the meanings of social life emerge and evolve into patterns, and to show how these configurations relate to one another. Weber was acutely aware that people live within subjectively defined and created social worlds. And although he appreciated the search for scientific laws and causal explanations, he also stressed the importance of subjective experience. In fact, he warned that the search for scientific laws might result in trivial generalization or, more often, might obscure the researcher's understanding of unique cultural and social innovations. From this base, Weber set out to establish how explanations that incorporate both subjective experiences and their meanings can be made.

The Weberian social scientist, then, attempts to understand and interpret people's worlds as the people themselves experience them. (Weber characterized his method by the term *verstehen*, German for "understanding.") These goals are achieved by observation and then, through sympathetic understanding, by thinking, feeling, and even acting as the people being studied do. But as observers, we can reach only a partial understanding of others, for we are always bound by our own personal histories, lifestyles and places in society. We could actually convert to the lifestyles of those we study, but that would limit our range of interests, and we would probably lose the desire to communicate what we know to an outside audience. We can, however, experience a kind of controlled conversion. By thrusting our imagination into another's way of life, we can know vicariously what it is like to live under a particular set of social circumstances. Weber referred to this imaginative exercise as the *mental experiment*, and although he suggested using it with extreme caution, he regarded the exercise as a powerful method for achieving an understanding of social phenomena.

By compiling and comparing the results of many such experiments, the social psychologist can begin to portray the organization of values and systems of meaning for larger constellations: groups, societies, and even cultures. For Weber, the culmination of such studies was the identification of the unique happening, the singular occurrence that sets a group apart. Thus, with this method the social psychologist can say what characterizes a group, what is distinctive in one group and missing from another, and, with good fortune, what constitutes the emergence of new social forms that influence the course of societal development.

Knowing that imaginative endeavors are highly individualized, varying with the creative impulses of each experimenter, Weber gave us some guidelines to follow in the performance of the mental experiment. We need not worry about endlessly searching for understanding on an individual basis then, for some criteria exist that allow us to communicate to others the operations by which we achieve our understanding and that likewise allow them to evaluate the accuracy and usefulness of our work.

In Weber's research, the primary tool of imagination is the ideal type. Such a "type" is a composite sample case (the epitome of a personality, social situation, or institution) fashioned by the researcher from the knowledge available on the relevant aspects of the investigated subject. The ideal type is, in fact, a caricature that likely will never be found in the real world; instead, it is constructed for the purpose of comparisons with "real" types, which do exist, or for the discovery of some unnoticed dimensions of a phenomenon.

For example, in order to learn more about sexism in American society, we may invent the character type of a male chauvinist. All the aspects of male chauvinism, such as the unquestioning association of housework with women and the uncritical payment of higher wages to males than to females for the same labor, are concentrated and exaggerated in the type. If you saw the film *Nine to Five*, you will remember the boss caricatured there as a good example. But as we have noted, in reality no single ideal type can characterize all the aspects of the phenomenon.

Ogles uses the television parody of the working-class male, Archie Bunker, from the 1970's "All in the Family," to identify some aspects of bigotry as they are typically understood in American society. Ogles first identifies two characteristics of bigots: their derogatory language and their imperviousness to criticism. He then shows how Archie can be considered a specimen case (1980, 159–64). The distribution of these two characteristics as they are empirically grounded in the remarks and actions of Archie allows us to depict a form of bigotry flexible enough to permit recharacterization. It is also suggestive of hypotheses, our expectations of how Archie would act in various situations, and it is sufficiently clear to serve as a concept in the language of social psychology.

Now, whereas Ogles's specimen case does describe reality, Weber's ideal type is a carefully designed distortion of it meant to uncover essential meanings. As such, it can be modified by constant movement between actual descriptions of the reality and the type itself. But although an ideal type does not contain descriptions of actual behavior, that is, of a person who actually exists, the thoughts, actions, and patterns it does describe must be theoretically possible. We refer to this as the plausibility of the type. That is, while we may not be able to find a male chauvinist who actually passes over a competent female for a less-qualified male in every executive promotion, we know that kind of action is a possibility.

As Weber exemplifies for us, part of the work of a social psychologist is the construction of types. These are not just classifications of the facts of social life or mere moral judgments about how things should be; they are selective, conscious arrangements of facts chosen to make a point, to achieve a state of understanding. Such types are always provisional and can be discarded if they do not operate to produce understanding. Framed by the researcher, they are imaginative projections of consciousness into other times, other situations, and other people's minds.

The Calvinist Experience

Now we can explore the way in which Weber himself used the ideal type. For Weber, the modern industrial order was the most significant social development in human history. But he believed that the advent of this social order in the nineteenth century could not be fully explained by the usual references to factors such as cheap labor, deep river ports and navigable rivers. He reasoned, instead, that the industrial revolution and the economy of capitalism that accompanied it resulted from a unique contact between two independent configurations of meanings in the lives of people. Namely, the merger of religion and the economic aspects of societal phenomena had shaped a new reality.

Weber saw capitalism as a rational system of calculated exchange that ensured individual profit. A certain type of person, the successful businessman, symbolized this system. He—or she, as we update Weber—is hardworking, well organized, fastidious in habit and mannerism, and above all, goal oriented. The existence of such persons impressed Weber as unique in world history. To him, the entrepreneur seems overcommitted to his work. In a figurative sense, he *becomes* his business. He defines his personal qualities, aspirations, hopes, and dreams in terms of its continued and spectacular success. This person drives himself, working day and night, and is totally consumed by economic enterprise. His private and public lives merge into one reality. Indeed, Weber's description brings to mind the workaholic and the current studies being done on Type A and Type B personalities. The Type A person, prone to heart attacks, is a contemporary version of Weber's business person.

Reasoning that such a total merger of self and outside activities could not be motivated solely by concern with making a living, Weber imagined that such zealous activities go beyond economic necessity, they seem to characterize men anxious about the destiny of their souls. So he tried to determine how these fervent men emerged and why they were part of such a frantic economic system.

Having established his description of the economic reality of capitalism, Weber now located a special mentality among zealots whose religious belief systems rested uniquely on practical concerns. Without interest in the truth or falsity of religious dogmas, he focused on what happens in the everyday lives of people who hold particular beliefs. From Weber's perspective, such beliefs occur within a complete social context, and religious principles have meanings in everyday life that go beyond their strictly theological significance.

The specific belief he examined was the Calvinist doctrine of predestination, a belief that God is all-knowing, grants eternal life, saves souls and plans in detail the outcomes of the lives of all mortals. Now since He has established His great plan, the salvation or damnation of all souls is preordained. There is, then, an election of souls, something like a celestial ledger, which enumerates the saved and excludes the lost. According to the doctrine, all of this is basically outside the control of the individual believer. It is God's business and beyond human comprehension or interference.

Weber was interested in the reasoning this doctrine engendered as people made practical decisions in their everyday lives. He asked his readers to imagine what it would be like to live among people who fervently believed in it. He himself concluded that a person would experience anxiety and a perpetual battle of faith to believe that he or she really was one of the chosen. One could not actually prove this to oneself or others, so every believer faced the problem of reconciling daily activities with nagging doubts about personal salvation.

How would you react? What would you do? How would you live your life? Imagine yourself always under the canopy of the doctrine, always in the presence of others whom you presume share your religious convictions. Weber's imagination identified three possible reactions, which are portrayed in the following soliloquies.

Life with Reckless Abandon Since I have nothing to do with my soul's destiny—that's God's affair—why do I worry about it all the time? This anxiety is burdensome. I can't take it anymore. What does it matter? My preacher says I'm saved by the grace of God. Seems to me I've got that or I don't. Doesn't matter what I do, so why not just do what I want? What's to stop me from just having fun? Drink, dance, and revelling! Why not? These things don't really have anything to do with my soul.

But wait, what will others think? The reverend, my friends, my family. If God predestined my life and I do all these sinful things, how will others think of me as one of the elect? They will never believe it. How could God will such a life of indolence, waste, and self-indulgence for one of his children? Aw, what the heck! Nothing really matters; can't do anything about it. Don't worry; be happy. Let's party!

Religious Questioning I just can't go on this way. I guess I never will know if I'm really chosen—if I'm really one of the flock. My parents tell me, "Stop doubting, it's God's affair. He will take care." But I can't get the picture of that list out of my mind. That list without my name on it. What can I do? Nothing seems to matter. I don't see any reason for doing anything. Why not just wait? My faith is strong, at least as strong as other people's. I guess I really believe. Wait! I know it. I am chosen. My heart rejoices. There is no more fear. So I will wait for my destiny.

Now it has been four months since I worked down at the shop. My father was patient at first. I told him it was God's will. He listened, but now he says that God never sanctioned such laziness, that God gave me talents; He could never have intended this kind of life for His chosen few. So my father says things like, "Maybe my son is not one of us."

Activism: By their deeds you shall know them Sure, everybody has doubts. God told us that, but we must overcome them. It's all in God's plan. If our faith is strong, if we are really in the flock, then God's will be done. God is good.

Always, He is there to show the Way, the Way He planned. He tests us with bad times, but He has a purpose; we must accept. Yet, I know He is good. He will help me, my life will be rewarded, and this will be evidence of my soul's security. I have a seed faith. It grows and God reveals more and more of His divine plan to me. My good fortune, my hard work, my toil is what He intended. Its fruit is His, I share it and put it back into the earth. Such a good life, full of all my talents, full of activity. This is what God wants for His children. How could a sinner and a cursed heathen be so blessed?

Each of these three ideal typical reactions is objectively possible. All could and to some degree do happen. But our purpose in formulating the types is to discover which one fits best with the self-driven, committed business person of modern capitalism. We are after a kind of relationship we can understand that informs us about the similarities between two previously unrelated configurations of meaning.

The Spirit of Capitalism

The third reaction is the one that made the most sense to Weber. The easiest way to convince your fellow believers of your soul's salvation is to prosper on earth, to use your God-given talents, and to realize His ambitions and wishes for you— ambitions and wishes that can be recognized only in terms of earthly success. The harder one works, the more accomplished one becomes in this world, the more certain he or she can be of preordained success in the next. Living under these conditions produces frantic activity and total immersion in work. By their hard work, frugality, and judiciousness you shall know them.

For Weber, then, the mentality necessary for the development of an economic system takes shape and is nurtured in religious beliefs; and his ideal typical example was the relationship between the spirit of capitalism and the Protestant ethic. According to him, historical circumstances led to an intersection of economic and religious meanings for human action. The two systems for deciding the sense and structure of human existence had an elective affinity for one another. They merged to form a unique meaning system composed in part of both previously independent ones.

Looking for another ideal type to illustrate the merger, Weber found the life and writings of Benjamin Franklin. This man, Weber believed, clearly represented the consequences of the historical intersections of capitalist and Protestant systems. Here was a secular, businesslike man whose ethical proclamations and zeal for work were like those of the earlier Calvinists. Franklin gave "hints to those that would be rich" and advice to young aspiring businessmen. He wrote of money "in almost idolatrous terms" (Zeitlin 1990, 125). He emphasized a commitment to industry, frugality and punctuality. He ascribed his recognition of the utility of virtue to a divine revelation intended to lead him in the path of righteousness. Why should men make money and what should men make of money? Franklin's answer was near biblical: "Seest thou a man diligent in this business? He shall stand before Kings" (Weber 1958, 53).

Weber showed that even in the rational economic system of modern society there is a heart, one that comes from the psychological burden ordinary Protestants carry. Unsure of their fate, they seek outward signs of their inward grace. These signs they find in hard work, frugality and the result they produce, worldly success. And while the sacred meanings may have slowly eroded with the advance of modern society, the zeal and frantic spirit of becoming economically successful remained.

Georg Simmel (1858–1918)

We move a step closer to a fully developed concept of social psychological reality with the teaching of another German scholar, Georg Simmel. Simmel is yet a third eyewitness, with Durkheim and Weber, to the upheaval resulting in World War I, so it is not surprising that he, too, maintained an interest in competition and conflict and the role of a sociological social psychology in helping foster their positive and ameliorate their negative effects. Simmel wanted to identify a set of conditions that together make up the state of affairs we refer to as society. He borrowed from philosophy the term "a priori" to name such a set of conditions.

For Simmel, individuals act, know and feel in many different ways, but when they meet in a concerted social activity, their individuality merges. For example, people thrown together in situations that require their cooperation, or even those who enter such situations voluntarily, will work to discover or create new ways to interact. It is as if they act to find or fashion a vessel to contain whatever elements of themselves they decide to introduce into the situation. They mix together parts of themselves to form yet a new, third entity—a part of and yet apart from each. And that new entity, or vessel, as we have called it, will act to shape whatever is put into it in the future. Simmel referred to these containers or vessels as *forms*, and what went into them as *content*.

Social activities have definite forms that can be identified and described separately from the action they contain. Competition, for example, can occur between siblings, athletes, or economic or political rivals, but we need not talk about any of these to talk about competition as a form. Statements made about forms, then, are depictions of a priori conditions of social activity, or "sociation" as Simmel called it. Nevertheless, talking about form without reference to content is a little like describing a glass of wine while ignoring the liquid inside: it can be done, but it's more meaningful, and a lot easier, if you include the liquid.

So a complete social psychology requires a description of both form and content, and most importantly of the interaction between them. The first step, though, is the identification of the forms or a priori conditions.

Social forms can be identified in every area of a society. In order to illustrate Simmel's concept of form, let us look at one type: conversational forms. Often the smoothness and ease of social exchange depends not so much on what is said as it does on the form, or the way in which the exchange is organized. "Stop the car." "Stop the car!" and, "Stop the car?"—each has virtually the same content, but the forms suggest quite different meanings. And in the same way we use a grammatical form for organizing written words into sentences, we learn to use conversational forms for organizing our encounters with other people. We talk not merely to transmit information but to accomplish social ends, including talking for the sake of talking. As with Kim and Derick in our earlier example on dating conversation can be an end in itself.

Take the case of two old friends who live in distant cities but meet for a brief time in an airport as each changes planes. They exchange information about the weather in their respective cities, the nature of their travels, and their families. Two things have taken place: the exchange of information and the participation in a conversational form. On other occasions these two friends may meet simply because they want to talk, to pass some time with someone each knows is another like-minded individual. A person without such a friendship to serve as a form may tune in a favorite talk show that is actually based on this same social form, as show hosts are considered to be friends by many of their regular listeners.

The guests on a standard talk show are selected for something distinctive in their identity, an accomplishment, or a reputation. They range from witty and informative to dull and ordinary. They are selected to cover a wide range of social backgrounds and occupations. The nature of the form of a talk show becomes especially apparent on call-in shows where anyone can phone in and be on the air. The various backgrounds of invited guests and callers appearing on the show, as well as who these people are and what they say, can be thought of as content. But the variety of this content hardly influences the form at all. Guests know the rules of breaking for a commercial, of turntaking, and of what can and cannot be said over a public medium. On call-in shows, moderators assume control over the conversations to make sure they conform to the form. One may chide a caller to hurry with his or her question or comment, or another will talk over the caller to preserve an appropriate format for the show.

In a careful study of radio talk shows, Ellis et al. (1981) show how there are rules for tying together statements, demonstrating who is talking to whom, and requesting additional information. All operate to create an organization for radio talk shows that allows the listener to recognize and even participate in the talk as conversation.

Perhaps most significantly, all parties to this form of communication realize the obligation to keep up the talk, to talk through errors or disruptions of speech, to allow no "dead air." Hosts and frequently invited guests develop favorite stories and techniques for moving the show along, thus establishing formulas for creating the illusion of fresh talk (Goffman 1981). So familiar are we now with this form that we have no difficulty at all in recognizing a talk show and the usually friendly chitchat that comprises both the character and the appeal of the form.

Social psychology has as one of its goals the discovery and portrayal of social forms. Simmel showed us that the contents of activities alone would never provide us with sufficient information about social life. Forms must be isolated and grammars of social interaction must be written in order to reveal the a priori nature of social life. With these grammars we can achieve an appreciation of the finely grained nature of our everyday affairs.

Charles Horton Cooley (1864–1929)

Although Charles Horton Cooley lived at approximately the same time as the other writers we have thus far considered, he was born and raised and lived virtually all his life in the same midwestern American city, Ann Arbor, Michigan. Given this, we can guess that his view of the world, and certainly his experience of World War I, was substantially different from that of the Europeans discussed earlier. While America did go to war, and our human losses were dear, our soil and our society were never seriously threatened. During Cooley's youth, America was still burgeoning as the land of the frontier, of opportunities where the rugged individual with a few skills and enough confidence to be willing to take risks had a good chance for fame or at least fortune. So although his work reflected an understanding of the societal emphasis of European sociology, it is not surprising that his most significant contributions were in the areas of small groups and the self.

Cooley, then, was familiar with the European conception of society as a superindividual, and especially with the ideas of men like Gustave LeBon, who thought of society and the crowd as having minds and vitalities of their own. Furthermore, Cooley could not relegate the human imagination to external forces or natural instincts. For him, societal and psychological matters were inseparable.

He wrote that society actually consisted of the imaginings that people have of one another. When two friends meet and embrace or shake hands, each brings to the encounter a wealth of images and ideas of the other, and both bring also the ideas they have of their own selves. Because we think of society as an objective thing, it seems strange to say that society exists in our minds, but this is what Cooley meant when he suggested that the solid facts of society exist in the minds of people. "Society exists in my mind as the contact and reciprocal influences of certain ideas named 'I,' 'Thomas,' 'Henry,' 'Susan,' 'Bridget,' and so on" (Cooley 1922, 84).

In order to describe what society is like then, we must discover what people think, how they think, what categories they use in thinking, and most important, how these categories are interdependent.

The Looking-Glass Self

As we see our face, figure and dress in the glass and are interested in them because they are ours, and pleased or otherwise with them according as they do or do not answer to what we should like them to be; so in imagination we perceive in another's mind some thought of our appearance, manners, aims and deeds, character, friends and so on, and are variously affected by it ...the thing that moves us to pride or shame is not the mere mechanical reflections of ourselves, but imputed sentiment, the imagined effect of this reflection upon another's mind. (Cooley 1902, 183–85)

The concept Cooley articulated in this passage is referred to as the *Looking-Glass Self*. According to him, just as we make contact with our image in a mirror by knowing that it is a reflection of ourselves, so when we make contact with others we see our own images reflected in their actions by the ways they approach and react to us. Here the term "contact" does not refer to direct physical touching, of course, but to a symbolic meeting of minds through the medium of imagination. Sometimes imagination alone, of how others would react to us, is enough to affect our behavior.

If you talk to your mother on the telephone and she tells you how lonely she is and how much she longs for you to visit her, you understand this request through your own qualities reflected in her request. The qualities may be ideas of your obligations toward your parents, or even more generally your views of kindness and being a good person. Your own feelings about being alone, and the opposite, of enjoying the comforts of companionship, are mirrored in her request.

You may decide not to visit, but you and your mother have contacted each other in a symbolic act. Although we rely on our own particular ways of knowing, the social sense of knowing, which Cooley called society, depends on the imaginative reflection of ourselves in others. When you imagine turning down your mother's request, you hear her disappointment or the disgust in her reply. What is heard really is your own understanding of how you would act if the positions were reversed. You hear over the telephone line your ideas about yourself as a good son or daughter, or as a responsible adult. Thus one way to think about society is as a result of individual minds in reflective contact.

Self and Society

For Cooley, society and the individual are inseparable, and likewise the organic whole of society is more than just the sum of the individual minds that make it up. Instead, the human capacity to extend consciousness, to guess at what is inside the heads of other people, creates society. In this manner, individuals derive a sense of what society itself is all about; but just as important, they also make judgments and come to conclusions about their own worth as they feel it is reflected to them from others. To summarize briefly Cooley's ideas: "We imagine our appearance to other people. We imagine their judgment of that appearance. We feel some self-worth or loss of it—pride or self mortification."

Each of us acquires a sense of our belonging in society by slowly accepting over long periods of time the social character and personal history assigned to us. This is not to suggest that we acquiesce in this process but that our consciousness merges with those of others around us. Cooley believed this process took place in what he took to be the cornerstone of society, the *primary group*.

Like a family or a group of teenage girls in a boarding school, primary groups involve intimate, face-to-face contact, not casual acquaintances or impersonal relationships, such as the ones one might find riding the bus to work each morning. Also, primary groups demand their members' undivided attention. Having spent a great deal of time inside each others' minds, people in primary groups share a wide range of subjective meanings. These groups are not like the groupings of people who gather on the street corner to wait for the bus. The urban world, as we later learn, is basically a world of strangers (Lofland 1985), but the primary group is a world of the familiar and intimate.

Given its requirements that interaction be both face-to-face and intimate, it is natural for the primary group to encompass the entire person. Such groups provide the direct mirror images of newly forming individuals (the young), as well as of the stable, historical images of older members. Thus our sense of self-identity emerges from and continues to be maintained by our membership in primary groups.

Lastly, the primary group produces and develops a character from the total society of which it is a part. So the quality of a society can be assessed by a careful examination of the primary groups in it, an insight that underlies much research in social psychology. In the primary group individuals learn the meanings and shared realities of society as these have been created and maintained over generations.

In sum, for Cooley society and the individual are two versions of the same phenomenon. Society is collective consciousness, the organization of individual minds in concert, thoughts arranged in categories and related to one another. On this point Cooley concurred with other early social psychologists, the most important of whom for our study is George Herbert Mead, whose work, as we noted earlier, we discuss in the following chapter.

William Isaac Thomas (1863–1947)

It is fitting that William Isaac ("W.I.") Thomas be the last of the founders we consider in this chapter, for he lived to be the grand old man of them all, the only witness to both world wars. Unlike his fellow American Cooley, Thomas studied in Germany and so had a firsthand appreciation of European sociology. Later Thomas taught at the University of Chicago, where during the first two decades of this century he won acclaim for his *Source Book for Social Origins* (1909). But it was *The Polish Peasant in Europe and America* (1918–20), coauthored with an eminent Polish sociologist, Florian Znaniecki, which assured his historical niche. This work, which studied immigrant adjustment and maladjustment, pioneered the life-history technique and focused on the individual through the authors' concept of all people's "four wishes"—for response, recognition, security, and new experience. Beyond this, Thomas's major contribution was his analysis of the part consciousness plays in giving meaning to social life. He was especially concerned with identifying the social situations in which people carried on their daily lives and with their definitions of these situations. These latter concerns are the subject of our discussion here.

The Social Situation

Thomas thought of social situations as composed of objective conditions, including the physical aspects of a room or the buildings of a city, as well as the intangible objects of human attention. Thus any social situation may be thought of as a physical shell within which are found people with attitudes and values— the objects of attention. For Thomas there are no unchanging attributes of the social world. Instead, it is continuously created and re-created by people who act in it. According to him, the social world is defined by people as real; it is composed of their definitions of how things actually work. We may think of it as the arena of action, the place within which the processes of society unfold.

Thomas's social situations are of two varieties: those created and defined by tradition, and those we create for ourselves and others. But even though we sometimes deal with novel situations, every activity may be thought of as a "solution to recurrent problems." The people involved in the situation of social action always bring with them their experiences, and they apply these to give meaning to the present. So each creation is at least in part a re-creation. Furthermore, to maintain the continuity of social order all individuals have to define situations in ways consistent with the definitions of others.

On Defining Situations

Thomas believed there is always competition between the spontaneous, personal definitions of situations and those provided by society. Although we are always deciding for ourselves what a setting means, we do so within preexisting meanings we have learned. Our social experiences, then, are organized both by preconceived definitions and by emergent, or for-the-occasion definitions.

Thomas suggested that such mental exercises actually create situations, for whenever people define situations, these definitions influence behavior. This is true, for instance, in the example in the first chapter in which police officers attempted to revive a woman, the victim of a heart attack. The officers defined the situation one way, as the practice of emergency medicine, while the spectators defined it another, as an instance of police brutality. People's respective interpretations, then, provided bases for action. For Thomas, when a situation is believed to be real, it is real in its consequences, that is, in the reactions of the believers.

Thomas's work shows us the constant interrelationship between the social world as it has been defined in the past and as it is collectively defined at the moment. His research was in part a description of the characteristic ways in which these definitions of situations took place for different people.

Summary

The works of the Europeans we have discussed converged on core concepts. They stressed a full appreciation of the autonomous nature of the social aspect of human life. This does not mean these men overlooked the part the individual plays in social life. Each in his own way dealt with the constructed qualities of social reality. Nevertheless, compared to the Americans, they clearly wanted to expand their understanding of society as a compelling and influencing agent in the lives of people. Taken together, the thinking of these giants of sociology points toward a description of social reality.

The Americans we discussed emphasized the indivisibility of society and individual, that society and the individual are best comprehended as two aspects of the same phenomenon. Each thinker expressed this idea according to his own focus. Both wanted to depict the continuing interplay between social and psychological reality.

From the ideas of these early social psychologists we identify several basic propositions:

1. Society is essentially a creation of human minds. Cooley called society a "psychic phenomenon," and Thomas gave many illustrations of socially defined situations. Relying on some preconceptions, they demonstrated the mind in the presence of other minds as inventor of the social world.

2. Society has an autonomous existence . Once created as content, society acquires a history to be passed on from moment to moment and generation to generation. Both Durkheim and Simmel stressed that the product of persons coming together does not equal the mere sum of what each brings to the encounter. Instead, the product of social interaction exists as an entity capable of making itself felt in subjectively experienced, real ways.

We must recognize, however, that a great intellectual problem is embodied in how we are talking about social reality. The interactive outcomes produced when people mentally and emotionally take each other into account constitute social reality; and those outcomes do not merely derive from the backgrounds of the respective people. Still, the danger here is a kind of thinking philosophers call reification, or thinking about social reality as a type of inanimate phenomenon. The student should be aware of the long-standing debate about precisely what social reality is. For our purposes, as Thomas teaches, a thing is real in its consequences if it is thought to be real. People do think of society as real in a variety of significant ways. In this sense, society has "autonomous existence."

3. Knowledge of society requires understanding. To achieve a genuine, workable body of knowledge about society, we as social psychologists involve ourselves in the lives of the people we study. Weber's treatment of the origins of modern capitalism illustrates this. Since understanding may emerge from imagining the interplay of intersecting circumstances, it is often the once-occurring situation that sheds light on major societal and psychological phenomena. Thus social psychologists seek out the details of life.

4. Society consists of forms that provide a structure for ongoing activities. These forms give meaning to individual lives. Many different things can happen within a given form. Forms allow and disallow thoughts, feelings, and actions according to their appropriateness to the form.

5. Society may be understood from the perspective of the individual and from the perspective of organization. The first step in understanding is to describe individual and collective processes of intentions and actions. The second, to analyze the forms of organizations, builds on the first.

Exercises Using Concepts Of Social Psychology

1. Write a brief description of yourself—your looks, intelligence, how well you get along with others, and so forth. Now ask another member of your social psychology class to write a similar description of you, and you write one of him or her. Both of you write what you think the other thinks of you. This exercise works best if you know the person outside class.

According to Cooley's concept of the looking-glass self, you should find your description of yourself agrees more with what you think the other person thinks about you than with what they actually think. Did your results show this? If not, can you think of why not?

2. In our society, homeownership is very important. Yet, the average price of a home far exceeds the yearly earnings of the typical American family. Still people buy and sell homes using a complicated way of thinking about money that we call the "mortgage." See if you can depict the idea of a mortgage as a kind of definition of the situation?

Suggested Readings

There are many excellent secondary sources introducing the concepts of symbolic interaction or sociological social psychology. Larry T. Reynolds deals with some of the same scholars we discuss in his *Interactionism: Exposition and Critique* (Dix Hills, NY: General Hall, 1993). In addition, he treats contemporary contributions from various schools of thought and deals with substantive studies of emotions and organizations.

In a recent and exceptional treatise, Richard A. Hilbert *The Classical Roots of Ethnomethodology: Durkheim, Weber and Garfinkel* (Chapel Hill: the University of North Carolina Press, 1992) demonstrates the historical connections between the classical concerns of Durkheim and Weber and those of one major figure in the study of the everyday life, Harold Garfinkel. Hilbert suggests that the study of the practice methods whereby individuals act socially is centered squarely in the classic literature of sociology. Hilbert's work shows that the study of ways people accomplish meanings is not secondary to sociology but is at the core of the discipline's origins.

These two books will take the reader far beyond the current chapter to a greater appreciation of the rich and significant theoretical efforts of sociologists to state clearly and programmatically what the concerns of the discipline are. Both books are accessible to the serious undergraduate reader.

Chapter 3

George Herbert Mead (1863–1931)

We devote this chapter to a single early symbolic interactionist because his influence has been so strong and enduring. George Herbert Mead taught a generation of sociologists and social psychologists at the University of Chicago and in so doing informed the philosophical foundation for an entire program of analysis. His direct influence on Blumer, and his indirect effect on Goffman and the large group of contemporary symbolic interactionists, has not just fashioned an intellectual style associated within social psychology, but has shaped the very conceptual heart and art of our discipline. We explore Mead, the man and his ideas, to appreciate better our task of understanding social phenomena.

Mead and Early Social Psychology

George Herbert Mead was a contemporary and close friend of Charles Horton Cooley. Also American-born, Mead even taught with Cooley for three years at the University of Michigan. But, unlike Cooley, Mead studied in Germany under Wilhelm Wundt, whom we meet later in this chapter, and perhaps because of this he had a greater sense of the role of society in the emergence of the mind and the self. Also unlike Cooley, and other contemporaries of theirs, Mead wrote very little during his lifetime, with his major literary contributions to the field being compiled after his death by former students who essentially pooled their lecture notes from his classes (*Mind, Self and Society*, 1934). Because he wrote so little, it was not until late in his career, after 1920, that Mead's ideas became well recognized even within professional circles.

Mead was acutely aware of the ravages of war and the difficulties of achieving lasting social stability in a changing and often conflict-ridden contemporary world. He considered his work an attempt to avert a second worldwide conflict and along with his fellow social scientists envisioned a broad understanding of the nature of social life, one that would allow a new social order composed of diverse people who could maintain their sense of identity while avoiding the negative consequences of national chauvinism, ethnocentrism, racism and parochial pride. For this and more philosophical reasons, his work is often associated with American pragmatism and appeals to many who share a

41

similar idealism, one tempered with realistic assessments of the legacies of history and personal experiences.

Except for his three years at Michigan, Mead spent most of his career in the Philosophy Department at the University of Chicago, where he regularly taught a course entitled Social Psychology. The impact of this course on Mead's students has been among the most significant influences in the field. In his class, Mead tried to show that although people are endowed with solitary, contemplative powers, a person is typically not alone in his or her quiet world. Here Mead anticipated the writing of Ortega y Gasset, who pointed to "man's power of virtually and provisionally withdrawing himself from the world and taking his stand inside himself" (1973; 217). But, ironically, the same power that allows this sense of individuation makes possible the creation of a distinctively human phenomenon—society.

For Mead, the primary problem of social psychology was to unravel the relationship between the individual and society. Which came first, the individual with contemplative powers and individual ways of doing things or society with its organized and customary ways for individuals to think, feel and act? This is no chicken-and-egg question in Mead's estimation. The pure case of one being within oneself, without some reference to shared categories of thought, even if these are simply words, cannot exist. Mead's position was clear: without society, there can be no individual. Any apparent individual escape must itself depend on some aspect of a pre-existing social life. Harvey Farberman (1980) makes a similar point with regard to the role of fantasy in the modern world, pointing out that just when we reach out to achieve our innermost fantasies, we become vulnerable to the forces of society.

The sum of the ideas we all have of our own worth, of who we are and what we do, is the reflection that, in the aggregate, we call society. In the final analysis, we are society; it is in us. It may even teach us to value withdrawal from it. Herbert Blumer restates Mead's thinking as follows:

> For Mead, the self is far more than an "internalization of components of social structure and culture." It is more centrally a social process, a process of self-interaction in which the human actor indicates to himself matters that confront him in situations in which he acts, and organizes his action through his interpretation of such matters. The actor engages in this social interaction with himself, according to Mead, by taking the roles of others, addressing himself through these roles, and responding to these approaches. This conception of self-interaction in which the actor is pointing out things to himself lies at the basis of Mead's scheme of social psychology. (Blumer 1975, 68)

We return later to the conceptualizations of Mead that form the basis of his symbolic interactionism. But because of Mead's own importance, we continue with some historical antecedents of his thought, utilizing in our effort the all-important concept of "self" as our vehicle.

Some authors (cf. Diggory, 1966) prefer to cite first Homer and Aristotle or at least Descartes's "Cogito ergo sum" and trace the concept of self to the present. Our approach is to consider a number of the recent (from the late nineteenth century) antecedents of the concept of self and then explore its development toward and within symbolic interaction theory.

According to James Diggory, through the mid- nineteenth century, "ideas about self and ego had been developed almost exclusively on the basis of reports of direct conscious experience, usually the experience of the theorist himself" (1966, 10). The philosopher C.S. Pierce (1958) first began the break from introspection, arguing that every cognition includes the object of which one is conscious and some action of the self, an action that produces the object in consciousness. The object is, then, the objective element of the cognition and the mediating action is the subjective element. But Pierce felt that one cannot distinguish present sensations from memory images, therefore "the only way of investigating a psychological question is by inference from external facts" (1958, 110).

For Pierce, knowledge of one's self is based on one's contact with the world of objects and on the actions of other persons toward oneself. In studying the development of self-consciousness in children, for example, he concluded that the child becomes aware of itself through the concept of its own body-as-cause and through trial-and-error learning. In adults, Pierce believed, knowledge of self is based on a conversation with another part of one's self or with "society," which he thought of as a sort of loosely compacted person, represented to us through actual people. As a philosopher, Pierce may not have been as concerned with operational definitions as is the social psychologist; for this reason perhaps, his definitions remain rather vague. Nevertheless, in his writings are the foundations of symbolic interaction's concept of self.

The German psychologist Wilhelm Wundt (1880) advocated a view of consciousness similar to that of Pierce. Wundt called attention to kinesthetic factors and the role played by tension in one's muscles. He believed that some muscles in one's body are always tense and the permanent mass of feelings that arises from such tension is the consciousness of self. In growing to adulthood, then, one gradually comes to believe that one's "permanent" mass is subject to one's own will, and thus "apperception" or awareness of self develops.

Perhaps a greater contribution of Wundt to symbolic interaction theory is his concept of "gesture," which was considered of much importance by Mead. For, as the latter said, "Wundt isolated a very valuable conception of the gesture as that which becomes later a symbol, but which is to be found in its earlier stages as part of a social act. It is that part of the social act which serves as a stimulus to other forms involved in the same social act" (Mead 1934, 42). As we see later in greater detail, it is actually in terms of "language" that the gesture becomes important in the development of the self.

William James's contributions are an important part of Mead's understanding of the self and self-consciousness. According to Diggory (1966, 14), "his (James') writing is a transition-point between older and newer ways of thinking about (self). He was militantly objective in his treatment of the problem." James assumed all experience, self or not-self, is object-oriented, and being able to make an object of the self is a significant step in the direction of self-development.

James actually believed there were three types of self: the material, the social, and the spiritual (1890, 292). James's material self is made up of one's body, clothes and even one's immediate family; thus, "our father and mother, our wife and babies, are bone of our bone and flesh of our flesh. When they die, a part of our very selves is gone" (1890, 292).

A person's social self, to James, "is the recognition which he gets from his mates" (1890, 293). He goes on to say that "a man has as many social selves as there are individuals who recognize him and carry an image of him in their mind" (1890, 294). Here, Diggory interprets James to be saying that a "person has as many social selves as there are groups about whose opinion he cares" (1966, 15); the implication for a basis for "reference groups," to be discussed in a later chapter, is apparent here.

By "spiritual self" James meant a "man's inner or subjective being, his psychic faculties or dispositions" (1890, 296). Realizing the problem of making the self an object, James believed that "considering the spiritual self at all is a reflective process, is the result of our abandoning the outward-looking point of view, and of our having become able to think of subjectivity as such, to think of ourselves as thinkers" (1890, 296).

Harrold Hoffding, a Danish psychologist at the turn of the century, examined the developmental aspects of empirical self-awareness in attempting to answer the question of how we come to "distinguish between our own self and the things outside us" (1891, 3). He believed body and self had, initially, the same boundaries, but gradually the body is discovered by the senses and comes to be subject to the individual's will. Thus the notion of "self as the subject of thought, feeling, and will" is established (1891, 6). Nevertheless, Hoffding felt one's idea of oneself is not derived from immediate perception but is inferred from the general nature of consciousness.

Because it was so important to Mead's own thought, we return briefly to the work of Cooley regarding the role of consciousness in self and society. Actually, Cooley's ideas about the power of imagination can be quite useful in understanding the relationship between aspects of appearance and the self. For example,

Davis (1992) suggests that fashion reflects changing images of self in modern society. We can "read" the content of fashion socially and understand the relationship between what people wear and who they think they are. For example, by affecting a "bizarre" appearance, by having a particular hair-do, or by wearing a coat inside out, a young person imagines how he or she will appear to others. But more than that, the youth imagines how a group of people will evaluate that appearance, perhaps as having a meaning of resistance to any efforts on the part of authority figures who want to influence the way people dress and otherwise appear in public. Most important for his or her consciousness, our young dresser will react emotionally to these imagined adult evaluations. By dressing in a way one imagines to have a particular meaning to a group of people, an individual attributes a quality or character to himself or herself and achieves a sense of belonging or social membership.

In *Human Nature and the Social Order*, Cooley stated, "I do not see how anyone can hold that we know persons directly except as imaginative ideas in the mind" (1922, 120) and "I conclude, therefore, that the imaginations which people have of one another are the solid facts of society, and that to observe and interpret these must be a chief aim of sociology" (1922, 121). Previous to this, in his *Social Organization*, he suggested

> at least three aspects of consciousness which we may usefully distinguish; self-consciousness, or what I think of myself; social consciousness (in its individual aspect), or what I think of other people; and public consciousness or a collective view of the foregoing as organized in a communicative group. And all three are phases of a single whole (1909, 10).

As we have already noted, Cooley believed one's consciousness of oneself was a direct reflection of the ideas about one that one thought were in the minds of others; thus, to reiterate, a "self-idea of this sort seems to have three principal elements: the imagination of our appearance to the other person; the imagination of his judgement of that appearance, and some sort of self feeling such as pride or mortification" (1902, 184). This, of course, forms the basis for Cooley's famous "looking-glass self."

Before Cooley, writers had already seen the self as emergent from and spreading across a social environment. But, according to Mead, " the superiority of Cooley's position lies in his freedom to find in consciousness a social process going on, within which the self and others arise" (1930, 696). Thus, both self and other exist as imaginations in the minds of individuals and can develop not just within a social environment but only through a social process.

Mead described in detail the emergence of the human mind and the self through the process of social interaction. Like Cooley, he believed in a looking-glass self. "It is only by taking the roles of others that we have been able to come back to ourselves" (Mead 1925, 268). Mead felt one must stand outside oneself in self-reflection and that the only points of reference the individual standing outside had were those attitudes other persons had of him or her. One then sees oneself as others do, or better, as one thinks they do.

Also like Cooley, Mead believed the self developed in a social situation. "It is further implied that this development has taken place only in a social group, for selves exist only in relation to other selves, as the organism as a physical object exists only in its relation to other physical objects" (1925, 262).

Almost immediately in infancy, one begins to interact, reaching out to nearby surroundings. The child soon discovers that even involuntary things, like crying or cooing, bring facial expressions and other responses from others. This earliest learning involves the ability to discriminate among people, the sounds they make, and finally one's own sounds and movements. According to Mead, only as the child's self begins to emerge from the society, usually represented by the family, does he or she begin to become an active, self-conscious family member. In this process, society begins to enter and inform the consciousness of the child.

The Emergence of the Social Self

In his discussion of the social conditions under which the self arises as an object to the individual, Mead presents his conceptualizations of language and what he called the "play" and "game" stages of a child's social development. Regarding language to be critical in the process of self development, Mead begins with Wundt's concept of gesture as that part of any particular act that will influence the behavior of others who must adjust to it. But even a dog fight would qualify as a conversation of gestures. For example, one dog growls and bares its teeth. In response, the other snarls and barks.

There are times, however, uniquely human times, when the gesture, especially the vocal gesture, becomes what Mead called a significant symbol. "The vocal gesture becomes a significant symbol . . . when it has the same effect on the individual making it that it has on the individual to whom it is addressed or who explicitly responds to it" (Mead 1934, 46). When, for instance, one individual says the word "table," the image or concept called up in the mind of a listener is the same as that called up in the mind of the speaker.

The role of language in the emergence of the self becomes apparent in the play and game stages of child development. To Mead, the play stage of early childhood is that particular part of playing in general where invisible, imaginary companions are produced in the child's experience. "Play in this sense . . . is play at something. A child plays at being a mother, at being a teacher, at being a policeman; that is (he or she) is taking different roles" (Mead 1934; 150). Here the child is being both self and other, saying something in one character and responding in another, having a conversation with an imaginary other conjured up and embodied in his or her own self. In this situation, from which the self arises and develops, the interaction can occur only through the use of significant symbols; thus the role of language becomes obvious. As Mead said, "I know of no other form than the linguistic in which the individual is an object to himself" (1934, 142).

Mead's play stage is followed by the game stage, in which the child must take part in an organized game with real others; that is, "the child . . . must be ready to take the (role) of everyone else involved in (the) game, and these different roles must have a definite relationship to each other" (1934, 151). In the play stage there is no basic organization, and the child may change the situation whenever he or she pleases. In the game (Mead used the example of a baseball game) the child "must have the responses of each position involved in his position. He must know what everyone else is going to do in order to carry out his own (task). He must take all of these roles" (1934, 151). Out of the game there arises for each participant an "other" made up of the ideas all the other individuals in the game have toward a particular participant. This "organized . . . social group which gives to the individual his unity of self may be called the 'generalized other'" (1934, 154).

The I and the Me

For Mead, during this play-game developmental world of symbolic interaction, there emerges in each of its participants a structured self that is more than just the sum of the attitudes and actions of others toward them. Mead contended that there are two parts to every social self: one that is the result of having absorbed others' attitudes and actions as one's own, and another that is unique to the individual. The first part he called the "me" and the second, the "I." The me is most easily understood in terms of self-consciousness in that the me is the part of the person, or self, that encompasses self-awareness. For Mead, self-consciousness is an awareness of all the attitudes about oneself that an individual arouses in others. One's me, then, is derived from the attitudes of others toward oneself—with the most important "others" in one's life being his or her "significant others." In this sense, the me is one's understanding of one's generalized other, or Mead's version of Cooley's looking-glass self.

The I, in contrast, is the individual's subjective perception of and impulse to respond to the me. One is aware of one's me and therefore knows what is expected of him or her in any given social situation. To return to the baseball game, when the ball is hit to someone, that player understands how he or she is expected by the other players to make a play on it (me); but the outcome of the individual's impulse to make the play (I) is not known. This is why Mead felt the I was creative or uncertain. It will determine how the attempt to complete the play will be made, but it remains uncertain until the play is actually completed, at which time it becomes a part of the me, depending on how the play was completed and how the other players reacted. Thus Mead said, "It is because of the 'I' that we are never fully aware of what we are, that we surprise ourselves by our own action. It is as we act that we are aware of ourselves" (1934, 74).

One way to think about Mead's division in the self is to imagine ways in which the direction of one's thought, feeling and action might be influenced. For Mead, the me represented those instances when influence originates outside the self; first pressures are put on us by others, and then those pressures are taken in as part of our self. When we share with our boss the belief that bosses have the right to tell employees what to do and thus we do what we are told, the direction of influence is from external to internal. Social psychologists refer to the process of absorbing external social pressures and influences as *socialization*.

But the I, as we have said, represented for Mead the creative, spontaneous, and even impulsive aspects of the self. So while the me suggests to an individual, "according to the boss, you should act this way in this situation," just how one will finally act is never fully determined. The I sees options, "you could do this, or you might do that or that." The I's sense of choosing what to do, or of sometimes acting impulsively and even surprising oneself, means that internal influences can affect behavior. In fact, behavior often involves a negotiation, as it were, between I and me. So although much social action is predictable, there is a paradox; for precisely what behavior will occur is never known until it actually does.

Older children and adults are somewhat discriminating compared to youth about whose attitudes they will take on as their own. Consider serious joggers, for example. Such persons don't care if most persons they pass remark that their running style is sloppy and tense. But after a daily workout, when a fellow runner discusses the merits of relaxed hands, arms and shoulders, when a running colleague points out that these matters increase the benefits of running and so further decrease the chances of heart failure, the jogger attends, notices, ponders, and incorporates the attitude of the other (Nash 1980).

Perhaps because of the creative and therefore elusive nature of the I, most research in this area has focused on the acquisition of the me. For example, many studies and experiments have been conducted to show how in some situations it is alarmingly easy to get people to take on attitudes other than their own. Zimbardo (1973) and his associates once set up a simulated prison and randomly assigned to students the roles of playing prisoners and guards. The researchers were shocked by the ease and rapidity with which the students lived up to the expectations of these roles, by the harassment and even brutality the role-playing "guards" imposed upon the "prisoners," and by the willingness of the "prisoners" to acquiesce as if they were in a real prison.

Even some of the students' family members were unwittingly taken in by the experiment. Some visited their sons during "visiting hours," and in one case, where their son appeared visibly affected, one family sent a priest to see him. Although they consented to be in the experiment and could have voluntarily dropped out at any time, at some point the "prisoners" seemed to forget this was the case. They continued to allow themselves to suffer the harassment of the "guards." Finally, before its scheduled completion but after one "prisoner" seemed to be having a nervous breakdown, the experiment was terminated by the investigators and each participant was put through a hastily arranged "debriefing" process.

Other researchers have demonstrated that the qualities we attribute to ourselves are those we think others attribute to us. Our belief in our own attractiveness seems to be directly related to our beliefs about whether others think we are attractive, whether or not they actually do. Miyamoto and Dornbusch (1956) once conducted a study in which they asked sorority sisters to evaluate themselves and other members of their sorority on such qualities as physical attractiveness, friendliness, and intelligence. They were also asked to say how they thought others evaluated them. The strongest relationships were between self-concepts and what the sisters believed their fellow sisters thought about them, rather than what they actually thought.

Mead's distinction between the me and the I tells us these studies are focused on the me and that they therefore provide an incomplete picture of the social self. On the other hand, if we were to compare, behavior by behavior, a me-derived action with a similar one derived from the I, we would discover the two seem externally indistinguishable, even though they may have been motivated by quite different forces. It is this aspect of his social psychology which makes Meadian analysis of social settings sometimes difficult. We follow here with some ideas on analyzing love from a Meadian perspective.

The I and Me in Love

A person with self-control can act sincerely or can feign an attitude or feeling and play act, and all such matters could be discussed as autonomous phenomena. Let us consider the example of a courtship, one in which a man and a woman play, rehearse lines and act like lovers. The two can speak and act in similar ways, but the meanings of their actions could differ in terms of their intentions and motivations. The situation might involve any of three separate but interrelated phenomena: the intentions and motives of the woman; those of the man; and, those both accept as sufficient grounds for the accomplishment of "good times."

One may say to the other with genuine assurance, "I love you," and the other may reply just as sincerely, "I love you, too." We could observe both acting similarly, their verbal utterances accompanied by embraces, smiles, laughs, and what the two consider to be a good time in general. Yet each knows they both have different reasons for their actions and emotions, and they know the actions each expects from the other are different. One partner believes love can be exercised with many different partners without adversely affecting the various relationships. The other person is a "monogamist," yet for intimate and personal reasons accepts this particular shared partnership in spite of the other partner's belief.

The woman may never articulate her feelings of love for this one man, nor how these differ from those she has for other men. The man may never make explicit his version of fidelity. Nevertheless, when they are together each accepts what happens, the things they say and do, the ways they look at each other and the way they hold hands, as manifestations of a good time.

Consider also the insightful essay by Judith Katz (1976), in which she illustrates how the conditions of our perceptions of love can be quite a problem in American society. We might be able to understand how two people may love each other in different senses, but when one partner wants evidence of the other's love, problems develop.

We assume that someone who loves us knows what we want, understands our tastes, likes, and dislikes, and wishes to perform unselfish acts on our behalf. Whenever we have to ask obvious questions, or remind our partners of our tastes, or whenever the nice things they do for us turn out to be something they wanted to do for themselves, we find our belief in their love fading in its credulity, and so we begin to question their feelings. If she has to ask, maybe she really doesn't love me; if he gives me something he should know I don't like, or if he asks me to go to his mother's for dinner when he knows we don't get along, maybe love is lost.

Mead maintained that we cannot truly understand social interactions without probing the consciousness of the parties involved. This is why a primary technique for Meadian analysts is participant observation, where researchers become so closely associated with those whose lives they are studying. External influences, like the strong cultural importance of love as the primary and sometimes sole criterion of intimacy in our society, find their way into the details of personal relations and even one's inner life, transforming that private place into a social gathering with the symbolic presence of the others. But in spite of the sometimes overwhelming presence of socialization processes, individuals always retain their unpredictable uniqueness. Mead felt this to be an essential aspect of human social life, its creative and spontaneous nature.

Mead's Theory Of The Social Self: A Closer Look

Mead was, first and foremost, a philosopher. By today's standards, his ideas lack empirical grounding—they are neither deductive nor inductive scientific concepts. To say this, however, does not mean his thoughts about the social character of human existence have not inspired scientifically grounded research about the social self. As we have noted, his work is perhaps the most inspirational of all the early social psychologists.

To appreciate why this is so, we need to restate his thinking systematically and formally. In doing this, we rely on many excellent secondary sources (see especially Martindale 1981; Reynolds 1993), but we wish to underscore that our situation is probably even more difficult than that of Mead's students when they attempted this task. At least they had heard him lecture and so also had the opportunity to question him. Our advantage lies in the years of retelling that preceded ours, and most important, in our knowledge of the ways that interpretations of his ideas have been translated into social psychological research.

Propositions of Meadian Thought

The self, as an entity that can be an object to itself, is essentially a social structure, and it arises from and develops through social experiences. In a certain sense, after a self has arisen, it provides itself with social experiences, however imagined or fantasized those might be. So we can conceive of the eventual existence of an absolutely solitary self. But it is impossible to conceive of a self originating outside social experience (Mead 1934, 140).

Minds and selves arise only in the process of social interaction and communication. Mead reasoned that the capacity to interact and communicate is a biological endowment of the higher orders of animal life. Furthermore, only human beings have created a language of significant symbols, a medium through which they internalize the attitudes of individuals with whom they interact and the social groups in which they participate. Through such socialization, the internalization of social meanings originally external to the individual, there arises a sense of social control, where the influence of one or more persons over one or more others is effected. Ultimately, the distinctive task of social psychology is to explain how society "gets into" the individual, determines one's behavior, and thus becomes a part of a person's psychology or selfhood.

Stated as formal generalizations, the following are the essentials of Mead's thought about the social character of human existence:

1. *Social interaction precedes language, mind and self-consciousness.* This statement reflects the fact that Mead starts from a given; that is, he regards society as an accomplished fact. In some measure, this suggests how Mead thought about

the way in which society was influenced by evolutionism, the thinking of biologists about the processes through which contemporary life forms have come into being. Drawing on the work of Charles Darwin, whose analysis Mead studied carefully, he focused on the principle that living organisms are engaged in a continual struggle for mastery over their environment. Each existing life form is based on some successful way of achieving environmental control. Biologists refer to this as adaptation. The color of a salamander, the speed of a deer, or the nerve down the side of a fish that senses vibration in the water—once an organism has developed or evolved adaptations such as these, that organism uses its adaptation to control its environment and be more likely to survive in it.

Human society, Mead thought, had also evolved, but since it is a subjective phenomenon, it rises out of a distinctive adaptation of human beings, namely, intelligence. The human mind is, then, a naturalistic phenomenon even though it differs in function and structure from other phenomena. Mead accepted this Darwinian "conception of intelligence, and saw the mind as engaged in an elaborate instrumental process to insure the organism's survival" (Coser 1971, 348).

While Mead's conception of social phenomena is far from any old-fashioned uses of biological analogies, he was uniquely influenced by evolutionism. First, as Coser suggests, Darwin's theory is the foundation of Mead's pragmatic philosophy. In this pursuit, he modeled his understanding of scientific thinking after Darwin's, characterizing intelligence, society and the self all as emergent and evolving.

So our first generalization is tantamount to a biologist's acknowledgment that what is seen as the natural world is the result of processes that occurred in the past. The social psychologist sees people, their senses of who they themselves are and of who they think others might be, and takes these as the results of processes that have occurred in the past. The social world has evolved out of complex processes involving the human mind, and as we become selves we discover it. Or in other words, the social world is a given, to be discovered by us through our being a part of it.

2. *Nonverbal communication precedes language in the form of natural signs and gestures.* In the genesis of the self, Mead reasoned that language is developmentally dependent on nonverbal communication. Later we devote an entire chapter to the importance of understanding language and the role it plays in human social life, and Mead clearly foresaw not just the kind of sociolinguistic work that we discuss there but even recent experimental work such as that of Cathryn Johnson (1994). Although she does not cite Mead, Johnson's findings from the experiments she conducted to determine the relationship between gender identity and legitimate authority point to Mead's insistence on the primacy of nonverbal communication in the meanings of the social self. For example, Johnson designed experimental tasks of complex decision making to

be carried out in four different settings: (1) a female manager with female employees; (2) a female manager with male employees; (3) a male manager with male employees; and (4) a male manager with female employees.

She designed these tasks so that some subjects were paid more than others and were given more say in the final task decisions. Students from introductory sociology classes participated in the study and were videotaped interacting in the various settings. Johnson then analyzed the tapes to see if patterns of conversations, such as interruptions, using tag questions ("you know?"), back channeling ("yeah," "mm-hmm," and "right"), the use of disclaimers ("I know this sounds stupid but" and the like) would be associated either with the gender of the conversational partners (men interrupting women, women using tag questions, back channeling and disclaimers) or with the authority roles played in the experiment. She reasoned that if authority roles are more important, managers will tend to interrupt without accompanying remarks, while employees will interrupt with remarks that support the formal leader and will use the other conversational practices; and all of this will occur regardless of anyone's gender. If gender identities are more important, then women managers will persist in the use of tag questions, back channeling and disclaimers. Thinking there might also be nonverbal aspects of communication at work, Johnson also measured the smiling and laughing that took place during the experiments. According to Johnson, her results

> clearly show that formal authority is more important than gender in understanding conversational patterns, supporting the situational/ authority explanation [that roles of authority suggest certain ways of talking for both genders]. Subordinates exhibit more conversational support (i.e., have higher rates of back channeling and positive interruptions, and talk less) than formal leaders and are less directive (i.e., have higher rates of qualifiers), regardless of sex. (Johnson 1994, 122).

Johnson's research also shows, however, that on the dimensions of nonverbal communication she measured, the gender of the subjects did make a difference. Admittedly her results are complex and difficult to interpret. For example, smiling and laughing appeared to be associated with gender, with women laughing more and smiling less with male rather than with female managers. Johnson suggests that gender stereotypes about how women should behave (be supportive and submissive in all relationships) may be stronger for nonverbal behaviors than for verbal ones in an authority context (1994, 122, 133). Perhaps actions do speak louder than words in some contexts; or it might be that in certain settings if women *act* submissive they may not have to *talk* as if they were.

Mead's ideas would support such an interpretation because, according to him the nonverbal behaviors we learn are more central to the core conceptions of who we are; they are developmentally important prior to the instrumental use of language. To the degree that men and women have different early socialization experiences, the behaviors that mirror these primary events will be more categorical and so more difficult to alter—that is, closer to the heart.

Mead appreciated both the biological basis of social life and the symbolic nature of it. While we are not suggesting that the nonverbal communication of women is determined by biological factors, we do note that research such as Johnson's might well lead to discovering some fundamental differences in the way males and females think about themselves and each other. Mead believed that the ability to communicate intent and motive is an important result of the evolution of higher-order animals. Just as dogs "walk around each other, growling and snapping, and waiting for the opportunity to attack [here we add that male and female dogs have different behaviors in this regard]" (Mead 1934,14), so we read meaning into the glance of an eye, the attitude of the body, or the configuration of one's mouth. Perhaps one day we will see that this reading of meaning into one another's social behaviors is shaped by the ways in which higher-order processes operate for males and females. In no way will this discovery, if it ever comes, justify stereotypical actions, but it might help us understand the origin and development of these behaviors.

3. *Language creates mind and self.* Given Mead's recognition of its importance, it is indeed surprising that social psychologists have been so slow to examine language in its own right. Typically, social psychologists acknowledge the role of language in social interaction as symbolic. Hence they look for the mediating role symbols play in human interaction. We recognize immediately who another person is as "male" or "female," "young" or "old," "black" or "white," and eventually we know them by a host of other words that carry the meanings we give to those with whom we interact.

Mead's insight was that in fact these words have meaning only to the extent that we use them in the general process of "self-indication" and that this process of knowing who we are appears to be twofold: when we indicate something to ourselves we also make that something into an object. We understand a person as female in terms of what we have learned to think of as "femaleness" or, in contrast, "maleness". So our thinking about the other depends on our prior knowledge of the thing we are encountering. In our world, these "things" are given, and we discover them through thinking about them, about others, from the vantage point of ourselves. Children have rudimentary versions of the aspects of objects, and they develop more sophisticated understandings of themselves and others as they grow. As they have more experiences with different objects in their world they differentiate among and between them. There are many types of women, for example, and there are many ways to characterize them. A small child with limited experience will have a rather fixed and inflexible version of the nature of objects, but will grow into an understanding of the general nature of things. Originally, who "women" are depends on who "mom" is, but eventually the child realizes there are many different kinds of women.

This exemplifies how the social world is not merely imposed on an individual, but is built up by virtue of the individual's thinking. As Reynolds puts it,

> One interprets things largely on the basis of action one is prepared to direct toward them, instead of this being a stimulus-response. The individual "remakes" [through symbolic thinking] each stimulus and responds only to a stimulus of his or her own (social) making. Mead sees people as having a fairly large measure of control over their social lives. People respond to their interpretation of things and not to things themselves; hence, the person can respond differently to the same object on different occasions, but can also respond in the same way to objectively different things if they are similarly defined. Self-indication takes place in a social context, in a context of symbolic interaction (1993, 68) .

So mind and self are dependent on the existence of language. Our world is given to us and we think about it by manipulating the significant symbols that represent it in our minds. And we come to see ourselves as objects in the world only through our symbolic interaction with others

4. *Mind and self are social.* This follows in a forceful way from Mead's conception of language's role in understanding and comprising context. The biological basis of thinking and knowing is insufficient to complete a picture of human existence. Who we are and think we are is as much a part of the way we learn to talk, the symbols that order our perceptions and way we use them as is the capability of our brains. To study an individual is, then, to study the society of which he or she is a part.

What we see when we study human interaction is always to a great extent a mirror image of the interactants' different social worlds. And whatever anyone does, whether it is the way someone walks or talks or the term paper one wrote last semester, says something autobiographical about that individual. Since each of us has a unique history, each one of us is slightly different from the next; but all of us have been socialized according to the same interactive process, so in some ways we are all the same. Because mind and self are social, and socially interdependent, always with some shared history, by studying one we must learn something about the other.

5. *As individuals mature, they develop the capacity to respond to a "generalized other."* In fact, this process entails both generalized and differentiated patterns of learning corresponding respectively to the "generalized other" and

"significant others." Since human understanding is self-referencing, all under-standing of others stems from self-understanding. Since self-understanding is itself social, however, society becomes complex, with a multiplicity of meanings developing through the ever increasing social web, of individuals trying to understand (objectify) each other.

Mead followed the discoveries of behaviorism about the process of learning, but he modified them to fit with the symbolic character he believed defined the very essence of human existence. As humans learn, they, like all animals, differentiate and generalize. We learn that fathers are a type of male; we differentiate between types of mothers and sisters and cousins and uncles, and we know about the differences among houses, cars, computers, and so on. So we learn to differentiate our world symbolically in ways similar to how an animal learns that a certain stimulus will evoke a particular response.

Unlike animals, however, we invent our responses and our stimuli, and this process results in two types of others—the significant and the generalized. To Mead the generalized other is the response of an individual's consciousness to others, that is, all the others in one's life a person has learned about. In this sense, the generalized other is similar to the general response an animal learns to make to different external stimuli.

Here the distinction between the way animals learn and how humans do becomes crucial. An animal learns through the consequences of its behavior, consequences measured largely in hedonistic terms (whether a particular behav-ior results in pain or pleasure).

The human creature, uniquely thoughtful and social, makes an environment of and with those who count and those who do not, those who count for a specific situation and those who count for all situations. In short, the human knows who is significant for a particular situation and who for a general one. For example, if you have ever taken music lessons, you will quickly grasp Mead's conception of the significant other. At first, when you were a young novice musician, your recital was a success when your parents approved of your performance. They were the audience to whom you played. You might have disliked performing, having your own unique reasons for taking lessons, but virtually anyone could approve of your performance; however, it was the approval of your parents that was important, significant.

As your competencies as a musician improved, that is, as you learned to think of yourself as a more accomplished player, you began to play simultaneously to both a more general and a more particular audience. While you still liked to please your parents, you learned that your father is "tone deaf" and did not notice when you played a "wrong" note. Your teacher and finally the generalized music critic, the knowledgeable music audience, became significant to you—your symbolic reference point for deciding whether your recital was successful. As mature social individuals, we can construct for the particular situations of social life, however temporary such situations might be, those to whom we refer to shape the senses we have of who we are and what we are doing; these are our significant others. We also know the various kinds of others who can respond to our performance, some of whom we may appreciate positively and others of whom we might deny. In the last analysis, the totality of our understanding of our entire listening audience is our musical generalized other.

6. *The social self has a creative, spontaneous aspect, thus the process of being social is internal as well as external.* We have already mentioned this very difficult aspect of Mead's sense of being social, but it is important to review it here. Mead reasoned that every person is unique, possessing a particular energy that allows us to identify the individuality in the social roles each individual plays. A social self is both one's understandings about others, about the similar patterns of thinking, feeling and acting that make up society, and one's unique attempts to act given these understandings. The first sense of self Mead called the me and the second the I.

As Reynolds (1993) mentioned, Mead thus acknowledged that individuals have considerable control over the way they act socially. While we are like each other to the degree that we have similar conceptions of both significant and generalized others, we are also unique in that understanding. No two conceptions and thus no two reactions are ever exactly the same.

Mead was fond of sports and a particularly avid baseball fan. It is appropriate then to follow his lead to illustrate in some detail the distinction between the I and the me in the game of baseball. Let's say we're at a major league game. There's a man on first with one out and a hard ground ball is hit to the shortstop. An accomplished player at his position will react according to his me. He will respond to his understanding of the "double play." He imagines what he would do if he were the runner and the hitter. He "takes on the attitude of the runner" and knows that the runner will attempt to advance to second in a effort to get to the base before the ball, thereby avoiding the force-out and foiling the double play. The shortstop fields the ball and throws to second base, acting also in anticipation of the second baseman's being there to play out his role. The ball is thrown not to the second baseman, but to where the shortstop believes the second baseman will be. Likewise, the second baseman takes on the attitude of the others in the play and moves to take the ball, touch the base and throw on to first, again based on his understanding of what hitters and first basemen do in this situation.

While we have glossed the complexity of thought and action that occurs in a double play, we can see that the play is actually an intricate interaction based on the ability of the players to take on the roles of each other and act on the basis of the symbolic meaning of the double play. Each player may be a significant other depending on his direct involvement in the immediate action of the particular play, and the overall understanding of all players, and even fans, of the double play is a generalized other. All this is an interaction of me's, that is, of the sense each player shares of the reciprocal nature of the roles involved in the playing of the game.

The double play is an instance of society (a game) made possible by virtue of players consciously knowing each other's role. Yet some shortstops, some second baseman turn the double play with a distinctive style, a way of handling the ball and posturing that allows us to see the "signature" of the player on the play. Fans can see the difference in the players because of the I, which is difficult to define but can be seen and known. It is the *way* that a role is enacted when nothing in the role itself determines the style of the play. Surely all short-to-second-to-first double plays are the same in one sense—they occur only under specified conditions and they must take place in a sequenced way. But some double play combinations are special, with three men moving as one unit, each adding a unique meaning to the sequence of motions.

The I or the me may be highlighted by the organization of an activity, or it may be subdued by it. In the Meadian view, organization is a preconceived or ready-made arrangement of roles, the enactment of which depends on their internalization by players and fans. Hence we learn the rules of baseball or football and the positions of the respective contests; and from our awareness of and abilities with certain skills, we can play a game, or at least understand it when we see it.

The complex, subtle, and varied interaction of I, me and organization can be illustrated by comparing baseball, an I-game, and football, a me-game. Although baseball is clearly a team sport, because it is played in an open space and because it has rules that make the playing of the game highly visible, fans and players are aware of the individuality of the players. The pitcher stands in full view of the batter. He studies his opponent—the batter—consults with this teammate the catcher, and makes a conscious decision about how to "pitch the batter." Pitchers have knowledge of batters who can't hit the change-up, who stand too close the plate and must be "brushed back," and so on. The positions of the outfielders are adjusted (right or left, shallow or deep) on the assessment of the hitting capabilities of the batter and the situation of the particular play (the number of outs, the inning in the game, the score, etc.). While the role taking and mutual understanding discussed here are a part of all games, in baseball the players and knowledgeable fans are keenly aware of the mental aspects of the game. The players are isolated in their playing, they make plays in the open, and the long dimensions of their throws and hits further define them as isolated individuals who perform the game mentally.

Baseball, of course, is an American game, once known as America's pastime, and in a society of intense individualism we should not be surprised to see the cultural understandings (the most general of categorical ways of objectifying the world) forming the mental background for both the meanings and the structure of the game. And football is also American, yet in football individual players seem purposively lost to the identities of their teams, with eleven men from each of two teams dressed in identical uniforms, each covered, almost disguised, in equipment and each performing a highly specialized task in the play. If it weren't for the different numbers they wear, many players would be indistinguishable from each other.

In football, the solid defensive lineman reacts to a play, he fights within the rules to tackle and cover his opponent. While he has an understanding of the roles of the offensive player, the nature of the action of the game, with its misdirection and deception, makes the equivalent of baseball's double play hard to discover. On every play a successful team executes plays, operates like a well-oiled machine, and each man plays every down for the team, giving up his identity for the collective goal of playing the game. The I's of the players are present and even highlighted in some positions (quarterbacks and running backs showing the I), but compared to baseball, the I is buried in the organization of the game.

George Mead saw that the organization of a game can be discussed as having a logic, and he gives us a way to think about it. Mead pointed to the game as an arena of self-development, and he insisted that the social self was composed of two complementary processes: one part of it due to taking on the attitude of the other and one to the unique features of the individual. Whereas social order itself, and, of course, games as manifestations of order, requires that an individual lose his or her distinctiveness to the logic of the game, there is still a sense in which an individual becomes unique by virtue of belonging to a collectivity. Different games stress me or I meanings of the self for those who participate in them.

Children are encouraged to play the games of baseball and football—girls are more likely encouraged to play softball or soccer—and find themselves attracted to or repelled by them partly in relation to their sense of themselves. A boy attracted to baseball no doubt lives in a home where the sounds of baseball on the radio are part of the normal sounds of summer. Likewise, the Pop Warner youth league quarterback surely has cheered for the local university or professional football team. Here we refer not to the direct influence of father on son, or mother on daughter, but to the tie between types of social situations and social character. Of course, within a single household there are often dual loyalties, even mutually reinforcing characters, as a family moves from summer games to ones popular in the fall. And we do not suggest that games necessarily determine the qualities of the social self, but they do make different demands on social competencies and they do have different ways to foster the display of the meanings of being social.

In the game of baseball, the individual player is isolated from the team. A high fly ball shifts the focus of the game squarely on the outfielder. He must cleanly and confidently display his individual skills in order to show that he is a worthy member of a collectivity. As Mead said, in each successful play the individual becomes the social reality. Consider the "error" in baseball, a game where there are many ways to make a mistake—the obvious are the "booted" ball, the "wild throw," the embarrassing "miffed grounder" that goes through the player's legs, and the "misjudged fly ball." While all these "mistakes" display that the player lacks the requisite skills to complete that moment of the play, none represents the serious error that reflects a player's missing the logic of the game. It is in children's games that the latter kind of mistake most often appears. Here we think of the kid in right field who cleanly and even spectacularly fields a fly ball, only to hold it in his glove expecting congratulations while in the meantime the runners on base advance. Baseball requires, as coaches are wont to say, that a player's "head is in the game."

This means each individual act on the field gives the player the opportunity to show that he knows what is going on. So the center fielder must concentrate not just on making the catch but simultaneously on setting up to make a throw in anticipation of a runner "tagging up" to advance to the next base. While each of these anticipated moves clearly illustrates the necessary ability of the player to take on the attitude of the other players (a me function), the individual player's inserting himself into the logic of the game underscores his way of understanding it (an I function).

In football, in contrast, mistakes are often hidden in the mass of the collective activity of the game. Of course, infamous examples like Jim Marshall's wrong way touchdown do happen, especially with some frequency in youth sports. But Marshall, as a defensive lineman, was not expected to know what to do with the ball. Likewise, when a quarterback is called on to make a tackle after he "errs" by throwing an intercepted pass, he has an opportunity to show that he is a "complete player"—something he is not required to be by the logic of the game. Whereas opportunities to show that one understands what everybody else on the field is supposed to do are the exception in football, in baseball they are the rule.

Baseball is a game of individuals acting in concert to make socially grounded decisions that anticipate the thinking and actions of other players. But football is one in which individuals lose their distinctiveness to the well-executed play, to the team effort of forcing the opponent to give up ground in a warlike setting. Baseball idealizes individual play and football the collective form of the complex organization. While both games are of course social, baseball is an I-game and football is a me-game

7. *The enlargement of the self is dependent on and in turn supports the breadth of community values.* By this point in our discussion of Mead, his pragmatic moralism and idealism about world peace and order should be apparent in his analysis. The more roles a person learns to take on, the greater the expanse of his or her generalized other, and in turn the greater is the possibility for a new, emergent social order. Narrow people are so because they lack the capacity, or simply reject the opportunity, to take on the attitude of the other, thus they are less likely to participate through mutual concerns in the creation of new symbols and, hence, new ways to enact roles.

Mead's home university was situated in the middle of one of America's most diverse and rapidly changing urban environments. Chicago had become a city with a high profile of immigrants, people from Poland, Jewish people, people from Italy—most important, people who did not share the ethnicity, religion, or language of the "native" midwesterners. Whereas early Chicago was a rough-and-tumble cow town, by the first decade of the twentieth century it was a cosmopolitan city, still rough-and-tumble, but the actors were more diverse and less homogeneous. Mead and his contemporaries were aware that many of these immigrants had been enemies in their European homelands. How could they coexist and how could they create a new social order out of their differences?

This is where Mead's analysis comes into its own, for Mead discovered the symbolic roots of social order in the individual. He shows us that both the individual and society are outcomes of the same process. From him we learn that people *make* their worlds in addition to *finding* them; and above all else, as we discuss shortly, he taught that acts of concerted individual consciousness can empower people to make new social orders. And for him, the form and character of these new worlds would rest on the same process that created the old, namely, the symbolic interaction between human minds.

Mead as a Social Reformist

We would be remiss if we were to conclude our discussion of Mead without devoting some attention to his concern regarding the issues of democracy and social reform. We recall here that virtually all of the founders upon whom we have based our social psychology felt the need for their work to make a contribution toward the common good. Nevertheless, the reader might wonder why such ideas as social reform would be brought up under the auspices of social psychology, for are they not more appropriately the business of sociology proper?

In fact, most social psychology texts, even sociological ones, do omit them. But throughout his own professional life, Mead was a staunch supporter of and often an activist for democratic social reform. The son of a Congregational minister, Mead himself thought seriously of following in his father's footsteps before he chose the academic life. And even though he did choose academia, all of his work was guided by a powerful humanistic ethic. This is readily apparent in his teaching and writing, and outside the university he aligned himself with several progressive organizations. He was involved in such a way that one Meadian theorist refers to him as a "radically democratic intellectual" (Joas 1985, 10).

But what is important for us to note here is that Mead's theories of democracy and social reform were intimately intertwined with his social psychology. And though he would not be one to support the expression of society at the expense of the individual—he was too much of a democrat for that—he did realize that an ordered society was possible only to the degree that individuals could take each other's place in some symbolic fashion. In his own words, "social control depends, then, upon the degree to which the individuals in society are able to assume the attitudes of others who are involved with them in common endeavor" ([1924–25]1964, 291).

In this fashion, the individual in taking the role of the generalized other, in this case of society, incorporates or internalizes society within his or her self and becomes not just an object but also a personal agent of the social order.

Given his firm belief in democracy though, it was critical for Mead that all individuals have the right to choose freely, from opportunities equally available to all, how to become such an agent. According to Shalin, Mead was one of several reformers at the time who, while they may have maintained individual differences on the causes of current social problems, still "all agreed that the gap between democratic ideals and American reality had grown intolerably wide" (1991, 35).

We reiterate here how Mead lived the greater part of his life in Chicago, and this at a time when it approximated a city of immigrants, many of whom were poor, uneducated and uncared for by a society to which they came with hope and a willingness to work. But to Mead Chicago exemplified what was occurring in most major American cities at that time, the failure of the American citizenry, and especially its leadership, to live up to the high ideals of Jeffersonian democracy. His conclusion, according to Shalin, was as follows: "If modern America is to fulfill the democratic aspirations of its founding fathers, it has to 'eliminate the evils to which economic inferiority exposes great masses of man,' it has to provide equal access to cultural goods for all members of the community, and it must imbue the laborer's work with meaning" (1991, 37).

Surely there are many who would echo these sentiments today, and perhaps justifiably so; for we in America continue to suffer from many of the problems evident during Mead's own life.

If this is true, then the question arises of how to resolve the social ills which have continued to dog us in the century since Mead began to practice his social psychology. In his day — Mead went to study in Germany in 1883, the same year Karl Marx died — Mead identified with many of the ideals of socialism, once writing, "Socialism, in one form or another, lies back of the thought directing and inspiring social reform," (1899, 367). But if he set himself apart from the socialists it was over means rather than ends for, as Shalin points out, he also renounced "all versions of socialism that sanction violent means" (1991, 32). As a pragmatist and a member of the Progressive movement Mead rather placed his faith in the ability of people to evolve social reforms non-violently.

We have already referred to Mead's close association of his social psychology with the concepts of evolution, and as a pragmatist he maintained the belief that society itself, in the present, was always in an emergent state. Furthermore, he saw in a country such as the United States a nation which, through its Constitution, offered its citizens the means necessary to foster reform, and, if they deemed it necessary, even revolution.

For the individuals of a citizenry to be in touch with their me, a common generalized other embodied by their society, is for them to identify with the social ills of their time. If we align this Meadian social psychological view with a conception which suggests the sense of a social or societal I, "the pragmatist vision of the world-in-the-making—the world that is perennially indeterminate, continuously emergent, and wonderfully malleable" (Shalin 1991, 38), the stage becomes set for the addition of a progressivist perspective which would suggest the potential for a populace to take voluntary non-violent action to improve their social condition.

That is, unlike the Marxian socialists who argued from the standpoint of economic analysis, the progressive view held social ills to be products of a flawed system of social organization. So in America, any public — for Mead, any "body of citizenry, well informed, conscious of its interests, and ready to take the problems of society as their own" (Shalin 1991, 41) — had at its disposal the constitutional means and thus the democratic freedom to foster non-violent social reform. All that might be needed was the proper guidance and the means to deliver it. And perhaps this is why early in his career Mead tried to convince a friend to join him in what would have been an attempt to gain control of a newspaper, namely, the *Minneapolis Tribune* (Discussed in Shalin 1991, 30). But they did not make such an attempt and Mead rather chose the academic life and so concentrated most of his efforts on education, which he believed involved the systematic broadening and expansion of the self and held the hope of fostering more inclusive senses of community.

In a way, Mead developed a highly sophisticated version of what is suggested by the old maxim "walking in your enemy's shoes." To know another means to take his or her role, to recognize and be able to use that person's sense of selfhood. To know another person is to speak his language, understand her history and the like. Ultimately for Mead, properly guided concerted action will produce new sets of symbols and a new order.

Mead, of course, had his own political orientations, and he saw the process of the emergence of a new order as both pragmatic and spontaneous. But as we have noted he was no socialist utopian. Although he believed the new order would arise from symbolic contacts among diverse others, he did not think social policy and governmental plans would necessarily succeed in forming it. Although he applauded some of the ameliorative programs of his time, such as the juvenile court system and the enactment of compulsory universal secondary education, he thought reformers would likely never be able to shape the world just as they wanted to see it, because the shaping of the world was for him always an interactive outcome, to a degree necessarily encompassing the societies of those involved.

According to some Marxists, Mead simply justified well-meaning but only piecemeal reforms to the negative consequences of immigration and social change (Schwendinger and Schwendinger 1974), thus they decry his failure to appreciate the social structural conditions that perpetuate the very problems he and his fellow pragmatists wished to solve. Indeed, this debate between the utopians and the pragmatists seems quite contemporary as today we struggle with the problems of large cities, race relationships and ethnic conflict. From Mead, we see a distinctively American "boot strap"approach—in the doing is the solution. And we all must consider just what this means for each of us as we pursue our own social psychologies.

Summary and Conclusion

George Herbert Mead may well have been one of the pre-eminent philosophers and social psychologists of late 19th and early 20th century America. Unfortunately, the amount of written work he himself produced was minimal compared to what it could have been—as we have noted, the works for which he is best known were completed from students' notes after his death. Perhaps this is why Mead was so often misinterpreted, a condition which led Maurice Natanson to conclude of Mead that "the work of a truly major American philosopher is today largely unknown, frequently misunderstood where it is known, and, more often than not, simply ignored" (1956, 1).

Fortunately, since Natanson's conclusion of nearly four decades ago, there has been a surge of interest in Mead's work, spurred particularly by the publication of Goffman's *Presentation of Self in Everyday Life* in 1959. And more recently, the work of Joas (1985) and a newer edition of articles by Aboulafia (1991) have begun to do justice to Mead's thought.

Overall though, and in spite of various limitations, Mead's contributions to a sociological social psychology are numerous and wide-ranging. We selected to address a number of these and to cover them in some detail from more than one perspective. In this we hope to have demonstrated some of the ways they have provoked research and how they comprise a core set of assumptions critical to our understanding of social psychology. Meltzer (1964, 30–31) provides us with a list of Mead's contributions:

The essence of the viewpoint of a sociological social psychology is that human behavior is behavior seen in terms of what situations symbolize.

Mind and self are twin social emergents and not biologically given.

Language acts as the mechanism for the rise of both mind and self.

Self-development illuminates a process whereby the individual is both caught up in and extricated from society.

The specific functional, processual development of the mind is characterized by the importation within the person of the social process of interaction.

Social action is behavior constructed in such a way that during the course of activity individuals can structure or select their own environments.

Through the development of common meanings, understandings, expectations and objects a common social world is formed.

Individuals actually share one another's behavior rather than simply respond to it.

The study of the inner, subjective aspect of human behavior is vital for a full understanding of human conduct.

In our concluding remarks we characterized Mead as a social reformer intent on practicing what he also taught, the use of social scientific knowledge both in the pursuit of truth and to foster the common good. George Herbert Mead was born not two months after Abraham Lincoln signed the Emancipation Proclamation, and he died on the eve of Adolf Hitler's election as Chancellor of Germany. Raised in a religious environment which emphasized the christian duty of doing good works to better the condition of humanity, it is no surprise that Mead blended his rigorous approach to social psychology with his strong humanistic spirit in an effort to ameliorate what he saw as a world often overridden with conflict. Obviously our social psychology is to a great extent informed by that of Mead; and it is for each of us, readers and writers alike, to choose the direction in which to apply our respective social psychologies.

Exercises in Meadian Thinking

1. Many of you have had a driver education class, perhaps in high school. In that class, you learned about defensive driving. Compare the basic task of defensive driving with Mead's ideas about how essential the task of "taking on the attitude of the other" is to social relationships. Does this way of conceiving of social order tell us anything about traffic regulations and the nature of accidents?

2. Recently, Ultimate Frisbee, or Ultimate, has become very popular on many college campuses. If you know about this game, you might want to think about whether it is an I or me game? To answer this question, think about the rules of the games and especially how fouls are called?

3. One way that researchers assess consciousness of the self is to gather descriptions people give for themselves. A simple way to do this is to ask people

to write ten sentences in response to the question "Who am I?". Ask ten of your friends to do this. Then, look at the sentences and see if you can assess the degree to which these sentences reflect the I or the me.

Suggsted Readings

Mead's major work *Mind, Self and Society,* (Chicago: University of Chicago Press, 1934) is still available and readable. Reading it certainly reminds one of contemporary efforts to link our knowledge of infra-human behavior to that of human beings. Mead was a master at drawing contrasts and examples from animal behavior, and we recommend that the serious student look at part 4 of *Mind, Self and Society*, entitled "Society: The Basis of Human Society: Man and the Insects."

An excellent secondary source is Bernard N. Meltzer's "Mead's Social Psychology" found in *Symbolic Interaction: An Introduction to Social Psychology*, ed. Nancy Herman and Larry Reynolds (Dix Hills, N.Y.: General Hall, 1994). Finally, we suggest J. Peter Rothe, *Beyond Traffic Safety,* (New Brunswick, N.J.: Transaction Books, 1994) as a compelling and exciting application of social psychological perspectives to modern issues in traffic. He deals with the symbols and selves of drivers and shows us how this aspect of daily life carries potent meanings of the self and society.

Chapter 4

Consciousness and Social Interaction:
The Contributions of Alfred Schutz

Every human association, from an intimate two-person group to an entire nation and now our global culture, is constructed from ideas or as some sociologists put it a mental "fiction" (Collins and Makowsky 1993) shared by the members of the particular group, nation or culture in question. It is difficult to think of society as an intangible object, an idea that exists only insofar as it is held in people's minds. In fact, most people go about everyday life, including social life, without giving it a second thought, that is, without thinking about the nature of what they do with one another.

Because we live in it and because it is such a part of our being, society becomes second nature to us. And to an extent, it is fortunate that we can and do take it for granted. If we were to think constantly about the nature of what we do, we really wouldn't get much done. Yet, if we were never to think about it, we would risk becoming automatons to the mechanisms of social life. We would become programmed to act in certain ways, and so would act without thinking, without even considering that we might have some control over our lives, and without having, or wanting, to take any responsibility for what we do.

But to say society is "only" an idea is not to suggest it is "merely" that, just a thought that can change as easily as people change their minds. As we have noted, society is part and parcel of a group mind—whether that group be of two or two million or two billion people. And because of our ability to symbolize objects, like groups, in language used to store ideas, first in our minds, but finally "on paper" and perhaps for all time, we have the capacity to institutionalize society and make it, for all practical purposes, permanent. The thought of something being "etched in stone" is not just a cliché.

In brief, while some ideas of society, like marriage, are relatively easy to change by the mutual agreement of the parties involved, changing nations is a much more difficult proposition. Tragically, as we see in the nation that once was Yugoslavia, people are fighting and dying to establish or maintain national identities. And this illustration can be multiplied many times over as we look around the world at, for example, South Africa, Northern Ireland and the Middle East.

Of course, it is presumptuous to think that an understanding of social psychology could bring an end to world conflict. But, without some understanding of how and why we act as we do, we are condemned to repeat historical errors, even in our own lives. By developing for social psychology students a conceptualization of the cognitive nature of social life, it is possible to present them with an alternative for understanding their daily lives and the decisions they must make to survive well in them. And this may be a beginning toward understanding the larger issues that must be addressed to affect positive social change.

Alfred Schutz (1899–1959)

The ideas of Alfred Schutz are central to any appreciation of the nature of social life because they provide a way to ground the study of social interaction in cognitive phenomena. Trained in law and the social sciences, Schutz knew many of the great European thinkers of the 1920s and 1930s, including Edmund Husserl, the father of modern phenomenology, the study of the nature of things. When the Nazis came to power, Schutz escaped to America, where he established a successful business and kept up his academic interests in New York, at the New School for Social Research.

Because of his knowledge of Mead and Cooley, as well as influential European thinkers, Schutz was able to articulate his own synthesis of theories for establishing a vital phenomenological sociology. His way of conceptualizing social science makes possible a strong cognitive version of social psychology. We follow his lead by considering the nature of interaction.

Interaction among human beings is a universal experience. People touch one another, hold hands, embrace and make contact in other physical ways. We also have visual experiences of others as we see their actions and as we watch them even when they are unaware of our presence. We talk with people in close, intimate conversation or speak into electronic devices that carry our words across the street and around the world, or even into outer space. These diverse and far-reaching human happenings all embody one universal feature, social interaction.

Here we define social interaction as a process of communication and mutual influence involving contact between two or more minds. As does any definition of social interaction, ours includes assumptions about human nature. In order to make our assumptions clear, let us look first at the "interaction" of some physical objects in a bowling alley. As we enter, we see at one end of a lane a group of brightly colored wooden objects, which, although only a few inches apart, are not in contact. They are not desirous of each other, nor do they think about making contact. They do not know of each other's presence. On initial inspection, as naive observers we would attribute only inanimate qualities to bowling pins.

Suddenly, a black ball rolls down the floor toward the group of wooden pins, striking some of them with considerable force, and a chain of reactions follows rapidly. The pins begin to influence each other in a jumbled confusion of movements. Some pins fly up in the air, knocking others into motion. Their positions change in relation to each other, and in a fraction of a second the once orderly group lies in a new formation, some pins resting on others, some lying horizontally in isolation. One solitary pin remains standing. In all this violent commotion, its position was not influenced by the movement of the others.

How should we study this kind of interaction? Given our assumptions about the inanimate, nonconscious nature of such objects, we would want to maintain a detached, outsider's vantage point. We could study the motion of the pins by recording and measuring angles, lines of force, and points of contact. In such a study, we do not need to assume anything about the objects' desirousness or anything whatsoever about the pins as active agents in the process. To be sure, the motion of any particular pin can be appreciated only in terms of its complex relationship to the others, the speed of the ball and other matters of the laws of physics. But no social interaction took place.

At the other end of the lane is a group of people engaged in animated conversation. They touch each other, make noises, change their positions, push, shove, laugh and show in their actions, or lack of them, their awareness of each other.

Bowlers and bowling pins are different qualities of phenomena. If one of the bowlers clasps the hand of another, pulls her to a standing position, and gently pushes her toward the line of bowling balls saying, "It's your turn, honey!," this sequence of events carries with it a tacit history and a hidden world of thoughts, intentions and meanings. Not only have two bodies briefly touched, not only has sound traveled between two persons, but contact has occurred between two minds. And the others, those who have observed this happening, have participated in it.

Human Consciousness

To understand the special nature of social interaction as a conscious, mental encounter we must first examine consciousness. As you may know, human consciousness has a physical foundation in an electrochemical process based in the central nervous system. Recently, the subject of much research has been the brain and how it operates, which portions of it are the sites of which functions, and precisely how information is used and learning accomplished by it. This research is of utmost importance, especially for its implications in treating aberrations of the brain. But it is not necessary for social psychologists to understand the physiological functions of the brain in order to explore consciousness. It is enough to know that as a medium for the work of interaction, human consciousness must allow for receiving, encoding and actively manipulating information. However the brain itself works, it succeeds in providing the mechanisms necessary for imagination and attention sufficient for the construction of the social world, the subject of social psychology.

Receiving Information

In order to survive, all life must coordinate its activities with its environment. In the animal world, such coordination, whether for reproduction, protection, or acquiring food, requires that the animal have some awareness of itself as well as of its external world. Human beings share with the rest of the animal kingdom this capacity to receive information; thus human consciousness allows for and enables the receiving of information from outside the organism.

Encoding Information

An important and distinguishing feature of human consciousness, making us unique among animals, is our ability to encode information. To encode means to make one object, event, quality, or relationship stand for some other object, event, quality, or relationship. For Mead, this capacity to create symbols and share their meaning with others was the basis for human communication. Instead of depending on our immediate awareness of temperature, for example, we can let such things as our seeing snow, the wind blowing through the trees, a mercury column in a thermometer, or hearing the words "It's twenty below out there" stand for a certain state in the environment—coldness. This capability makes possible the element of social life Goffman referred to as *theatricality*. In a theatrical mode we become sometimes even physically aware of how certain information has a referential relationship to certain other information. This knowledge allows us to act as if we were someone or somewhere else. The images out a window or even on a screen can evoke in us meanings and even feelings of coldness, even if the actual temperature in the house or the theater is comfortably warm. Another illustration is how the ideas of, say, Steven King can evoke in us a feeling of fright, even though we are safe reading at home or watching from our theater seats. In everyday life, theatricality may refer to a person's attempts to ignore the insulting intent and pay attention to other aspects of someone else's remarks, or disregard them altogether.

While there are many ways to encode information, human consciousness makes predominant use of linguistic symbols to accomplish this important task. Since a symbol is any object or event that has been assigned meaning, even a smile, the simple human act of turning up the corners of the mouth, can take on such connotations as "I like you" or "I won and you lost." Symbols, then, couple with their referents the meanings or things they represent. Language is a complex system of symbols allowing us to encode anything conceivable in human experience. But human consciousness makes use of other symbol systems, such as the clothes we wear, the arrangement of furniture in our houses, the way we move our bodies, and even the distances we stand from people when we talk to them. Symbols allow us to talk about the past and the future, to imagine and be aware of things outside our immediate presence. As we have suggested, perhaps the most important feature of human consciousness is this capacity to encode information into socially relevant symbols.

Actively Manipulating Symbols

Animals dependent primarily on direct input from their environments or strictly limited in their encoding capabilities tend to respond only to the immediate world. Stimuli are taken in that may or may not stand for other things; and with little thought, wondering or debate over what it might mean, the animal selects some behavior from its repertoire. Although human beings can react in this fashion, most of our behavior is symbol manipulative. We think about things and we work with our environment, attempting to use, change, modify, or in some cases ignore it. Some researchers have discovered, for example, that people who live in northern climates in large urban settings often dress and act in a way that communicates to their follow residents their disdain for winter weather. They do this by simply displaying symbols of warmth. Hence they will resist putting on boots even if it means ruining a new pair of shoes (cf. Nash 1981).

Especially in the modern world, great stock is put in the art of arranging symbols to create new worlds having no external reality at all. Novels and films are the more obvious examples of this. And these constructions of reality can play important roles in the practical affairs of everyday life. Just listen carefully to the talk of friends at school or co-workers on the job and you will hear many references to images from television and movies, and to words and phrases that come from these purely fictional sources. Such fictions become part of the cognitive basis of social life. The nerd laugh, the affected talk of the characters on "Saturday Night Live," the fictional roles played by popular actors such as Arnold Schwartzenegger—all can be part of what people know, which they in turn use to express themselves and build relationships with one another.

People may have faulty memories, misuse the images from television, or reason in ways that would get failing marks in a college logic class, but these things do not mean people are "judgmental dopes" (Garfinkel 1967, 66–75). Most of us at some time or other invent stories, believe in stereotypes, lie to others, or change the reasons we give for our conduct. Human consciousness always includes an active, creative element, and when utilized as part of our symbolic interaction, this feature distinguishes us from all other animals. Chimpanzees can respond to arbitrary symbols. They can be taught to communicate with gestures or colored chips, but they are not able to employ these devices to create some new myth about the origin of the universe and the history of chimpanzees.

Typical Knowledge and the Social Organization of Consciousness

What we take for granted such as our presumptions of memory in others, the styles of thinking we enact, our commonsense attitudes—is all socially organized. The mind without interaction with other minds remains merely a potential, an empty form. Consciousness involves systematic relationships among minds.

The process by which we come to think of the world as typical reveals the meaning of consciousness as socially organized. As Weber taught, in practical action sometimes the typical understandings people have can combine into new and more general ways of thinking about the world. According to him, a form of religious consciousness was a necessary accompaniment of modern thinking about capitalism. And in everyday life we all place our actions and those of others within categories of typical knowledge. Alfred Schutz wrote that this typical knowledge is what in the vernacular we refer to as common sense. For example, the runner who speaks of a "steady pace" is referring to part of an organized body of knowledge shared by other runners. He or she knows what it means to run with a steady pace, and how to tell if his or her own movements fit this category. When we explore the full context of the expression "steady pace," we discover several typified ways of thinking.

First, runners use this expression. As a type, they assume certain identities and attitudes. They think of themselves as people for whom running is a, perhaps the, dominant organizing theme of their routine, everyday worlds (Nash 1980). They have a runner's attitude. They judge running as a central or core value in their awareness of the world. Thus all other occurrences are interpreted from that stance. To a male runner, the birth of his baby means, among other things, missing a few training runs.

Second, the phrase points to an organized set of categories. A steady pace assumes its meaning within those categories that are part of the runner's consciousness. It contrasts with a "jogging pace" and a "racing pace"; the first refers to a warming-up exercise and the second to a deliberate, studious running style. The steady pace can be used during a training run but not in speed work. It can also apply to different paces, like a "steady racing pace."

Consciousness, then, is composed of typified knowledge—classes of events and things, and most important, the ordering of their contexts. One runner's steady pace differs from another's, and the outside observer can know the meaning of the term only by discovering how runners as a type of people think about the various running activities they engage in. The following example illustrates how typifications may operate within a given context.

During mid-July in suburban Hopkins, Minnesota, several thousand runners congregate for the Raspberry Festival Five-Mile Open. The race is held in conjunction with a community celebration. There will be a parade, shops will be decorated, and the town officials will speak. For the runners this is a popular race, one in which the finish is defined as fun because there is always strong competition, and of course there is a crowd. But while most people come to party, for the runners, Hopkins means a race, not a festival. Racers ignore or reinterpret the signs all around them of different ways to understand the event. The people who line the street may be parade watchers. They are there anticipating the start of the parade; watching the runners is secondary. Some may even taunt the runners; and spectators with small children must placate them by reminding them that soon after the runners finish the parade will start. To drivers on their way to a summer outing or heading to the office for some catch-up work on this Saturday summer afternoon, the racers are an annoyance. What is typified as the place for a parade by some is seen as nearing the finish, a place to pick up the pace, for others, and for still others, as an unnecessarily crowded intersection.

Often social markers indicate the shift from one typification to another. Consider the parade route at Hopkins. Ordinarily it is a street with typical understandings of its use by residents and visitors. It is a two-way street with no parking; it has four stop lights and a speed limit of twenty-five miles per hour. For a few hours on the day of the Raspberry Festival, these typical understandings are suspended and another set comes into operation to transform the meaning and use value of the street. The regular speed limit is relevant to usual street traffic, but not to a parade, and certainly not to a foot race. The bus stop posted on the street means nothing, except that would-be riders must look for a new stop today—something they know if they have ridden this bus regularly or something they will discover if they try to behave as usual on this day. The consciousness of which typification operates, "street" or "parade route," defines one typification as relevant and the other as irrelevant. While the parade is in progress, but not usually otherwise, the curb may be used as a seat. Goffman (1974) suggests that we think of shifts in the set of typifications employed to define the appropriate meanings for a situation as a process of "framing." Our discussion of how meanings shift on festival days depicts a reframing process.

In the case of the parade, the social marker is often dramatic, helping people understand that a reframing is taking place. People who know of the coming of the parade gather to see it; others merely wonder what is happening. Children not yet experienced in reframing see the street without traffic as an opportunity to play. The confused bystanders and playing children learn what is happening when a motorcycle, flashing its red lights and mounted by a uniformed police-man clears the street, proclaiming that the transformation has fully taken place.

The Life World

Consciousness is organized around life situations. According to W.I. Thomas, our social experiences are influenced by predefinitions of situations. By "predefinition" he meant the situation is thought of before interaction takes place. If we extend this idea, we realize that each of us lives in various worlds of ready-made meanings associated with persons and events encountered in the pursuit of the pragmatic objectives of living (Wagner 1970, 320). These worlds can be described according to the characteristic consciousness they engender. After Schutz, we call the patterns of consciousness life worlds. A life world may be thought of as a form of ready-made meanings. Every person has at least one life world, a typical way that he or she begins the understanding of social life.

An example of one life world will help show how this concept informs our analysis of everyday life: Fred rolls out of bed at five A.M. It's still dark, and anyway, after last night's six-pack, his eyes can't focus enough to see what kind of day it is. He switches on the radio to catch Earl Finkel's "meteorological forecast." Earl says over the radio: "Well, people, we are lucky again—mid-November, no snow, and low 40's. How much longer can it last?" Fred disagrees. He moans and swears. "I could've used the rest," he mutters.

Fred is a construction worker. The company he works for landed a good contract to repair the sewers in an old neighborhood. Fred operates a crane and makes good money. Construction is seasonal here in Minnesota, just as it is affected by weather conditions virtually everywhere (cf. Reimer 1979). Workers can't do certain jobs in inclement weather, so the men and women working on this project have been pushed to finish excavating before the first hard freeze. The work is hard, and recently, with union approval, they have been pulling down time-and-a-half pay for overtime, trying to finish. Fred is beat. He could use the day off. November is usually a slow work month. Some years it means lots of beer and ice fishing. This year it's a different story. "Looks like another beautiful day." Fred is depressed. Here what counts as beautiful can only be understood from the perspective of Fred's life world.

In modern society most of us operate comfortably and uncritically in many life worlds. We use the concept of life world much as the older concept of role was used by Mead and other early social psychologists. We have learned to be different people according to our definitions of the situations in which we find ourselves. In the concept of role, the ideas we have about what is the expected behavior for a particular situation guide what we actually do. With the concept of life world, we account for ideas and their influences on actual behavior by locating expectations in an agent, namely, a conscious person.

For example, let's imagine a middle-aged woman and the various life worlds in which she could live. On occasion she may think of herself as a wife and mother. On other occasions she may think of herself much differently. During any ongoing occasion, whenever she simply makes sense out of her world, the mentality she assumes for that occasion is called by Schutz a "natural attitude." In an average day the natural attitude of the housewife-mother may well end with breakfast being finished or dropping the kids off at school. When this same woman dresses for a day at the office and goes to the corner to wait for the bus, she becomes a bus rider. As a bus rider she knows how to read a schedule to time the arrival of the bus and where to sit to avoid conversation while riding, or conversely, how to encourage it. She is familiar with the objects of the bus world—tokens, passes, transfers, route maps, side seats, rear seats. When she arrives at work, she then becomes an executive, instructing her secretary, setting meeting times, pondering the consequences of cutting out part-time people employed in her school district, and thinking up strategies for going after federal grant money.

In the language of social psychology, this woman is doing much more than acting on expectations. She is symbolically and literally becoming a different person with each varying situation. She is able to make transitions from life to life because she has mastered the art of gearing into and out of qualitatively distinct communicative settings. In order to accomplish this feat, she must be capable of applying rules, making judgments, and interpreting correctly the intentions of those with whom she interacts. Each different life situation is organized, and in each there is a given consciousness we can uncover only by observing and describing the perspectives and competencies of conscious persons in their respective settings. We make no judgments about the contexts or interrelationships among these forms before the descriptions are completed, but we do expect personhood to be multidimensional.

The Life Plan

Thomas showed us that if we take a very broad view of individual lives, we can see patterns in how people organize their social worlds. He called this patterning "life organization." Such an organization underlies the often conflicting realities of the everyday world. The life plan does not necessarily unite these life worlds, but even if only in vague ways, it does serve as an overall objective and guideline for an individual's life as a whole. This can start with specific or limited plans and motivations provided for in the life world. We call this supreme system a "life plan" and note that it does not need to be deliberate or self-determined. It may be imposed and it certainly can change throughout a person's life (Wagner 1970, 319).

A father advising his son speaks from a confidence he believes one acquires only with maturity. He advises from his vantage point. He and his son may share many life worlds. They both are football fans, fishermen and bus riders, but the overall sense each makes of their respective worlds, the underlying consciousness of each, differs. The father recommends trust and faith that "all things will work out." The son may not be able to articulate his stance, but he is sure it is different. The father's roots, his sources of security, and the signs of his happiness—a home, provisions for the son, and even the son himself—are for the son unbearable chains, symbols of dependency. The son's frustrated attempts to change his father's understanding highlight the operation of two different life plans. Life plans, with their varying interpretations of the same events are sometimes associated with age or cohort grouping. When this occurs, we speak of generations and, in this sense, of generational conflict (cf. Mannheim 1938).

Forms of consciousness, the organization of everyday life worlds, and the judgmental activity of social life take place on a tacit level. If you ask some people what their life world for the moment is, they cannot necessarily tell you. Just as I do not need to know the formal rules linguists use to describe the grammar of a language in order to speak it, so in everyday life people do not often formalize their knowledge systems.

Conditions for Social Interaction:
Thinking about the Other Person's Mind

One of the primary tasks of social psychology is to show how the unspoken knowledge people have of each other makes social interaction possible. We can, like Cooley and Schutz, think about this knowledge as assumptions we make about what is in the minds of other people. In some situations, so much is assumed that what people do or say makes no sense to someone who is not a party to that specific conversation. Consider the following example:

Jim: Your SL-76s looked great—did they help?
John: A little, but I still have that quad problem.
Jim: Though that was taken care of?
John: Me too, but that's why I got the SL-76s; they did help, but I can't say they're worth the bucks.
Jim: In the kick I thought I saw you pull up.
John: Yeah—same old story.

In order to understand the meaning of this conversation, we would have to know about the context of the interaction between Jim and John. Because they assume, correctly, that they share the social knowledge of a certain life world, the runner's world, they do not have to explain everything to each other when they talk about running. They both know, for example, that SL-76s are special units of a class known as running shoes. SL-76s are one of eight different types of training "flats" manufactured by one shoe company. A flat is a shoe that uses the whole of the foot. Flats contrast with "spikes," which are designed for short fast races, putting more of the stress of running on the toes. Flats are either "racing" or "training." Racing flats are lighter and provide less support for the foot. Some training flats, like SL-76s, are popular for use in long-distance races, of two or more miles.

Jim knows John recently purchased the 76s because they have a reputation among runners for having a well-supported heel. The reputation takes on significance when paired with John's allusion to a "quad problem." He means he has been having pain in the front part of his thighs while running, and he believes this has something to do with the worn heels on his less well supported Brook-Drakes, another type of running shoe. He switched from the Drakes to the 76s because of their specially shaped, rounded heel which he thought would minimize wear and help prolong his running life through a less painful heel-striding posture. Jim knows this as well and was curious about the outcome of the experiment. John and Jim thought the 76s would fix the problem. Apparently John feels he has experienced less pain, but is unsure of the advisability of the purchase of the more expensive 76s.

Jim and John also share a long history of competitive running. Their emotional involvement in this competition is controlled. After all, they belong to many other life worlds; they hold jobs, have families, and belong to organizations. John has never beaten Jim at a race. A "good race" for the two friends is one in which Jim pushes John to run faster. John's "quad problem" has prevented him from running all out (at top speed). Eight-miler John's leg hurt on the final half mile, preventing him from catching Jim, even with his SL-76s. "Same old story."

Jim's remark, "In the kick I thought I saw you pull up" was not a reflection of just the good sportsmanship, interest, or controlled exhilaration of the winner. Within their running relationship, Jim acts like winning is unimportant to him, and he periodically acknowledges John's accomplishments, his personal record times, and his role in pushing him to run faster. Winning is important, but not as important as having a "good race."

The friendly competition between Jim and John is part of the reality of their relationship as runners. To uncover the meaning of their conversation, we must be aware of the unspoken understanding between them. In this example, its expression is so subtle that if we were just looking for general rules of good sportsmanship, we would miss the richness of the interaction. When observing social relationships and describing them as life worlds, we must recognize the operation of many idiosyncratic ways of talking, double meanings, implications and general rules.

John and Jim presume a common life world between them. They assume each possesses similar knowledge of the objects of the runner's world, like shoes and personal records. Each thinks the other knows more or less the same things about running. In the conversation, Jim guesses about whether John understands him, and John allows any vague comments that Jim may make to pass on the grounds that they will become clear in future remarks. These assumptions allow their interaction to continue.

Recent writers have singled out an essential aspect of these assumptions, which they refer to as mutual intentionality recognition (Cegala 1982, 83–85). They suggest that human beings signal to each other their intentions to engage in communication. When people recognize their mutual intentions, they give each other a certain latitude in the precision of what is said; any "slack" is taken into account in their respective knowledge of their common experiences. Without this mutual recognition, persons engaged in conversation tend to turn inward, touching their own faces or folding their arms as they talk, without regard for whether their remarks are being received. Alternatively, gesturing away from the body and toward one's communication partner is thought to reflect an outward intent to communicate.

Jim and John interact with ease as they feel secure in their assumptions about each other's intentions and the level of understanding between them. They make good guesses about each other's motives and intentions. Without the ability to make, recognize and act on such guesses, the social world could not exist at all.

With our example we have begun to demonstrate how interaction depends on one's mastery of a particular way of understanding what others are thinking. In brief, communication requires an individual's being able to recognize when and how he or she knows what other persons in the conversation are thinking. As we have suggested, how well such a skill is mastered and how much we can guess we know about what others are thinking depends on various tacit assumptions that underlie any conversation we might have. Schutz identified several assumptions people make about the thoughts and intentions of others, and we analyze four of them here: reciprocity thinking, filling-in, typical experiences, and temporality. The contemporary sociologist Aaron Cicourel (1974, 52–54) first discussed these in systematic fashion for the purposes of social psychology. And while they are basic to social interaction, we cannot go out and observe them, but only infer their existence from what people say and do.

Reciprocity Thinking

Reciprocity thinking occurs when one person assumes that for the moment—for the sentence being spoken, say, or while something is being requested—the mind of the talker is interchangeable with that of the listener. For the purposes of interaction, this assumption is taken as valid by both parties until further notice (Cicourel 1974). Reciprocity thinking about others is never validated in the sense that we can somehow test and know that we know the other person's mind. We guess at what is on the person's mind. We have guessed this way for a long time, since probably even before we could talk, and so we boldly decide what others intend by using our confidence in our own ability to know others.

When we say "pass the salt," and someone hands us the salt shaker, we assume an interchangeability of standpoints with the person of whom we made this request. When we receive the salt shaker we hold that in fact, for this limited purpose, we have interchanged mental stances. But did we really? Whether it is really possible is irrelevant to social life, for the reality is defined or constructed by those who live within it.

In our example of the runners, John responded in a way that Jim interpreted as appropriate for his question, so John continued to assume his subjective, conditional way of thinking was true. Had John replied about the SL-76s, "Yeah, but it uses too much oil," Jim would have been puzzled. Jim knows SL-76s use no oil and presumes John also knows it. But John's response is inappropriate; it does not make sense. Therefore, it is possible that either Jim's presumptions about John are false, Jim made a mistake, John has misunderstood Jim, or John is joking, putting Jim on. In any event, the remainder of the conversation cannot proceed. In this instance, Jim probably would take John to be joking or to have misunderstood and then request a clarification; that is, a different way to establish reciprocity thinking must be found, or else the interaction ceases. Jim might reply, "Sure man, my pair are down a quart all the time," and move on to the rest of the conversation; or else Jim could say, "Not your TR 3, man, your SL-76s." John might then say, "Oh, I thought you were talking about my car." Both examples function to restore the form of thinking we are calling reciprocity.

Filling-In

Although it is fairly easy for people using the same language to make themselves understood, human beings are not computers, so when they talk to each other their communication is not usually precise. In fact, people depend on a certain amount of vagueness in each other's talk in order to engage in conversation at all. This reflects the assumption that one person can fill-in what the other does not express. In other words, if people were to require of each other definitions of all the terms used in everyday conversation, there might be no meaningful social interaction at all. The dialogue between Jim and John would expand to one hundred times its present size if Jim were to have to specify things like what quad problems are. Instead, Jim assumes that John knows. If there are misunderstandings in future conversations, Jim can always find out what John means; or at least he assumes he can!

Of course, this all means a great deal of talking and social action can take place on very little knowledge. Often only a name or label is required to serve as sufficient grounds for the continuation of a social world. New words never heard before or events never seen can be interpreted and can acquire meaning.

Police, for example, know well the territories they patrol; but they still must fill-in in order to interpret objects in their environment. They know that open drapes in a certain home mean trouble. The light off in the second tier above the shop means something is wrong. Neither of these events occurred before; they are novel. Sometimes without even realizing just what it was that was out of the ordinary, a police officer can say, "I felt something was wrong." The officer has acquired a history of idealizations about the appearances of his or her beat. He or she notices kids darting around the corner of a building because the movement of the kids is an instance of a "unique feature emerging from the background of routine features" (Mehan and Wood 1975, 78). The police officer may not fully understand the movement, but takes it to be suspicious and investigates without completely knowing whether a law has been broken. Police officers decide law violation neither from a formal legalistic vantage point nor from consciously applying their background knowledge of their beat and its typical appearances. They judge such problems by filling-in their routine practices with the web of practical, ever-changing circumstances and thus decide on incidents that necessitate applications of the law.

In a recent study of the role of the citizen caller in initiating direct police action in two large suburban towns, Mehan (1993) deals with the details of just how police interpret and use these calls in their efforts to manage various juvenile activities (drinking and hanging out/disturbing the peace). Generally, he finds that police don't prevent crimes, they "prevent calls." They know or think they know what kids are up to, and through certain practices they attempt to prevent disorder. For example, they "broom the sector," which refers to keeping kids "moving along," and they "show themselves" by driving up to groups of young people simply to let them "see us." Through these practices they attempt to control the activities of young people, to move them into a specific area to do their drinking so that citizens will not call in about it.

Mehan deals with some of the paradoxes in these practices, first noting that normally police prefer to deal with large groups of young people rather than singles or pairs of them. But in fact the very practices they employ to "breakup" groups, such as "brooming," may create more difficult situations for them (they have a harder time finding the kids after they broom a sector). In this case, then, we appreciate the complexity of the judgments police make about the character and activities of juveniles, and how the job is actually one of "control and management" rather than enforcing the laws.

A law, then, is not evenly enforced from one time or from one officer to the next, just as Jim and John do not really know about SL-76s in precisely the same way. The meaning of the law, or of a particular law, and the reference to the shoes both depend on being within a context of other meanings, assumptions, and sketches of knowledge that are sufficiently vague and incomplete, a context that becomes clear only after future events take place (Garfinkel 1976, 210–213).

Typical Experiences

As we discussed earlier, people organize their social worlds into categories, sometimes grouping together things that appear to be different and unique and treating them as if they were the same. In interactions with other people, we make assumptions about whether experiences are typical. Police officers who decide something is wrong from some clue in the appearances of their normally perceived environments make judgments on the basis of contrasts they draw between typical and extraordinary features. They rely on their own stocks of knowledge to determine a sense of what is routine and what is not. "Things are quiet tonight," the officer tells his partner. "Let's take one last swing around by the liquor store . . ., then request a Code 7 (coffee break)." As the patrol car pulls up in front of Tom's Liquor Store, the officers look at the store's appearance and notice that the lights are on and the doors look locked. "Looks ok—let's go," they agree. The judgment, "looks ok," depends on an attitude or commonsense assumption that social life can be normal or routine. In order to arrive at any judgment regarding meaning, an assumption that there are "normal" or "typical" experiences must be made.

Frank tells his son, six-year-old Bobby, that the family might purchase a Jeep. But Jeeps are expensive, and Frank is not sure the family budget will allow such a large expense. One Sunday morning Frank says to Bobby, "Let's go look at Jeeps. Probably the showrooms will be closed, but we can look around." Frank and Bobby head for the local AMC-Jeep dealer. Upon arrival they find the showroom locked and the particular model they want to price inside. Bobby reads the sign on the door, "Open 2:00—8:00 Sundays." It is now 11:00 A.M. He grabs the door and pulls it hard. Frank looks at Bobby and admonishes, "It's locked. Please don't pull on it." Bobby stops. They decide to go out on the lot once more, to read sticker prices on the new cars. Frank walks back to the showroom window and thinks he hears the faint sound of a bell, perhaps a phone, inside. He does not give it a second thought.

They continue browsing the lot, commenting on the costs of cars. "This one is $17,000," says Frank. "Let's get this one, Daddy!" Frank ignores Bobby and walks to the next car. They see two men drive up in front of the showroom and look through the windows, then glance around the grounds. They spot Frank and Bobby and say nothing. They talk briefly to each other; using a key, they go inside the shop through a side door, then they depart. Frank and Bobby peer longingly one more time through the showroom window at the green Commando inside. Frank does not hear the bell but doesn't really notice it either way. They get back into the old family sedan and drive home.

This episode rests on assumptions of typical experiences: shopping, Frank's fatherly attitude toward Bobby's behavior, the cost of the vehicles, and the like. We want to show how the principle feature of the story, the meaning of what was an alarm bell, relates to typical understandings. Bobby set off the burglar alarm when he pulled on the door. The two men, on-call security guards, did not suspect that a crime had been committed. They did not call the police. Instead, they simply inspected the property themselves, pronounced everything to be normal, and went back to their homes. Now, what typifications, or normal forms, underlie this decision-action sequence?

From the guards' thinking, real criminals rarely set off a frontdoor alarm. The shop is equipped with a dual alarm system, one wired to windows, side and back doors (typical entrances for criminals), and the other to the front doors which face a busy city street. Second, Sunday morning is not a typical time for a burglar, especially for one using a frontdoor entrance. Third, criminals engage in purposeful action; they plan their heists. In short, they come prepared with equipment they need after having completed the planning required to carry out the burglary. Generally, such planning does not include bringing children on the job.

Upon arrival at the dealership, the guards found no open doors, nothing disrupted inside, and no one who looked like a burglar on the scene. They concluded, therefore, that the alarm might have gone off accidentally and that they should recommend it be checked for mechanical defects first thing Monday morning (when repair people typically work). Or they decided this was another instance of rowdy children or curious pedestrians jerking overzealously at the door, and the appearance of Frank and Bobby did not suggest that either of these two were criminals. The guards close the sequence for the moment by thinking of the incident as a case of an infrequently occurring, but nevertheless typical, false alarm.

From Frank's perspective, the faint noise he heard was not understood as an alarm until several days after the incident when it dawned on him what had happened. The presence of the two guards in street clothes did not precipitate an unusual scene for Frank. The men had keys to the showroom, which they knew how to use. They also knew each other, were looking around and came to check the place out—two typical occurrences.

In this example, we see how participants in interaction make assumptions about the existence of typical experiences and how these assumptions become the basis for their social action. They do not treat all the events and actions of others as entirely unique or of equal importance. Some things are routine and ordinary—even false alarms. No false alarm is like any other in all its details; still, every false alarm has common features that can be described. The meaning of the event derives from these features.

Temporality

Social time is another feature of the conditions of consciousness that make possible social interaction. In our natural attitude, we have a variety of ways of experiencing time, such as calendar time and clock time and setting aside some time to do something. For the purposes of understanding experiences social psychologically, however, as Schutz pointed out, a person's sense of lived-through dimensions of time is what is important.

Contemporary writers of social psychology have turned their attention to describing how time is experienced. Weigert (1980) shows how meanings of time derive from the social purposes to which time is put: hence, we try to be "on time"; we have "time to kill"; we "put time into" a job; and we "take time out" from our daily rounds. The multiple and varied meanings that time can have in everyday life and the continuity of social interaction itself depend on a state of mind that Cicourel referred to as the "retrospective-prospective" sense of occurrence (1974). This rather awkward phrase suggests that while we live in the present, we understand it according to our assumptions of what both led up to and will follow from it.

Primarily, we make the assumption of "it-can-happen-again." This way of thinking about the future allows us to assume a continuity of time: What has been proved to be adequate knowledge so far will also in the future stand the test (Schutz 1971, 286). We assume, until proven otherwise by actual experience, that the future and the past are connected in a way we can understand. Our ability to expect both routine and novel occurrences gives us the confidence to go about the task of reciprocity building. Our anticipation and expectations do not refer to future occurrences in their uniqueness, but to the future as typical.

For example, even though we know our plans could go awry when we arrange a Friday night party, we invite friends over, buy beer and wine, and prepare food on the assumption that a good time is possible in this fashion, as it has been before. Such a way of thinking links our understandings of what has happened with our projections of what will happen next, thus allowing us to anticipate the future, in this case giving us sufficient grounds to go ahead with the planning of Friday's party. Still, as Schutz put it, "any experience carries its own horizons of indeterminacy" (Schutz 1971, 286). We hope, therefore, that the party will be a success, but we cannot be certain until Saturday morning. Hence all social interaction depends on assumptions about the past having relevancy for the future. An attitude of "having done something in the past, I can go and do it again, more or less" grounds social life.

Basic Elements of Social Interaction

The work of Schutz and Cicourel is reminiscent of Simmel's search for the a priori conditions of social interaction. The continuation of that search in social psychology has led to descriptions of how consciousness operates to establish the conditions out of which interaction emerges. Since they are essentially assumptions, these conditions are not directly observable; however, they constitute the foundations for all prospective social interaction. What actually transpires between persons in interaction will depend on the individual participants' definitions of situations and the precise nature of the typical thinking they practice.

Even so, the outcomes of social interaction, what actually gets done in interactive work, can never be anticipated in every detail. Instead, the meanings of interaction must be thought of as a result of what people bring with them to the interaction, together with their individual contribution to it.

In any communicative encounter, each party comes prepared; for each has prefabricated meanings that they intend to use in any given situation. These stocks of prefabricated meanings contain memories, knowledge systems (some of which are widely shared by the members of society and others that encompass much smaller domains), special skills and approaches to communication, and motivation. Any encounter among socialized persons can involve many levels of meanings often layered one on top of another (cf. Goffman 1974), and they can occur sequentially or simultaneously. These levels, as the illustration with Frank and Bobby at the car dealership shows, need not be shared in the sense that all parties actually think, feel, or act in the same manner.

In order to engage in interaction, there are elementary skills and experiences that a person must possess and must presume others possess. These break down into memories and background knowledge, linguistic and other communicative skills, and motivations and emotional involvement. All three elements are contained in what we call the individual's *biography* (Berger and Berger 1974; Schutz 1961). A biography is a personal and public social history of the individual. Interaction between two persons entails the contact of biographies.

Memories and Background Knowledge

Human beings both know things and remember what they know. A detailed description of the knowledge of everyday life for even the most trivial of happenings is an elaborate undertaking. A simple greeting such as "Hello! How are you?" activates our knowledge of the appropriate organization of conversation in which certain responses are admissible. Several researchers have identified the characteristics of this organization. For example, Susan Ervin-Tripp (1972) has isolated the tacit rules we have for addressing one another in American society. She depicts these rules as alternating in their application depending on several factors, such as how participants read and interpret such matters, whether the setting is a status-marked one, whether one person is at least ten years older than the other, and what the sex and kinship of the person being addressed are.

In the performance of the rituals of everyday life, such as a greeting, the organization of the exchange is so powerful that, in a sense, "everybody has to lie" (Sacks 1975). For example, we may reply to "Hello! How are you?" with "Fine! Thank you" when in truth, we have just learned some distressing news. In her personal account of the trials of becoming a widow, Lynn Cane reports her own loss under stress of the ability continuously to enact the knowledge of the amiable greeting. On a business trip, when she was asked by a total stranger why she seemed nervous on an airplane, though a noncommittal response would have been appropriate, she replied, "No, I'm not scared of flying. My husband has cancer. He's dying" (1974, 31), whereupon the conversation ended.

In crossing a busy intersection, we act on the basis of pertinent information, such as our knowledge of traffic, the meaning of different- colored lights, and the time of day (rush hour, for example). Some of us become specialists in interpreting traffic, perhaps hypothesizing that "raked" cars, ones with oversized tires on the rear and "dropped" in front, are more likely to speed through a red light and hence must be watched more carefully than station wagons. We guard our exposure to the raked, modified auto, but stroll in front of the wagon without a second thought. Of course, our knowledge of the behavior of cars may be inaccurate, or we may forget something about cars we once knew, but we act toward the car as an extension of the qualities we attribute to drivers. That is, we think we know what types of cars go with what types of people.

Our enactment of what we know depends on what we can remember. When police officers become specialists in reading the intent of people from their demeanor, dress, and general appearance, they must remember fine details pertaining to these matters. In order to make a judgment about whether a person should be stopped for questioning, officers must remember what constitutes a normal appearance and compare the appearance of the suspect to this normal or typical case. On discovering an incongruity—such as a person dressed as a postal employee "delivering letters" on a street known to receive its mail by way of a central distribution system—they feel justified in making a stop and inquiring about the suspect's motives and actions. Under such conditions, they feel they are minimizing the chance that they will bother an innocent person or, in the converse of this problem, fail to stop a guilty one. Likewise, a dentist must be able to recall every detail in the steps of doing a root canal, even though he or she forgets a patient's first name. Obviously, in our modern society those actions that require the more detailed recollection are least likely to be left to informal recall; that is, instructions on how to act are written down and stored in a fashion allowing them to be displayed when the situation requires detailed knowledge. The expression "write that down" is synonymous with "that's important."

Linguistic and Communicative Skills

In the social world, memories and knowledge are expressed symbolically. The medium of language transports knowledge, capturing it in phrases and sentences and making it useful for whatever purposes people have in mind. Hence, the precise linguistic skills and knowledge possessed by the people involved in interaction becomes a major contributor to the character of the interaction. In a conversation with a friend, you may wish to express a delicate point which you know is contrary to your friend's own views. Strongly committed to your own opinion, you feel compelled to speak out. Still, you value the friendship. To escape what may become the negative consequences of your remarks, you prepare your friend with a few well-chosen remarks: "You and I are good friends, and we are both moral people, but your objection to a neighborhood abortion clinic is simply outrageous." This verbal device has been called a "credentialing disclaimer" (Hewitt and Stokes 1975) and is one among many tactics designed for a speaker to smooth over the anticipated negative consequences of a remark. By acquiring skill in such verbal techniques, we can present our knowledge about a subject such as abortion without implying an identification with some undesirable group, like radicals, rednecks, pro-lifers, or whatever designation might be judged offensive in a particular setting. The skill we possess in such talking allows us to avoid pejorative associations and thereby maintain the integrity of the assumptions that ground the interaction in the first place. In the preceding example, you are telling your friend that his friendship is of higher value than your view of abortion, but that you do have strong feelings about abortion and these feelings are a part of your general relationship.

Even after having been caught in the performance of some unacceptable act, we can try to talk our way out of its consequences. Two analysts, Scott and Lyman (1968), provide a classification of types of "accounts" they define as linguistic devices intended to justify or excuse a person from the consequences of his or her actions. Sleeping though an important chemistry examination may be excused if the offender can "talk" to the professor in the correct manner. For example, a student may say, "I just can't understand it. That clock of mine never failed before. I've used it all semester and on this of all mornings it breaks down! Must be a broken part, and it's a new clock too."

The way in which something is said, the mannerisms, gestures, and facial expressions accompanying an utterance can be just as important as the actual words. We refer here to styles of communication, nonverbal elements such as gestures and postures. Any account, whether it is an excuse or a justification, must be framed in the appropriate style. A professor may not lecture his wife, nor a lawyer brief her husband. In both instances, the same information can be conveyed in different styles. The professional, consultative, or lecturing style must be switched to a casual or intimate one, a style that highlights the character of the relationship of that occasion. All persons express in language at least part of what they know. They may be inept or clever in anticipating the reactions of others to what they say. They may avoid the negative attitudes of others by disclaiming or accounting for their intentions and actions, or they may become trapped by others more skillful in the games of language. Those lacking communicative skills often find themselves in sympathy with the line from an old popular song that referred to lawyers who could "put you where they choose by the language that they use."

In the end, the character of any interaction is judged at least partially on the communicative skills of the participants. The give-and-take of testing the conditions of social life, the searching for mutually sufficient grounds for interaction, the shifting of those grounds from impersonal to personal—all occur within the framework of symbolic communication. Talking, then, is the currency of social interaction. It is through conversation and its related phenomena that the character of interaction is discovered.

Motivations and Emotions

Each of us possesses the potential for different levels of involvement with others, and we are capable of having a variety of reasons for our involvements. Although we have learned that all interaction rests on tacit background features, varying degrees of tacitness are required for interaction. Thus, our relationships with other people may entail a rather thoroughgoing and encompassing way of thinking about them. An example of minimal involvement occurs whenever we purchase an item at a large discount store. We expect the clerk to have rather limited knowledge of us, knowledge pertaining only to the act of exchanging money for goods; our personal histories become irrelevant in the task of acquiring a tube of toothpaste. In contrast, when we complain to a close relation, we expect that he or she will interpret our disgruntled disposition in a fashion consistent with our relationship. For instance, if we think someone "should know I feel rotten if I don't get my morning coffee," then we could point to interference with our morning routine to aid our friend's interpretation of our state. Such a tactic used on a testy clerk by an irate customer would probably yield quite different results.

Depth of emotional involvement ranges from superficial to intimate, the former requiring minimal presumptions regarding the other and the latter maximal. The actual qualities associated with involvement vary from situation to situation. Clerks in hardware stores may feign helpfulness in order to make a sale. One partner in love may exploit the vulnerability of the other that comes from assuming common states of mind, perhaps to procure some object or information that would be regarded by the other lover as outside the scope of the relationship. A classic example of this situation is the female spy using her wiles to extract secret attack plans from an enemy general.

Motivational systems provide the reasons for engaging in interaction, reasons taken for granted in such a way that parties to the interaction are not tempted to wonder why they are doing what they are doing. Reasons for interaction also emerge from the character of the interaction itself and are transitory and highly situational.

Motivation is a key concept, and there are two types of it: the reasons people have as to why they will do something are referred to as "in-order-to" motives, and the reasons they give for why they did something as "because" motives. The intentional stance of any act will be preserved by describing whether the actor is attributing motives to himself or herself or to another. Weigert, et al. (1992) have written about the various concepts of motivation Schutz developed. These are important because they capture the lived-through sense of the reasons we discover and devise for our own and others' actions. It is through a description of the motivational systems operating in interactional encounters that we understand why people do what they do and say what they say about what they do.

Although we have discussed the elements of social interaction as if they were separately occurring components of a social situation, they actually are interdependent, intermingling, and mutually influential. Any social interaction may be discussed in terms of background knowledge, communicative skills, and motivations, but a single instance of a social act contains all these aspects and no doubt many more. Our descriptions of an encounter or social event must be attentive to each of these elements and to their interrelationship. Of course, the task is doubly complicated by the basic requirement of the word *social*. We always deal with at least two persons, even if one of them is imaginary.

Summary

This chapter introduced the central concepts of social psychology for understanding the basic elements of social life. These concepts were depicted as ways of thinking about the nature and the actual practice of social interaction. After conceiving of interaction as part of a conscious process, the social organization of consciousness itself was described in terms of typified knowledge, the life world, and the life plan.

Moving to a treatment of how people accomplish interaction, necessary conditions of thought were identified. These are reciprocity thinking, filling-in assumptions, assumptions about typical experiences, and a sense of time. When we understand interaction as a process of thinking about other people, we can further appreciate and describe the range of elements implied when people interact with each other. We attribute to those with whom we interact backgrounds of knowledge and linguistic and communicative skills, as well as motivations and emotions. The versions of these elements that we impute to others become the material for building social meanings.

Exercises in Understanding Interaction

1. *a.* How are you today?
    b. Fine! Did'ya get those papers?
    a. Didn't have time. Too much goin' on at work.
    b. That's OK—probably too early anyway.

What are these two people talking about? Of course, you can imagine a variety of topics that this conversation would fit. Select one and rewrite the conversation so that it is not ambiguous. Now identify the precise forms of the conditions necessary for interaction. What is the version of reciprocity thinking operating in the conversation; what matters are purposefully left vague, what typical experiences are assumed; what sense of time is used by the people talking?

2. Look at the above conversation again. Repeat the exercise, but this time show how the conversation can take place even though the two people talking actually have two quite different things in mind. If you saw the movie *Being There*, you will recall many examples of this happening in conversations between Chance the gardner and the people he interacted with, including the President of the United States.

Suggested Readings

Much of the literature establishing the cognitive foundations of social life is quite complicated and makes for very dense and slow reading. But several secondary sources both go deeply into the approach and provide solid examples of why studying thought in its social context is so important. Helmut Wagner's edited book, *On Phenomenology and Social Relations* (Chicago: University of Chicago Press, 1970), including excerpts from Schutz' writing is widely available in libraries and still in print at this writing. And an excellent introduction to the field of inquiry most influenced by Schutz is Warren Handel's *Ethnomethodology: How People Make Sense* (Englewood Cliffs, NJ: Prentice Hall, 1982). In this short text, Handel illustrates the complex thinking that makes practical action possible. He relies heavily on published empirical reports on police work, the juvenile justice system and the classic case of Agnes, the first sex change patient at the UCLA medical center. Finally, there are several excellent journals specializing in studies which stress the symbolic bases of social life. For example, *Symbolic Interaction* 15, no. 4 (1992) recently carried the article on police work with juveniles that we referred to in this chapter. See Albert J. Mehan, "I Don't Prevent Crime, I Prevent Calls: Policing as a Negotiated Order." pp. 455–80.

Chapter 5

Learning How to Interact:
The Process of Socialization

Individuals are born into an already existing society and thus face the task of becoming part of a continuous social order. We have already addressed how society exists in individuals and how, in accord with their definitions of it, society is acted out by them. Our concern in this chapter is with the process by which society comes to be inside of us; that is, with *socialization.*

The term socialization itself suggests individuals are born asocial, without society, and that they are somehow "made social," that is, socialized, by the world around them. Yet, a good argument can be made that we are born with a certain potential for sociality, for becoming and being social, and that as we grow through the normal stages of human development our potential is naturally and inevitably realized. Even the Wild Boy of Aveyron, whom people believed to have been raised by wolves, appeared to have reached a certain level of socialization by the time he was discovered at the age of ten or twelve (Lane 1976).

In social psychology, then, there are two distinct meanings for the concept of socialization. One stresses how individuals adapt to social expectations, the opinions of others, and the norms and values of society (Gecas 1981, 165). From this perspective, we think of the individual as malleable, shifting in form and content as a result of contact with others. Here socialization is a means by which society as an overwhelming external force perpetuates itself, a means that by definition operates against the natural dispositions of the individual.

The other meaning of socialization emphasizes personal development and how all individuals grow through the same stages and confront various crises. In this view, people are different at different points in their lives. How they deal with the pressures of society depends in large measure on how well developed their competencies have become. Here we may see the individual as relatively stable but undergoing routine changes in a patterned fashion. Such changes can be initiated and influenced by the demands of the social environment, but the organization we call society is rooted in characteristics inherent within individuals. In this conception, from the perspective of one writer, socialization is "largely . . . a matter of the shaping of self concepts" (Stryker 1979, 177).

The question of how social organization comes about at all is answered differently depending on the vantage points of one or the other of these two

91

conceptions. Is order imposed from without, an outcome of forces that operate on individuals? Or is it the resultant effect of individuals realizing their potential through interaction; in other words, is it something that emerges from the basics of social life?

We recall here how the founders of social psychology all saw the inseparability of society and the individual. And just as Mead and Cooley insisted on tying self and society together in a continuing process of emergence, we also see socialization as a concept describing how, through the social competencies they have mastered, individuals learn to adapt to the social pressures they experience throughout life. Socialization, then, refers to a lifelong process, one often patterned into phases and stages, in which people acquire the skills necessary to interact with one another. Different social competencies operate in respectively appropriate contexts, and these can be characterized by the qualities they manifest. The contexts of socialization themselves vary from intimate and informal to impersonal and formal, from family and peer contexts to those of school and occupation.

Even from birth, human infants can be engaged in simple social interaction. Although part of an elaborate social network, the objects of much conversation, and even the recipients of greetings and questions, infants cannot respond in kind. So adults often do the responding for them, answering their own questions and providing their own cooing sounds. But as children grow physically they also grow socially. First come smiles, usually in response to a parent's presence. Next there are responsive sounds, movements, and finally words. And these eventually give way to fluent conversations and the complex process of social interaction. But learning how to interact does not stop at childhood or adolescence. It continues for a lifetime.

Language, Mind and The Self

As children acquire language, they accumulate knowledge and become aware of motives; they also develop individual ways of thinking and selves. A very young child may say, "Julie want cookie." Implied in this seemingly simplistic utterance is a motivation that goes beyond a child's mere hunger. Both "Julie" and "cookie" reflect the child's growing awareness of the world, a knowledge about herself as an object in it and about a particular edible substance. In this simple use of language, Julie reveals that she has taken an important early step toward acquiring a sense of self.

As we have already noted, fundamental to the development of the self is the complex task of what Mead (1934) called "taking the attitude and role of other." The primary task in this is thinking reciprocally. The child must learn to think what others are thinking—to project himself or herself into another person's position, or mind, and try to see the world from that other person's perspective. At first a child engages in reciprocity thinking in a childlike fashion, a manner not only less complex than that mastered by adults but actually distinctive. Most of us have learned to imagine distant places and persons with relative ease. Although we usually take this skill for granted, we tend to become aware of reciprocity thinking when we interact with children. Consider the following example:

> Six-year-old Ann's mother tried to explain to her why she should eat whole grain wheat bread, rather than the white bread she begged for. "Ann, honey, scientists say our bodies need roughage to stay well. White bread has all the roughage removed. So when Mommie says you should eat whole bread, it is for your own good." "But Mommie," Ann replied, "I like white bread; it's softer."

This misunderstanding between mother and child suggests that, in a strict sense, the mother's thinking and the child's are not comparable. Ann may try to think what her mother is thinking, but she is unable to go very far with it. Her mother, in contrast, projects her confidence into the imagined activities of distant scientists she presumes work for the purpose of improving human health. The mother thinks in complex reciprocities. She assumes she knows "scientists"; she can guess the importance of their work, and she can interpret that portion of their knowledge of nutrition that pertains to feeding her family. Qualitatively, the six-year-old daughter is also capable of reciprocity thinking, but at a much different level. To her, bread has meaning only insofar as it relates to some immediate action, such as the amount of energy she must expend chewing food. We can say her thinking lacks detailed knowledge and a long-term future orientation. She does not give consideration to what the health of her colon will be when she is fifty years old. So the conversation between Ann and her mother has a note of futility about it. They talk past one another, each operating from different knowledge systems, with disparate levels of linguistic skills and from distinctly different motivational vantage points. Ann's mother operates from a base acquired through years of refining the application of knowledge, and Ann from recently acquired skills barely tested out in the practical consequences of daily living.

Children learn about the world by extending their imaginations beyond their immediate concerns, that is, their minds grow socially. Adults have developed extensive repertoires of different modes of imagining the presence and the nature of other persons. The problem of what kind of bread to eat must be resolved on grounds mutually understandable to mother and daughter: "Mommie says you have to eat the wheat bread" or "Do what you want, it's your colon." In the first instance, the threat is mutually understandable; in the second, mother and daughter may maintain their respective views. Ann gets her soft bread. Her mother continues to believe that wheat bread would be better for her health; but Ann still is able to make decisions about her body. This latter position may be interpreted by the child in several ways, including, "Good, I get white bread" or "Mommie won't love me anymore."

Children mature socially as well as physically, moving from a phase marked by an inability to think or even be aware of any perspective or interpretation other than their own to an increasing capacity to "take on the attitude of others." Two- or three-year-old children might bang around the house relentlessly or seem to pay little heed to parental requests. But a seven-year-old boy may request of his friend playing outside in the front yard, "Please be quiet. You have to realize my father is a writer." Or a young girl might reply to her father's request that she clean up her room with, "But Daddy, I only got my cast off today" (adapted from Cook-Gumperz 1975, 157—58).

As they acquire language, children develop the ability to identify with others. In learning to use the language of their culture, children develop the mental capability to become the other person or persons with whom they are conversing. So to the extent that others carry the culture of the group, children learn about how to be social beings by interacting with them. Formally in social psychology we say this process entails "learning to play a series of roles, to assume a series of conducts or linguistic gestures" (Merleau-Ponty 1964, 109).

The development of language parallels and is indistinguishable from the growing ability of the child to perceive other people. O'Neill (1973) sees this demonstrated in childhood jealousy. For example, the birth of a new baby in the Jones family results in behavioral regression on the part of three-year-old Billy, the older sibling, seen in incidents such as his bed wetting or reverting to baby talk. There is even some open hostility toward the baby, as when Billy raises his hand as if to strike it. Billy sees the new baby as an affront to what he assumed was his own "eternal presence." In other words, he thought of his family as a constant, making up the totality of himself. Before the new baby, he was not required to distinguish between himself as a member of the family and the family itself. To him these two phenomena were identical. Now, with the presence of the younger child, this reasoning is called into question. Billy must learn to think, "My place has been taken," which in turn necessitates a new form of linguistic expression. Technically this process can be referred to as a verb conjugation, from present to future perfect. Socially the process takes the form of "I have been the youngest (member), but I am the youngest no longer, but I will always be the oldest (child)."

While language and emotion are interrelated, this example should not be taken to imply a causal relationship between learning grammar and overcoming jealousy. Their actual relationship depends on many factors, like the developmental level of the older sibling and the parents' responses to the jealousy. What should be made clear is that the mastery of language and the mastery of socially appropriate action develop together. It is through language that we think; that is, we give meaning to our ideas and feelings by putting them into words. If we couldn't do this, we would constantly be overwhelmed by our emotions, slaves to our every impulse. Thus all our knowledge, the accumulation of our ideas, is embodied in our language. From the social psychological perspective, then, language functions as a social principle. It literally is society, not just a representation of it. Given our example, the rules of language usage and the socially appropriate actions required of the jealous child are identical at this phase of socialization.

The function of language in the socialization process is substantiated by some important psycholinguistic research. The child's early speech can be interpreted as iconographic, as if it represented an illustrative picture; that is:

> The setting, (the) shared history of the participants as well as presently occurring events for the participants are treated as a single communicative context in which verbal utterances and their (syllabic and grammatical) features form a single unit for interpretation by the child. All parts of the message and context contribute equally to the possible interpretation. *All components are considered to contribute similarly to the understanding for both the child and his reciprocal partners* (Cook-Gumperz 1975, 151; italics added)

Another way to grasp this complicated point is to think of the differences between child and adult speech. The de Villiers (1979) sum up these differences according to three features. In adult language there is a freedom from the here and now, as well as an ability to take into account variation in shared knowledge, and finally an awareness of language form. In the earliest manifestations of a child's language, communication is bound by circumstances. Even seven- and eight-year-olds have difficulty communicating when their view of one another is obscured by a screen placed between them. Likewise anyone who has called a family household and tried to relay a communication through the child who answered the phone knows how tedious this task can be. But, with the acquisition of language comes the ability to escape the confines of the moment. In the end the adult human uses language to create circumstances (de Villiers 1979, 86).

Language contains all the necessary knowledge for making assumptions about the character of others and for assessing their intentions and motivations. Its mastery and its many varieties and uses provide us with the keys to understanding social life, and in the light of that knowledge, to our own decision making, insofar as we, too, act with intent and motivation. Language and mind are, as Mead taught, part of the same social process.

Primary Socialization

Although the linguistic aspects of communication, like learning the use of tenses and moods, are important parts of the process, the full development of the social self involves much more. It includes all the influences, both subtle and explicit, that come from the social context of communication. Eventually virtually all of us learn to adapt. We do what is appropriate most of the time, take our chances and break the rules in some situations, and sometimes work out relationships with other people, even when we'd rather not.

Obviously most early childhood learning occurs in a rather close setting peopled by parents, siblings, and extended family members or others who are with the child on a daily basis. But this represents only one side of the coin of socialization. In characterizing socialization it is convenient to distinguish between two levels, each highlighting the importance of varying social contexts; these two levels are commonly referred to as primary and secondary socialization. The former includes all the learning experiences that occur within the family and the other social forms known as primary groups. The latter refers to socialization that takes place in less intense, less involving contexts, in social forms such as those found in many classrooms and sometimes called secondary groups. This secondary socialization is also called adult socialization, and in its effects on the individual it can be as profound and compelling as the primary form.

Earlier we introduced Cooley's notion of the "looking-glass self." That concept helps us understand how we think of ourselves as we believe others think of us. Cooley felt the primary group, the social context characterized by face-to-face contact, demanding all of a person's consciousness and thus encompassing the entire person, produced society. Groups with these characteristics constitute the context for primary socialization.

Let us consider a typical interaction between a father and son to see how self-concepts are formed in primary groups. Sam, the father, says, "I don't know why you always make such a mess? Why can't you just leave things alone?" Son Freddie answers sheepishly, "I can't help it." Sam then relates the history of Freddie's development for the child's benefit. "Sure, always been that way. When you were three you got into some old paint cans in the garage and poured all the paint out, all over the floor. Took me a week to clean up that mess. Guess you can't change a leopard's spots." Freddie's only response is silence.

We do not intend to convey the impression that Freddie is messy just because his father always thought of him as such. The formation of self is more complicated than that. Nevertheless, in this passage we can see that Sam does offer an interpretation of his son's behavior. He characterizes it, casts it in biographical relief, and judges it with implications for the future. In their daily lives with their families children receive literally thousands of such character references. They are told they are bright, sensitive, dull, clumsy, quick, or slow. Depending on how and how often these definitions are represented to a child, they can take on great importance in influencing actual behavior.

A series of experiments by Rosenthal (1966) demonstrated the part played by the fulfillment of social expectations in both laboratory and classroom settings. In studies with both animals and humans Rosenthal found that the definitions researchers or teachers had about the nature of their subjects (the animals and children they were working with) influenced the subjects' actual behavior in the experiments. For instance, in one experiment teachers were told falsely that certain children's IQ tests indicated they were about to "spurt ahead" in their school work. Those children presumed by their teachers to be late bloomers often surpassed their classmates on IQ tests taken a full year later (Rosenthal and Jacobsen 1968).

Perhaps fortunately for children in "real life" (outside experimental settings), parents' and other adults' reactions are often inconsistent and get expressed in forms not immediately comprehensible to the children themselves. Such vagueness about what the parent or teacher really means leaves room for children to select and formulate personal ideas about who they are that are sometimes at variance with their parents' judgments. Freddie may think his father is a "neat freak" and just "bitches all the time" so that he, Freddie, does not think of himself as messy at all. After all, his friend Adam is the biggest mess in the world. As Freddie likes to say, "Adam's room is so dirty he sleeps in the living room."

Primary socialization, then, is crucial to the acquisition of self. Within intimate social contexts, whether dominated by the family or fragmented among different people and groups, the materials necessary for becoming a social self are found. These materials are assimilated, organized, and used by individuals to reflect their personally unique experiences and endowments.

Learning the Meanings of Gender

One of the most salient features of the social self and dominant lessons of the socialization process involves gender, or sexual identity. This conclusion is supported by a fascinating exercise in which a researcher dressed an assistant in a large green bag. Though she could walk in the bag and there were holes in it through which she could see, the bag reached from head to toe and completely concealed the assistant. The bag went to school, sat in a classroom during a regular class, and moved about the halls of the classroom building between classes. The researcher and the "bag" were attempting to make evident the basic assumptions people make about each other. In interviews with those who had encountered the bag, and through observing the reactions of people to it, the researcher and her assistant found that a primary concern of those who tried to make contact with the bag was not so much what it was supposed to be, or what was going on, but what sex it was.

This experiment serves to show us how powerful the learning of sexual identities is and how crucial it is to interactive competencies (Nelson and Jorgensen 1975). And until fairly recently—before the 1970s, "unisex," women's liberation and gay pride—most people felt they could take others' sexual identities for granted. But it has become obvious that this is not the case.

In the modern world the meanings of sexual identity have become ambiguous, and a rather remarkable amount of negotiation may be possible around what it means to be a male or female, boy or girl, man or woman. Sharp differences still do exist, even if they are regarded as vestiges of more traditional ways of deciding the meanings of personhood.

One of the most reliable ways to learn about something behavioral is to watch it happen. If we are interested in the differences between girls and boys in modern society, a powerful way to document and study these differences is by observing their natural occurrence. Janet Lever (1976, 1978) conducted such a research project, which consisted primarily of simply watching children play. She focused on a group of fifth graders in a Connecticut town. In addition to watching them play, she interviewed them, administered a semistructured questionnaire, and kept daily diaries of the children's play activities. She wanted to show what children do when they are relatively uninhibited by adults or other figures of authority; and she followed many of the early social psychologists in choosing "play" as the arena for her observations.

By developing detailed categories for classifying the content and organization of the children's play, Lever noticed many subtle differences between girls and boys. Her findings can be summarized by six generalizations: (1) boys play outdoors far more than girls; (2) although both boys and girls play alone about the same amount of time, when they are involved in social play boys more often play in large groups; (3) boys' play occurs in more age-heterogeneous groups, meaning that they play in groups composed of older and younger boys, while girls prefer groups of girls their own age; (4) girls more often play in games we usually associate with boys than boys play in "girls'" games, an example being that girls play baseball more than boys play jump-rope; (5) boys play competitive games more often than girls; and (6) boys' games last longer than do girls'.

Lever's study also shows girls are more imaginative and more interested in other people being involved in their play than boys are, and boys indeed are more rough-and-tumble. As we have suggested though, these findings do not imply that boys are "by nature" more active than girls. In fact, most social psychologists believe such differences in play reflect the definitions of self that the children learn from their parents and the wider social worlds in which they participate.

Some years before Lever's work, Kohlberg (1969) theorized that children form images of sex-appropriate roles and role models based on what they have observed and have been told about what it means to be a boy or girl, with those features most visible and easiest to understand making up a child's viewpoint. So a child's gender-role conceptions are sketches—oversimplified, exaggerated, and stereotyped; and their play reflects these ideas even if they are not totally accurate. Kohlberg illustrates by relating a story about one of the girls he studied. She was a four-year-old who insisted that only boys become doctors, even though her own mother was a physician.

The notion that children's understandings of their social world shape their concepts of gender is known as self-socialization. According to exponents of this theory, there is a critical period for acquiring a sense of gender. By age six, some argue, a child's gender identity is already fixed and provides an organizing focus for social interaction. Allan Katcher (1955) reports that although four- or five-year-olds cannot assemble dolls by sex anatomically, they know the categories of "boy" and "girl" exist, and they can identify with their own gender category.

Kohlberg's theory differs in essence from an exchange perspective, whose premise is that we learn what we are rewarded for doing and which suggests further that society rewards children for "sexually meaningful" behaviors. Kohlberg believes, instead, that self-attribution of a gender identity comes first—hence the thought sequence for a young male is, "I am a boy, so I want to do boy things; therefore, the opportunity to do boy things (and to gain approval for them) is rewarding."

An exhaustive survey of the literature dealing with sex differences seems to support the self-socialization explanation. Maccoby and Jacklin (1975) conclude that available data seem to fit with the theory. They cite, for example, research that demonstrates children are not directly affected by the behavior of their parents. A boy will choose to play with cars and trucks, even though he may see his mother drive a truck. Girls play hopscotch and jacks, even though they do not see their mothers doing so. The learned images of what it is to be female, and not male, can have far-reaching effects in everyday life, in the very ways we see the world as gendered.

Gender Displays

Males and females present themselves to others in fundamentally different ways. Goffman (1979) showed us how we can understand such differences between the sexes by turning our attention to what he calls "gender displays," by which he means behaviors associated with a sexual identity but also rooted in an emotional motivation.

We have already learned society encourages different types of play for the sexes. Aggressiveness, assertiveness, and activity seem to us to be masculine. Likewise, we recognize the impressions of nurture, of emotional sensitivity, and of domesticity in females. The question Goffman raises concerns whether there are differences in how the details of everyday life are arranged by gender. He answers affirmatively and supports his response by looking at the display—action so simplified, even stereotyped, that it can be recognized through almost any social context. The "smile," the "leer," the "seductive posture"—all are examples of displays. A display communicates an emotional message to the person witnessing it. A gender display refers to "culturally established correlates of sex" that are "conventionalized portrayals of these correlates" (Goffman 1979, 1)—television situation comedies aimed at the thirty-and-under age groups tend to utilize these quite often; and most soap operas seem to be based on them.

By analyzing advertisements from magazines and television, Goffman hopes to uncover the gender displays that are certainly there for the unmasking. He documents "the feminine touch," the "ritualization of subordination," and other meanings tacit in advertising. He observes that a woman's hands are seen just barely touching, holding or caressing—never grasping, manipulating or shaping. Men instruct women in these pictures of interactions between the sexes. Women recline more than men. The head or the eye of a man may be averted by some object or occurrence, while female attention is usually on the man she is with. Women are shown as "drifting" mentally from the scene in which they are set, while males are more physically in touch with their surroundings. Finally, women more than men are pictured with a kind of psychological loss or remove from a social situation, such that the viewer gets the impression they are frozen, unable to act.

Goffman's contribution in this analysis "is the continuous, ever-deepening connection he makes between our image of women and the behavior of children" (Gornick 1979, viii). According to his analysis, women are linked to children, if not through the sense of family, then through the posture and attitudes they are supposed to assume. The female display connotes "play," a lack of "serious-ness," and a strong sense of the leisure and emotional context of private lives—in the beer ad, for example, the men are sailing the boat, and the women enjoying it. Goffman does not argue that advertisements cause these displays to be acted out by women in real life, nor that the real world is accurately depicted in such venues. But, he does write: "Although the pictures shown here cannot be taken as representative of gender behavior in real life...one can probably make a significant negative statement about them, namely, that as pictures they are not perceived as peculiar and unnatural" (Goffman 1979, 27).

In a society such as ours, where material possessions, down to the labels they bear, are so important, we see these displays often in everyday life. That is why we recognize and accept them so easily in advertisements; and it is why those advertisements are effective and appealing to most of us. Women are typified as being able to cope with emotions, but not to suppress or control them. The playthings of girls are not as mechanical, as able to be manipulated as are those of boys. While at the same time dolls for girls show the pleasurable side of ordinary life, the fantastic creatures of outer space, the conquerors in war, and the masters of galactic adventure are for boys.

A major part of gender learning, then, is learning how to present oneself in interactive exchanges. In American society, males are taught to control and master their surroundings, even if only in imagination. Females, in contrast, are taught to invest in emotions and interpersonal relationships. Such differential socialization results in varying rates of interest in the objects and happenings of the social world. Boys tend to occupy themselves with their bicycles, exciting play, or more recently, the family computer. Girls, while also interested in bicycles and computers, are focused more on friendships, matters of reputation, and the displays of these concerns.

A study of video games and arcades produced results that support these generalizations. Not only do boys play these games more than girls, male games predominate in the video world (Kaplan 1983). Games appealing to boys are those with violent themes and requiring a great deal of concentration and practice. An early very popular game, Defender, for example, had five separate controls. Some games have graphics that offer the illusion of a third dimension. In order to play well, the player must learn to see depth in the graphics.

Games that have themes of everyday life, chase-and-run games, like the famous Pac Man, Frogger, and Ms. Pac Man, do not require as intense an involvement with the game and do seem to have a greater appeal for female players. Although these generalizations may seem strong, Kaplan reports on the results of a survey he conducted with 430 male and female college students. In his study, he found that women acknowledged their lower level of skill as compared to male players, and his findings revealed, as other observational studies have shown, that although girls are present and playing at arcades, it is the boys who amass top scores and who are engrossed in the difficult games that invariably have military and space themes.

To find out why this sex difference exists, Kaplan conducted another survey. He speculated that perhaps females saw arcades as undesirable places, and because of this interpretation simply avoided them. His data did not support this conclusion. In fact, he discovered that females gave arcades a generally favorable evaluation, seeing them as relatively safe places to go for having fun. He accounted for the strikingly significant male presence in the video world in terms of differential socialization. Females thought the males were simply being macho while playing the games. And, "females were seen as being more interested in activities conventionally defined as being appropriate to females" (Kaplan 1983, 98); hence, females saw males' intense involvement in play as "wasteful." They repeatedly said they preferred shopping to playing video games in mall arcades.

It appears that even among college students some stereotypical ideas about gender still operate strongly enough to explain differences in behavior. Men are seen as game oriented, interested in science and machines, and relatively unconcerned with what others think about them. Women are defined as more conventional, focused on social relationships, and less apt to become engrossed in a world as artificial and plastic as the video arcade. And although the names of the games will surely change, and those whose business it is to predict, create, and sell to the youthful consumer will work hard to extend the appeal of video games, the differentiation of emotions and activities by sex seems to be deeply ingrained in American society. Changes occur and opportunities for educational and professional development broaden, but these social trends do not seem to signal the demise of gender.

We return to a point made by Goffman. Women are associated with children in American society in ways that run deep into the meanings of self. Here Goffman means more than just the association of women and children in commonsense thinking. He exposes very subtle processes and comparisons that occur in both same sex and cross-sex interactions.

Secondary Socialization: Reference Groups

After people develop selves, they still confront groups that make demands and exert pressure on them; and the impact of these groups on one's self can be profound. But these groups usually require distinctive competencies of the individual. Generally we meet them when we step outside the door of our homes. They are composed of our neighbors, strangers, friends, and enemies. Primary socialization is a necessary condition for secondary socialization, as the latter builds on the former to extend the self. In primary socialization children learn to identify the other, now they must learn to differentiate kinds of people. The learning that occurs once a child knows how to identify others allows for the classification of people into categories and for the development within the child of an understanding of how to relate to these new groupings. This is the essence of secondary socialization. Having acquired the rudiments of language use and self, children will mature into discriminating adults, eventually picking and choosing the groups toward which they compare their behavior. Such groups are called *reference groups* (Merton 1957), and all of us identify with several of them throughout our lives.

Every reference group supplies the basic information and experiences of secondary socialization. Such a group can be defined as those persons in the social world whom an individual uses as standards for making sense of his or her own actions. Besides providing actual behavior as a basis for comparison, a reference group can also serve as a symbolic guide to producing behavior. That is, people's interpretations of others' behavior play a role in the decisions they make regarding the significance and direction of their own actions. We understand our own identities by referring our selves to our reference groups. In reference groups we find public, objectified and typical answers to questions about who we are. The reference group allows us to refer to publicly known groups (Wiegert 1983, 152), and as Shibutani (1955) put it, they supply us with a social perspective for viewing the world and evaluating ourselves and it.

As the child moves out of the primary context of immediate family, friends, and relatives, the influences of these people are replaced by others less intimately known. Important gropus of others become reference groups—peers at school, the boys down the block, the girls in Campfire, the members of an athletic team or of the lodge to which one desires admission. Even if a person does not actually interact in face-to-face contact with these others, they may be an important influence on the self.

Now let us look more closely at how reference groups operate in secondary socialization. To be selective in our discussion of groups possessing referential significance for the individual, we can begin by pointing out how such groups enter into the scenario of socialization. The process described here encompasses the transformation of the capability for thinking reciprocally in general ways into one of thinking about the other according to very specific contexts.

For the child, everybody's opinion matters. When a seven-year-old boy becomes preoccupied with whether his outfit for the day "looks funny," he is worried about people in general thinking he is strangely dressed. The teenaged boy who knows his blue-jeaned, layered-shirt, torn-tennis-shoe look is offensive to his elders disregards any potential adult censorship in favor of the positive judgment he believes his peers give to his style of dress. Both the seven-year-old and the teenager are capable of knowledge of the generalized other, but only the teenager distinguishes significant others from the array of possible groups. The teenager has selected a reference group.

The process of becoming more and more discriminating about who is significant for the purposes of acting is a developmental one. The adult may distinguish many different significant others for particular situations. Thus, at the corner store, in the presence of clerks and neighbors, the jump-suit leisure attire of the lawyer gives him the feeling of being properly dressed. On returning home with the groceries for the night's dinner party, he changes into a casual denim look, with boat shoes. The next morning, as he prepares for a day in court, he chooses a white shirt, a subdued tie, a dark suit, matching socks, and black shoes. Each of these outfits has been carefully selected with reference to each different group.

The adult's ability to imagine himself or herself in different situations is the hallmark of secondary socialization, for it involves the internalization of specific forms of reciprocity thinking, forms that possess definite limits and partial application. Groups of people whose standards are imagined and then referenced by the socialized person may or may not actually adhere to those standards. The lawyer may be regarded as overdressed by his colleagues or as an out-of-date, unhip casual dresser by his dinner guests. As Cooley, Mead, and Thomas taught, it is what the lawyer thinks others think of him and his reaction to this imagined opinion that determine his actions.

The importance of self-concept in mediating the actions of people has long been recognized in social psychology. For example, studies of the American soldier during World War II indicated that the morale of troops could not be assessed by objective factors, such as how readily promotions or pay rate increases were given. Instead, such objective factors were interpreted by soldiers according to the way they compared themselves with others (Stouffer et al. 1949). The meanings they attached to slow or fast promotions depended on which reference group was used to compare their understanding of their own position. In the Air Corps, where promotions were rapid, airmen who had advanced a grade in six months might express discontent because some of their fellow corps members advanced two grades in the same time period. In the Army, where promotions were slow in coming, advancing one grade to corporal in three years was regarded as normal progress, and the fact that one was still a private after six months was no cause for discontent. Of course, the mere knowledge that one was in the Army instead of the Air Corps could be just cause for low morale among members of the Army.

During the Vietnamese war, many Army officers were dismayed when what they thought was their humane treatment of recruits failed to produce an appreciative attitude. The officers, many of whom were career soldiers ("Lifers") since the 1930s and early 1940s, remembered well the often dangerous and clearly arduous training they had received as young recruits. During World War II, training consisted of long hikes, experience with live ammunition, and uncomfortable living quarters. Indeed, many deaths were the result of training accidents. In the modern Army, training routines are monitored and evaluated. Whenever live ammunition is used, it is under the strictest supervision. Long, forced marches no longer are used to push recruits to the limit. Trainees ride in trucks on hot days, take shorter marches, and enjoy much greater freedom on base than was the case in the Army many Lifers recalled. All the new, managed training routines appeared to be "soft living" to the career soldier. But they were still interpreted as horrors of Army life by the draftees who did not judge their present lifestyle by previous Army practice, but by the civilian life from which they had been snatched and that was still being enjoyed by friends back home not so unlucky as to be drafted. To the career drill sergeant, the award of a meritorious service certificate meant a high honor. To the draftee such an award became evidence of how well he was able to "pull the wool over the sergeant's eyes," while making the best of a highly undesirable, hopefully temporary situation.

The sergeant would be angered, or at least confused, at the draftee's ridicule of or outright disgust for the award. He would expect the certificate to be honored in a special place, perhaps framed and hung on the wall. The draftee instead might hang it upside down in the bathroom or simply throw it away.

These differences in the interpretation of meaning and the attribution of significance can be explained according to the different socialization experiences of Lifers and recruits. Each came from a learning background that provided identification with different reference groups. Since people evaluate their present circumstances by comparing themselves with those whom they regard as relevant points of reference, feelings of deprivation are relative. The young draftee regards the practices of World War II basic training as irrelevant to his current plight.

This concept of the relativity of feelings of deprivation helps us understand why African Americans in the 1960s, though "absolutely" better off than their ancestors, were angry enough to riot. It also reminds us of the importance of the immediate standards from which people derive their judgments of having been wronged. Consistent with our use of the concept of relative deprivation is the conceptualization by George Homans (1974) of the sense people have of the just distribution of rewards.

> Distributive injustice occurs when a person does not get the amount of reward he [or she] expects to get in comparison with the reward some other person gets. He [or she] expects to get more reward than the other when his [or her] contributions . . . rank higher than the other's, equal reward when his [or her] contributions and investments are equal to the other's, etc. Though many men [and women] in many societies implicitly accept this rule, they may still disagree as to whether the distribution of rewards is just in particular circumstances, because they do not admit the same dimensions of reward, contribution, and investment as relevant. In their assessments of distributive justice, persons are more apt to compare themselves with others that are close or similar to themselves in some respect than with others that are distant or dissimilar. (Homans 1974, 268)

A major consequence of adult socialization is the shifting that occurs almost daily among the various standards of different groups with which the individual comes into contact. Some shifts are total, entailing dramatic conversions; others are minor, involving matters of taste and preference. But regardless of how trivial a shift in a reference group might seem, it may become an integral part of the complex method a person uses to judge how he or she is doing. So whether we are talking about the child's sense of having been wronged or the adult's concept of injustice, we can understand how the way a person feels is bound up in one's symbolic powers of comparison.

Our discussion of significant references and their acquisition in the adult's life emphasizes that a person need not actually achieve membership in it for a group to become a significant reference. In fact, all that is necessary is anticipated membership. "For the individual who adopts the values of a group to which he [or she] aspires but does not belong [conformity to nonmembership group norms] may serve the twin functions of aiding his rise into that group and easing his adjustment after he has become a part of it" (Merton 1957, 265).

But as Merton suggests, there are several consequences of this type of reference group behavior that may be dysfunctional as well. If people shape their behavior in accord with a group to which they want to belong and then fail to acquire membership, they may become marginal. Though still not members of the new group, they will have changed their behavior so that they now act in ways inappropriate to their old one. It is only in relatively open social structures, ones that provide for relatively easy mobility, that anticipatory socialization operates smoothly.

Interpretations of Rules: Action and the Reference Group

To understand fully reference groups, it is important to describe the precise form of reciprocity thinking that results from identification with specific groups. We do this here by examining how rules for action are interpreted by group members. In fact, a single, explicitly stated rule can manifest itself in many different forms of action. Our understanding of the use to which a rule is put depends on a number of factors, including a full description of the context in which the rule is used, the specific interpretation of the rule, and perhaps most important, the socialization level of the persons involved in the group.

Consider the application of rules of behavior at a public swimming pool. Even if only for legal reasons, these rules are usually written down and displayed on bulletin boards near the pool—we have seen as many as thirteen rules for a single, small motel pool. Let's look at some of the more common ones. "Don't eat or drink near the pool." This rule seems clear enough and straightforward in its application until we sit by the pool and observe the actions of people. We see a mother fully dressed, sitting at a table six feet from poolside, sipping a Coke. The lifeguard, we note, makes no comment. On another occasion, an eight-year-old boy clad in swimming trunks walks to within fifteen feet of the pool, sandwich in hand, and the lifeguard yells, "Hey kid, don't eat near the pool!" Obviously the rule is applied differently in the two instances; what we might see as the mother and child in the same "poolside" context, the lifeguard apparently interprets as two—one for the mother and a different one for the child. Such matters of interpretation distinguishing applications of rules may be expressed as questions: What does "near the pool" mean? To whom, or to what kind of person do the rules apply? What constitutes eating or drinking?

With regard to the first question, we see that in the mother's case, position in relation to the pool is defined as "not near," probably because, as the lifeguard tells us, she is "not a swimmer." Thus the application of the rule to situations depends on a judgment with respect to who is swimming and who is merely poolside. This seems to be decided on by the attire of the person, although even this determination becomes complicated by the presence of people clad in swimsuits who do not swim. Thus a nonswimming person wearing street clothes may actually move closer to the pool than a swimsuited "non-swimmer" and still not be "near" for the purposes of the rule.

"Eating and drinking" depends on what is eaten or drunk and under what circumstances. Regarding what constitutes eating and drinking, drinking pool water while swimming is not "drinking." And a person who walks to the side of the pool and with methodical intent begins to sip pool water through a straw would presumably come under a different rule than "Don't eat or drink near the pool." Or a formal poolside dinner for which tables are set up suspends the rule. An adult may consume food in small quantities, sunflower seeds from a plastic bag, for example, without prohibition, while the consumption of a candy bar by a child would evoke blasts from the guard's whistle. The lifeguard's interpretations may be supplemented by the assumption that adults will be responsible for their food and litter, while children "can't be trusted."

From our observations, we conclude that the meaning of a simple rule depends on the lifeguard's interpretation of nearness on the part of different kinds of people and under various circumstances that can be ranked in terms of how certain actions depart from what is presumed to be the normal activities of swimming. Careful adults who know the rule may therefore break it judiciously or with formal sanction. Irresponsible children, in contrast, ignore or willfully flaunt the rule and must be admonished.

Similar points can be made for other rules, such as "No Running!" In this case, children are usually more sophisticated than we realize in how they apply rules. A six-year-old girl gleefully and repeatedly diving from the pool's board develops a gait from poolside to boardline that looks like a race walker's waddle. She beats other children to the head of the line for the board and still avoids "running." On one occasion the guard blasts a whistle at her, to which she replies, "But I wasn't running!" "Running," then, is not merely a matter of the technical definition of foot-pavement contact and forward motion. It necessarily includes the realization of a motive. The crucial question the guard must decide is, "Did the girl intend to run or is she really running even if she does not appear to be running?" Such everyday applications are only partially related to official reasons for the rules, such as safety. They always reflect both some degree of personal involvement, here of the people at the poolside, and the interactional character of such encounters, in other words, contacts among socially defined selves—life guards, swimmers, and the like.

More often than not, how we apply rules for making preliminary definitions of the meanings of particular situations depends on the cultural definitions available for the situations themselves. Stebbins (1969) hypothesized that individuals enter any setting with particular intentions and that certain aspects of the setting will tend to confirm these intentions. Taken together, those confirming aspects of the surroundings, along with the individual's intentions, will lead her or him to select a cultural definition of the situation. This definition will then direct the individual's actions.

In order to demonstrate how regular and uniform the culturally given interpretations of situations can be, Stebbins staged a classroom disruption. In this enactment, two "visitors" to a lecture class interrupted the instructor and accused him of polluting the students' minds, calling him an outsider, an atheist, and a communist. The subject of the day's lecture had been evolution, and this in a school located in a "community where religious matters are taken seriously." After a heated five-minute debate between the instructor and the visitors, the two were expelled from the classroom. Then the experimenter entered, explaining how the confrontation had been staged.

The students who witnessed this scene then filled out open-ended questionnaires on both their initial impressions of the pair's intentions and their personal feelings about what happened. The remarkable consistency in the students' accounts was interpreted by Stebbins as reflecting culturally given definitions of the situation. The students' general impressions were that the two men were religious figures of some sort whose beliefs were being challenged by the lectures, and as a result the men wanted the lectures corrected or stopped; their activities were considered outrageous and highly resented. Some students felt these two men were only nonstudent intruders who somehow decided that the lectures were having a bad influence on the students and as a result wanted the lectures either corrected or stopped. Their activities were regarded by these students as mildly disgusting.

Although this research does not prove that culture provides ready-made interpretations of situations, it does show how in ambiguous situations people tend to rely on what they see as generally applicable interpretations. Thus our interpretation of the meanings of situations and the specific way in which rules are applied is conditioned by generally available cultural meanings and the concrete applications of rules to given situations.

Extreme Cases of Secondary Socialization

Sometimes in the course of one's life, major changes occur in how people identify themselves, thus producing a different organization in the self, an altered identity. Others recognize, or recognize again, a person as a social object according to his or her own announcements about such alterations (Stone 1962, 93). Hence a person may announce a religious conversion, a new identity that varies from an older one but is equally complete. These extreme changes in identity, usually in adulthood, take place only after a person has already accumulated considerable socialization experience. They are, however, similar to ones that occur in primary socialization because they involve the entirety of the person, the total social self.

As we have inferred, secondary socialization tends to complicate and fragment the self. It gives us many life worlds, adding some and causing us to drop others. Our primary socialization experiences function to provide the basis for the organization of these many facets of the self into a whole, or a life organization. Now we focus on secondary experiences so extreme they function to alter life organization in a radical fashion.

American soldiers taken as prisoners of war during the Korean and Vietnamese conflicts, for example, soon discovered they lived in profoundly altered life situations. Everything about their lives was externally manipulated by their captors. Old routines like grooming habits or sleep patterns were controlled by strangers. Even encounters with soldiers from home, other POWs, were transformed into occasions for mistrust, since a buddy could have turned out to be a collaborator.

Studies of the reactions of prisoners of war to extreme brainwashing techniques reveal that coercion frequently produced a "ritualization of belief" (Schein, Schneier, and Barker 1961). That is, the prisoner often transformed the focus of his beliefs from matters of primary self-concern or relevant life plan expressions to secondary levels of verbal expression. He said what he believed he was supposed to, but only ritualistically and without inward conviction. He learned to feign, to express himself and his beliefs, often ideological precepts, moral dogma and the like, in ways that would satisfy his torturers. Those of us who might have seen an Air Force officer on national television denouncing the American system as imperialistic might not have been able to tell that the testimony reflected ritualization. To many of us it rang with authenticity; but the officer's friends, those who knew him well, noticed a strange difference in his manners, speech, and posture. On returning home after release, the officer had to account for his action to the armed forces authorities. But in most of these cases the military courts ruled that such expressions of belief were the result of duress and did not reflect a genuine conversion. These decisions seem to recognize the social psychological distinction between primary and secondary socialization.

Another finding from similar studies concerns a different phenomenon of secondary socialization, prisoners' ritual identification with their captors. During the atrocious treatment of Jews in Nazi concentration camps, prisoners frequently esteemed articles of Nazi clothing worn by the guards. They would bargain for these articles and wear them under their own clothing. Or they would even fashion symbols of their captors, like swastikas, and display them outwardly. As with the study of ritualized belief, close examination of these practices indicated that they did not represent a genuine or deep-level reorganization of the prisoner's self. His or her primary experiences remained intact to resurface and manifest their true nature after the concentration camps were liberated and the extreme pressures of imprisonment were lifted.

In less dramatic but similar fashion, extreme pressures for conformity exerted by schoolteachers over students, or the close supervision of a foreman over his workers, can produce a characteristic ritual adaptation. Irving Rosow has termed this form of adaptation "chameleon conformity" (1967), pointing out how extreme external pressures for the proper behavior, without regard for internal beliefs or value states, produces a self-presentation in which people do what is expected of them for the sake of potential or actual rewards. They behave as they do for instrumental reasons, for their actions are merely a means to an end and are not necessarily an expression of their deeper self-identities. We all do what we must—work at a summer job or accept menial after-school work to earn extra money. We do not regard these activities as reflecting our real selves. A student may drive a cab at night, but does not think of himself or herself as a "cabbie." He or she is, instead, a "student." In another instance, someone might go to school to become a lawyer, but does not really think of himself or herself as a student. At some time or other, virtually all of us act as chameleons, changing our colors to conform to the demands of a situation, but we retain our underlying identities.

According to Rosow, these identities show up in times of stress. If another summer job becomes available, we do not forego wages to stay with the first one on the grounds that the former job is "really me." We simply move on to the other job. Top-level executives express loyalty to the firm until a better job comes along and their loyalty shifts accordingly. This does not mean that executives have no life plans, but just that affiliation with a particular firm is interpreted as progress toward a more basic personal goal, such as career advancement or "success."

The work of theorists like Goffman represents an effort to assess the effects of socialization in societies where major portions of everyday life are taken up in interaction with strangers. When we interact with those whose core self-attributes we do not know, and whose authentic selves are largely irrelevant to the instrumental purposes of going about our daily rounds, we tend to present only a version of our selves to others, a version we consider appropriate to the situation. Goffman formulated several concepts designed to help understand the nature of interactions in an impersonal world. His theory has been referred to as dramaturgical or, more colorfully, as the view of society itself as the "big con." His ideas are discussed in more detail later; however, his cynical view of socialization as impression management is consistent with what we single out here as the effect of secondary socialization, namely, the ritualization of the self.

To understand chameleon adaptations we must know whether the experiences in question involve deep-level identities or secondary ones, essential attributes of self or techniques individuals have developed simply to get along. Both deep and surface, private and public attributes of self are acquired through reciprocity thinking and taking the attitude of others, but the reciprocity thinking itself functions to organize the experiences of taking others' attitudes. The experiences of prisoners of war, like the instrumental actions of employees who so readily change jobs, represent learning that modifies the self, making it more complex, adaptable or manipulative. There are, however, some secondary socialization experiences that apparently modify core self identities.

In light of the secular character of most youth movements in the 1960s and the early 1970s, the popularity and vitality associated with the Jesus movement surprised many observers. The very youth who had rebelled against the puritanical moral code of their parents now embraced the brotherhood of those who knew the love of Jesus. Yet often they kept their long hair and hip clothes, or changed them for wardrobes even more unconventional. Jesus people were not the Christians of the First Presbyterian Church. Still, their conversion to Christianity rang with authenticity as they changed their ways of life, giving up drugs, forgoing the use of "swear words," and most important, devoting much time and energy to "the work of the Lord."

It appears that we have, in this case, an instance not just of an individual passing through stages that shift the focus of self but of changes in the core of the self brought about through secondary socialization. At least we can conclude that significant alterations have occurred in the way these believers think of themselves. On the other hand, detailed descriptions of the types of belief changes characterizing the Jesus people show that primary socialization continues to play an important role. In fact, one observer hypothesizes that "the Jesus movement combines elements of the moral code into which these young people were originally socialized" (Gordon 1974, 159). Gordon illustrates that a self-change called "consolidation" takes place and apparently contradictory socialization experiences synthesize into a new self-identity.

Jesus people use a language that is a synthesis between religious discourse and the argot of the hip. They are hip Christians. Their dress and casual styles of work and worship reflect the impact of youth cultural values, while the religious belief system itself represents a conventional expression of the more basic institutional values of society. But, the changes necessary for becoming a Jesus person may involve movement from the conventional secular life or from Christian fundamentalism. A move from conventional, not-saved backgrounds to Christian fundamentalism represents an ordinary conversion. Here the values of the institutions implicated, like family organization and marital fidelity, remain unchanged. Typically, a person finally espouses religious values that have been indirectly introduced earlier in his or her life.

When a fundamental ("saved") Christian becomes a Jesus person, though, the belief changes often symbolize rebellion against conventional or institutional expressions of belief. He or she assumes a new identity built upon old belief systems. The change from fundamental to youth-drug and then to Jesus person activates the consolidation experience. Drifting from the ways of the Lord or straying from the fold is only temporary. The return is affected by the style of life picked up while in the wayward world of the hip. Jesus-personhood reconciles these background features, sometimes indirectly: a person loses faith and becomes a conventional, secular person only to regain the lost faith of childhood by way of a hip expression of it.

We mention these phenomena of conversion and consolidation to demonstrate how consolidation usually involves only a modification of the self. Most adulthood learning, even if it appears to have radically altered the self, builds on the interactional effects of primary and secondary socialization.

Duplicity, Deception and Fraud: The Real Self and the Other

Socialization is the process of acquiring senses of self through social interaction based on the subjective judgments of who people are and how they go about accomplishing relations with one another. Given this and the fact that the motives and desires people bring to encounters with one another are established for particular interactions, we see that it is the illusion of consensus which makes social life possible. If social life rests on illusions or fictions, then the possibility that both who we think a person is and what we think that person thinks of us may be contrived. This basic insight was best developed by Erving Goffman's work on "humanity as a big con" (Cuzzort and King 1980).

Goffman questioned the relationships between what people do to manage the way they are perceived by others and who they really are. He distinguished between the content of a performance (what one *intends* as the meanings for others to attribute to one's action) and symptomatic behavior (what one *does* to validate those intentions). When someone manages to establish the image of who he or she is through actions that validate that image, others accept that person's version of the self. Undercover cops, for example, may manage to fool drug dealers into thinking they are users or dealers by acting as if they are users or dealers. They may carry drug paraphernalia, talk about how they used to "use drugs" but discovered that their use interfered with conducting their business, "But man, I'm a dealer just like you," or cite obligations such as to a parole officer or a regular job they say they are trying to keep. Undercover cops, then, have an elaborate repertoire of ways to simulate drug use and otherwise talk so that they may "give off" the impression that they are users or dealers (Jacobs 1992).

Obviously in Goffman's terms it is only when undercover cops manage to perform well and conceal their "true" identities that they can make an arrest. Only at the moment of the "bust" will the criminals know they have been deceived. In everyday life, Goffman observed, the same dynamic occurs between the images of self that people manage in their interaction and the way they are perceived by others. People may wish to appear "hip" or "politically correct" but may continuously say the "wrong" thing or act in ways inconsistent with the content of their performance. Or, as in the case of some undercover cops, or a salesperson, one may actually be "phony," obviously giving off the impression of being sincere and committed when "everybody" knows that one is simply "doing ones job."

Goffman appreciated that the way people wish to be seen varies from situation to situation and that the sociologist cannot tell which self-presentation is authentic. Instead, the sociologist must attend to the dynamics of impression management, showing how what one says meshes with the meta-messages one gives off, that is, manners of dress, style, tones of speaking, bodily posture and the like. Goffman shifts our attention to the dynamics of social interaction.

With Mead and the modern symbolic interactionists, one's self is the result of socialization, and that self refers to the regularities and processes of the individual's organization of behavior, what we have called primary and secondary characteristics of the self. Goffman stresses that our understanding of interactions depends less on knowing a person's self, that is, what one brings to an encounter with another, and more on the identity or image of a person that arises in interaction. Socialization, then, is in part a process of learning how to interact, how to establish a particular image for the purposes of a particular social situation.

In his major theoretical work, *Frame Analysis* (1974), Goffman offers an analytic language for examining the fit between performances and their social organization. For example, he suggests that performances are framed or organized as experiences. We can be "astounded" whenever those with whom we interact manage to convince us that something truly extraordinary has happened, a supernatural occurrence, a "believe-it-or-not" event, and the like. He also considers stunts and muffings and fortuitousness, "meaning that a significant event can come to be seen as incidentally produced" (Goffman 1974, 33). So for Goffman the meanings of our interactions depend on the skills we have to shape and reshape, frame and reframe our experiences with others. Frames of experiences in turn may be "played" almost *as if* they were something else, as our "keying" of certain acts as if they were play, such as when a sporting event is keyed as "elementary combative activity" (Goffman 1974, 57). As he develops his idea further, he discussed designs and fabrications as outcomes of the attempts of interactants to accomplish impressions in one another's mind.

With Goffman, we see socialization as a dynamic process of accomplishing interaction. Interaction consists of interpreted experiences organized into units meaningful to the actors. While social life is not completely theater, it is surely likened in his view to an actor's performance. We may frame and fall out of frame (off the stage), we may err in performance, confusing lines or reciting them incorrectly or inappropriately, or we may be truly adept at managing for our own design and purpose who people think we are. How people learn to do these things socially is a part of the process of socialization. Learning to be sincere, to be sarcastic, to be authentic, to joke, to "come on," to "loosen up," and the like, are all part of the marvelous skills people employ to do things socially.

Summary

Socialization is a term used to refer to the lifelong process in which a person becomes a self and acquires the skills necessary to interact with others. Children accomplish the task of learning through the mastery of both social and linguistic problems. Socialization proceeds according to the ever-increasing complexity in a person's capacity to think as though she or he were someone else. Of course a variety of factors can modify this trend toward complexity, such as psychological aberrations and senility.

Interactions, then, are influenced by the uses to which people put their version of reciprocity thinking. Those skills acquired within the context of the primary group generally result in core qualities of the self, whereas with some extreme exceptions experiences mediated by specific ways of thinking about others complicate and diversify the self. We call the first type of socialization primary, where the fundamental skills of interaction and identity, such as gender, are learned; and the latter secondary, where skills of interacting with strangers in situations that are formal and rationally oriented are learned. While the skills of impression management may be acquired in the secondary group context, they can pervade all aspects of life in modern society. Goffman shows that socialization is more a matter of learning to perform and organize performances than it is one of self-concept. So we recognize that socialization is both a "concrete" result (the social self) and an interactive competence (skills at acting socially).

Exercises for Socialization

1. Two very important skills acquired throughout the socialization process are our senses of time and space. These are fundamental to many of the processes of

comparison (reference group membership, distributive justice, etc.) discussed above. By using techniques designed to help you recall your primary socialization experiences, you can gain a greater appreciation of how these senses were formed and sharpened in our childhood. James Spradley devised several exercises that accomplish this appreciation.

a. The task is to select a period of your childhood, say when you were ten to thirteen years of age. Then recall where you played, along with associations between play and area of play during this period of your life. Professor Spradley suggests that you draw a turf map. This map will represent your recollection of your territory of play. It should include your home, a sketch showing the layout of your friends' homes, playgrounds, etc. Of course these will vary with the person's experiences, the kind of neighborhood, the family composition, and other factors.

b. Compare your completed maps with those of others in your class. Notice if there are differences between men's and women's maps, between those of people who grew up in cities and of people who were socialized early in rural or suburban environs. You can spend hours with these maps. You should discover that they tell you a great deal about how you acquired a sense of membership in groups and the general notion of who you are.

c. Professor Spradley used a device he called the life chart to illustrate how we mark and sense time. To draw one of these, first sit down with paper and pencil and make a list of the events in your life that you think represent significant changes; Spradley called these "marker events." Pare them down to categories that gloss the events (e.g., neighborhood life, junior high dating, making the cheerleading team, etc.). Now arrange these according to the lived-through sequences of your life experiences.

d. Again compare life charts with others in your class. You will discover how these charts convey the sense of self that you currently hold. How you mark your life can be seen as representing the core attributes of your sense of self. Notice how there are both similarities and differences in life charts. Generally, people with similar charts share interactive competencies.

2. Much of the socialization experience consists of learning how to use rules. Spradley invented an exercise to help students appreciate the great variation and complexity in the practice of "rules in use." A simple version of this exercise requires that you recall how eating took place when you were, say, fourteen years old. Recall a typical weekend at your home. Write a paragraph about each meal of the day. Then state the rules that governed eating at your house. For example, there may be assertions like, "Don't chew with your mouth open," "Food will be served to mother first, then boys according to age," or "Sunday is the big meal; everybody must attend." By comparing these rules for eating among your classmates, you will discover the consistency and the variation of rules in use in

everyday life. You will also discover there are often rules for not following rules, times specified for when certain rules are suspended. These make life interesting on occasion.

Suggested Readings

Bruce A. Jacobs's (see "Undercover Drug-Use Evasion Tactics: Excuses and Neutralization" *Symbolic Interaction* 15 [1992]:435–53) research on undercover cops and the tactics they use to evade the issue of whether they are actually using drugs is an excellent introduction to the kinds of problems Goffman's approach alerts us to. He shows that out of necessity undercover cops become very skilled at tricking drug users and dealers into believing they are one of them. These processes are learned and involve developing competencies in talking, dressing and acting according to the requirements of a particular social situation. It is worth the effort for a student to read at least portions of *The Presentation of Self in Everyday Life* (Garden City, NY: Doubleday Anchor, 1959). Goffman changed the way we think about interaction with his emphasis on the role the actor plays. A person accomplishes images and presents himself or herself to others. Socialization involves, therefore, who a person is and what that person can do. Studies of everyday life demonstrate how complex the accomplishment of interaction actually is. For example, Clark and Pinch describe the strategies and interactional skills required to conduct a "mock auction," which is "a form of confidence trick where money is obtained by a salesperson lulling a crowd of shoppers into buying goods at prices that are much higher than what they had been led to expect. See Colin Clark and Trevor Pinch, "The Anatomy of a Deception: Fraud and Finesse in the Mock Auction Sales 'Con'" *Qualitative Sociology* 15 (1992): 151–76.

Chapter 6

Knowing Others:
Group Phenomena

How we think about groups derives from our understanding of social phenomena; and just as we do of all objects of commonsense knowledge, we think of groups as real. Actually, they are seen at times in the organized form of teams on a field engaged in athletic competition, or just in the similar clothing worn by kids "hanging out" on a street corner. But groups also can be invisible, for sometimes rather abstract boundaries mark people who "belong" from those who do not. Groups also can be understood as outcomes, ever-changing with each manifestation of their members' activity, but they still remain compelling components of the context or background against which individuals experience themselves in the presence of others.

So far we have introduced interaction, socialization, and self as the three principal concepts necessary for understanding the nature of social life. Among actors, the results of the interrelationships among these phenomena emerge as groups. Although groups originate in individuals' thought and feeling processes, they are finally the outcome of people's shared thinking about and imputing of motives to each other in more or less regular ways. Given that their members share a sense of what has meaning to them, it is natural that groups exhibit clearly identifiable patterns of self-other relationships. Most of our founders, particularly Mead, Cooley and Simmel, recognized this and so devised ways to think about the group social psychologically. Mead's concept of significant others and the generalized other, Cooley's primary group and Simmel's social form are some examples of how they conceptualized group phenomena.

The Nature of the Group

According to Simmel, social form is somewhat independent of content. As we have noted, one can discuss many different topics, such as sport or religion, within a recognizable form known as *conversation*. But the form of any conversation is distinct from its content as well as from other ways of talking; for example, lecturing a college class about sports differs from talking about baseball with friends at the barbershop. Or children may engage in games—some simple, others complex, some cooperative, others competitive—but all of these games constitute forms of "playing."

To talk of different groups is to discuss social forms; and whereas the content of various groups may show enormous diversity, there is both order and stability in the form. Hence in the task of analyzing social life, social psychology pays attention to form over content. Of course, this does not mean content never influences form or that form never changes; for some very subtle interactions can take place between content and form. By stressing form over content, though, researchers simplify the amount of observation and description necessary before analysis can begin, and in observation they follow powerful concepts to depict human sociability.

What distinguishes groups from being mere aggregates of individuals or simple reflections of the behavior of specific individuals is the forms they display. In a situation where three people stand together talking, what they converse about—doctors, politics, sports—is usually unimportant to the form of their group; but the manner in which they converse is quite relevant: they seem to presume a great deal about one another, using first names only; they touch each other frequently, patting backs and poking ribs; they laugh at remarks that do not seem funny to the outsider; they use words that sound familiar but apparently convey special meanings for them. Although we cannot comprehend all that transpires in this group, we do gather from the tone and character of the interaction we observe that these people arc friends.

In another instance, we see three other people. They are dressed quite differently from the first three, and they speak in formal terms of address, using "Doctor," "Professor," and other honorific verbal designations. One of them is called only by the initials K.C. The only body contact we notice is handshaking. They seem distant, intent on a specific purpose. One remarks repeatedly, "So what have we got so far, K.C.?" and, "Now let's sum up progress on that." It is obvious that in character these two groups differ significantly. The first is informal, familiar, and expressive, in the direction we have identified as primary; the latter is formal, instrumental, and in the direction we can call secondary. Friends and business associates, even if they are actually the same individuals, manifest distinctive forms at the group level of reality. The character of the social interaction reveals the form or nature of the group.

Groups and Their Organization

Every group possesses a characteristic organization depending on the manifestations of three features of interaction in the group's form: background knowledge, which ranges from tacit to explicit; communication skills, which vary from casual to formal; and motivational or emotional involvement, which varies from compete and intense to partial and superficial. The various combinations of these features define the group form. The primary group, for instance, manifests tacit knowledge backgrounds, casual communicative expressions, and intense, complete motivational involvement. A secondary group displays explicit knowledge systems, formal articulations, and requires only partial and incomplete motivational involvement with the group. Further, mixed combinations of features are possible, producing forms that, generally speaking, are predominantly primary or predominantly secondary but that, in practice, are neither. We now turn our attention to a description of the features of these group forms: primary, secondary, and mixed.

The Primary Group

We have already learned that the primary group is characterized by intense, intimate, usually face-to-face communication and tacit understandings among its members. Given how much early learning occurs in them, it is not surprising that the theoretical importance of the study of primary groups has been developed by several sociologists. Among the most convincing work is the classic 1950 study by Homans, *The Human Group* (1992). According to Homans, it is in the primary, small group that the observer can find the origins of norms, the very rules that make social order possible. Furthermore, by studying the human group, the elementary features of all social life can be uncovered; for the accomplishment of social order for whole societies is, in part, a process of transferring the order and strength of the small group to society itself.

> At the level of the small group society has always been able to cohere. We infer, therefore, that if civilization is to stand, it must maintain, in the relation between groups that make up society and the central direction of society, some of the features of the small group itself. If we do not solve this problem, the effort to achieve our most high-minded purposes may lead us not to Utopia but Byzantium. (Homans 1950, 468)

Such a high-minded charge requires some clear thinking about small groups, and Homans supplies just that. He draws on some classic studies from social science literature: the Hawthorne bank wiring room studies, the Norton Street gang study, and the ethnography of the family in Tikopia, each of which is famous for providing us with theoretical insight.

The study of the bank wiring room was conducted by groups of researchers at the Western Electric Company's Hawthorne (California) plant during the 1920s. It focused on the relationship between group organization and worker productivity. As reported by Mayo (1933), the researchers originally expected the physical characteristics of the work situation along with matters of employer-employee relationships to determine productivity in a bank wiring room (where workers wired the bottom parts of telephones). Much to Mayo's surprise, however, regardless of which factors he varied, even when he introduced such presumably counterproductive ones as severely dimming the lights, worker output tended to increase. Mayo concluded that more important than any variable consciously applied as part of the experiment was the mere fact that attention was being paid to the work groups. The workers may not have known what the researchers were up to, but they were bound and determined to show how proud they could be of the work their teams could produce

This finding, know as the Hawthorne effect, is generally interpreted as showing that workers in any setting cannot be viewed as isolated individuals but must be seen as parts of well-organized small groups. Further studies on the work groups at Western Electric demonstrated that management efforts to control productivity, say, through worker incentives or new company policies, were often thwarted when they conflicted with the norms of the work group. Hence, members of the work groups who either overproduced or underproduced were brought back in line through the exercise of informal social controls. An effective means of control at Western was "binging," a practice male employees had of hitting each other on the shoulder. Whenever a person departed from the group's standards for what was a good day's work, he found that the friendly hits on his shoulder became more violent, or he might even be ostracized.

William Whyte's *Street Corner Society* (1981) is an early study showing that street gangs are not just random collections of boys with time on their hands. Instead, they are elaborately organized social systems adapted to their environments. The Norton Street gang had a complicated leadership structure and rules that were so powerful they even influenced the leisure time activities of gang members. For example, Whyte found that the results of bowling contests were correlated with the young men's ranking in the gang.

Homans cites these studies, as well as Firth's description of the complicated kinship structure of the Tikopia, as evidence for his theory that the small group is best understood as a system of four interrelated elements: activity, interaction, sentiments, and norms. Activity he defines as what people do. The essential feature of interaction is contact with others, and sentiments include the emotional states of people relevant to the activities of the group. Norms incorporate both the inferences people make about what is expected of them and their use of these inferences to establish conformity to inferred group standards.

Homans uses these elements to constitute a set of hypotheses, arguing that specific predictions are possible based on the nature of the small group as a social system. Theoretically, the more people engage in the same or a similar activity, the more they will come into contact with each other. With this increased contact, they will experience sentiments, sentiments that must be controlled if the group is to cohere. This requirement then results in the creation of norms; and the norms are exceedingly important because they in turn govern the activities of the group. This theory allowed Homans to formulate the hypothesis that the more frequently two persons interact with one another, the more probable it is that those people will like each other; and when a system of norms emerges (as it must) to govern their liking, their sentiments for each other actually become an outcome of that normative structure. College classes provide a good example here, for students often enter a class not knowing anyone else in it. But after a few weeks of the students seeing each other every Monday, Wednesday, and Friday, friendship groups, complete with normative structures, are clearly distinguishable.

Although Homans's theory has been subject to criticism, and he himself modified the basis of this theory in his later writing, the underlying rationale of his ideas is consistent with our viewpoint. It is out of mutual contact and recognition that the rules governing social action emerge. Rules emerge within the context of groups, and they are applied and interpreted within these same contexts. Hence, the practices of everyday life in the primary group setting offer keys to understanding the nature of the entire society. In the primary group, selves develop and skills in interpersonal relationships are acquired. In the setting of the small group, the very essentials of social life are revealed.

What we learn in such groups subsequently affects other relationships and interactional encounters we might have. In fact, the total arrangement of all parts of society, of its institutions and even the forms these parts assume (the structure of society), rest on the work, interpretations and learning developed within primary or small groups. A society in which individuals have lost their capacity to form primary groups is in danger of failing to transmit itself from one generation to the next. Without the vitality of the primary or small group, members of society may lose their ability to know and trust each other.

Although the primary form may express itself through many different contents, for the purposes of describing the form itself three will be mentioned: the love couple, friendships, and family groups. Now while it is fairly readily apparent that each kind of primary group has definitive characteristics, what is more subtle is how the form a group takes is not rigidly set but rather is "worked out." That is, friends can become lovers, and sisters can become friends. Like all social life, the primary group depends on constant negotiation among people as they work out their interactional encounters.

A Love Couple Sally and Ivan remember when they first met; they laugh about it. He was nervous because it was such a conventional date. He dressed up, grooming for more than an hour and rehearsing his conversation. He thought about which topics he should discuss and what "she" might think about him. He had been surprised that she accepted his invitation to go to the movies. After all, everyone agreed that Sally was the most gorgeous woman in their senior class.

That first date was fairly typical. Everything they talked about seemed artificial. He avoided saying anything he imagined might be offensive to her, and she waited for him to take the lead, to suggest where they should eat and which movie they should see. Still, it was a pleasant evening and warranted a second date.

The second date was an improvement. Each began to relax, to try to be more natural, and that is when, as Ivan put it, "things began to click." They discovered, for instance, that both liked health foods and yoga and that they seemed to believe in similar life philosophies. They discussed for hours such topics as "tactics for survival in a hostile world" and "the meaning of life" for them. And what is possibly most important, they had a similar style in discussing these weighty matters. Each had a sense of humor and each was able to frame what they said in a way that communicated that they were serious about the topic, but still having fun with it. Perhaps we could say they both enjoyed sarcasm. Continued meetings became more and more informal. Soon they could introduce topics by using shortened phrases or words. If Ivan said, "I think there's a new angle of high impact exercise," Sally knew what he meant without further explanation. Sally could ask, "Could you bring me a loaf of bread," without fear he would buy white bread. As they became "closer," they decided to live together. Long discussions ensued about whether to tell their parents:

> *Sally*: My mom's cool, very up-to-date. She didn't do it herself, but I think she would have—I mean, if it were today. She'll understand.
> *Ivan*: Maybe so, but hostility depresses me. I really want to avoid confrontations if possible.
> *Sally*: She knows I love you and she trusts me. She doesn't want me hurt. All I have to do is say it's what I really want. It'll be OK.
> *Ivan*: I hope so. My parents are no sweat. They live so far away. Besides my Dad lived with this second wife several years before they got married. We'll hold off telling them to see how things work out.

In the conversational form of the primary group, most of the meanings associated with expressions are tacit: "It'll be OK" and "to see how things work out." Sally and Ivan mutually presume the meanings of these remarks are clear to both of them in more or less the same way. They decide to live together and change their names to mark the new era in their lives. Both take the nickname "Skipper," a singular designation for the new reality, the oneness, they have created. They are now "together," a couple serious about one another. When friends inquire, they explain, "Yes, we've got a relationship."

As this newly built social reality endures, it will expand the degree of tacitness that grounds it. It will be renegotiated as crises threaten the assumptions from which the meanings and reality of the relationship derive. For example,

Ivan gets a job in another town and Sally must decide whether she will continue her schooling or accompany Ivan. They argue:

> *Sally*: Skipper, you know I love you, but I have one year left to finish my thesis.
> *Ivan:* I know, Skipper, but if you really love me, you'll quit and come with me. You know I need you.
> *Sally*: Oh, Ivan, you're just being self-centered and old-fashioned. I don't want that kind of relationship.

By discontinuing, perhaps unconsciously, the use of "Skipper," Sally indicates to Ivan (and to herself) a change in her understanding of the meanings that undergird their relationship. As problems force each person to be more explicit, it becomes clear that their understandings of "love" are not identical, so the assumed reciprocity on which the relationship was originally founded must now be renegotiated, or perhaps the relationship ended.

Like all primary groups, this one rests on trust and a certain degree of unqualified acceptance (Garfinkel 1963). The love couple presumes an intensity of interpersonal involvement in which the meanings of the cliché "love is never having to say you're sorry" becomes clear. As we can readily guess, building such important primary relationships from "scratch," that is, based exclusively on the feelings and interaction between two persons, results in a fragile relationship easily influenced by outside pressures. Conversely, whenever something happens to upset the routines within such groups, it is more likely that one party or the other, possibly both, will respond emotionally (Handel 1982, 69). Similarly, one or both may also be willing to do a great deal of work to restore the trust that grounds the relationship. This was exemplified in studies we can recall by Garfinkel, in which people's routines of social life were purposefully upset. In these experiments, Garfinkel (1962) began by recruiting subjects to address personal questions to people whom they thought were counselors. But the responses of the "counselors" were random, with their answering yes or no to subjects' personal questions without regard for what the questions themselves might be. Garfinkel discovered that under these conditions subjects searched for underlying patterns in the random yes/no sequences, trying desperately to use what they believed about such settings to instill sense in a trusted relationship.

This may be analogous to what Homans was suggesting about the vulnerability of a civilization that does not protect and support primary group formation. That is, all new members of a society are born into primary groups, and from these groups they receive their understanding of how their society makes sense. Furthermore, the society itself is built up from and therefore based on the strength of its primary groups. If its primary groups can no longer make sense for individual members, the society itself will eventually fall.

Friendships Friendships are also classified as primary groups; and in fact, the difference between love and friendship is often obscure. We may love our friends, of course. But generally the difference between having a friend and being in love with one involves degrees of tacitness, informality, and involvement. We presume less of a friend than of a wife or husband. As Goffman might have said, those with whom we are in love are allowed "back stage," are privy to matters of the self behind the "front." For example, if we experience a radical change in mood, this is more likely to be misunderstood by a friend than by a lover. Rage may be interpreted by a friend as the termination of the friendship, but by a lover as a mood change signaling the need for intervention, or simply as evidence in support of the proposition "that's the way he is sometimes."

Friendships can develop in unlikely situations, such as on an assembly line, in a bar, or during a bus ride; however, we can describe any typical friendship according to a particular process. In other words, a friendship does not depend on specific kinds of activities; and thus it resembles the love relationship, generating a complete environment for itself, as the following example shows.

Bud and Gene grew up together on the Sand Springs line, a working-class suburb of a large midwestern city. They played together as children, shared the experiences of trouble, joy, disappointment, and grief. When they were growing up neither really imagined an existence without the other. But when Gene went to war, Bud stayed home, disqualified from service because of a medical problem. They corresponded for a while, but soon they simply stopped writing. Gene wrote home to his wife frequently, and Bud would occasionally find out from her how things were going. When Gene returned, they revived their relationship, spending long evenings together telling stories about their childhood adventures and sharing Gene's tales of his wartime exploits. Bud had married during Gene's absence, and the wives accompanied their husbands on visits to each other's home. But the men carried on their conversation, and the women often left the room whenever Bud and Gene started talking about old times.

There was more to this friendship than just conversation and reminiscences. Bud worked at a local high school in the athletic department. He was able to get tickets to all the football games, and since he managed the concessions at the home games of the local university, he could allow Gene and his family free admittance. In return, Gene, a handyman, installed central air-conditioning in Bud's house, kept his plumbing in repair, and helped out with jobs Bud could not handle himself.

There were also limits to the friendship. It was lifelong and it endured many crises and even bitter quarrels, but where each other's family was concerned, a "hands off" agreement existed. Bud's children had troubles growing up. Much to Bud's chagrin, while still quite young his son "came out" in the gay community and moved to California; his daughter dropped out of high school and had several run-ins with the law. Finally, family tensions over these problems led to divorce. Throughout these difficult times Gene was there to listen, sometimes for hours on the phone, but never did Gene give Bud explicit advice. Each understood that such matters were part of family life, and mixing family and friendship could have a devastating effect on their friendship. Bud remarried after several years, moved from job to job, state to state, finally reappearing in their hometown where Gene had remained since his military experience. The two men resumed contact and their respective lives, which by now were considerably different, seemed to have little effect on their friendship. The content and operation of their friendship had been established long ago. The version of reciprocity that served as the foundation of their friendship was stable and enduring, protected by an elaborate defense from outside pressures.

Family The family is the primary group form par excellence. It is in the context of the family that the strongest, most consistent manifestations of tacitness, informality, and intense involvement are found. In essence, no one *achieves* a family. Families are given, members find them ready-made, appropriate for reinterpretation, reorganization and renegotiation. A husband and a wife do invent their relationship out of a social base composed of mutual assumptions; but this family is their second, built to some extent on experiences of each one's first. A marriage reality is created and sustained through years of practice, usually developing a distinctive and even idiosyncratic character (Berger and Kellner 1964). It is children and others who confront it who must discover its nature.

As we know, Durkheim suggested that a fundamental fact of all social life is the degree to which interactions and meanings of everyday life are integrated into the structures of society. Homans's work also suggests how the identification and discussion of forms of primary groups must include an understanding of how closely such organizational forms are integrated with patterns of the larger organizations of the society in which they are located. For our purposes, the love couple as a form is the least well integrated, the family the most well integrated, and the friendship an intermediate form. In other words, and even in spite of the increasing number of persons "living together," the meanings for a love-couple relationship are somewhat problematic, since they are not part of taken-for-granted, commonsense knowledge—what everybody knows. In contrast, family forms—of both dual- and single-parent families, and including married couples without children—are precisely understood in terms of what everybody knows.

One way of thinking about integration then, is to focus on the problematic character of form. The less problematic the form the more integrated it is; and conversely, the amount of ambiguity associated with the form is a reliable indicator of its low integrative linkage to other societal forms. Keeping within a Durkheimian idiom, we can say that dyads like the love couple are egoistic.

Given that each of us has or has had so many of them, we should not be surprised to find a wide variety of meanings for our primary relationships. A study of blue-collar patrons of a bar (LeMasters 1975) provides some indication of the variety of content possible within the family form. To young middle-class couples who attempt to use the love relationship as the sole foundation for their families, the practices described by LeMaster may seem strange. For example, the men who became regulars at the bar spoke of their wives and their marriages in terms like these: "My wife is a good gal, but I just don't know anybody I'd like to be married to for thirty years"; and, "Hell, man, you can't live without 'em and you can't live with 'em." The wives often talked of the "raw deal" that marriage was for them and commented that if they had known then what they knew now, they would at least have "waited awhile to marry."

In short, wives and husbands may actually interpret their involvement in marriage quite differently. But the segregated sex roles that mark these blue-collar families "can be quite stable and satisfying if both sexes accept the arrangement" (LeMasters 1975, 45). The reasons people have for staying together vary. For the wife from a conservative rural background, "catching" and staying with a man who can provide "a good living" may be the motivation; or the husband may be satisfied with a "homemaker" and a "good mother" for his children. Within the marital relationship these reasons remain tacit and function to the mutual satisfaction of the couple. Since the form is primary, we expect tacitness to prevail and should not be misled by pronouncements from the individuals involved. Like the author of this study, we must search for the "bedrock" features of the relationship. For example, LeMasters reports this conversation with a married couple:

"You know, Professor," one of the older wives said to me, "Bob and me have never had an argument in our forty years of marriage." "That must be a record," I said. The husband looked at his wife and said: "That's a lot of bull-shit—what are you trying to do, feed the Professor a lot of crap?" The wife stopped talking, resuming her beer drinking, and the husband took over the conversation. "I'll tell you what, Doc," he said. "Marriage is a 50–50 proposition and people who don't know that better stay single." He drained his beer and ordered another one. "Now you take this wife of mine—she's a good sport. During the depression when a man could hardly earn a dime, she stuck right by me and saved every penny she could." He paused to light a cigarette. "Another thing—she always took care of our kids. If I had a woman that let her kids run around dirty the way some women do, I'd kick her right out of the house." The wife didn't say anything. The husband continued. "Her only trouble is she talks too damn much—and some of the stuff she says don't make sense—like that thing she told you tonight about us never having an argument! Christ Almighty, I wouldn't have a damn woman in the house if I couldn't fight with her once in a while." The wife was looking in her purse for some snapshots of their grandchildren she wanted to show me.

I looked at the pictures and admired the children—they were handsome. "A hell of lot better looking than their grandparents," the husband said. He turned to his wife, "Come on, Mother, Harry [the bartender] says that all grandparents have to be home in bed by ten thirty. Let's go!" The wife protested that she wanted another beer. "Nope, you've had enough for an old lady"—and out they went. (LeMasters 1975, 45)

Our point about primary groups is dramatically illustrated; for here the primary group form functions within a context of informality, of unspoken understandings, and it rests on an assumed content that cannot be explicated without changing the nature of the relationship. As with any relationship built on degrees of tacitness, as long as the parties involved do not question their basic assumptions, the relationship endures, though, as in the case LeMasters reports, perhaps to the detriment of one member. Informality demands tolerance and unquestioned loyalty to the emotional basis of the relationship. It requires familiarity and long time interactions that can be patterned and intuitively grasped by the participants. Primary forms occupy a major portion of every person's social existence. They provide continuity for social life.

Secondary Groups

In a complex society where there are many different primary groups and persons from them must interact both within and across groups, the basis for interaction cannot always be tacitness and informality. People who do not know someone's background cannot assume to know the other's self and cannot relate to such persons immediately in a way that allows the assumption of a mutually intuitive understanding. But of course it is often necessary to interact with those with whom we have no prior knowledge. A particular person may have a commodity we desire, or he or she may play an important role in an activity we intend to complete. So it is obvious that grounds other than those provided by the primary group must be established if the affairs of everyday life in a world of strangers is to be carried out (Lofland 1985).

The German sociologist Ferdinand Toennies (1940) wrote systematically about the social psychological basis of interaction in social contexts varying in degree of formality and tacitness. He was particularly concerned about the changes that occur in a social system as the relationships within it evolve from those built on familiarity and natural association to ones constructed on objective, rational grounds. Modern sociology thinks of these differences in the character of social encounters as expressive and instrumental. Although both groups exhibit some of both characteristics, primary groups are essentially expressive (an end in themselves) and secondary groups instrumental (a means to an end).

Writing at the beginning of the twentieth century, Toennies noticed how the railroads that connected small German villages were bringing together for the first time people of markedly different backgrounds. The social problem of the stranger, the person whose motives and intentions could not be readily ascertained, become paramount. We can think about this as a problem of trust. Although the railroads were constructed for the purposes of commerce and industry, their effect was far more profound. How could lifelong residents of a village tightly knit into a community relate to other people about whose character and identity they knew little? In short, Toennies focused on the problem of people finding grounds for interaction that could substitute for the natural, taken-for-granted grounds of common experience that were crucial to their sense of community. He discovered that such a basis existed in the thought patterns that had already developed among people concurrently with the increasing industrialization of Germany and Europe. He pointed out that if a set of specific goals could be defined by the persons involved in the interaction, then a form of organization relevant to these goals emerged.

The storekeeper and the customer are one example. The storekeeper need not know a stranger to take his or her money in exchange for an item. All that is required is a precisely defined and delimited reciprocity thinking between them. All the two need to know is the setting of the store, some minimal standards of civility, the kind and availability of the desired item, and the manner necessary for an economic exchange. A customer does not have to know about the storekeeper's family life, the details of his or her children's activities in school, or their mischief at play. The storekeeper does not need to know about the purchaser's recent good fortune in a card game.

Toennies's observations led him to suggest that within given societies two basic forms could be identified: one in which the diverse primary group form prevails, and one in which the form is "rational" or "goal specific." The first, he believed, was "natural" and engendered feelings of belonging and security, while the latter resulted in mutual suspicion and distrust. The first kind of society he called *Gemeinschaft* and the second *Gesellschaft*. Composed of secondary group forms the *Gesellschaft* society solved the problem of how people with radically different backgrounds could interact, that is, by offering a superficial and artificial foundation for social relationships. Toennies referred to this foundation as "rational will." In the extreme, Weber might say the "ideal," the *Gesellschaft* society requires that we learn to treat all persons as strangers. In the language we have chosen, we say the basis must be explicated or formalized so it can be learned readily, without regard to differences in socialization experiences. Such a secondary group form establishes minimal requirements for interaction. It generates a formal system for interpersonal relationships, a system with a definite reason for being.

As with the treatment of primary groups, our aim is to describe the form; therefore we have selected the case that most clearly demonstrates the characteristics of a secondary form, the bureaucracy. Its basis is explicit; its language is formal; and its requirements for involvement and the motivational system it activates are minimally specific. In the *Gesellschaft* society, the bureaucracy functions as the standard for all social relationships, and social life within it retains a secondary character. Finally, it comes after something else, building on experiences already present in those it recruits as members. In essence, one does not "belong to" a rational exchange; instead, one "works with it," or "puts it to use."

Properties of Rational Social Forms

Precisely what are the properties of rational organization? The classic German sociologist whose writing has already been discussed, Max Weber, depicted the form of bureaucracy in explicit terms, enumerating five basic features. For him, the bureaucratic form is (1) formal, (2) impersonal, (3) technical, (4) based on an ideal of merit, and (5) hierarchical. By formal, Weber meant that organizational principles transcend any person or the activities of any person connected to the organization. These principles are made formal when they are written down and essentially expressed as abstract guidelines for the determination of admissible practice and policy. Any rational organization has a charter and a constitution detailing its statement of purpose. Of course this is expected in the secondary form, for it must accommodate and educate newcomers, and in some standard fashion, and the procedures for doing this need to be formalized. The conscious characteristic of the behavior of those interacting within this form is ordinarily known as bureaucratic action.

A judge, for instance, can be removed from the bench for unprofessional conduct in affairs of law. While acting out the role of judge, a person must follow abstract rules that define a set of actions to encompass events, like hearings and trials, relevant to the courtroom. In the end, actual judgments depend on abstract legal notions being processed and then enacted through the minds and behaviors of certain people. A judge who consistently rules in a biased fashion violates the principles defining a court and may be admonished by a higher authority, thus reflecting the intent of the phrase "equal justice under the law."

The feature of impersonality signifies the requirement for equal relationships among people within the boundaries of the rational exchange. This property forbids primary experiences, or at least forbids their playing any role in the functioning of the bureaucracy. It requires background knowledge to become relevant only if it is consonant with the abstract principles presumed to govern the occasion. Thus if two people are neighbors, close friends, or even relatives, these facts are not to be considered pertinent to any rational operation of a bureaucratic nature. An automobile dealer's special deal for a friend is officially forbidden; a separate set of books used by a social service worker to allow friends to avoid administrative steps at a welfare agency likewise is "against the rules."

A third feature of rational exchange in everyday life is the influence of technical competency. Durkheim's early writing referred to this as "the division of labor." Within any given social organization, there are major tasks to be accomplished and the manner in which the group separates and assigns performances relevant to the accomplishment of those tasks is the division of labor. For example, no one person designs and builds a car from start to finish. Instead, the labor required is divided into various kinds of work and assigned to various workers.

In societies without a rational foundation, ones predominantly primary in group form, there may be little technical skill required to work. For example, clearing a patch of jungle for planting corn and the actual planting of the corn may require the same tool, an ax; nevertheless, the group may sharply delineate "clearing" as masculine and "planting" as feminine. In this instance though, it is not just the technical basis of the activities that separates the two kinds of labor; customs, religious beliefs, or other elements of culture function to define who does what.

With regard to the accomplishment of *its* task, however, the bureaucracy minimizes the role traditions play in any particular group. In this ideal type, the rational grounds for task accomplishment is the technical requirement of the work. Thus, if a division exists within an organization, it is due to some technical reason. A motor pool platoon within an army division is organized with a person in charge, a staff of trained mechanics, and a parts inventory because the division needs motorized vehicles and this equipment must be maintained. Or a corporation selling information-processing machines must have a research branch to develop and improve computers and software to do that job. This rationale for the ideal expression of the bureaucratic form rests on a technical requirement, whether it involves hardware or knowledge of a technical nature.

Weber's fourth bureaucratic feature states that merit predominates in a bureaucracy. This means that in a rational organization the occupant of any technically created position has the job because of his or her skill in its performance. Ideally, personnel who fill the positions should be those individuals with the best skills and the highest accomplishments. Hence the best mechanic gets the job on the motor pool or the brightest research technician heads the study of the latest miniaturized computer circuitry.

Finally, the bureaucratic levels within the naturally derived organizational form are ordered according to a principle of hierarchy. Each level is accountable to the one directly above it, and in like fashion, higher levels are responsible for lower ones. More fundamentally, not only are all the divisions or levels technically grounded, but they are also stacked one on the other in accord with the abstract principles defining the rational properties of the organization. Hierarchy by position is a constitutive feature. It pertains to the general demand that all segments of the system make sense in terms of the stated goals of the organization. If a segment makes sense—that is, if it fits into the overall plan or purposes of the organization—we say it possesses the properties of accountability and responsibility. Official reasons for its existence can be readily expressed and they are generally acceptable to persons at higher levels of responsibility within the organization, with the chief executive officer charged with ultimate responsibility and accountability, sometimes to the public at large. In the extreme, we have seen even heads of state resign for what they thought was no fault of their own, but to take responsibility for an error made by some high official appointed by them.

We can easily understand how the bureaucracy demonstrates secondary forms of social interaction. Yet, as we describe its ideal features, we begin to suspect that a neat distinction between this form and the primary is impossible. We have stressed before how social life should be seen as dynamic and unfolding in character. Secondary and primary forms contrast in provocative ways; each counterpoints the other. In everyday life, whenever people actually try to act in the presence of others, conflicts emerge; the form in which much of this conflict takes place is called the *mixed form*.

Mixed Forms: Emerging Conflicts

The study of work groups in industrial and formal settings has reaffirmed the importance of the persuasiveness of primary forms. Considerable debate has been generated over this issue. Investigators initially attempted to study the performances of workers in terms of job incentives and rational matters only. But they soon discovered how such factors themselves took on meaning within the context of primary or informal groups created by the workers; for instance, an efficiency rating for the accuracy of its shelling achieved by a ship at war may not be a totally valid indicator of the gunnery practices of that ship.

Altheide and Johnson (1980) describe the practice of "gundecking" in the U. S. Navy. Gundecking refers to the falsification of official written reports to make it appear as if certain requirements were carried out, but without the required procedures actually having been met. For example, one could gundeck the daily reports the night before an inspection. The authors contend that gundecking cannot be fully understood as merely a matter of dishonesty. In fact, gundecking is often built into the normal operations of a ship. There are, for example, formal requirements to test both sonar equipment and full engine capacities, and Navy regulations instruct that both tests be conducted at the same time. But engines running full out make so much noise that accurate sonar readings are virtually impossible, so the tests are routinely done at separate times and reported as if they were done according to regulations. Likewise, the battle efficiency of a ship (the ratio of rounds fired to targets hit) depends on a complicated decision-making process involving a spotter and the ship's gunnery personnel. To avoid having to average in so-called lost rounds (shells that the spotter never saw explode), ship personnel have been known to classify these shells under the category "target of opportunity," to indicate that indeed the round had fallen on target (Altheide and Johnson 1980, 217).

The emergence of such intimate forms of knowledge in a strict bureaucracy is a remarkable demonstration of how the relationship between primary and secondary forms can be exceedingly complex. Another example comes from Gouldner's research of a "wildcat'" strike, one not authorized by a union. He studied a mining operation (of the General Gypsum Company) and discovered that a major cause of the wildcat strike among the miners could be traced to the workers' reaction to a management policy that ignored preexisting informal group relations (Gouldner 1954). Over time, the miners had developed a procedure among themselves for making judgments about what counted as "a good day's work." This procedure was grounded in an understanding between the foreman and the miners, a tacit agreement that only a certain amount of work is to be done in a single day. The workers had to mine enough ore to satisfy the minimal demands of the "boys at the top," in other words, an amount that would keep the bosses off their foreman's back, and hence him off theirs. The agreement took the following form: we, the workers, will do the necessary work, if you, the foreman, do not ride us too hard, allow us to pace ourselves with frequent breaks, and perhaps most important, tolerate the informality of our attitudes toward work. Gouldner called this mode of interpreting work the "indulgence pattern" (Gouldner 1954, 18–23).

The indulgence pattern defined a satisfactory workday and allowed strong friendships to develop among the workers and between the workers and the foreman. So with the untimely death of their trusted foreman, the workers of course clamored for one of their own to replace him. They wanted to be able to continue the indulgence pattern and knew a foreman coming from the outside would have to be trained, and might even require them to work at what they regarded to be dangerously fast rates. But upper-level management policies prevailed and an outsider from the above-ground processing plant was appointed foreman. Predictably, he went by the rules, formalizing work breaks, demanding maximum efficiency, and being generally intolerant of informality between himself and the miners; in short, he behaved in a manner dictated by the official bureaucratic structure but inconsistent with the indulgence pattern. The workers' reaction to this violation of their primary form and the norms generated by it were so intense that the conflict exploded into a wildcat strike. The strike was eventually resolved when management agreed to institutionalize some portions of the old indulgence pattern, like work quotas and more frequent breaks. The settlement also resulted in a curious formalization of the primary form that undermined the nature of the work group itself. In social psychological terms, the resolution of the strike explicated once-tacit knowledge, expressing formally what before was merely understood, and this essentially relieved the men of their social obligations to each other and to their foreman. One no longer needed to become an accepted member of the group in order to understand work arrangements, for such arrangements were now instituted through formal applications of the contract agreements.

In each example of a mixed form, either the primary or the secondary dominates. The goals of the company may be subverted by friendships among the workers, with their ways of interpreting work winning out, if only temporarily, over the rational procedures of the company. In the Navy, rational requirements and incentives get renegotiated in such ways that gunnery targets are redefined. Or, as in the settlement of the wildcat strike, there is a transformation of the tacit meanings of social life into a formal contract. In this case, the goals of the company were fostered by promoting an experience of primary group membership.

The mixed form can be either an arena, or a mask, for conflict. One can always be fired or laid off from the mine if coal sales drop or the cost of production rises. These reasons for termination do not necessarily create a self-crisis, but expulsion from a formal friendship circle, like breaking up with a lover or being rejected by a parent always goes to the heart of the self. According to Hummel (1987), the investment of self in secondary group forms can only lead to problems for the person and for the organization. A lifelong, loyal employee of an oil company suddenly finds his accounting section has been replaced by automated, modernized procedures; he or she is without a job and feels deprived of the reason for social existence. Or there is the other extreme, the chameleon who in moments of solitude anxiously ponders what he or she really stands for, what his or her life is all about.

Jackall (1977) investigated how people sense pressures to conform in commercial bureaucratic work situations. He found that the bank employees he studied not only were aware of pressures to shape their behavior and demeanor according to standards of dress and appearance but they also recognized that these standards varied in proportion to contact with the public. Hence tellers and loan officers who had the most contact with the public had to dress most conservatively and conform most closely to bank rules. The consequence of all this pressure was a kind of alienation, a detached cynicism about oneself and one's relationship to the organization. Jackall identifies this alienation as a kind of self-artificiality, an employee's consciousness of unauthentic role performance. A payroll clerk's remarks during one interview illustrate this feeling:

"How do I see myself at work? Well, I wouldn't associate with me given a choice. Tie, suit, sports coat. Everything toward doing what somebody else wants" (Jackall 1977, 285).

Standardized public faces are an integral part of secondary form interaction. In the bank, workers experienced this conformity to organizational demands as partially negotiable. Their response was to "dissemble" themselves, "both to do their jobs and get along at the office." For example, the rules might say "sports coat and tie," but not restrict how outlandish one's tie might be. Most employees felt uneasy about their alienation but saw no alternative to such "internal detachment from external behavior" (Jackall 1977, 285). On more than one occasion Jackall found employees who resolved the problem by exemplifying Goffman's (1961) belief that in a bureaucratic world the ability to manipulate whatever public face a situation demands is not only a necessary means of survival but may even be considered a personal virtue. In such extreme cases we see the victory of the secondary over the primary form.

More frequently, adaptations to conflicts take on the shape of chameleon conformity and a very strongly felt sense of self-alienation. Alienation between self and the group is a consequence of the conflict often created by mixed group forms. It refers to a separation between self and others, a fundamental failure to achieve reciprocity thinking, and it occurs whenever the features of the self oppose those of the other. Thus alienation results from a tacit, informal, and deep commitment to a secondary group form, like that of the faithful clerk for the oil company who, when automated out of a job, suddenly realizes the company doesn't feel that same sense of loyalty. Alienation also develops when a rational stance is taken toward the primary group, as we saw in the settlement of the wildcat strike. In the primary relationship there is a merger between self and group. The person's identity and, most crucially, the principles of organization and the expression of that identity are rooted within the character of the group form. In effect, a person becomes a member of the group—a regular at the Oasis Bar or half of a couple. The relationship between self and group membership functions smoothly.

In the secondary form, reliance on rational grounds of exchange is not necessarily alienating, at least not in a fundamental sense, for the secondary form presupposes the primary. The shallow commitment that the bureaucracy demands of the individual is not conducive to stability in the organization of the self. This is true to a certain extent because the bases of the secondary form thrive on change, such as the kind we have seen recently in many organizations with the introduction of technological innovations. The primary form resists change; each modification calls for a renegotiation of the tacit group supports. Thus the alienating consequences of the secondary form derive either from the individual's investment of self in the form—without a corresponding investment from the form itself—or from the absence of a primary grounding in the individual prior to contact with the secondary form. Of course the latter results in an investment of self in the form, but the first consequence differs from the second in that one may rebel against one's past primary experiences or at least may confront them without forsaking them altogether. While the primary form embraces the self, the secondary forsakes it.

Although strains and conflicts may emerge from the mixed form, we may have to recognize it as an inevitable part of the "way things are" (Dayton 1957). The consequences of mixed forms in groups are variable. The literature is rife with examples of how a primary form may be at cross purposes to a secondary one. Many sociologists suggest this phenomenon as "bureaucracy's other face" (Blau and Meyer 1987). In still other cases, primary forms within a formal organization may inadvertently further the rational goals of the organization. Sometimes friendship ties among executives influence them against accepting positions with better remuneration in competitive firms. But our point aims at the essentials of group form. One must distinguish between the consequences of forms and the forms themselves. It is in the nature of forms and their interrelationships to generate opposite forces and so foster conflict.

We can summarize as follows: formality is out of place in the primary form; informality is out of place in the secondary. The relationship between the butcher who throws in a little something extra for his favorite customers and in return is remembered by them on his birthday, represents a reciprocal arrangement not permitted in self-service supermarkets. The person who experiences mixtures of forms in everyday life must go through the difficult and taxing task of interpreting the meanings of conflict. In the final analysis, these meanings become the definitions of the situations out of which are created the realities of lived-through consequences.

The Company as Reference Group

The consequences of working within the complex and dynamic forms of bureaucracies can go to the heart of the social self. For many people in today's world, the companies they work for demand more and more time and commitment from them. In our view, the workplace can become a major point of reference for the meanings of many aspects of a person's life, including moral decisions. From our earlier discussions of the concept of the reference group and especially following the contribution of Shibutani (1955), we learned that people formulate many ideas and plans of action in reference to groups to which they belong or aspire to belong. It follows that as competition for jobs and keeping jobs become intense, the company may well assume the role of a major reference group in the social lives of its employees. Its impact on the subjective side of social life may not be so obvious.

Jackall (1988) studied how corporate managers think the world works, and how big organizations shape moral consciousness. The hierarchic authority structure of organizations is the "linchpin" of bureaucratic dominance, and the way managers understand personal relationships reflects their position within the organization. For example, within the complicated and sometimes ambiguous authority and social structure of a bureaucracy, moral questions are translated into "alliances, fealty relationships, networks, coteries, or cliques, as circles of affiliation, or simply managerial circles" (Jackall 1988, 39). This means that whenever questions about a policy come up (and these include such famous cases as the "Dalkon Shield Affair" and the "Pinto Case," involving Ford Motor Company), they are judged less in terms of how they fit within the abstracted rules of the organization or standards of community safety and more in terms of who is loyal to whom or how a decision or action will affect a particular alliance of managers within the organization.

The managers Jackall interviewed and observed in several large corporations illustrate how the social life that emerges within these organizations is the major determinant of what members regard as "morality." For them, it is highly important to be a "team player," to be ready to affiliate with others who have been successful and to distance oneself from those who have not. Skill is acquired for talking one's way to success, which means survival by the negotiation and manipulation of social relationships within the organization. A successful manager learns a dexterity with symbols. When one says "exceptionally well qualified" he or she might mean "has committed no major blunders to date." Or, "tactful in dealing with superiors" may mean, "knows when to keep his mouth shut." As one of Jackall's managers put it: "By the way, in the corporate world, whenever anybody says to you: 'I'm going to be completely honest with you about this,' you should immediately know that a curve ball is on the way. But, of course, that doesn't apply to what I'm about to tell you" (Jackall 1988, 161).

Jackall is able to show us that the corporate world is a social world in its own and even grand right, requiring that its members become integrated into its structure. But in virtually all bureaucratic organizations, while following most rules most of the time, members still choose to modify some. They learn survival skills, and most important, they develop a strong sense of what is right and wrong, which may readily correspond to everyday ideals about moral practice. Of course as the difference widens between the corporate world and the everyday one where it finds its customers, there is the possibility that from the standpoint of daily life the corporate world looks "immoral."

Summary

Social interaction may be characterized according to three interrelated components: background knowledge, communicative skills, and emotional dimensions. In a person's lifetime various amounts and degrees of skill in these components are acquired. The process of acquisition, know as socialization, produces consequences in the individual that we call the social self.

Groups require interaction between self and others. These interactions exhibit typical forms that can be depicted using the same three components of social interaction. Each group type (primary, secondary and mixed) predisposes a self-other relationship. These relationships in turn either synthesize or antagonize the identities of self and others implicated in a given social encounter. Morality within the social form of bureaucracy is a particularly difficult concept since the standards for making moral judgments develop within the context of the organization and may differ from those used in everyday life.

Exercises on Groups

1. One way to appreciate the power of groups is to recall from your own life experiences the groups that influenced you. Professor Spradley devised a technique for doing this. He suggested that you focus on a period of your life, for instance ages eleven to thirteen, and begin by writing down the names of your friends. Then arrange these names into activity groupings. You should discover that you interacted with some kids only for certain activities while others appear in all of your groupings. Finally, think about which of these friends and acquaintances exerted control over you and which you could control. This exercise should provide you with vivid illustrations of reference groups.

2. Homans's theory suggests that people you interact with are people you probably like. List the names of people you know fairly well. Then rank these names in an order that reflects how well you like them. Look at the results of this exercise and see if Homans's theory works. If it does not, think of why not. Often we may interact with family members whom we do not especially like. Does Homans's theory of group dynamics help explain the problems arising from such interaction?

3. All of us have had experiences in secondary groups. If you were a member of a scouting association or a church youth group or even if you attended a summer camp, you have probably experienced the problems of mixed group forms. To document these problems, think about the ways in which what you and your friends actually did in these groups differed from what you were supposed to do. Write a few examples. These will make exciting topics for discussion, and they should dramatically show the problems of mixed forms.

Suggested Readings

Several of the classic sources we have cited have been reexamined recently. For example, an entire issue of the *Journal of Contemporary Ethnography* (April 1992) is devoted to assessing the contributions of Whyte's *Street Corner Society*. We recommend especially the study that revisits the locale where Whyte conducted his study in the 1940s. Some very important issues about the factual matters in Whyte's report are raised. Whtye himself responsed to these criticisms, and through the interchange the reader can gain insights into the complicated and often controversial character of field research. The business of finding and telling the sociological truth can be quite interesting.

Also, in Helen Schwartzman's discussion of the Hawthorne study, *Ethnography in Organizations* (Newbury Park, Calif.: Sage, 1993), she points out the contributions of anthropology. She outlines a strategy for seeing organizations as social settings much like the organization of folk society. She shows how it was through interview data that the major discovery of the effect of the informal social system on work habits and production was made. She further illustrates the power of ethnography in her own studies of hospitals, research laboratories and factories. Finally, we highly recommend Robert Jackall's *Moral Mazes* (New York: Oxford University Press, 1988) which gives the reader a keen appreciation of life inside the corporation.

Chapter 7

Talk as Social Practice

As Schutz (1971) pointed out, the routine talk people engage in, their vernaculars, are indexes of the social organization of their experiences. Moreover, the words, phrases and organization of what people say and the way they speak and hear the meanings and intentions in one another's utterances are the primary data of social psychology. And while we sometimes elicit language from those we seek to understand, that is, we ask them to respond in a restricted way to a question we formulate (an item on a questionnaire or a specific question in an interview), we are learning more and more to appreciate that rich sources of information about the elemental social processes are to be found in "naturally occurring" speech. Consider this example.

> On the early morning shift at the county hospital two residents converse as they walk down the hall toward the rooms of their patients.
> "Did you buff that gomere?"
> "Sure thing, I buffed her, and they turfed her to urology, but she bounced back to me!"
> "Well, they must think she's an LOL in NAD. Tell you what, see if you can turf her to some slurper, buff her as an interesting ortho, maybe that'll turf 'er."
> "She's a tough one, but I'll give it a try."

These doctors are talking about a difficult-to-treat female patient ("gomere"). They want to transfer responsibility for her to another branch of the hospital (turf her). They attempted to transfer her to urology by modifying her chart (buffing it) to request urine tests, but the doctors in urology sent (bounced) her back. They thought she was just a little old lady in no apparent distress (LOL in NAD). In hopes that an ambitious, upwardly mobile doctor (slurper) will accept her as a patient, one resident suggests to the other changing her chart to make her seem like she has an interesting bone problem (ortho).

This "doctor talk" (a linguist would call it a *variety*) tells us a great deal about how doctors see patients, but it also reveals the social organization of individuals' experiences working in a hospital emergency room. It tells us about what "trouble" is (patients who cannot be transferred), and about attitudes doctors

139

have about each other—a "slurper" is a doctor, usually a resident, who wishes to gain favor in the eyes of high-status doctors—and it hints at liberties doctors might take with the formal rules of the hospital (buffing a chart means falsifying it).

Without learning the unique language doctors use while working in the emergency room, we would not be able to recognize the complexity and natural power of the way doctors talk about their patients. We might dismiss their talk as slang, or we might simply take for granted that people "have" language and that languages themselves differ from one another. Most social psychological studies build on a structural view of language—that language is a systematic, rule-governed competency a person displays mostly through vocal performances. The structure of what is said is multilayered or, as Goffman (1974) put it, "laminated." By this we mean that by virtue of its organization talking does many things at the same time. Talking carries the meanings of words and the forms of sentences, and it conveys a sense of who the speaker is and how he or she conceives of an audience. It also can be a means for people to do things with one another—most of us know people whom we just enjoy talking to. In other words, given all of the above, talking is the fundamental device of social interaction.

The Things People Do with Language

When we see talking as the tool of human invention most significant for the construction of social reality, we are including language as part of the general process of social interaction. We appreciate that through using language people build larger social contexts for their activity. One way to understand this point is to look at the social functions of language.

The word "function" itself carries many connotations. It has specific meanings in mathematics and biology and a variety of meanings in the social sciences. We use it to denote the results of language usage, to identify as precisely as we can what people do with language.

We usually associate language variation with ethnic or nationality groups. We refer to the organization of the linguistic performances by groups of people as the language of that group. Italian, English, German, and Hindi—each refers to both political and cultural phenomena. And like all languages, they are shared by all the members of the groups using them, thus providing the basis for communication in daily life. But within political and cultural groupings there is a remarkable variety of language performances—accents, slang and dialects represent only a few. Even small groups tend to develop special languages, ones clearly derived from a national or ethnic language but which include special terms and meanings. The discovery of the widespread existence of special ways to use a language led students of language to coin a special term: *argot*. Argots are sublanguages organized by members of social groups engaged in activities that mark them off from other groups. The way members use language is an important part of their group, and in instances where the group might be engaged in clandestine activities, such as crime or sabotage within the larger society, knowledge of the argot is used to identify group members.

We can illustrate how language functions by examining in detail a special group of youngsters in American society who call themselves "BMXers"— BMX meaning "bicycle motocross." Literally thousands of young people, mostly males, participate in the recreational and competitive riding and racing of BMX bicycles. BMXers know a kind of argot, speaking for example of "endo" when their bikes flip over forward, either by accident while racing or as part of a skilled trick maneuver. They suffer a "medical" when they hurt themselves in accidents. But why do BMXers, or members of other subgroups (we recall the hospital residents at this chapter's introduction) develop special argots? Does the national language not provide a sufficient means of expression? The answer to this question lies in what language can do besides just communicate linguistic meaning. Like most languages, argots reflect the special needs found in the social world of their speakers. For BMXers, this means the argot must permit them to name and talk about special technical aspects of their sport. It must also meet social needs, such as enhancing a sense of group membership, and permit the BMXers involvement with others, such as business people, parents, and new recruits, while still allowing insiders the advantage of remaining special and elite.

BMXers usually range in age from four to the early twenties; however most are boys between the ages of seven and fifteen. These boys' bicycles are their most precious possessions (virtually all of them have several, many in parts lying all over the family garage). If they work, say, throwing newspapers or mowing lawns or even in "real" jobs, their bikes are the reason. If they can't figure out ways to get money for parts, they barter with other BMXers; they learn to work on the machines and most important, to ride them with style. Modeled after the motorcycle motocross, BMX has become organized at national and international levels. Races are sponsored virtually every weekend all across the nation. While the sport has experienced waning popularity in recent years, it remains a part of the youth scene in Australia and several European nations. Like motorcyclists, BMXers race over dirt tracks laid out with jumps, sharp turns, and bumps. The sale of special BMX bicycles, competition clothing, and racing accessories has become a multimillion-dollar business influencing the styles of dress as well as the values of young people all across America.

We can refer to BMX as a social world, for participants in BMX both share knowledge about and focus their interaction on bicycles, equipment, riding techniques, and all the other activities making up their sphere of interest. As in all such groups, they use language to communicate with each other about these things, but unlike members of the general public, they use a special argot to do so. When BMXers talk about racing, they use phrases such as "wire the start," "get the hole shot," "wipe out," "get medical," and "cross up." They may say that they "dusted the pack" or "swooped" a competitor at the "zookers." They may complain that they "tweaked" something, "slipped" a pedal, or perhaps worst of all, were "cherry picked."

Presumably BMXers could say these things in standard American English. They could say that "they got a fast start out of the gate" (wired the start) and had the lead into the "first turn" (hole shot) or that they "they fell off their bike and got hurt" (a medical trash). They could note that they "broke a piece of equipment" (tweaked it), or that they "lost a race because an older kid lied about his age in order to race in a younger category" (got cherry picked). But they don't; instead, they seemingly insist on using their specialized way of communicating with their unique vocabulary to name things. Many of the things they want to identify are difficult to name, or so they believe. A perfectly tuned bike—one that rolls with ease, pedals well, and has that "great feel"—is said to be "dialed-in." There are well over fifty different types of frames for the component BMX bikes, each with its own name. And features of tracks (whoopdeedoos), attitudes (rad), and other aspects of BMX all have corresponding words in the BMX argot.

In addition to its communicative functions, language, including argots such as BMX talk, functions to increase a sense of group identification, mark group boundaries, and instill group pride. The need for special groups is especially acute for children and adolescents in our modern society. Many scholars have suggested that the rise of a peer-group culture in our complex society is at least a partial adaptation to changes in traditional institutions. For example, families relocate often, reorganize when both parents obtain jobs, and divide when parents are divorced. As children find it more and more difficult to feel part of a family group, they turn to other young people who are uprooted or unsettled. They form such groups as BMXers, which are often organized in a formal way by aging members and other adults.

BMX language is an efficient way to mark the boundaries of the group. To an outsider, words like "zookers," "whoopdeedoos," and "ant hills" are parts of a foreign language. On the other hand, when a BMXer advises a fellow racer that a "berm" on a particular track is a place where "you can get medical," not only is he telling his friend that the turn is dangerous, by speaking a shared insider's language he is also reaffirming a sense of membership. Consider the conversation between two young racers, Jim and John:

Jim: Hey, you chasing points? (Are you racing as often as possible to pile up points toward your year-end standings in your district?)

John: Nah, but I'm goin' to the triple pointer. (I am going to the upcoming race which awards triple points for first-, second-, third- and fourth-place finishes).

Jim: That's a real rad track. You can wire the starts but you'll bum out on the berms. There's an awesome European there you can really get medical on. (The track is very good. You can get fast starts there. But some of the turns are dangerous).

Using the argot gives these two racers a shared feeling of mutual experience and belonging. It permits them to compare their sense of being special and test their degree of involvement in BMX. At the same time, a non-BMXer listening to Jim and John talk might be impressed by the insider knowledge of the speakers, but he would also be reminded of his alienation from their group.

Another important function of language is that it does allow a group to deal with outsiders. In the case of BMX, a highly commercialized scene, insiders must recruit new members or at least encourage the purchase of BMX items and bikes. Therefore the language must sound exotic enough to be attractive to potential BMXers and at the same time be specialized enough to enhance the sense of group membership. Linguistically, BMX argot accomplishes this by building up a special vocabulary, but one that is nevertheless used according to grammatical forms widely distributed in society in Standard American English. Many such argots serve the dual functions of both building membership and demarcating members into core and marginal ones. A BMXer can talk some BMX to his father for the purposes of influencing what his father will give him on an upcoming birthday. In addition, the BMXer must know enough of the argot to order parts and stay up with the fashions in clothing and equipment. And true insiders, those who initiate and refine the terms of the argot itself, always feel secure with their place in the world of BMX.

Sometimes the way an argot functions to tie insider and outsider together is quite subtle and difficult to appreciate. In his study of a halfway house, Wieder (1975) discovered that the residents (who thought of themselves as inmates) communicated with each other and understood their experiences in prison and prisonlike settings according to a code, which here means beliefs that support an argot. In the inmate code, the men would speak of not "sniveling" (not trying to ingratiate oneself with the authorities). The code also required that inmates not tell authorities about the activities of other inmates (never "squeal") and that they obey the norms of inmate life (stay in line).

Wieder understood the actions of inmates according to his understanding of the code. He saw the reluctance of inmates to participate in activities encouraged by the staff as instances of code conformity. As he began to pay closer attention to the situations in which inmates talked the code, however, he found that more was happening. In one instance, a staff member asked an inmate to organize a pool tournament, to which the inmate replied, "You know I don't snivel." This remark did not seem to make sense according to the code. Inmates liked to play pool and the activity was not generally seen as "official." The inmate's reply did not seem relevant to the code.

Wieder began to notice other instances in which inmates talked in code-appropriate language, but in situations where it did not seem necessary or called for. By interviewing the inmates and observing what was happening in the halfway house, Wieder learned that the inmates were aware that the staff knew about the code and that they generally honored it unless it led to serious violations of the rules. Staffers thought that if they forced an inmate to violate the code, they could actually be endangering the well-being of the man; and inmates knew that staff thought this way.

Whenever the staff would request that an inmate do something he did not want to do, one way for him to get out of it was to say that the activities would violate the code. But the inmate could not say this outright because that would force the staff to acknowledge the power of the code. Hence the inmate would "tell the code"; that is, he would use code words and phrases to create the impression that what was requested was indeed code relevant, when in fact it was not. In this fashion, inmates exercised considerable control over the staff. Telling the code could cover up the real motivations of inmates, which often were to get out of the halfway house as fast as possible. By telling the code inmates could hide from the staff a number of practices which if discovered could even lead to one's return to prison. For example, in order to obtain a release from the halfway house an inmate needed to have a place of residence and a full-time job. Recently released inmates would write to officials at the house with false offers of jobs and false addresses to help their buddies out of "the joint." These practices could be covered by telling the code. For example, if a staff member questioned an inmate about the stationery on which a supposedly official letter was written, the inmate could avoid giving a response by pointing out that if he did, other inmates might think he was "trying to get close to staff"; so again, "I don't snivel."

We see that argots are associated with special groups within larger, more complex societies. They function to name the special cultural categories that make up the knowledge and social reality of the group, and they permit precise and economical conversation among group members, giving them a sense of sharing common interests and experiences and at the same time setting them apart from outsiders. They signal commitment and elite status, and by their unintelligibility create an attractive and mysterious aura about group members. Finally, they function as a cover for the pursuit of both individually defined and group interests.

Motive Talk

More than forty years ago, C. Wright Mills (1948) suggested that the words people use to describe their purposes and intentions contain all the information we need to assess their motives for various actions. He referred to such talk as a "vocabulary of motives." Building on this idea, that "talk is the fundamental material of human relations," Scott and Lyman (1968) proposed that basic questions of social analysis could be answered by looking at a particular kind of talk, which they called an "account." An account, they wrote, "is a linguistic device employed whenever an action is subjected to valuative inquiry" (Scott and Lyman 1968, 46). It is a statement made by a person to explain unanticipated or untoward behavior. In short, it is talk intended to reveal why a person did something he or she was not supposed to do.

By examining this type of talk we can see more clearly what kinds of assumptions ground social life, how a particular kind of thinking operates as a foundation for social order. Scott and Lyman examined various written and audio transcripts containing examples of such talk. They used published materials as well as tapes from interviews conducted for their own research purposes, and generally they looked at talk occurring within a wide array of different situations of everyday life.

In their study, the authors classified accounts into two types: excuses and justifications. They defined excuses as "socially approved vocabularies for mitigating or relieving responsibility when conduct is questioned"; and they identified four kinds of excuses: appeal to accidents, appeal to defeasibility, appeal to biological drives, and scapegoating. Justifications, though, are accounts in which "one accepts responsibility for the act in question, but denies the pejorative quality associated with it," and there are also four ways to justify an untoward action: denial of injury, denial of victim, condemnation of condemners, and appeal to loyalties.

We will illustrate each instance of motive talk and suggest what function it can perform in the "shoring up" of the "timbers of fractured sociation." Regarding excuses first, we note that when people use appeals to accidents they try to talk their way out of unpleasant consequences or the negative responses that might come from others; that is, they aim to dissociate themselves from the meanings of their actions. In one situation a person might say, "Sure, that gravy I spilled does seem to have spoiled my shirt, but the ladle simply slipped out of my hand," providing an account that points to some recognized hazards in the environment or some understandable incapacity of the body. Blaming some feature of simple humanness arranges what everybody knows (commonsense knowledge) in such a way that the consequences of the action are not linked to the intentions of the actor. Pointing out how "clumsy" an act was—that, for instance, one missed an appointment because of a memory lapse—means that the act under question was simply "by accident." Children may employ this device in a kind of overkill when they claim that everything that gets them in trouble with adults is "by accident."

When one appeals to defeasibility, he or she arranges commonsense knowledge according to assumptions people make about the mental elements that make up the world—the ordinary understandings of "knowledge and will." One can defend oneself against an accusation by saying "I didn't know" or "I can't help it."

> "Why did you make her cry?" asks the accuser. The presentational strategies in reply to this question allow several modes of defeating the central claim implied in the question, namely, that the actor intended with full knowledge to make the lady weep. However, men ordinarily impute to one another some measure of foresight for their actions, so that a simple denial of intent may not be believed if it appears that the consequence of the action in question was indeed what another person might expect and therefore what the actor intended [so, we may resort to several simple and complex devices]. I did not know that I would make her cry by what I did . . . I knew matters were serious, but I did not know that telling her would make her weep. (Scott and Lyman 1968, 49)

We can also excuse ourselves by appealing to biological drives and pointing to features of what is understood in our culture about the "fatalistic" or "natural aspects" of life. "Boys will be boys"; "he's just feeling his oats," and the like are statements that attribute qualities or meanings to acts based on an understanding of nature. Scott and Lyman use an example from the research literature on the beliefs first- and second-generation Italian men have about their sexual appetites. That is, they believe themselves to be naturally motivated toward sexual aggressiveness and that this aggressiveness can become an uncontrollable impulse. Similar beliefs are widespread in Latin American cultures.

In American culture there are many manifestations of fatalistic thinking For example, homosexual preferences are often thought of as "natural," as are differences between the behaviors and tastes of boys and girls. All manner of accounts can be built on assumptions about the validity of such thinking.

Scapegoating is a form of thinking in which a "person will allege that his behavior is a response to the behavior or attitude of another" (Scott and Lyman 1968, 50). By pointing out that one's untoward actions were not directly one's own, that is, that they were the result of some characteristic or trait of another person, one can dissociate or excuse oneself from the negative consequences of his or her actions. For example, in Oscar Lewis's research on Latin American cultures, we read of how a Mexican girl who was constantly in trouble blamed her tendency to fight on the nature of other girls, or of the young Mexican boy who scapegoats by explaining how it was a girl's fault that he got into trouble for showing off on his bicycle.

Justifications are socially approved vocabularies that neutralize an act or its consequences when one or both are called into question. In contrast to an excuse, a justification asserts that the consequences of the act were in fact positive or at least not as they appeared.

One way a person can attempt to justify an act is by denial or injury, saying it was permissible because no one was hurt—hence the exchange, "Did you set off that firecracker under the gasoline can?" "Yes, but there was no fire." Another way to use this same device is to suggest that the person allegedly injured cannot really be hurt by such action. A younger brother says of an accident on the Fourth of July, "He got in the way when I was lighting my firecracker. Sure the punk burned him, but you know how tough he is. He's not hurt."

In denial of the victim one argues that the injury to another resulting from one's own actions was somehow deserved. Members of certain groups—"whitey," "rednecks," "pimps," or "homos"—occupy a social status so low, so despicable (according to the one arguing) that they are legitimate targets for attack. A policeofficer making an arrest may feel less restrained by his training and the law that prohibits him from handling the suspect roughly when he is dealing with a particularly odious criminal. In other words, cops may rough up certain criminals and not others. When questioned by authorities about this brutality they may reply, "He was just street scum."

In condemning a condemner one simply points out that others do these or worse acts and "these others are either not caught, not punished, or even praised" (Scott and Lyman 1968, 51). And finally, in appealing to loyalties one says one's actions were permissible or even right because they served the interests of another to whom one owes an unbreakable allegiance or affection. From history, we are all aware of how this justification has been used to "make seem right" some of world's most hideous crimes, like the executions of the Jews by the Nazis.

For the sake of analysis, Scott and Lyman illustrate some of the variety of accounts for unanticipated or untoward behavior may assume. The importance of their analysis lies not so much in whether they have correctly identified the full range of types of accounts, but in the point they make that talking in a certain way can be understood as a device for accomplishing desired social ends. They show how a successful account, or one that is honored, is one consistent with the background knowledge of the group to which it is offered and balanced with the gravity or severity of the alleged action. To further illuminate this point they make a distinction between "illegitimate" and "unreasonable" accounts.

> An account is treated as illegitimate when the gravity of the event
> exceeds that of the account, or when it is offered in a circle where its
> vocabulary of motives is unacceptable. An account is deemed
> unreasonable when the stated grounds for actions cannot be "nor-
> malized" in terms of the background expectations of what "every-
> body knows." (Scott and Lyman 1968, 54)

Further, the authors show how the effectiveness of a verbal device depends
also on how well the account is performed. Using the work of Joos, they identify
five styles of discourse: intimate, casual, consultative, formal, and frozen. These
styles, which amount to different ways of presenting information, differ in
vocabulary and grammar, but more important, they rest on different social bases.

In the intimate style, one uses specialized words and phrases to communicate
whole ideas or emotional states. This is the language of the couple, the restricted
or in-group code, which is virtually unintelligible to another not intimately
familiar with the person talking. The casual style is similar to the intimate but
usually involves larger numbers of speakers. This is the language of the peer
group. Most argots are used in a casual way. The consultative style is "that verbal
form ordinarily employed when the amount of knowledge available to one of the
interactants is unknown or problematic to the others." It conveys an air of
"technicality." In the formal style, there is an audience too large to permit one-
to-one exchange. A speaker therefore adopts a presentational style to "hold the
attention" of his audience. Goffman (1981) refers to this form of talk as the
"lecture."

Finally, the frozen style is an extreme form of the formal, used by those who
are simultaneously required to interact and yet to remain social strangers. The
communication between pilot and control tower is in this frozen style; likewise
the talk of CBers is largely managed by a frozen style that allows the impression
of community without the intimate or casual contact required in face-to-face
interaction.

Obviously, an account must be proffered in an appropriate style. A father's
account of why he is late to pick up his daughter from her dance lessons must be
formulated one way for the ten-year-old daughter and yet another for the mother
who waits for them at home.

> *Father*: I'm sorry, honey, I had some stuff to do at the office. Hope
> you didn't get too bored waiting?
> *Daughter*: It's OK, daddy; I just practiced with the next class.
> or
> *Father*: Sorry, honey, we were running late on that monthly report
> and the computer was down half the day.
> *Mother*: Well, you should have called or made other arrangements.

Father: I know, I'm sorry. What's for dinner?

Human talk is very complex and cannot be fully understood on formal grounds alone. In the social psychology of language, we must also look at the functions of talk, that is, at what is accomplished by it. This often requires looking at both sides of communication, at both the reasons people have for communicating and the relationships they have with one another while communicating. One final illustration of human communication involves looking at how people use a sense of time in their talk. Of the many ways they do this, perhaps the clearest mode and probably the one most often used by us all is the practice of disclaiming.

Everyday life is full of potentially embarrassing situations. There are serious and trivial departures from role obligations, as well as some downright troublesome occasions on which some aspect of one's self is revealed at the wrong time, in the wrong situation, or to the wrong people. All of us have experienced such unpleasantries; and as we gain more experience in less than desirable interactions with others, we learn to recognize cues to what might happen, what a person might do or say if we pursue a certain line of conversation or course of action.

Just as giving accounts to excuse or justify certain actions can shore up fractured relationships, there are ways of talking thta can "ward off and defeat in advance doubts and negative typifications which might result from intended conduct" (Hewitt and Stokes 1975, 3). These verbal devices are called "disclaimers," and we use them when we know something we are about to say or do might offend or embarrass someone, or even incite conflict. Yet we must say what is on our mind. Unlike the account that mends the result of untoward deeds, the disclaimer looks into the future and so involves a form of "if . . . then" thinking. When we use a disclaimer, we imagine an interactive occasion.

> If I say my wife's new dress is too revealing for the formal party we are to attend, then she will feel that I have insulted her judgment and taste. I know, nevertheless, that if she wears the dress, I will be embarrassed, even if she is the hit of the party. Therefore, I must say something about the dress, and at the same time avoid any remarks she might take as critical.

This is a real interactive problem, and Hewitt and Stokes have inventoried some of the available solutions to it. First, I could "hedge," meaning I could preface my remarks by impugning my own identity. I could say something that tells her I'm really not all that concerned about the dress (my identity is not really at stake in the matter)—I am not fully, unalterably opposed to her wearing the dress, but still I have an opinion about it. When I hedge, I also communicate a sense of openness to compromise, along with my understanding that other people's reactions to the dress might be negative and hence call into question the impression I think she wishes to give. I know she wants to appear stylish, not brazen.

So to hedge I say, "I'm no expert on fashion, but . . ." or "you know how I think everything you wear is sexy, but this dress . . ." or "it's just my first reaction to the dress, but . . ." If it works, she may save me my embarrassment—or even hers, were she to have to deal with unwanted advances from males at the party—perhaps by changing to a more conservative outfit.

I could also use a device Hewitt and Stokes refer to as "credentialing." To credential, I must know that what I say will offend her but still remain strongly committed to saying it. I must establish myself as a person with a particular identity to which I am strongly committed. "You know I am no jealous husband, but . . .", or "I have never led you astray before, so hear me out." When I attribute a credential to myself, I establish myself as someone who knows what he is saying. "You know I'm a social psychologist of everyday life, and I can tell you that dress will make you look like a hussy."

Or I could use another device, the "sin license." This device wards off my wife's critical response toward me by its recognition that I know full well what I say to her will be seen as boorish and none of my business, but I do not care how she will react. I simply must have my say. "I realize you might think I'm criticizing your taste in clothes, but . . .", "I know we have independent lives and what you do is your business, but this dress is just too . . .", or "Sure, I'm going to break a rule of our relationship, but . . ."

I could also use a "cognitive disclaimer"—that is, I could point out something about the unique way I see the world, my peculiar empirical grasp of it, that might account for what I am about to say. "This may seem strange to you . . .", "Now, don't react right away to what I'm going to say . . .", or "I know this sounds crazy, but I think that dress will make you look . . ." By demonstrating through advance knowledge that a negative consequence might result from an action, I can show the purpose for my behavior, an action that otherwise might be interpreted as without purpose or as "reflecting a loss of cognitive control" (Hewitt and Stokes 1975, 5).

Finally, if I assume my wife and I have a common purpose to pursue at the party, I can appeal for a "suspension of judgment," "Don't get me wrong, but . . .", or "Hear me out before you explode." What I have to do is show that her action (wearing the dress) might negatively affect our common goal, which is to appear as a happily married couple.

There are of course many different ways in which people can respond to accounts and disclaimers. Accounts can be honored and disclaimers heeded; thus persons can get themselves excused and so manage to avoid potentially unpleasant circumstances. Disclaimers are heeded when they seem reasonably valid. If they smooth interaction, they succeed in one sense by facilitating interaction and allowing things to go on in spite of obvious differences of opinion. Much of this interactional work depends on reading clues in interaction. My wife sees that I am really concerned about her, even if I seem childish. There is a constant signaling and a finesse in interactive sequences whereby we can tell each other what kind of person we want to be seen as in a particular exchange. Disclaiming is one powerful way of signaling identity.

In the case of the failure of an account or disclaimer, the identity a person seeks to establish is simply not accepted by the other. The person becomes an irresponsible juvenile or a coward who always tries to get out of the mess he or she makes, or is cast in another identity by those with more authority.

Forms of Talking

Language is the medium through which identities are exchanged, negotiated and changed. These functions go beyond the formal properties of language and turn out to be what is truly human about communication, and perhaps about social organization. Erving Goffman dealt in detail with the social organization of talk in *Forms of Talk* (1981), where he developed a social psychological approach to everyday communication by stressing the importance of three characteristics: "ritualization," the unintended and yet regularized movements, looks, and vocal sounds we make when speaking and listening; "participation framework," the full range of potential listeners and speakers for a given instance of talking; and "embedding," the existence of inherent messages in our sayings over, above, and within their strictly formal or linguistic content.

Goffman illustrated how these social dimensions operate in the form of talk we recognize as the lecture. When we walk into a classroom, hear a friend begin to speak about a favorite subject, or see someone, like a parent who's car we just scratched, coming toward us, we know we are about to be lectured. As all of us have learned, this particular way of talking is not so much a matter of grammar and vocabulary; instead, it has more to do with the social organization of what is said. Goffman defines a lecture according to its social dimensions. A lecture is an institutionalized "holding of the floor" to present a "text." And even if no actual written text exists, the speaker presents material in such a way that the impression of the existence of a text is maintained.

The primary intention of a lecturer is to "format" a text. Formatting does not require those in the participation frame to be engrossed in the presentation. Those of us who listen to a lecture need not, and know that we need not, be fully attentive to what is being said. We can think of our own text, interpret what is happening idiosyncratically, simply daydream, or even go blank. This contrasts markedly with other activities that require engrossment. Think of where your attention would be if you were playing cards for money. Without engrossment in the game, you wouldn't be in it for very long.

In the lecture, the person who makes the text come to life is the same person who is assumed to have authored the text and so is the principal of the occasion. Other presentational formats are quite different. Actors are not necessarily authors, newscasters do not make the news in a literal sense, and usually no one person is supposed to dominate a conversation—we do not normally chit-chat with the focus on a single person as a source of information.

Lectures cannot just be given. Instead, they are "celebrative occasions." They are usually the main business at hand, even though other things commonly happen along with them, such as a luncheon or the giving of an award. Some event, educational or patriotic, or even some form of entertainment, is being highlighted with the collective intention of communicating the message that what is happening is worthwhile, indeed, worth an organized happening.

Formal organization is often a prerequisite to giving a lecture. The college, university, civic group, or political party provides the literal or figurative platform on which the lecturer stands and derives some identity. Organizations thus foster a star system. They seek out lecturers who give off a good impression. Of course the interests of the lecturer and those of the organization need not be identical, but the lecturer must have something to offer relevant to the organization.

Lectures are social as well as linguistic phenomena. They can be defined according to their social features, and most important, we can analyze the lecture by describing how the social meanings of it are achieved. Goffman himself lists ways in which a speaker "animates words," that is, uses the devices available to make one's speaking appear to be alive, energetic, and personal. These include "memorization," "reading aloud," and "fresh talk."

Memorization means simply to commit to memory what is to be said, thus allowing the speaker to give off the impression of a person "who knows the material." But even the well-rehearsed lecturer is well advised to glance at notes occasionally, so as not to appear to be merely talking off the top of his or her head. This impression would violate the form of the lecture and transform it into something less formal, perhaps seen by the audience as less important. We are well aware of how many students stop taking notes when lecturers look up from a prepared text to offer an aside or a further explanation of a point.

This tendency to display too much of oneself can be counteracted by reading aloud, verbally holding up the text for all to see. By reading from a text, the lecturer reminds all of the organizational features of the presentation. Too much reading, of course, hollows the performance of any element of self, and the presenter runs the risk of becoming unanimated.

Since many lecturers are on tour, making the college circuit, for example, much of what they say is actually old to them. But all try to give the impression that what they have prepared for their audience is something new, really fresh talk. But although lecturers often depend on a fresh talk illusion, they must take care not to be seen too distinctly from the content of their speech. The lecture form must maintain the content as primary, or else one is "left with the box and the cake," or too much of self and not enough of the occasion.

By digressing, or telling a story, the speaker can enhance the image of giving off fresh talk, new materials, things never said before. As Goffman writes of the image of talking freshly:

> There is irony here. There are moments in a lecture when the speaker seems most alive to the ambience of the occasion and is largely ready with wit and extemporaneous response to show how fully he has mobilized his spirit and mind for the moment at hand. Yet these inspired moments will often be ones to most suspect. For during them the speaker is quite likely to be delivering something he memorized some time ago, having happened upon an utterance that fits so well that he cannot resist reusing it in that particular slot whenever he gives the talk in question (Goffman 1981, 178).

Goffman continues his analysis of lecturing by discussing how the lecturers align themselves with the underlying identities of the occasion. This process, which he calls "footing," usually involves devices for work that goes on prior to the performance, the advertising or announcing of the lecture, its sponsorship, or the actual printing of the text in its entirety or in sketched forms. Goffman also points out how footings can be accomplished during the actual delivery of the lecture by making tongue-in-cheek remarks, using sarcasm, changing styles, using props, or making parenthetical remarks.

Under Goffman's treatment, we learn to appreciate how forms of talking carry with them a host of social meanings, and of how a person works with the forms to achieve a desired effect. One can break a form to give off an impression. For example, a lecturer can discard his notes in order to speak face-to-face about matters of grave importance. In Goffman's view, talk is an accommodative social form in which the business of impression management is carried out.

Analyzing Conversations

Through the detailed study of conversational practice we have seen how to analyze and understand communicative interactions among people. Just as language has structural and social organization, so too do the exchanges between and among people talking to each other (Perinbabayagam 1992). For example, during a conversation, as opposed to a lecture, speaker change recurs, or at least occurs; overwhelmingly, one party talks at a time; occurrences of more than one speaker at a time are common but brief; transitions from one turn to the next with no gap and no overlap or with slight gap or slight overlap make up the vast majority of transitions; and, turn-allocation techniques are used—a current speaker may select the next speaker, or parties may self-select (Sacks 1974, 700–701).

These observations suggest that patterns exist in communicative exchanges, and these can be depicted in terms of both their composition and the rules that govern them. We can identify "turn–constructional units" (Sacks 1974), which are devices of talking used to signal turn taking or a change in speakers. Two examples are "single-word turns" ("What's you last name, Jerry?" "Smith." "What?" "Smith.") and "single-phrase turns" ("Oh I have the—I have one class in the evening. On Monday? Y-uh Wednesdays. Uh-Wednesdays. An' it's like a Mickey Mouse course.").

Sociolinguists (Schegloff and Sacks 1973) have identified specific aspects of talking that order exchanges and provide information about what is to come next. For example, "tag questions" ("I know that song, don't you?") require that one's conversational partner respond. There are also "repair mechanisms" such as excuses or apologies that can be used to correct errors or interruptions, and "backchannel cues" ("yeah," "right," "uh huh") that are "referentially meaningless but have great pragmatic import by indicating one's attention to and ratification of the speakers talk" (Bonvillain 1993, 115).

All the dynamics in conversations are set within specific social situations and cultures. For example, with turn taking in America, most of us follow a minimum-gap rule, that is, we allow little or no conversational space between replies. In some cultures, like the Native Cree in Western Canada, rules allow for and even encourage longer gaps between replies. In their estimation, if someone has said something of importance, it requires a pause to register and evaluate what has been said. This shows respect for one's conversational partner. In America, where we are highly individualistic in our views of who we are, much of our conversation is organized to allow us to participate as much as possible. We know that others are highly "taken with themselves" and that they want our attention as much as we want theirs. If we do not respond quickly, they will simply add what they want to say. Hence much of the organization of our everyday talk is directed at "the pursuit of attention" (Derber 1979). So general cultural meanings of membership in society condition conversational practices.

This is especially true of the rules of politeness in talking. While the specific terms of politeness will reflect the culture of the speaker, some universal principles seem to apply. Brown and Levinson (1987) compared linguistic data from English, Tzeltal (a native language of Mexico), and Tamil (spoken in India) and suggested that assumptions of cooperation are the bedrock feature of politeness (Bonvillain 1993). In all three of these speech communities, politeness is concerned with "face," which is an "individual's self-esteem" or the "public self-image that every member wants to claim" (Brown and Levinson 1987, 161). Brown and Levinson think of these assumptions of cooperation as "face wants" of which there are two varieties: positive and negative. Positive face wants are desires to be approved of, and negative ones are desires to be unimpeded in one's actions.

To be polite, then, means to follow strategies in a conversation that allow people both to be who they want to be and to do what they want to do. Of course this can be difficult if one's self-presentation is at odds with what one's conservational partner thinks about him or her. Three strategies work to allow these face wants to be accomplished in talking:

1. Positive politeness: talking so that the speakers recognize each other's desire to have their positive face wants respected. These strategies express solidarity, friendliness and in-group reciprocity.

2. Negative politeness: talking that conveys the speakers desire not to be imposed on, that is, that recognizes the participants' rights to autonomy. These strategies express a speaker's restraint, his or her avoidance of imposing on the hearer.

3. Off-record politeness: Here a speaker uses indirect talk to avoid making any explicit or unequivocal imposition on the hearer (from Bonvillain 1993, 132).

We can appreciate the dynamics of politeness by looking at face-threatening acts, that is, acts that infringe on the hearer's face wants. If I ask someone to do something he or she would not ordinarily do, I am requesting a face-threatening act. A father videotaping his son's wrestling match needs to get a drink of water and does not wish to carry his heavy camera case with him. He asks another dad sitting next to him in the bleachers, "Would you mind watching my camera for a while?" He could say, "Watch this camera, I'll be right back?" or "Man, I'm thirsty, watch this?" In any case, he is asking the other person to assume responsibility for the video equipment, something that could result in a problem (a stolen camera). At the least, he is requesting that the other person restrict his own action (not move until he returns). The request threatens the self-presentation of the other as a mere spectator.

The linguistic form a person uses will depend on who he or she thinks the person being talked to is, that is, the speaker's assessment of the hearer's identity. Other conditions, such as the perceived urgency of the request, the circumstances of the face-threatening act, and any cultural expectations about cooperation are part of the decision that a speaker makes about how to be polite. Brown and Levinson show how politeness strategies can be located in the three languages they examined. For example, what they call "bald on record" threats to face exist in English: "Help!" (as in an emergency) or in Tamil: *eRu! eRu! periya paampu!* (Get up! Get up! There's a big snake!) or in Tzeltal: *Yakuk. la? cuka tey ?a.* (OK.

Come tie it there!) These strategies would be employed when it is not necessary to be concerned about face threatening. Examples of positive politeness (the speaker wishes to indicate that he or she respects the hearer) are from English, "You must be hungry, it's been a long time since breakfast. How about some lunch?" And in Tamil, *vviTu payankaramaa KaTTirukkiraar* (He built the house lavishly); and Tzeltal, *ma ya?we wah me?* (Won't you eat, mother?).

The strategies Brown and Levinson list are extensive, covering a wide variety of communicative interactions in the three languages. Their work illustrates that forms of discourse used in talking reflect interactive quality, that is, the outcomes sought after by the conversational partner, and that the assumptions around types of acts condition the talking. In the case of politeness, assumptions that people will cooperate with each other as long as neither threatens the face of the other shape the sounds of being polite. The identities of people are reflected in the structure of the conversation they use.

Varieties of Talking as Identity Markers

Differences in forms of talking and conversing have practical significance for social identity and for the interaction that takes place between persons of different identities. We recognize as markers of identity details of speech that tell us we are listening to a female speaker, a black speaker, or a speaker of a status different from ours. These markers of social identity are often confounded with the forms we discussed above.

Ultimately, the task of understanding how talking marks identity requires that we look at the interactions between speech and social phenomena. West and Zimmerman (1977, 1983) and others (see Coates and Cameron 1988) have examined how interruptions, turn taking, the length of silences, and intonation patterns are used differently by men and women. We start with some simple generalizations: When men and women converse, generally men interrupt more than women. Likewise, the degree to which a man will arrange his comments so that they overlap those of a woman is greater than that for women overlapping men. Women remain silent for longer interludes in cross-sex conversations than do men. And finally, according to the authors, there is a definite "female" habit of raising one's voice at the end of a statement. When making an assertion, a man usually drops the tone of his voice at the end of it. It is possible, of course, to express the assertion as if it were an exclamation or to speak it as if it were a question. Hence, one can say, "I told you that paper was incorrectly punctuated!" Or "I told you that paper was incorrectly punctuated?" It seems women are more likely to use these latter two forms.

In another study, Fishman (1979) placed tape recorders in the apartments of three male-female couples. The couples were aware of the recorders and could control when they operated. Over several weeks, Fishman was able to collect a considerable body of ordinary conversations between men and women. She found women asked questions nearly three times as often as men, and used the question as a device to ensure continued talk. "Know what?" and "Do you know what?" were common forms used by women to open conversations. They used this device to initiate conversations twice as often as men.

In these cross-sex conversations, women also tended to use conversational fillers such as "yeah" and "huh" more frequently than did men. From these data, it appears they used filler methods of talking in two instances: first, to discourage interaction at the end of the man's statement, and second, to punctuate conversations at pauses and thereby encourage more talk. Whereas women's short responses tended to come during the man's turn at talking, men's short responses marked the end of the woman's turn. Fishman believes these data illustrate the kind of work women must do in cross-sex interactions. That is, she argues women must do extra work to ensure that topics of their choice get talked about. Without this effort, women's interests become subordinated to those of the men with whom they are conversing. The parallel here to the position children occupy with adults is obvious.

Although the Fishman and the West and Zimmerman studies report results based on samples not representative of our entire population, their findings are interesting and provocative. Generally, they describe asymmetrical conversations, ones in which the contributions of the parties involved are not the same, and they take this situation to be a reflection of unequal power relationships. At this point we might conclude that we are simply looking at another manifestation of male dominance; for certainly such dominance does appear in many relationships. But, gender differentiation can be very subtle, and some of its consequences may be unintentional and even unknown to the parties involved in a conversation. A man may be following what he has learned to take for granted as his usual manner of speaking, while a woman may likewise follow her conceptions of what makes for ordinary talking. The practical results, though, what the conversation brings to both parties, may be something neither one anticipated or realized.

Handel (1982) offers an alternative interpretation of the data on cross-sex conversations. He reexamines the West and Zimmerman data, finding that what appears to be a one-sided exchange between a man and a woman may not be as asymmetrical as one might think. Men do interrupt women, but this does not mean they will be successful in the long run in changing the topic of talk. In fact, on further inspection the very same data we just reviewed indicate that the topic introduced by a woman but interrupted by a man was typically reintroduced by her later in the conversation. It seems then, that men and women react differently to interruptions. Men, when interrupted, tend to move on to new topics. Women are much more persistent, reintroducing their topic when the opportunity arises later in conversation.

Handel suggests these studies demonstrate how conversational style is an important way in which men and women differ, especially since one's style can become a central medium for getting what one wants. However, as he also points out there are many unresolved questions about the asymmetry of talking between males and females. According to Handel, "it is not clear whether women acquiesce in the abridgment of their rights relative to men's" (1982, 144). Actually, what we may be observing are very different rules for conversing, with simultaneous attempts at the implementation of both the male and female versions:

> Suppose, now, that men and women define the (meaning of the) word "enough" differently as it applies to various qualities of talk. If men, on average, preferred less talk than women and if men and women applied . . . conversation-limiting norms without attention to the sex of others in the conversation, all the (following) observed phenomena would occur. Women would tend to talk more than men would prefer. That should lead to less frequent encouragement by men to continue, more interruptions by men, and less frequent follow-ups by men on proposed topics. Men would tend to talk less than women prefer. That should lead to fewer interruptions by women, to more frequent encouragement by women to continue, to more frequent follow-ups by women on proposed topics, and to the reintroduction by women of interrupted topics. Also, since these quantitative preferences are linked to gender, conversations between people of the same sex ought to display less asymmetry. (In such cases) people would still interrupt one another but would do so approximately equally (Handel 1982, 145).

What is significant for us in Handel's explanation is the proposition that following rules that are functional in one situation can produce unintended results in another. Handel tells us how simply "doing what comes naturally" can create interactive situations characterized by gender inequality.

Throughout this book we have emphasized the primary role consciousness and active thought play in social life. It might appear that now we are saying something else; however, this is not the case. While it is true that asymmetrical conversational situations often involve the unintentional consequences of following taken-for-granted rules, this does not imply "mindless" sexist practices. What Handel suggests has to do with minds at work, minds molded from the different gender worlds because the learning experiences of males and females reflect many subtle and tacit differences in their socialization. Something as seemingly trivial as the way a man and woman talk to each other can embody years of habits and, indeed, actual skills—skills that differ by gender learning.

Nevertheless, although an action is taken for granted and thus is performed as if it were out of habit, it may still be participated in willfully and with conscious intent. In fact, we usually want to act the way we do in everyday living; it is what we have learned is "the right way" or "just the way it is," and in any case, we condone or acquiesce to it. So it is only when someone steps outside the boundaries of what we have taken for granted that we realize things are "not the way they're supposed to be." At such times we are reminded of our conscious intent to have things the way they have been, even if they are as apparently trivial as the way we address each other or otherwise behave during our daily conversations.

How Forms Interact with Identity

Every day we make comparisons and use forms according to how we understand the composition of society. Often such uses are dramatically tied to the perpetuation of socially unequal identities. Here is how this works. Different ascribed positions within American society are associated with identifiable linguistic and communicative expressions. Blacks in urban America use a version of English so unique and pervasive that many linguists refer to nonstandard Black English as a variety of American English—perhaps somewhere between a dialect and a separate language (Dillard 1966; Hecht, Collier and Ribeau 1993). Actually, Black English has its own rules for tensing and inflecting verbs, for expressing possession, and so on; but because of the way it is distributed in the population, its use is often taken to mean that the person using it is "illiterate," "uneducated," or perhaps even worse, "unsocialized." Hence, people may be known not only by the company they keep but by the way they keep it, that is, the way they communicate. From a linguistic point of view, there is no reason any version of a language should be taken as superior to any other. Any language may exist in multiple varieties, and any one of these varieties can serve intrinsically as the carrier of all the information necessary for complex learning and social experiences.

In practice, as sociolinguists note (see Hecht, Collier, and Ribeau 1993), comparisons of the varieties of a language are made by members of a speech community while they are speaking, and often these comparisons are invidious. Let us imagine the situation of a well-educated black man, a successful engineer who knows that his chances for that big promotion will be diminished if around the office he speaks Black English or displays his childhood skill at "doin' the dozens." Since he was raised in a poor black community, but completed his education through the master's degree, we can assume he knows Standard

English as well as Black English. Thus, as with most people who have mastered more than one variety of their language, he is in a position to code-switch, meaning he can change varieties of language performance to fit what he thinks is the appropriate form of talking. To a certain extent, we all know different varieties of our language and can and do switch manners of communicating. Whenever different status meanings accompany the different codes, as they often do, code-switching skills may be critical for establishing and controlling unequal relationships in interactive encounters.

But what of the black man whose economic position and life experiences precluded learning Standard English? He may well be a bright, articulate, and capable person; but these qualities may go unnoticed when they are circumscribed by the vernacular characteristic of the inner-city black community. In fact, in contrast to much conventional knowledge, William Labov (1970) has shown that, indeed, Standard English in its middle-class usages may mask in verbiage the display of logical thinking, while nonstandard Black English lends itself to tightly reasoned and efficient storytelling. Labov's tongue-in-cheek treatment of the differences between the speech of a gang leader named Larry and that of Charles, an educated middle-class black man asserts that no form of language ensures lucidity and clear reasoning. Indeed, in this case Larry, while using a nonstandard variety, follows an intricate line of reasoning. Charles constructs a simple and logically flawed argument conversing in the idiom of textbooks and lecturers.

As Labov writes: "Our work in the speech community makes it painfully obvious that in many ways working-class speakers are more effective narrators, reasoners, and debaters than many middle-class speakers who temporize, qualify, and lose their argument in a mass of irrelevant detail" (Labov 1970, 167)

This may be true, but in the minds of most whites and many other Americans speech like the following means that the speaker lacks certain qualities of high intellect and good character: "He be white, man," and "'Cause the average whitey out here got everything, you dig? and the nigger ain't got shit, y'know? Y'unnerstan'? So...um...in order for that to happen, you know it ain't no black God that' doin' that bullshit" (Labov 1970, 167).

Such a manner of speaking ranks low among educators and most employers, of course, and its use may become the grounds for discrimination resulting in inequality that is best described as exploitative. For those whose speaking competencies restrict them to a form of communication that carries with it a low social rank, the chances of ever breaking out of the conditions resulting in the initial inequality seem locked in the habits of speech.

When it comes to linguistic variety and the choice of which to use for which situation of everyday life, our society is not very accommodative. Most institutional channels of competition assume competency in Standard English. As we have learned, however, not all members of society possess equal linguistic backgrounds, and they may well have unevenly distributed communicative skills. Many everyday interactive situations can be classified according to whether they require people to be equally matched in skills or to possess skills for interaction in different forms of talk. Hence, we can distinguish talk among equals and talk among unequals.

Some of the detailed devices and processes of interaction are referred to as modal and cross-modal communications. Consider two people of different ranks—a woman professor and a male custodian—talking to each other, each aware of the differences in their social rankings. The erudite scholar and the "semiliterate" janitor meet on the elevator on the campus of their large, prestigious university. The scholar wishes to be friendly, but she assesses the man next to her on the basis of his appearance, judging him to be of low verbal skill and limited intellect. She speaks to him in a manner that she assumes is understandable. The janitor likewise enjoys chit-chat with the professor and puts on his best speech. Each will be performing within a form assumed to be the other's. The scholar's mode of communicating is Standard English, perhaps bearing a hint of professional jargon; the janitor's is a nonstandard variety, one of several he may know. In this cross-modal communication the janitor or the professor or both must attempt to speak as they believe the other speaks.

We portray the interactional dynamics of situations like this one in Figure 7.1, by thinking of a sender and a receiver of messages and then imagining each has a visibly different social rank, and we can visualize a circumstance in which to describe the form of talking which might take place.

Even though we are focusing here on cross-modal comparisons, many evaluative comparisons are possible even within a mode. For example, ever since he "caught" his colleague "using 'data' as if it were singular!", Professor Smith did not think much of Professor Jones' writing and now has proceeded to tell him so. Jones may rebut, or become angry, refusing to dignify the criticism with further remarks to Professor Smith, and instead may bring it up with his colleagues. But whatever happens, it will occur expressly within a linguistic form: Standard English.

| | Sender's Ranked Social Identity | |
	High	Low
	HighStandard English	Hypercorrection
Receiver's Rank		
	Low Simplification	Black English

Figure 7.1 The relationships between social rank and language (adapted from Bernstein 1966; Labov 1966; Grimshaw, 1966)

Likewise, janitors tend to speak vernaculars of their social position, and within a vernacular many important comparisons do occur. A person may be a good conversationalist (see Kockmann 1972), tell a good story or joke (Labov 1970), or be an outstanding listener (Labov 1971), but within their rankings, people assume of each other equal backgrounds. As Gold's (1952) study of them indicates, janitors rank and model comparisons among themselves. They may even see themselves as of higher rank than their tenants, as in the case Gold found where janitors were generally better paid than the tenants in the apartment building they maintained. These janitors had definite ideas about the tenants, and they were acutely aware of the ideas tenants had about them. On the floor of the apartment building Gold studied, janitors regarded their services as professional and were resentful of tenants who treated them as inferiors. The tenants tried to degrade the janitors by forcing them to wait for times personally convenient to themselves to perform requested services and by blaming them for poor facilities and other general unpleasantries they attributed to their dwellings. This all happened in spite of the fact that these janitors often earned more money than the white-collar tenants they served. But the janitors seemed to accept among themselves a "public" definition of their work and duty. They experienced relative financial success but remained low in status in their own personal evaluations as well as those of their significant others.

It is by looking at instances of cross-modal interaction that we can better understand the mechanisms of inequality in society. A janitor may actually make more money than the tenants he serves; a street person may display elan and cunning that the social worker completely misses; a student may possess greater knowledge about the subject of the day's lecture than the teacher. But matters of comparisons are masked by the distortions created and perpetuated by maintaining an impression of rank.

Within modes, more or less accurate readings of the societal selves of others can be made. There, reciprocity thinking works to foster interaction that proceeds according to the shared knowledge about and similar rankings of the competencies people mutually attribute to each other. But if, as in the cross-modal setting, the societal rankings preclude the practical testing of ideas about the other person, then ranked inequalities are continued into the present and interaction and communication become increasingly distorted (cf. Habermas 1987). Whenever one person acts on the basis of misinformation about another, any possibility of either one finding out what the other means becomes remote, so neither party understands the other. If at the beginning of the interaction it becomes apparent that one party possesses a higher ranking than the other, that person usually controls the meanings that can make a difference in the interactional outcome; most often, such communication simply plays out preexisting social inequalities.

For example, Gold points out that the professionalization of janitorial services conflicts with the societally given meanings of clean and dirty work

(1952, 179). If someone can identify a man as a janitor by the style of his speech or his personal appearance, no matter what the janitor says, he assumes a subordinate position in the interaction. Many of those in subordinate positions in an interaction realize that such identifications invariably distort their intentions and interests, and often they attempt to correct for this. But these efforts usually result in what Labov has referred to as "hypercorrections" (Labov 1973).

Hyper or overcorrective responses occur whenever a lower-ranked sender tries to communicate in the "hyper" forms of the high-ranked receiver of the message. Labov (1973) illustrates this in his report on lower-status New Yorkers who were aware that they omitted the /r/ sound from such words as guard (thereby, for example, pronouncing "god" and "guard" the same). When they were asked to be formal, or otherwise were led to believe they held equal rank with the interviewer, who was middle class in appearance and seen by them to be highly educated, they inserted the /r/ sound much more frequently than did their middle-class counterparts, even in words where they only thought it might belong. Another common instance of overcorrection occurs when students attempt to use words they think will make them sound "intellectual." Unfortunately, some do not know how to pronounce (or spell) them properly. Another good example is the use of elaborate "incorrect" grammatical inflections on verbs to create the impression of being educated; and perhaps the most common overcorrective use of grammatical construction is the misuse of the pronoun I in formal speech. When trying to sound important or formal, a person who might ordinarily say, "Him and me went with her," will say, "Him and I went with her," or even more commonly, "She went with him and I."

People's motivations for the use of these linguistic devices reveal the inequalities they wish to avoid, the very ones we want to describe. Continuing with our example of the professor and the janitor, the lower-ranked speaker knows that the higher cannot speak his vernacular, and he knows that even if he can be understood, using his ordinary talking form will identify his social rank. This does not mean that he will just be ranked as a janitor, for instance, but that, as a speaker, he tacitly knows such an identification means inequality. To avoid what he rightly perceives as the consequences of being so typed, he attempts to assume the higher-status form. Since he is not fully competent in that form, however, he errs in ways that seemingly mark him according to his position in society. So overcorrection does not avoid distorted communication; it instead, reveals the societal meanings that underlie the communication. In this instance, forms of communication function to perpetuate inequality.

In contrast to the above, the higher-ranked sender's efforts to converse with someone of lower rank often unmask the inequality of this situation through the form of undercorrection, or simplification. Here the higher-ranked party imagines she knows the appropriate form of the lower-ranked speaker. But she does not really know it, for she invariably believes it to be simple, unsophisticated, and easily mastered. Proceeding to speak with the motivation to be understood as an ordinary person, she reveals only her social rank and her ignorance. Unaware of them, the professor will gloss over important distinctions among cleaning solvents to make a point to the janitor that the smell in her office is offensive. Thereby she establishes her ignorance and inadvertently reveals her possible disdain for such trivial knowledge. A white woman will "come on hip" to build rapport with a black man, painfully revealing her dilettantism in keeping cool (Lyman and Scott 1970, 145). At times, the lower-ranked person may chide or rebuke outright the higher. "You honky, y'can't rap like nothin'," or, "Hell, doc, you don't know nothin' about cleaners." But in terms of the systems of the given rankings of social status, the outcome of such antagonism is irrelevant. The professor still has higher rank than the janitor, and the white higher than the black, even though at the interpersonal level appearances give off the opposite impressions.

Undercorrection, like overcorrection, does not create equal conditions for communication. Instead it highlights inequalities as these are given in the ready-made meanings of rank. To anyone interested in describing social meanings, cross-ranked communications serve as strategic events for the uncovering of meanings people attribute to their part in social interactions.

Summary

Talking, its functions and forms reflect processes of social interaction and create the contexts that condition the talk. The way language is used can shore up fractured social relationships, as in the case of giving accounts, and using language in a particular way can ward off undesirable consequences, as in offering disclaimers.

Talk itself exhibits an organization that contains a great deal of information about its own social context. Forms of talk can be identified; and the way they are arranged, lectures, requests, replies, and so forth, both reflect and create the social context within which people hear meanings, motives, intentions, and answer questions about their own selves and the ones of those with whom they converse.

By examining the social organization of talk, we can appreciate that it is often more important for the social psychologist to understand the way something is said and the social context within which it appears than simply to understand the language. It may be that the practical needs of everyday life condition the strategies of talking in similar ways across different cultures and within social situations within the same culture. The study of politeness helps illustrate this point.

Forms of talk and conversation relate meanings that reflect the larger arrangement of social order in society. Talk and gender identities are interrelated as are identities of social rank. We can understand a great deal about being male and female, especially about the relationships between genders, by examining forms of conversing between genders. Likewise, we can see how attitudes and values about status and rank in society interact with the forms that talking assumes.

Exercises for Understanding Talking

1. Alfred Schutz wrote that the words we use in everyday life, our vernaculars, are "mirrors of social reality." He meant the way people actually talk, the words and phrases they naturally employ in routine communication, reflect the assumptions and values they use to build social relationships. Hence, if we wish to understand social life, we must start with the vernaculars of everyday life.

Select a particular activity you frequently engage in. This can be anything from watching television with others to working with automobiles to playing fantasy games. Collect a list of at least ten slang words or terms that pertain to the activity. Define the terms using Standard English. Then see if this translation exercise helps you understand something about the social world of the activity? For example, in some hospitals doctors, nurses, and other staff people refer to patients who are beyond help as "gomers." The fact that this word is a part of the working vocabulary of hospital staff reflects a consistent view of patients by the staff.

2. Accounts and disclaimers play an important part in the establishment and maintenance of social order. When order is threatened, these ways of talk come into play. From you own experiences, give examples of each of various types of accounts and disclaimers.

3. Just start paying attention to ways you try to be polite in the course of your everyday life. Also be attentive to the specific ways you hear others trying to be polite. Write down at least ten politeness strategies for these conversations. Identify them as positive, negative, or off-record, and then say what you think are the intentions of speakers (such as trying to avoid disagreement, assuming agreement, being optimistic, etc.).

Suggested Readings

The topic of language in society and the social psychology of language are areas of increasing research. For this chapter, we recommend readings focusing on the precise ways in which talk functions. The first is a classic by Marvin Scott and Stanford Lyman. Their paper entitled "Accounts," *American Sociological Review* 33, no. 1 (1968): 41–62, started a wave of research that attends closely to language in social context. Next, an article by David Paul Gordon, "Hospital Slang for Patients: Crocks, Gomers, Gorks and Others," *Language in Society* 12, no. 2 (1983): 173–85, exemplifies Schutz's assertion that vernaculars reflect social reality. Nevertheless, as Gordon shows, these realities may not always be as they appear. Finally, Deirdre Boden, "People Are Talking: Conversational Analysis and Symbolic Interaction," in *Symbolic Interaction and Cultural Studies,* eds. Howard S. Becker and Michal M. McCall (Chicago: University of Chicago Press), 1990, makes a case for the coming together of the study of talk and social meaning. She provides examples of talk as data and shows how the stories people tell provide insights into their lives in society.

Chapter 8

The Meanings of Being Different

The ways we think about one another, who we think we are, how we organize our experiences—until now we have addressed these phenomena, respectively, mind, self, and society, in relatively abstract fashion. That is, although we have used real-world examples, our primary concern has been with their appearance as pure phenomena, rather than with their existence in actual life. But in fact, in every society, all people's experiences are interpreted against a background of norms or rules that define what is "acceptable," "normal," "regular," "per usual," or "the way people are." And while these norms are far from static, at any given time it is possible to describe social life in terms of what is expected of the people governed by them. Furthermore, ideas about acceptability and appropriateness are expressed organizationally through the interaction of groups of outsiders and insiders. Every understanding of one's self is opposed to an understanding a "different" other, every thought of a typical experience implies the unusual, and "our" group has its form in contradistinction to "their" group.

There is, then, a sense in which normality and deviance, like self and society, are two sides of the same coin. We can understand this more fully by looking at what it means to be different, what it means to have committed an untoward act or to be understood by others as "deviant," a persistent "troublemaker," or "handicapped." In commonsense terms, we might be tempted to think of departures from norms as "necessary," or having to do what has been done, and there is a sense in which this is true. The act of discharging a bullet from a handgun into another person's body might be deviant, but it might not. For example, if this act takes place during the holdup of a convenience store, when a robber fires on the store attendant, we understand it as deviant. But if the store attendant fires at the robber, this act has a different meaning—it may be an act of self-defense and may even be called "heroic."

As Goffman (1971) shows, the determination of the degree to which acts depart from what is normative and the assessment of the seriousness of these departures are highly situational, sometimes generating elaborate interpretations of motives and intentions. Several students of deviance have generalized this observation in a principle that often has profound implications for the ways we deal with acts, thoughts, feelings, and categories of people whose doings, expressions, or mere presence call into question what we have come to regard as "normal." According to Becker(1963), "deviance is not a quality of the act a person commits, but rather a consequence of the application by others of rules and sanctions to an 'offender.' The deviant is one to whom the label has successfully been applied; deviant behavior is behavior that people so label"(p. 9).

More recently, in connection with a sociological program for understanding the meanings of having a disability, Higgins(1992) writes: "We make disability. Disability is not a natural quality of people or of their individual traits. Through responses to people with variations that we have made meaningful within a world that we have often uncritically built, we produce disability. Those of us made disabled and those of us not can make disability in an infinite number of ways, ways yet to be tried or even imagined"(p. 6).

Who is on the outside and who is inside, who is disabled and who is not, is largely a matter of which group in society can make its labels or meanings the dominant ones. All the while, this definitional process takes place within the opposition between ways of understanding what a particular set of occurrences, appearances or capabilities means. For instance, the acceptability of homosexuality has become a subject for open debate. As gays "come out" (publicly acknowledge their identities as so-called deviants) they attempt to refute the negative or stigmatizing meanings "straight" (heterosexual) society has attributed to them. This is one way some gays hope to remove the discriminatory consequences of being so labeled. The future some gays envision would require a singular set of meanings for sexual behaviors, separate from the current institutionalization of sexuality, that is, from the legitimacy of only heterosexuality within the sanction of marriage. Or some may seek an integration of sexual orientation into these institutionalized meanings. Being gay, in the first instance, would simply be another way to be sexual over against perhaps some new "deviant case" such as being antisexual, or, in the second homosexuality would be encompassed within marriage. Our point is not to enter a debate but to suggest that oppositional categories would still function to define what is "normal" and what is "deviant."

We are relating and perhaps extending a basic insight that Durkheim provided: it is impossible to imagine what is normal without some collective, readily available and widely used construct of what is not. And since there must and always will be real-world examples of the abnormal available, so that normality can be defined, social deviance itself is both natural and necessary. Now while numerous and large categories of people in society may be at odds with the structure of normality, and although certain constructs surely change, even radically in modern societies like our own, society does constitute the starting point for understanding the meanings of being different.

Societal Meanings of Deviance

We are born into ready-made societies, complete with, as Durkheim saw, a set of social constraints to keep us in line. The systems of widely distributed knowledge of its rules and regulations we have referred to as a society's institutions, or *societal meanings*.

Although no single individual or group is ever completely "normal," there are generally understood criteria that we learn beginning with childhood and continuing throughout life and that we use to judge our own appearances and actions as well as those of others. As members of society, we eventually take for granted certain physical, moral, and mental states as "normal."

Certainly the guidelines, models or analogies we receive from institutions or societal sets of meanings vary from society to society and even within a society over its history. In Western society the body was once thought of as the receptacle of the soul. And Byzantine medicine of the Middle Ages forbade dissection for such an act would defile the body and be a "sin." When in 1616 William Harvey dissected cadavers to provide evidence for his theory of the circulation of blood, his doctrine, while accepted in parts of Europe, was condemned by the Paris faculty as heretical. Anyone who professed it was threatened with excommunication by the Catholic church.

In the seventeenth century, Descartes suggested the concept of "the body as machine," and as the scientific and technological images of the body became accepted, everyday understandings of the body changed accordingly. Today, few of us would regard "medical students" as deviant for dissecting cadavers. Of course, as Goffman would no doubt have pointed out, situational variations in meaning remain paramount and the dissections (mutilations) that Jeffrey Dahmer performed on his victims would be a supreme example of deviance.

In contemporary society, our understanding of the body is defined biologically; but this does not mean everyone in society can correctly identify anatomy, cell structure, and other physiological facts. In fact, people have to learn that such identifications are possible, and most tend to use a lay version of biology to understand departures from the "normal body machine." For example, the body has parts named "organs" and the organs themselves are organized into systems, like the respiratory and circulatory systems. People believe the body works unless external or internal causes interfere (germs and diseases, for example). They trust that the senses are universal, that everybody feels, sees, hears, touches, and tastes. In this natural attitude, disease is universal and its distribution and causes are knowable (Manning and Fabrega 1973, 255).

In varying degrees of completeness and detail, members of modern society come to think of the body as a generally well-functioning biological organism. We judge any serious problems with our bodies as breakdowns or malfunctions probably requiring some intervention, ideally by a physician, an expert on the body. Persons who cannot hear or see, or who are not able to move or control their bodies in the ordinary fashion may be ascribed deviant roles, with the degrees of their deviance depending on various factors, like how impaired (different from normal) they might be and whether their so-called disabilities are temporary or permanent. Such ideas of what it means to depart from the normal contrast with different understandings in different societies and with earlier forms of development in our own, where at one time departures were attributed to "sin," or "fatefulness," that is, God's will, and therapy consisted of prayer, fasting, and repentance.

Although departures from normality are understood biologically, they may still carry moral meanings. Thinking of departures as "undesirable" may lead to stigmatization, a stigma being a literal or figurative symbol that a person, group, or kind of action departs negatively from the general expectations of what is normal. It may signify that someone has done something wrong and so represent a moral cross he or she must bear. The unmodulated, flat and often too loud noises that some deaf persons make in the effort to speak may be interpreted as a lack of grace or as stupidity; a blind person's groping posture might mean his or her loss of autonomy.

As members of society learn what is normal, they make assumptions about what other people can do or how they think and feel based on the knowledge of what normality means. In the end they attribute mental and moral states to those others who are "different"; and under certain conditions the result of these judgments is a special kind of stigmatization, often called labeling. A label is a shorthand term or catchword that characterizes what a person is, and it is special because, like a mailing label, it tends to "stick" to its target over time. Labels themselves can be official or legal designations, like a child being labeled "delinquent" by the juvenile court, or tacit, like a young girl with an undiagnosed learning disability constantly being called "stupid" by her classmates or kids in her neighborhood.

General and Specific Contexts of Deviance

Although members of society know what normality is in a vague sense, when they make specific judgments about themselves and others, immediate and practical consequences become important. Growing up with deaf parents, having a mentally retarded child, becoming involved in the intimate life of a criminal or an alcoholic—all these experiences shape specific judgments about what is normal. First-person accounts of people who have been labeled deviant often reveal to us the dramatic character of their everyday lives. A deaf man writes of the need to be recognized as a whole person (Jacobs 1989); a death-row criminal touches our hearts relating his sufferings and repentance.

What is normal takes on a more delimited meaning when we begin to describe the social context of deviance. In fact, we often discover that persons labeled deviant may be seeking social approval that we would regard as normal under other circumstances; yet the practical contexts of their life worlds provide them with meanings at odds with those of the institutions of their society.

For example, Carl Werthman (1969) in his early studies of youth gangs identified several values that seem all-important to gang members: "coolness," "action," "risk taking," "smarts," and one's "rep." In order to gain the esteem of fellow gang members, one had to display "cool." This means that in situations of tension and conflict, looseness, relaxation, and presence of mind are maintained. Threats from a rival gang are said to be met with "coolness" when someone can continue with his display of bravado and control in spite of real danger and fear. "Smarts" refers to knowing how to use cool. To be "smart" means to know when to fight, with what weapons, and how to handle the weapons. The "smart" man knows when to make a challenge and how to control his temper. Young gang members may actually seek out danger in order to display "cool." These young men are said to be "on the make," "coming up," or "looking for trouble," and should be avoided because they do not yet possess "smarts." Actually to fight such a young man would be too great a risk to the older gang member's established "rep" (reputation).

In this setting, to acquire esteem and loyalty a gang member may have to violate the law: to show cool, he must confront the police; to display loyalty to friends, he may risk parole violation by association with "known criminals"; or to gain a "rep" in the gang he must challenge and fight a member of another gang, or even one of his own.

Suttles (1969) portrays a similar situation for ghetto drug users. He points out that heroin users are at the top in the drug world because it is widely known that heroin addiction is a very expensive habit and hence requires the most skill at hustling (getting money for buying drugs). A heroin user may even suffer the pains of early withdrawal in order to remain "righteous" (to use only heroin). He or she will associate only with other heroin users, who understand the "true" meaning of the "flash" or "call" (the ethereal state that comes just after an injection of heroin), or of being "on the nod" (the state of relaxation and sleepiness heroin eventually produces). To maintain status in the world of drug users and not drop to the level of a "garbage junkie" (one who will use any and anybody's drugs), the addict must make connections, often in the world of crime. She will become a prostitute or he pimp for whores or engage in petty theft and both might become dealers themselves in order to stay righteous.

Problematic Relationships between General and Specific Contexts

We can understand that there may be conflict between societal meanings for deviance and the specific meanings of acceptable behavior for certain groups. For example, the practical matters of living in poverty within a society that values success and defines being poor as failure may set up circumstances in which a person becomes deviant. Hence in order to survive a homeless person must enter a "subculture of street life" (Snow and Anderson 1993) that teaches ways to find a place to sleep, eat, and avoid being assaulted yet forces a "deviant" status on those who do survive on the street. One consequence of being a good member of a bad group can be that an individual becomes a deviant; or learning the ropes of street life may result in becoming a homeless person, down on one's luck.

Returning to the description of gang life, we learn that members often challenge each other over becoming "smart." They may purposefully say things to insult or demonstrate a superior attitude toward other people. Such a display of "being smart" usually means one's place in the gang is being challenged; sometimes these challenges assume the form of rituals of verbal insult. Among young blacks this practice has been known variously as "capping," "sounding," "signifying," or "playing the dozens," and often it involves sexually vulgar language.

A teacher in a "black school" who is unaware of the meanings of such "contests" or who demeans a youth's way of life may inadvertently issue a challenge in what he or she regards as the routine discharge of teaching responsibility. In the school, of course, it is only the students' response to the challenge that is out of place and this may be the very act that labels them troublemakers or behavioral problems.

Werthman (1969) relates a story told by a gang member in which a teacher's demeanor was interpreted as "getting smart" and hence challenging the young storyteller. The boy explained that he played it cool and put up with the teacher until the opportunity to get even arose. A verbal duel came first.

> *Teacher:* You two shut up, or I'll throw you out on your ear.
> *Gang member:* The best thing you can do is ask me to leave and don't tell me. You'll get your damn ass kicked off if you keep messin'.
>
> A short while later the boy walked out of class, went out in the yard to play basketball; he walked back into the school with the ball and passed the classroom door. Upon seeing the teacher with his back turned, the boy threw the ball at the teacher hitting him on the back. The boy exclaimed, "I hit him with the ball. Got him. I didn't miss. Threw it hard too. Real hard!" (Werthman 1969, 625)

Snow and Anderson (1993, 198) relate a powerful example of how a stigma was applied to a group of homeless people following their own survival skills. In the course of their fieldwork, the authors were waiting with a group of homeless people for a Salvation Army center to serve dinner. A school bus loaded with Anglo junior high students being bused from an eastside barrio school to their upper-middle- and upper-class homes in another part of Austin, Texas, rolled past. As the bus passed,

> a fusillade of coins came flying out of the windows, as the students made obscene gestures and shouted, "Get a job." Some of the homeless gestured back, some scrambled for the scattered coins— mostly pennies—others angrily threw the coins at the bus, and a few seemed oblivious to the encounter. For the passing junior high schoolers, the exchange was harmless fun . . . but for the homeless it was a stark reminder of their stigmatized status and of the extent to which they are objects of negative attention. (Snow and Anderson 1993, 198)

The Police and the Deviant

The police occupy a strategic position in the relationship between the world of the deviant and the societal meanings of moral normality, for they symbolize the contact between the acceptable and the unacceptable. And although they deal with specific instances of deviance, they represent the general role of social-control agent. In the course of their becoming police officers, they learn a great deal about outsiders and their worlds. Yet their job is to represent the moral order of society. On occasion the line between "good cop" and "bad cop" becomes blurred as the officers who are simply "doing our job" allow the guilty to go free or arrest the innocent. In other situations, officers who contact the criminal world in intimate ways are afforded opportunities to go "on the take" or become "bad."

From their unique vantage point, the enforcers of moral order serve as labeling agents. As Aaron Cicourel (1968) suggested, it is the police, probation officers, and judges who transform gang boys into "delinquents." Becoming a deviant therefore may be looked on as an organizational rather than a legal process, "since the criteria used to contact, categorize, and dispose of boys often has little to do with breaking the law itself" (Werthman 1969, 626). Similarly, Snow and Anderson (1993, 78) trace how homeless people acquire a deviant status by dealing with the variety of organizations set up to deal with them, from the accommodative responses of the Salvation Army and Employment Commission to the containment responses of the police department.

Patrol officers face another interesting problem, and their solution to it has a great deal to do with the labeling of deviance whether they are dealing with juveniles or homeless persons. That is, they often must make judgments about the "moral character" of a person from appearances alone (Sacks 1972), and they do this basically by becoming specialists at being suspicious. Using a principle of thinking called the "incongruity procedure," they look for small details or larger features of the social scenery that do not seem to fit in. The man dressed as a mail carrier in a high-crime area of town may be stopped and questioned, because the officer does not know him as the regular route man and is aware that the postal uniform is a perfect front for "running numbers." Provocatively dressed women in front of a convenience store may mean "trouble with hookers." In like manner, the policeofficer comes to see gang members as potential troublemakers. Initially they may want to "give them a break" and help them "get straight," but then they risk losing the capacity to interact with such kids in ordinary ways. They cannot accept the intentions of suspicious characters or known delinquents at face value; police officers do not suspend their knowledge of the background of "gang bangers" as they deal with them in routine questioning. Instead, they keep an eye on them, watching for the first sign of trouble.

The police, then, are moral judges in modern society. Playing the unique role of enforcers who may actually create criminals, they hold great discretionary power in the definition of deviance. This position of moral judiciality gives police officers the power to "normalize crime," as well as to repress it. Sudnow (1965) points out that police and other legal officials come to think of crimes as typical. They understand a particular act according to whether or not it is like others. They accept categories of crime as normal and often plea-bargain and settle offenses by placing them within the knowledge system of what is a greater or lesser offense. In this system an offense is considered normal if it fits with what the police know about how that particular crime is ordinarily committed, under what circumstances, and by whom. A charge of burglary can be settled through a plea of guilty to a lesser offense, such as petty theft, if the burglary in question was considered normal—was committed in accord with the official's understanding of typical burglaries (e.g., no particular violence or vandalism was committed against the burglarized residence or business). For the most part, the specifics of typical burglaries will vary among police departments, and from precinct to precinct within departments. In one area, a type of burglary may be perpetrated by young blacks who fence to organized professionals in order to earn money for personal use—even to support their families. In another region, youths from "good families" may break into a house and steal "just for the fun of it." Judgments about the circumstances of crime are important to settlement. A police officer's intentions to "get a criminal off the street" or to "give a good kid a second chance" may be the determining factor in whether an actual arrest is made.

What becomes deviant and how it is defined as such is often the result of the complex relationship between societal and contextually specific meanings for actions. The deviant possesses knowledge and interactional skills in both meaning systems. He or she is a member of society as well as of a peer group, gang, or other subculture. What distinguishes the plural life world of the deviant from that of regular citizens is the antagonism between the two. Deviants are caught in a bind between what they know about societal normality in general and what they know about acceptable attitudes and actions within their specific worlds. When these relationships result in the application of the label of deviant to the total life world of the person or group, as in the case of the transformation from gang member to delinquent (which has a legal definition, not just a social connotation), we have observed the creation of what Goffman(1963) calls "discredited, virtual social identity." After that process has been completed and the label sticks, the identity itself is a stigma.

The Organization of Deviance: The Worlds of Outsiders

The socialization process introduces people to both general and specific ways of interpreting experiences. When there is consistency between these, the person will most likely not become deviant. Inconsistent and conflicting meanings for societal and group life offer the conditions for deviation. Actually becoming a deviant involves several steps and some rather common experiences. In fact, there are often rituals and ceremonies marking a person's entrance into a deviant life or identity.

After a person has been attributed a discrediting identity, the first step toward becoming deviant is the degradation ritual (Goffman 1963; Garfinkel 1967). In a degradation ritual, the change in a person's social status is publicly acknowledged. Further, there is an advance warning of the possible loss of self-creditability. A jail sentence functions as such a ceremony, as does a psychiatric diagnosis of mental illness, or even a medical diagnosis of cancer, or certainly of AIDS. In all these practices, a person is placed outside the everyday moral order and is defined as a threat to it. The accuser must be defined as morally superior, evoking moral values of normality that the degraded person is then persuaded to accept. The successful degradation ceremony forces the degraded person to accept his or her new status. This is one way in which the scales are tipped toward the eventual adoption of a deviant lifestyle.

Another ritual is initiation. Here a person undergoes a rite of passage that marks entrance into a group or into a new status with a group. A gang member achieves "cool" by "rippin' off" a car, or a boy's first arrest by the police functions to cement his membership in a gang. Life is deviant according to societal meanings, and a person becomes deviant by adopting deviant life meanings as the dominant ones for his or her own life. A ceremony may be negative, as with the degradation ritual, or positive, as in the case of the initiation. Either way, the person enters in more or less complete fashion into the life world of the deviant.

For the sake of our analysis, we can identify three deviant life worlds: physical, mental, and moral. The physical deviant is ascribed a stigma and must live life under the encumbrances of it. The mental deviant achieves a stigma and often becomes a career patient; and the moral deviant chooses a life of crime or a life in the vagueness between legality and illegality.

The Physical Deviant

Generally, there are two types of physical deviants: those born with a deficiency such as deafness, blindness, or mental retardation; and those who have lost their normality by becoming blind, deaf, paraplegic, and so on.

Invariably, social dimensions are associated with physical stigmata. Deaf people, for instance, live much of their lives in the company of other deaf people. Together they make up a vital social organization, known as "the deaf community," which revolves around their unique means of communication, sign language. Although not all hearing-impaired people join this community, most do by early adulthood through associations they make either in special education programs or in state-supported residential schools. Also, a small number of deaf people live in families in which all of the members are deaf. Learning the language of signs opens associations with other people and enriches the lives of the deaf. But, they live in a four-sense world, and "normals," or hearing people, assume that deaf people experience less of the world around them. The stigma of deafness, which is made visible to all by deaf people's use of sign language, consists of assumptions other people make about them, assumptions that deaf people are less capable, less responsive than "normals," and that they suffer from a "lack of maturity" (see Jacob 1974; Higgins 1980). Of course these assumptions can become the basis for decisions about the educational potential of deaf children and finally about the employment and career opportunities of deaf adults.

The stigma of deafness is reflected in the social organization of the deaf community in both negative and positive ways. Importantly, the community gives to deaf people a strong sense of belonging, but the blessing is mixed. Gaylene Becker (1980) writes that the deaf community helps the aging deaf person deal with isolation and depression; yet this very community isolates the deaf person from the larger society, thereby depriving him or her of opportunities to acquire "success."

In more subtle fashion, the stigma of deafness is reflected in the attitudes deaf people can have about their own language. Although attitudes are now changing, particularly among younger deaf people, there is still a tendency for deaf adults to devalue signs and encourage hearing-impaired children to be "oral," which means to learn to speak and lip-read.

Nevertheless, since they must use signs in everyday life to communicate with peers in their native language, forcing them to be oral risks overemphasizing the power of Standard English. Accordingly, the children learn two things: the importance of "proper" language and the meanings of being physically deviant. The effect of such dual meanings on the action of a stigmatized person is manifest by those deaf people who wear hearing aids even though given their particular form or degree of deafness the devices cannot possibly aid them in distinguishing or producing speech sounds. In such cases the hearing aid is a mere symbol, reinforcing for the deaf wearer, as well as the public at large, the normality of hearing and speaking.

As this example begins to demonstrate, physical deviants may possess extensive technical and social knowledge about how to manage their "spoiled identities." The organization of this knowledge and its incorporation into life worlds are the result of constant efforts either to achieve normality or to mask an actual social identity. It is only with those who share the stigmatized condition, or with others who already know and understand them, that deviants can share ordinary social interaction. Otherwise, physical deviants must learn to manage their stigma, which, if they are successful, may mean being able to pass as normal persons, such as when the victim of a mastectomy uses a prosthesis to alter the actual contours of her body. With a physical stigma, failure to pass may mean life in a degraded condition, holding a job for which one is overtrained, or being denied access to opportunities that presume normality.

The second type of physical deviant, one who once had but has lost normality, occupies a different place within the life world of those with spoiled identities. Such persons have been normal and unless they lost normality at a very early age know and remember the experiences of the insider. Such persons must master a new set of meanings for their physical appearances. If you are familiar with the film *Born on the Fourth of July*, you know how it is they who often become politically active, demanding that the stigma of being handicapped not only be made illegal but that it actually be ameliorated through accommodative legislation. On the other hand, people with adventitious hearing losses may never become members of the deaf community. They may resist taking up any behavior they see as embodying the stigma of their handicap, like using sign language or, as in the case of a blind person, carrying a red-tipped white cane.

Often the strain of the struggle with stereotypical thinking about handicaps is accompanied by acute mental distress that can place the individual under a double stigma. In such cases, a person who is a physical deviant may become a mental one. Again, the character portrayed by Tom Cruise in *Born on the Fourth* exhibits this.

The Mental Deviant

Laing (1969), Szasz (1961), and many others have written that mental illness is often the end result of complex interactions in which behavior, although not intrinsically ill, becomes so interpreted. Laing believes social situations come to be seen by people in general, as well as by such outside agents as social workers, physicians, and psychiatrists as ones where "something is wrong." In any given situation, it may be true that no one knows exactly what is happening. We often feel this in the "seedier" downtown sections of large cities where it is common to see people walking along talking loudly to other people who just aren't there. One task of social interaction is to "discover the situation" and unravel the chains of events that interlock or alienate people's self-identities. In the case of families, members may collude, however unwittingly, to practice and reproduce mental illness. Sometimes, for example, some will talk about others behind their backs or in hushed tones, and when caught will flatly deny doing it. In other cases, economic hardship, especially the sudden loss of a job by a parent, leads to the emotional or physical abuse of a child who has no idea what he or she might have done wrong. When these practices take their toll and attract the attention of outside agencies, certain family members, or as is more likely just one of them, run the risk of becoming stigmatized as mental deviants. Out of the social situation of family life emerge ways of deviant thinking (Laing 1969, 89).

Another example of how social contexts can exacerbate and even create deviant roles comes from literature on the sick role. Mechanic (1966) describes a process through which people learn to recognize illness behavior. When people begin to do erratic things, regardless of how temporarily, they exhibit symptoms associated with abnormal conditions. Then the people who make up their immediate social network treat these persons as if they were ill—that is, in ways they understand as appropriate for dealing with ill people. Consequently, the so-called ill are not held responsible for their incapacities. After that, they are not allowed to make decisions or care for themselves. Second, they are exempted from usual role or task obligations, such as parental supervision, housework, and job responsibilities. Third, if they demonstrate in attitude and behavior that they desire to leave the sick role, they are expected to talk about getting better, getting their heads together, breaking the habit, or licking the disease. And finally, they are obliged to seek and comply with technically competent experts.

Alcoholics, junkies, mental patients, and others may assume this role. So widespread is its interpretation in our society that Mechanic suggests the sick role or "illness behavior" functions as a form or outline for many particular deviations. Since we are referring to interpretations of diseases and not actual illness, our concern is with understanding how people impute to others certain traits and characteristics and how these imputations in turn affect social interactions.

These processes have special relevance to understanding the deviant careers of ex-psychiatric patients. Over the past twenty-five years in the United States, the movement toward deinstitutionalization and the development of community psychiatry have resulted in more and more people carrying the label of "mental deviant" on their return to their respective ordinary lives.

Herman (1990, 1993) has researched the strategies employed by these people as they deal with the stigma of being a "mental deviant." In her major study of how ex-psychiatric patients reintegrate into society, she discovered several ways that these people dealt with potentially discreditable information about them. Some practice selective concealment—the withholding or disclosure of information about being a "mental deviant"; others used therapeutic disclosures that entail disclosing information about the discreditable attribute to "trusted," "empathetic" supportive others in an effort to renegotiate personal perceptions of "failing." Other practices were preventive disclosures, where a person simply tells people "right off the bat" about a mental illness in an attempt to ward off negative evaluations and medical disclaimers that attempt to define mental illness as a random disease. Various strategies such as deception/coaching and education and political activism combine to socialize ex-mental patients into a subculture where they reject their deviant identities and statuses and adopt more positive, nondeviant identities.

According to Herman, while some of these strategies were aimed at altering society's stereotypical perceptions about mental patients and mental illness in general, they had the consequence of creating a viable context of interpretation where people who might otherwise simply fall back into the status of mental deviant are able to construct alternative meanings of the self.

Herman (1990) suggests that stigma, particularly for some types of discreditable attributes, may have positive consequences. For example, those who were once "mental deviants" may reinterpret their past identities as therapeutic opportunities that provide new meanings to the self, personal growth experiences, and expanded interpersonal opportunities. Herman corrects the tendency in the literature to see consequences of being stigmatized as all negative. In fact, in a fluid and dynamic society where typifications are often negotiable, a group of people once "spoiled" may find ways to enhance their integration into society. While in no way does this analysis diminish the suffering of those who bear the stigma of mental illness, it does add to our understanding of the interaction between the general and specific meanings of being "normal and deviant" in a modern society.

The Moral Deviant

In this form of deviance, stigma follows the departure from prevailing moral standards, and so in a sense it is earned through some act or series of actions. Such violations are often organized, so much so that some authors (see Becker 1963) suggest certain groups constitute "deviant worlds" or "deviant communities." In these cases, the moral deviant belongs to a social circle in which particular practices that are acceptable within the circle are unacceptable and therefore stigmatized in larger society. For the most part, criminals can be characterized as moral deviants, ones who people a loosely connected criminal world generally consisting of three types of "citizens": conventional criminals, white-collar criminals, and racketeers. Both the degrees and kinds of moral deviation in these categories vary from type to type.

Conventional criminals may be either professionals who live lives of crime on a daily basis and never work straight jobs or amateurs who commit crimes less frequently, but nonetheless regularly, usually to supplement any legitimate ways they have of making money. Violent crimes, such as murder and rape, can be classified as conventional, but they are not typically committed as occupational activities. Of course, some murders and many batteries are committed while their perpetrators are involved in more conventional activities, like burglaries and robberies. And some members of society do become skillful at violence and threats. Professional hit men and guns for hire are appropriate examples. Still others learn conventional criminal trades, such as picking pockets, running con games, shoplifting, safe-cracking, or stealing and stripping cars—all of which can involve refined skills and abilities and the willingness to take substantial risks.

White-collar criminals are morally stigmatized even though, according to their own relative worldview, they see themselves as completely ordinary or even as superior to other members of society. In fact, as has come glaringly to light in the past quarter century, many of them are persons elected or appointed to positions of political and economic power. Their crimes usually include moral offenses occurring in federal or state governments, higher education, regulatory and planning agencies, and even police departments. Although much white-collar crime takes place at lower levels and its practice may result in only small and short-lived pangs of conscience, we can speak of a morality of the job. For high-level jobs, a moral element may be an important aspect of the job itself. Douglas writes:

> The primary reason why the public is so outraged (at such offenses) is precisely because we do have higher standards for government officials. Each act of deviance which has been transferred from the private sphere to the government by the welfare state revolution has increased our degree of moral outrage over that one deviant act (Douglas 1981, 403).

Almost all white-collar criminals live most of their lives as respectable citizens in reputable social positions and economic or political occupations, and they commit crimes, however grandiose, only occasionally. Racketeers, in contrast, usually maintain apparently legitimate "front" operations, such as small businesses, but they mainly live and work in a domain of underworld activity: gambling, prostitution, and the fencing of contraband goods are examples of such activities, ones that may even serve the respectable world. Klockars (1974), for example, details the life of a racketeer he calls "Vincent Swaggi." Vincent spent a lifetime in the world of crime. He learned hustling skills as a child growing up in a large city, and he later established himself in the business of fencing. He had a store for a legitimate front and developed elaborate social and business connections in both the "legit" and criminal worlds. In Klockars's book Vincent relates in vivid detail how to run a store, possess stolen goods without danger of identification, make a drop (in which stolen goods and money are exchanged), and use other practices and procedures for running a fencing operation. From his own perspective, Vincent actually saw himself as a conventional person:

> The way I look at it, I'm a businessman. Sure I buy hot stuff, but I never stole nothin' in my life. Some driver brings me a couple of cartons, though, I ain't gonna turn him away. If I don't buy it, somebody else will. So what's the difference? I might as well make money with him instead of somebody else. (Klockars 1974, 139)

In his classic study of the professional thief, Edwin Sutherland shows how some criminals do contact the legitimate society and use their acquaintances with bondsmen, politicians, and lawyers; however, they are suspicious of all legitimate people. The professional thief believes that

> whoever is not with him is against him. Any noncriminal individual not personally known . . . is a possible danger . . . because of this the professional thief lives largely in a world of his own and is rather completely isolated from general society. The majority of them do not care to contact society except professionally. (Sutherland 1935, 166)

So the world of the criminal often has a definite organization, requiring special skills and knowledge; and within that world there are occupational specializations and networks of interpersonal involvement. There is also a division of labor within the underworld of crime, where conceptions of membership as well as degrees of shared moral stigma can be well defined and stringently enforced.

Another type of person often deemed by a society to be morally deviant is the one whose behavior is stigmatized primarily on moral rather than legal grounds. Groups such as homosexuals, traffickers in pornography, and massage-parlor employees make up this category. In this kind of deviance, the line between legal and illegal is blurred and constantly changing. Acts falling into this category clearly demonstrate that deviance results from the imputation of a moral stigma.

People who engage in stigmatizable acts are discredited and acquire appropriate moral characters. When people with similar characters congregate and develop particular norms for their social organization, we speak of deviant worlds; and, to be sure, we use the word "moral" here in a relative way. What is moral depends on the social context; some acts, such as homosexuality and white-collar crimes, are so widespread that the interpretation of their morality becomes very difficult to establish. For example, have you or has anyone in your family ever "cheated" on an income tax return form? And further, the worlds we describe are "immoral," not from the perspective of social psychology, but only from the vantage point of the larger society. Hence we refer to "immoral character" and "immoral worlds" only relative to the contexts in which they occur. But we have learned that relationships between general and specific meanings of morality are dynamic and the label of deviance can be fixed, removed, or altered.

One idea central to understanding deviance is that of the "career." The criminal worlds we depict are organized around the idea of a moral or immoral career, and any person who occupies a place and an identity in a deviant world has a career as a deviant. And while some careers are deviant, others are normal or ordinary. As in the case of the professional fence, the line between these careers may be fine; but from the perspective of societal knowledge (what "everyone knows"), virtually everyone, including the deviant, knows the difference.

Goffman summarizes the interrelated aspects of a career when he writes of how various worlds offer different career avenues (1961, 127–28). These are marked by entrances and accesses. A person's movement through these avenues is controlled, and there are clear phases and levels of involvement. Just as a person must meet recruitment, educational, and socialization criteria to become a physician, nurse, or police officer, so a person becomes a deviant by contacting the worlds of deviance, entering those worlds, and passing through them. Sometimes the avenues and entrances to them are specifically defined and can be described as a funnel that leads to conversion to a deviant perspective.

For example, Lofland and Stark (1965, 874) account for conversions to an obscure millennial cult in terms of a model that describes a funneling of social experiences toward more and more exclusive involvements with the cult members and their worldview. The authors depict a sequence of occurrences from a general tension coming from a life of disappointment or failures in a marriage or job, to religious problem-solving perspectives, to a self-identity as a "religious seeker," and finally to an encounter with the cult itself. All this leads to emotional ties with cult members. These interactions all tend to focus the individual's social attachments on the cult's activities, ultimately resulting in the person becoming a "deployable agent" to recruit for the cult. All the while the person's self-image, his or her acquired skills at interaction and newly assumed life biography shape the novice into a full-fledged member of the deviant world.

A full social psychological understanding of deviance requires a detailed description of the organization of deviance. Such a description in turn leads to the classification of patterns or forms of actions, thoughts and feelings that are somehow stigmatized. Persons who enter the deviant world assume identities and careers that result in characteristic thinking on their part ,which then helps to create and maintain those worlds. In some cases, just as with the general socialization process, individuals are actually born into and almost automatically become members of deviant worlds (through families that are a part of them), and in others, entering a deviant world is a more conscious choice made by an adult. In both cases, though, we can identify what we might call a deviant mind, or mind set, a consciousness about being different.

Consciousness of Being Different

How does a person who has been labeled a deviant think? And how does this thinking relate to the construction of social worlds of deviance? Social psychologists who study this aspect of deviance use the term *secondary deviation* to distinguish between societal labeling and the individual thought processes resulting from such labeling (Lemert 1967, 7, 40–60). We can think of secondary deviation as the individual's conception of and reaction to being labeled deviant. Generally, an individual's consciousness of what it means to be different reflects both the general meanings of deviance (say, what it means to be an undesirable person) and the specific version of it that pertains to a group (for example, what it means to be in a wheelchair, blind, deaf, etc.). Depending on their life circumstances, however, the interpretations persons make of the stigma they bear varies greatly, such as their degree of involvement with their particular world of deviance and their understanding of their overall place in society. Accordingly, we consider below two types of deviance: passive and active.

The Passive Deviant

One adaptation to stigma is simply to accept it according to its general meaning. Here one thinks of oneself in stereotypical fashion, that is, in terms generally understood in society. For example, a male homosexual accepts society's assertion that he cannot control his sexual impulses and hence feels he should not be allowed to teach boys, since such an opportunity could lead to an "immoral offense," which he wishes to avoid. Whereas this particular example becomes less applicable as the meanings of homosexuality are more particularized and people learn that the general notions do not apply with much accuracy to specific individuals, there remain situations in everyday life where stereotypical understandings define situations as real.

Perhaps a deaf man acquiesces to a lifetime of low-paying jobs because he believes he is language deficient, that his native language is less than complete, and that he surely is so immature that he cannot be entrusted with the responsibility of a high-paying job. Or a criminal knows that he will return to a life of crime once he is freed from jail, simply because in his mind that is all he is fit for.

In passive interpretations, the person labeled as deviant will take on the general societal meanings of deviance as the way he thinks about himself. This does not mean deviants like the discrediting connotations of their stigma or that they necessarily devalue their station in life. They simply begin to think of themselves as they think others do. A subtle part of this adaptation involves the consequences a deviant experiences, from having passive responses to accepting labels.

Deaf people, for example, may elect to join a community of their peers in which they can enjoy spontaneous and ordinary communication with others like themselves. Or young boys become gang members so they can gain stature and esteem in the eyes of their peers. In return for this refuge from the larger world, the person bears the stigma of being a deaf-mute or a juvenile delinquent. It is almost as if we are describing a tradeoff or barter in which a person receives the rewards of being like others as long as he realizes the others who he is like are not totally acceptable to society. In return for being strange, in exchange for calling into question the ready-made accounts of normality our society offers us, the stigmatized find opportunities to retreat from confrontations with the larger society. When deviants accept discredited or spoiled identities, general conceptions of normality for the nonstigmatized remain unaltered and the "able" person can continue to function in society without ever having firsthand knowledge of what it is like to be stigmatized. Whenever contacts are made between the world of the stigmatized and that of the "normal" or "straight," the two may coexist smoothly as long as the deviants retreat into the predefined meanings of their labels: "Well, he's a homosexual (or con man, crook, etc.), what can you expect?"

The Active Deviant

More often, though, contacts between the normal and the deviant are not simply a matter of the deviant's acquiescence or retreat. Instead, active confrontations mobilize forms of consciousness in deviants who actively oppose the meaning of being different. Through normalization, deviants attempt to normalize others' (normals' or straights') imputed interpretations of them by refuting or denying the stigma, usually through demonstrations that they are really not deviant; in neutralization deviants accept the label but reject the negative interpretations of it by offering an entirely different version of their actions; and by counterstigmatization deviants formulate a theory typically directing their assaults at the very basis of society, namely the taken-for-granted assumptions about what is normal.

Normalization: In this process, a person tries to avoid having a stigma placed on his or her actions or identity. A deaf person tries very hard to "speak normally," by wearing expensive hearing aids and attending lip-reading classes to become like everybody else. An amputee exercises and practices diligently to master the use of an artificial limb. In both examples it is not so important for the deaf person actually to learn to speak "normally" or for the artificial limb really to allow normal movement. Instead, a stigma-avoiding strategy is used. The goal of normalization is to pass, which means to mask the discreditable trait so successfully that no one recognizes it. In interaction, the person who passes does not demand of others a special knowledge of communicative systems or an appreciation of the difficulties of life without normal movement.

Of course, not all efforts to pass are successful. But our focus is on the intentions and assumptions that ground social life. Efforts are made to approximate the ideal of normality, to become or at least appear to be normal, by those who know or think their condition, if discovered, would lead to discrediting. Many studies of alcoholics and drug users show that sometimes the relatives of heavy drinkers or users will interpret their kin's drunkenness or otherwise altered states as normal—in the light of the pressure of a job or an illness—thus they, and perhaps the deviant himself or herself, can be said to apply their interpretations of what is a "routine life" beyond reasonable limits. A husband may see his wife's drinking as "normal," given the boredom of housewifery and the stresses of child care.

Other people who use more widely distributed and agreed upon meanings do not concur with the "normality" of these behaviors. An employer may be forced to ask an employee to seek counseling, or a husband to see that he has an alcoholic wife. Both the deviant and those who make up his or her immediate social context must learn to see their respective behaviors as others see them. In the case of current treatments of drinking problems, the deviant and those affected by his or her deviance learn to shift their thinking about drinking from "a practice of harmless fun" to "a symptom of a deadly disease."

We see that normalization can refer to the efforts of a person to avoid revealing a stigmatizable trait, or to accounts of an already detected character flaw. Crucial to active deviance of this type is a clear conception of normality used to interpret an aberrant trait or behavior, or to mask a condition. The deviant in either predicament knows what is normal and acts on the basis of that knowledge. The "closet queen," so long a stereotype of the male homosexual, exemplifies one form of this adaptation. This type of homosexual hides his identity behind ordinary role performances. He avoids stigma by managing any discrepancy between his being identified as a normal, a heterosexual, and his real identity as an abnormal, a homosexual.

Similar processes operate with the heavy drinker. In the early stages of alcoholism, the alcoholic works hard to perform job and family roles. In spite of excessive drinking, accompanied by blackouts and failures to perform the social responsibilities of family and workplace, the alcoholic continues to think of his or her social activities as normal. But for any real change to occur, the deviant must become deviant, that is, must acknowledge the problem,and then become normal again through the removal of the discrediting conditions of heavy drinking. The alcoholic must say he or she is a "drunk" and then "dry out" and "stay clean and sober."

Neutralization: Another active response to the stigma of deviance involves accepting the label but reinterpreting its meanings. The new meanings, ones the person accused of some discrediting act attempts to assign to it, neutralize the label.

Vincent Swaggi relates his autobiography as a professional fence in an apologetic tone: of course his actions were illegal; sure, his best friends and business associates were criminals; but in Vincent's view his work gave him a measure of respectability. According to Klockars (1974), Vincent was able to maintain an air of respectability as an impression, an effect of his mannerism and style. Vincent saw himself as a "businessman who never stole anything." In his opinion, clear distinctions could be made between "thieves-and-receivers" and "thieves-and-drivers."

> See Carl, what you gotta understand is when I say "driver," I don't mean "thief." I don't consider a driver a thief. To me, a thief is somebody who goes into a house and takes a TV set and the wife's jewelry an' maybe ends up killin' somebody before he's through. An' for what? So some nothin' fence will steal the second-hand shit he takes? To me that kind a guy is the scum of the earth. Now the driver, he's different. A driver's a workin' man. He gets an overload (on his delivery truck) now an' then or maybe he clips a carton or two (boxes of wares). He brings it to me. He makes a few bucks so he can go out on a Friday night or maybe buy his wife a new coat. To me a thief an' a driver is two entirely different things. (Klockars 1974, 140)

Vincent was also certain that "If I don't buy it [the stolen goods], somebody else will"; besides, he does not cause the goods to be stolen, and no one is hurt by his transactions. He sees himself as a part of the legitimate business structure. He "helps out" a large corporation by equitably distributing their goods. All in all, Vincent thought he was a "pretty decent guy."

Sykes and Matza (1959) suggest that deviants often employ "techniques of neutralization." They enumerate four:

1. Denial of harm—little or no real harm has been done.

2. Denial of the victim—the victim provoked the action and got what was coming to him.

3. Attacking the accuser—the police are corrupt, brutal and unfair and laws are unjust.

4. Invoking other or higher loyalties—such as loyalties to one's fellow gang members.

Others, like Scott and Lyman (1968) and Hewitt and Stokes (1975), have expanded these conceptions into their general notion of "motive talk." We recall from an earlier chapter how these authors point to processes whereby one's intentions for an untoward action, actually committed or only anticipated, can be displayed in such a way as to establish or restore a sense of social order. Within the context of understanding deviance, neutralization implies that the deviants' sense of guilt and the ideology of the deviant world used to recount it indicate how they are committed to the values they violate. Knowing normality and knowingly violating the rules of routine social life entail accepting both stigma and normality. Professional thieves who take this approach accept that what they do is wrong; thus they try to have good lawyers or a "fix" in at city hall. Failing this, they see jail and prison time as occupational hazards.Merton's (1957) analysis of innovation further describes this predicament. The deviant knows and accepts the societally defined goals but invents new ways to achieve them. For instance, Vincent Swaggi fully understands legitimate ways to achieve success, but thinking them unavailable to him he innovates. He is motivated by the same things driving other professionals, doctors and lawyers, say, but his longings for success lead him to the deviant world. He actively confronts the negative connotations society places on his life activities by reinforcing societal meanings through violation.

Counterstigmatization

When deviants begin not only to refute and deny the negative connotations of the labels they bear but also to question and attack societal meanings for them, we witness the final process of the active responses to stigma. Neither of the strategies we have considered—attempting to approximate normality or neutralizing the effects of a label through an ideology grounded in a deviant world—requires of the deviant a vocal and deliberate frontal assault on society's foundations. In fact, these two types of active responses actually require the deviant to embrace to some measure the meanings of legitimacy. This is not so for the counterattacking deviant.

Of course all deviants must be able to recognize normality and hence their putative departure from it; but they do not have to accept or acquiesce to the meanings of their condition. This is precisely the case for deviants who wish to counter their stigma by formulating new meanings, replacing societally given ones with those from an alternative, deviant, worldview. Such deviants then campaign, demand, rebel, and organize to establish a new version of the meanings of their particular condition. Ultimately they develop a counterstigma approach which includes both ideology and practice. It offers alternative meanings for the deviant's condition, ones which conflict with those available in the larger society. And it prescribes courses of action which are often political and confrontational. For example, many physically handicapped people lecture, write, and proselytize in their attempt to get society in general and especially those directly responsible for the labels they bear—physicians, psychologists, employers—to know the truth about their conditions. They want the societal meanings modified to include "whole social persons" and insist that definitions of an "able-bodied" person be based on a new set of criteria. Blindness does not necessarily mean dependency nor deafness a lack of intelligence; bodily impairments do not require social restrictions. These people want others to know that they consider themselves and have a right to be treated by society at large as full human beings.

A counterstigma theory requires action, and so we see political action by the handicapped—picketing, lobbying, and in the late 1970s occupying for weeks a portion of a government building in San Francisco. In their demands for full equality in the social world deviants use demonstrations like these to foster the symbolic, if not literal, removal of their stigma, arguing that such effects as they desire will be the consequences only of legal action and tough enforcement by government agencies. Counterstigma theory gives meaning to confrontational strategies and can serve as the foundation for wholly different ways to decide what is normal in society.

One paraplegic related the following story of his encounter with a "labeling agent":

> I had been working down at the state capitol trying to make legislators understand that we must have public access to buildings. I spent a lot of time getting appointments, doing research, mostly on my own. A friend of mine helped me get into the building because there was no way for me to get inside. Well, I had been parking up

close to the building in a loading zone—after all they were "loadin'" me. Over a period of weeks I collected quite a few tickets. I refused to go to court. Finally, there was a final summons to appear in court. Well, I called them up and told them to come get me. They did. A patrolman came to my house. I went with him. When we arrived at the courthouse we faced that long flight of stairs up into the building. The policeman started to pick me up from the wheelchair and carry me in. I said, "If you drop me I'll sue the state, you, and the judge." I demanded that the judge see me. Well, after a long argument, the policeman left me in my chair at the bottom of the flight and the judge met with me there! He left his chambers to see me on the street! I guess I got my point across. He dropped the charges on the tickets.

In recent years, many moral deviants, such as prostitutes and homosexuals, have also adopted a rebellious stance toward the meanings of their labels. For example, especially since the Stonewall incident in 1969, where police harassment in New York led to a standoff between them and the gay community, homosexuals have organized to contend that the civil rights movement and its consequences must apply to them. Saying their stigma is discriminatory, they present ample evidence to show that prejudice against gayness disqualifies them from jobs in many parts of the nation. Also with documented justification, they attack the stereotypes of themselves as child molesters or bad security risks. They reaffirm the naturalness of homosexuality through reconstructing a history of it and point out that some great men were homosexual and how other cultures accept the practice as normal. Some argue a biological or body chemistry cause, that homosexuality is as "natural" as heterosexuality. Of course militant factions of the so-called deviant world of gayness, like ACT UP, Queer Nation, the Pink Triangle Alliance and Does Your Mother Know? illustrate the counterstigma response.

It is interesting to note here even a counter-counterstigma reaction, which can occur in any counterstigma movement—where even some of the more militant activists feel others in the movement have gone too far. In the late 1980s, some gays made popular the practice of "outing," making public the names of prominent citizens in business, government, or the world of entertainment who were known homosexuals in the gay community but passing as straight in the general society. Of course the rationale for outing someone was that if the world knew how many highly respected people also happened to be gay, the stigma would be diminished. Others argued that all gays, especially prominent citizens who were gay, had an obligation to the gay community to be "out." As we have inferred, though, in the long run many gays, even militant ones, repudiated this practice, saying it was invading a privacy that should never be violated. Perhaps as a result, outing now seems to operate only minimally, and this primarily within the gay community itself.

In sum, the counterstigma approach aims to change society, not the deviant. Its goal is the total alteration of the general meanings of normality. Normalization and neutralization are defensive postures, the former conformist, the latter innovative. Unlike these two, thinking and acting counter to a stigma focuses on grand changes and is, hence, rebellious in nature.

Coping with a Spoiled Self-Image

Each of the three strategies for dealing with stigma and its deviant status (passive, active, and counterattacking) gloss over some complicated coping mechanisms that may be taking place in the mind. The strategies themselves are ways to understand one's own identity, and Snow and Anderson (1993) provide us with a fairly complete description of how homeless street people "salvage the self." Homeless people, as Snow and Anderson show, are often stigmatized. But they also receive compassion, help and even genuine concern from society. This context of both derision and sympathy allows homeless people a considerable range of ways to understand what is happening to them. For example, they often employ accounts of their lack of good fortune that revolve around two themes: "What goes around comes around" and "I've paid my dues."

Just as with other deviant subcultures, there exists among street people a code for interpreting what is happening to them. Among the people Snow and Anderson studied, this code took on moral significance as a version of karma, or the "golden rule": "If you don't want somebody to fuck with you, you don't fuck with them." Actually, the authors suggest that street people do seem to follow this rule which explains why they do not typically steal from or assault one another.

But the rule also applies to one's own misfortune and implies that somehow, somewhere, and in some fashion, "things will get better." As one of their informants told them, "I've been down on my luck for so damn long, it's got to change. . . . Like I said before, I believe what goes around, comes around, so I'm due a run of good luck, don't you think?" (Snow and Anderson 1993, 206). Similarly, street people feel they have suffered long enough, tried long enough, and are due a reward for their patience in dealing with bad luck. Thinking in these ways, they exempt themselves from responsibility for their plight and "hold the door ajar for a change in luck" (1993, 208). Their reliance on a notion of fate or luck allows them to salvage a sense of their own worth as people.

Of course, they also have available to them avenues of escape through the use of alcohol and alternative realities. A recurring account is, therefore, a familiar justification for "drinking problems." Homeless people blame their drinking on the hard luck of street life, believing that drinking certainly cannot worsen their already hopeless situation. Some of them also construct elaborate "alternative versions" of their existence. One of Snow and Anderson's informants was an avid reader of Carlos Castaneda's books and imaged himself as kind of spiritual sage with special powers to "read and understand people" and the ability to alter his experiences of the ordinary so that he lives in another dimension patterned after his reading of Castaneda's Yaqui Indian shaman. In this spiritual mode he could escape the consequences of being down on his luck.

More generally, Snow and Anderson (1993) suggest that street people construct "identity-oriented meaning." By this they refer to how street people think about themselves, how they fashion a version of who they are. While some consciously manipulate props and appearance, most accomplish "identity-oriented meaning" through talking. Through an analysis of the way they talked about themselves, three generic patterns could be depicted: distancing, embracement; and fictive storytelling.

Distancing is a technique that separates who street people think they are from what they and others around them are actually doing, that is, talking in such a way that they are distanced from other street people. For example, Tony Jones (an informant) said: "I'm not like the other guys who hang out down at the Sally [Salvation Army Center]. If you want to know about street people, I can tell you about them; but you can't really learn about street people from studying me, because I'm different" (Snow and Anderson 1993, 215).

Also in role distancing a street person self-consciously "attempts to foster the impression of a lack of commitment or attachment to a particular role in order to deny the self implied" (1993, 216). Hence when talking about why he quit a job as a dishwasher at a local restaurant, a street person expressed disdain about that type of job and its demeaning effects on him. Another variant of distancing is institutional distancing. Here a person who depends on the "Sally" goes to great lengths to critique the Christian ideology of that organization, pointing out how he is not really like that, and they do not live up to the Christian spirit, and therefore he can take their assistance because he is not really Christian. In this way, he can distance what he is actually doing from who he thinks he really is. Snow and Anderson (1993, 219) are able to demonstrate that a homeless person's degree of integration into the subculture of street life is associated with the kind of distancing employed—with recently dislocated homeless people using categoric distancing (dissociating themselves from a homeless identity), straddlers (those who are in and out of the homeless way of life) using role and specific distancing, and those most into the homeless life (the outsiders) using institutional distancing.

Some homeless persons simply embraced the identity, taking it on as their own. Again, this identity seems to be linked to the degree of integration into the subculture of homelessness, with outsiders using it a great deal. Finally, fictive storytelling involves using full-fledged fabrications and minor exaggerations of experiences. Hence homeless outsiders heavily used embellished stories to relate their personal experiences, while those straddling the identity tended to use more fantasized accounts of their plight that stress what they think will happen to them in the future—their prospects of "getting lucky" and the like.

We can see that the social circumstances of the plight of being down on one's luck affect inner life as well as physical well-being. And while people are not totally hopeless in the face of the stigma of homelessness, the ways they internalize its meanings are reflections of the social organization of those experiences. Generally, those whose lives seem most hopeless rely on escape, lies, embracing and distancing techniques from within the identity of being homeless to understand who they are as street people. Perhaps the consequences for the self are in the final analysis more tragic than those for the body.

Summary

Deviance as a meaning of social interaction is understood as a result of the definitions of situations people are able to enforce. Generally, this perspective is known as *labeling theory*. There are both general and specific meanings for being different in society. The concept of stigma covers the interactive aspects of deviance. Problems often emerge from attempts to define what is and is not acceptable. Studies of the relationships between police and deviants teach us a great deal about judgments and the control of judgments that may produce a social deviant.

There are outsider worlds made up of deviants and those who deal with them. This chapter described these worlds and offered a scheme for classifying deviants according to the primary meanings imputed to them. There are physical, mental, and moral deviants. Within each type there are several possible reactions to the label of deviant. These reactions are depicted as active and passive. The processes through which people attempt to give meaning to their situations of life as deviants are discussed as normalization, neutralization, and the counterstigma reaction. Also, the process of acquiring a complicated and changing self associated with a deviant status, and with salvaging a sense of self was illustrated through research on homelessness. Generally, the matters of being deviant are concerned with the acquisition of identities, attempts to avoid these identities, and, once acquired for better or worse, their management.

Exercises for Understanding Deviance

1. With a few friends, go to a restaurant where you have never eaten before. Select a place where you can be reasonably sure no one will recognize you. Go through

the entire evening without speaking. You can gesture, point or otherwise figure out how to order your meal, request water, and the like, just as long as neither you nor any other member of your group speaks. After you leave the restaurant, sit down and record everything that happened to you and how you felt during the experience.

Another exercise for those of you who are shy persons is to watch a popular television program without the sound. Do this exercise with at least three other people. After you finish watching without taking notes, try to reconstruct the story. Compare your version of what happened with those of the others in your group. Did you all have similar versions? If not, how do they differ? If you have access to a video recorder, it is a great idea to record the program you watched so you can listen to it after you have completed discussing what you think happened with the others doing this exercise. You should be surprised at what you missed and at the variation in the versions of what happened. This exercise should help you grasp a little of the experience of being an outsider.

2. In the course of a typical day, as you go about the routines of living at home or in the dormitory, working, attending class, and so on, record all the words and phrases you overhear that seem to label another person (examples of some common ones are "you queer," "jerk," and the like). Of course, the precise expressions will vary a great deal from place to place and time to time. Still, you should have no trouble hearing a few dozen or so in an active day.

Rank these words according to what you think is their power to label and what kind of deviance they connote (physical, mental, or moral). Also make notes about the situations in which you heard or used these labelling terms. This exercise should help you appreciate how prevalent these attempts to distinguish insiders from outsiders are in everyday life.

3. Imagine you have been caught with an "excessive" amount of a controlled substance on your person. You are about to acquire the identity of a deviant. According to your reading of this chapter, what can you do about it? In other words, what devices are available for managing the label of deviant. We listed neutralization techniques and there are many others that you can deduce from our discussion of the meanings of being different.

Suggested Readings

David Snow and Leon Anderson have written a comprehensive and detailed study of the lives of homeless people in Austin, Texas, entitled *Down on Their Luck: A Study of Homeless Street People* (Berkeley: University of California Press, 1993). They identify types of homeless people, showing the diversity of people on the street and their degree of involvement in the street subculture. They also place the experiences of homelessness within an organizational context. Here the reader will find an excellent social psychological study of the meanings and practical consequences of being homeless in the United States.

In Erving Goffman's *Stigma: Notes on the Management of Spoiled Identity* (Englewood Cliffs, N.J.: Prentice Hall, 1963), he defines stigma as a process of information about who a person is. He suggests that stigma results from discrepancies between how persons appear in terms of the standards of normality (a virtual identity) and what different and aberrant versions of their identities can be applied to them (their actual identities). Goffman is able to show us that we are all vulnerable to stigma as long as we do not have full control over what people think of us.

Chapter 9

The Meanings of Violence

The concerns of many philosophical and religious belief systems include the causes of aggression and the "base" emotions of humans; and of course these also represent grave practical matters. For the social psychologist, aggression appears to be so prevalent a characteristic of the human condition that it literally demands explanation. In fact, there are several approaches to explaining aggression, its nature and causes. One suggests aggression is natural, a survival mechanism intrinsic in the human animal. Those following this path, like the famous naturalist Konrad Lorenz (1963), draw parallels between animal and human behavior.

It is well known that aggression has considerable adaptive value in nature. But while most animals fight to establish and defend territory, in almost no instance do animals other than humans kill members of their own species. Animal aggression and violence are both fostered and constrained by learning and instinct; and Lorenz and others argue that humans act likewise instinctively with violent and aggressive behavior. Because the social realities humans have constructed are so elaborate and so persuasive, however, whatever instinctive controls homo sapiens might once have had are now covered over by layers of civilization. The trouble is, whenever civilization or societal controls become weak, the unbridled violent side of humans can express itself. According to Lorenz, humans have lost the fully developed, self-regulating instincts of aggression; and this places the control of aggression squarely in a social arena that merits distrust. This line of reasoning is similar to a Freudian approach in which it is also said that human beings are naturally animalistic. Accordingly, Freudians also look to social control in the form of customs and habits to regulate the "base" nature of humans.

Most social psychologists think Lorenz's explanation, as well as the Freudian theories, are too one-sided, primarily because they do not fully appreciate the role social reality and meanings can play in the expression and control of aggression. From a strictly social psychological perspective, while human beings are probably encoded to react in aggressive ways, there is no compelling evidence for a direct link between the social meanings of aggression and any biological conditions or genetic dispositions.

Explanations of aggression that enjoy more favor in the scholarly community of social psychology include two remaining but related approaches: the frustra-

195

tion-aggression hypothesis and a variety of social learning theories. We briefly survey each of these and then move to a discussion of the meanings of aggression and violence in several different social contexts.

Some years ago, Dollard, Miller, and Sears (1939) proposed an explanation for aggression that postulated violent and destructive behavior as responses to the experience of frustration. Both through laboratory experiments and in studies of racial relationships in southern towns, they tested hypotheses and refined their theory. According to the authors, frustration arises from interference with the satisfaction of some biological or social need. The result of such frustration, so the theory goes, is anger, and in the expression of anger the aggressor is rewarded, if only by a general reduction of the tension he or she experiences. For some years this view of aggressive behavior was the predominant one among social psychologists. More recently however, critics have reasoned that when persons experience frustration they may also respond with new or added nonaggressive efforts to realize their goal, substitute a new goal, abandon the goal, or just become apathetic. In short, they do not necessarily become aggressive.

To account for the variation in responses to frustration, social psychologists have expanded the frustration-aggression theory to include differential social learning. The influences of the social environment became important factors in the explanation of aggression as researchers began to compile evidence to show that when frustration occurs in certain social environments, people learn to act aggressively.

When violence and aggression came to be seen as learned, the attention of researchers shifted to the settings in which such learning took place. But in fact such a shift is apt to produce an incomplete understanding of social phenomena unless the environment is seen in terms of symbolic social interaction. Perhaps nowhere is this gap in understanding better illustrated than in the study of violence.

Two approaches explain how violent and aggressive behaviors are acquired. The first focuses on the early socialization experiences of children. For example, both Gelles (1974) and Strauss (1973) identify "violent families" through research that shows that some families commonly use aggressive and even violent modes of interaction with each other. A mother reports she "blistered" the small behind of her four-year-old daughter to teach her not to run into the street. Couples report they love each other dearly, but fight frequently. Some even use implements, like the proverbial rolling pin, in acting out their violent relationships. Generally, studies such as these conclude with a description of historical or habitual uses of violence, like hitting and punching, as means of communication and control in the complex and often subtle reciprocal relationships making up family interactions.

Unfortunately, according to these same studies children socialized in such families often continue to use the same or similar childrearing techniques and modes of dealing with frustration as they become adults. It is as if the learning of violence is passed on from adult to child by a social code, one that values nonverbal, tacit, and emotive modes of communication over verbal, explicit, and rational ones.

A second common way to explain violence has been to sketch a connection between individual behavior and the larger societal context. Most studies of this kind bring children into a laboratory setting and subject them to stimuli designed to induce violence. Some researchers have shown videotapes of boxing matches, military battles or fight scenes from movies to children who are then given an opportunity to act out any violent urges they might have received from the stimuli (cf. Phillips 1983).

These studies, which generally concern the effect of media on behavior, often yield consistent results. In fact, subjects do seem to imitate violence under the following conditions: (1) when violence is portrayed in a positive way; (2) when those (on the videos) who perpetrate the acts are rewarded, or seem to have fun or be excited performing the acts; (3) when the acts seem real and justified; and (4) whenever the perpetrator presented as intending to injure his victims is not criticized. After having viewed such violence in research situations, children typically will spontaneously strike a doll in the room with them, and measures of their emotional states will usually reflect more aggressiveness than had existed before they saw the stimuli (Comstock 1977).

Definitions of Aggression

Thinking about aggression usually takes for granted that we know what it is; but in the literature and theories we have reviewed violence means everything from striking an inflated doll to a well-timed body check, from a sharp left jab to the intentional taking of another person's life. In a sense, we understand what each of these meanings of aggressions is about, or at least we think we do; however, attempts to be specific about a definition of aggression usually result in a general gloss characterized by a variety of behaviors.

Lorenz (1963) defines aggression as a "fighting instinct," one that is evident in his analyses of attack behaviors, displays of emotions, and the energetic defense of territory. Dollard, Miller, and Sears (1939) seem to consider aggression to be any behavior that results from frustration, including as little as a well-formed obscene phrase and as much as a fist in a stranger's face, or more. Laboratory experimenters demand such specific definitions of aggression and violence that what qualifies is usually limited to the varying circumstances of each particular study.

If we were to attempt to synthesize typical textbook definitions of violence and aggression, we would see first that violence is generally understood as an instance of aggression. Violent acts are acts in which one person intends to injure another (physically, emotionally, or mentally); indeed, most textbook attempts to understand violence assume that aggression is an energetic effort to do harm. Furthermore, violence and aggression are bound together in such a way that violence always suggests something wrong, unusual, or even aberrant must have occurred. In the average study then, aggression seems to have to do with attitude and motivation, whereas violence refers to outcomes, ones that can be tied to actual harm or behavior that intended to accomplish it.

Although this way of thinking about violence and aggression seems to make commonsense, to have what scientists call a kind of "face validity," we consider it inadequate for two reasons: Primarily, it does not force us to look critically at our ideas about what are valued behaviors or desirable interpersonal relationships. And beyond this, it covers a multiple of routine acts that occur regularly in the course of everyday life, but that are not interpreted as such even though they meet the criteria of aggressive and violent behavior. Gelles (1974, 24–27) offers support for this criticism when he describes some of the methodological difficulties in defining violence. In his study of families, he acknowledges the great variation existing among meanings of, for example, members of a family striking one another. Striking can range from an angry blow delivered by a mother across the face of her child who accidentally spilled some milk on the newly carpeted living room floor to a stinging slap in the intimacy of a marital embrace.

Sometimes definitions serve as devices to facilitate discussions when analysts talk to each other, and this can be so regardless of the fact that what may be violent in one instance may not be in another, or that what is violent for one person is not for someone else. Reading Gelles, for instance, we discover his willingness to include as violence incidents of corporal punishment and other like exchanges between members of a family, even if these acts are not consensually understood as either harmful or intended to do harm. Gelles takes this position for the sake of getting on with his analysis of violence and its prevalence in the American family; and although he is sensitive to the role of context in relation to the meanings of violence, he believes strongly in the harmful features of what he defines as violence.

The fact that meanings vary according to situations is a given in our approach to social psychology; this means no general assessments of violence can be valid without careful descriptions of the contexts within which so-called violent acts take place. Still, we recognize that people within a given culture may well have a commonsense consensus about what consitutes a violent act. But the precise meaning of a particular violent act is frequently the result of decisions made by the people involved for the special purposes of the given situation. Furthermore, as we have suggested, the decisions and interpretations of what counts as a violent act can be quite different, even among the same people, from place to place and time to time. A technical way of expressing this conceptualization is to say that the meanings of violence are to a degree ad hoc and above all are highly situational.

Gregory Bateson (1972) wrote of a visit he made to a zoo to observe monkeys at play. To Bateson, the monkeys' play appeared to be quite aggressive as they wrestled, punched, and rolled with each other; but he reports he had little trouble, and the monkeys seemed to have no trouble at all, deciding when the boundaries of play had been crossed and play itself was transformed into fighting. Play, he then argued, always communicates a paradox: it is both serious and trivial, aggressive and passive, as is seen regularly in children's play. For example, an eight-year-old boy plays in the front yard with a friend from across the street. It's a warm summer's day and they wrestle with each other with great joy. One calls out in loud voice, "I'm Mad Dog Smith and I'm gonna body slam ya!" He attempts to lift his friend in the air, and with great difficulty manages to get the other boy's struggling body off the ground. He whirls quickly and falls on top of his friend. There is a brief moment of silence, until the boy on the bottom cries out in apparent pain and anger. Tearfully, he pushes the other off him and stands up, fists clenched and arms pumping punch after punch, mostly into the air. One finds the other's face. An adult, the father of one of the boys, intervenes. Play has stopped; aggression and violence have begun.

Commenting on the subtle shifts that seem to make the difference between fighting and playing, Bateson (1972) noted the role of gestures and other bodily communications in conveying the message that something has changed. He suggested that we can understand these transformations by seeing beyond the behavior itself and into its meaning as this is derived by its participants and manifest in the basic manner in which their experiences are organized. Goffman, following Bateson and others, carries this analysis further and offers the idea of a frame as a way of organizing experiences. For example, we can think of a "kidding" or "putting someone on" frame. As most readers can guess, this might involve certain words spoken in a certain way, a particular look in one's eye along with a smile, and perhaps a gesture, such as putting one's arm around someone. If someone is talking to another who recognizes and accepts this frame, one can say to the other, "Hey, you're really looking ugly today, baby," without the other feeling insulted.

Bateson used an ingenious visual device to illustrate the idea of a frame (see Figure 9.1). Everyday life, he contended, is understood as organized according to typical experiences; for example, most of us understand that there is "play" and there is "fighting." In play, things are not as they seem; in fighting, they are precisely what they appear to be.

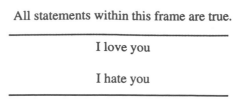

All statements within this frame are true.

I love you

I hate you

Figure 9.1 Frame From Bateson 1972, 184.

As important to understanding typical experiences is the fact that with their increasing skill at social life people learn to "key" framed experiences. Keying involves performing certain acts that change the tone, intention, or presentation of experiences. Even though the boys themselves might not have been fully aware of the mechanics of keying, we saw it in our example of their play on the lawn. In the beginning their activity was framed as play. But when the one boy keyed it, that is, screamed and jumped up punching, it was reframed as fighting. And perhaps the father's arrival keyed it back to play, or on to yet something else. In short, how an activity is understood depends on how that activity is framed and on the transformation the frame goes through. This basic insight turns out to be crucial to understanding violence and aggression.

To develop our perspective on how people come to understand activities as aggressive or violent, we must recall earlier discussions in which we depicted the nature of everyday life in modern society. Such words as "negotiation," "situated," and "socially constructed" remind us of the problematic character of establishing meaning in everyday life. And nowhere are the processes of attributing meaning more fundamental or more crucial than in the decisions that formulate an action as violent.

These basic social psychological insights can be illustrated by examining acts of violence found across widely different situations. From rape to the sport of hockey to the families in which members physically hit each other, we see how such acts are framed, keyed, and understood from the very different vantage points of those who take part in them.

Situations of Violence

A sociological truism guides our view of social psychology: there are no intrinsic social meanings. We have repeatedly demonstrated how the meanings of social acts must be seen as constructed; and now we add more information about what social construction is like. Goffman's idea of frame is very important in this task, as is the elaboration of his conceptualization of the key.

The meanings of sexual intercourse are complex and multilayered in our society. Such an act can be interpreted as a sensitive and intimate expression of a loving relationship; but the same act, under different situational conditions, becomes a vile, deplorable crime. The more room there is for negotiating the occurrence of an act, the more confusing and less clear-cut are decisions about what it really means, both for those engaged in the act and from the point of view of those who, for various reasons, must make an assessment about its social significance.

Imagine how silly it seems to ask a husband and a wife why they have sexual intercourse; it makes more sense to ask them why they do not (cf. Scott and Lyman 1967). Yet there are many circumstances of everyday life in which questions to the effect of "Why do you have sexual intercourse?" seem appropriate. Perhaps the most obvious concerns an issue that has had monumental significance throughout human history: what is rape? We approach this question by asking another, one that social psychology can more properly answer: how do people make decisions about what constitutes the commission of rape?

To provide at least a partial determination of the meaning of the violent and aggressive act of rape, Shotland and Goodstein (1983) conducted an experimental study of how it is perceived in dating situations. Through their research, they discovered that cultural assumptions and previously acquired attitudes about women influence decisions about whether particular actions could or should be called rape.

A review of existing literature told the authors that it is often difficult for policemen, jurors, and people not directly implicated in the act to say that indeed a woman had been raped. But Shotland and Goodstein did identify what they characterized as "acquaintance rape," referring to situations in which a woman is said to have been raped by someone she knows, who might range anywhere from a casual acquaintance to someone she is dating. In fact, in some instances a strong case can be made for marital rape.

Shotland and Goodstein reason that the confusion about whether a rape has actually been committed comes from cultural assumptions that govern sexual activity among dating couples. Some of these assumptions, often held by men, suggest that women conceal their genuine interest in sex in subtle and symbolic ways. In addition, cultural beliefs about the dating situation hold that a woman is expected to resist a man's advances, especially in the beginning stages of a potentially sexual encounter. These beliefs are further confounded by a widespread judgment among males that women enjoy being dominated.

Certainly no great leap of imagination is required to appreciate that these beliefs, operating together, might result in confusion about the meanings of sexual acts. It was to sort out how the effects of these beliefs that Shotland and Goodstein devised their experiment. In this, they constructed fictionalized accounts or "stories" of various dating situations.

These stories, depicting intimate sexual encounters, were read by 287 students in an undergraduate psychology course at a major U.S. public university. About equal numbers of men and women read the stories, and each story was selectively written for different randomly selected groups of students. Some read a version in which the male in the story became aggressive in spite of the verbal protest of his date. Other stories varied with respect to when and how much the woman protested. In each version, the story ended with the couple engaged in sexual intercourse. By arranging accounts of the sexual encounter in this fashion, the researchers were able to classify the depicted scene according to whether the male was forceful and how forceful he might have been.

Shotland and Goodstein also measured the students' perceptions of the roles of women in general. They classified students according to how egalitarian their attitudes were and according to how they judged the principals in the story. For the latter category, students were asked to judge the female's desire to have sex and the amount and kind of protest she gave to the male (from verbal to physical protest), and the male for the amount of force he used.

The authors' findings clearly demonstrate how cultural beliefs can influence judgments about whether a rape has occurred. They found, for example, that in the story where the woman protested late and was seen as desiring sex, a male's forceful sex act might still be seen as rape, but the female was more likely to be blamed for what happened to her. The man in the story was more likely to be seen as violent and the incident more likely to be seen as rape when he used more force and more and earlier protests were made by the woman. These differences generally held for both male and female students who judged the accounts.

This study leaves us with an interesting observation that helps inform us about the framing of violence and aggression in our society. Whether a female is seen as desiring sex and the judgments about the male's aggressive pursuit of sexual intercourse seem to be important considerations in making a decision whether the crime of acquaintance rape has occurred. We seem warranted in concluding that the cultural beliefs people have about female sexuality and male aggressiveness confound clarity about the meanings of intimate acts. As Shotland and Goodstein write: "We believe our results have important practical significance . . . (and) . . . it appears that people are reluctant to label these scenarios as rape, although they will admit that the male's behavior was wrong and the woman had a right to expect the male to cease his advances" (1983, 231).

Finally, the authors of this research concluded by calling for stronger and more flexible rape laws, ones that would better fit the actual situations under which a woman may be forced to engage in sex. But their project also underscores our point about violence in modern society. In spite of some very strong and widely shared feelings about the sex act and its meanings, the decisions people make about violent and aggressive acts are indeed highly complex and situational. This means many of us may well agree in general, for example, about how women who eventually "gave in" didn't really want to have sexual intercourse, yet we have a great deal of trouble agreeing about the specific meanings of particular acts; that is, was each of these cases an instance of acquaintance rape?

We can treat this problem as a matter of the organization of social experience. As Goffman showed us, the meanings we see in everyday life derive from presuppositions, states of mind, beliefs, values, and moods, both our own and those we surmise to be characteristic of the other person. But to impute a violent motive to another person is not only personally disquieting, it is objectively problematic. Since the meanings of social life are layered, laminated, and made to seem to be something they are not (Berger, 1979, refers to this aspect of social meanings as a "double floor," as in a magic act), it is no wonder we are somewhat troubled by our inability to achieve consensus about violent and aggressive actions.

By shifting our attention to how people make decisions, we can begin to understand the dimensions of the problem. Not only this, but we can also show how decisions made about the violent nature of acts are always couched in larger social contexts. Finally, we want to understand how much of the violence that occurs every day in our society is the result of incomplete understanding, mistakes, and unskillful actions.

How Violence Is Learned:
Ice Hockey, A Case of the Pros and the Kids

Early on a Sunday morning, cars begin to arrive at the ice arena. Eleven- and twelve-year-old boys begin to emerge from them. They carry bags stuffed with equipment and pairs of skates draped over long wooden sticks curved at one end. They are silent but friendly as they greet one another and head for the dressing room for final preparations. They put on padding and uniforms, skates and helmets, and "hit the ice" just as the Zamboni finishes cleaning it. The boys circle on the ice, warming up and taking "shots on goal."

A puck is dropped and the game begins; the action is fast and wild. At one point in the game the puck glides to a stop in a corner at one end of the ice. Two boys chase after it. They arrive at the same time, both lunging for the puck with their sticks. They collide with a violent impact. There is a groan from the crowd. One boy goes down but quickly recovers while the other controls the puck and, to the cheers of his teammates, parents, and friends, begins skating toward the opponent's goal.

Among sports fans and even throughout the general public ice hockey is well known as a violent game. The movie *Slap Shot* portrayed it as a cross between street brawling and sport. Perhaps the comedian Rodney Dangerfield expresses it best with his joke, "Yesterday I went to a fight and a hockey game broke out."

At the professional level hockey has dealt openly with the issue of violence. Lawsuits, brawls involving fans and players, and the exposés of journalists have focused public attention on hockey as the violent sport. Coaches, players, and owners are sensitive to questions about fighting, and deservedly they are seriously concerned with the image of the game.

In the past twenty years, programs in youth hockey have proliferated, especially in eastern and midwestern cities. Children, mostly boys but sometimes girls, as young as six years old are now playing organized hockey. Critics point to the violence of pro hockey and caution parents and organizers about the deleterious effects of the game on children, generally arguing about the "contribution" hockey makes to our already violent world. "Why add such an aspect of sanctioned experience to the images of fast cars and fighting that the children see on television?" they suggest. Defenders of hockey and of youth sports in general counter with claims about the teaching of character, the value of competition, and the power of sports to keep children, particularly energetic young boys, "out of trouble."

There seems to be validity to both claims. Young hockey players are not generally as deeply involved with drugs or identified as troublemakers as often as other students are (Vaz 1982). Still, most of these claims are made by parents and coaches, and there is little empirical evidence to suggest that involvement in sports does much more than extenuate already learned behaviors. That the environment in which children grow to maturity is laced with violent images cannot be doubted. But the crucial question here is the same encountered in our treatment of the effects of violence portrayed in the media, only now we are concerned about the actual experience of violence. A few years ago, a riot in which several students were injured occurred at the end of an important high school hockey game in eastern Massachusetts. The riot took place the night after the infamous Minnesota North Stars vs. Boston Bruins "brawl," a hockey game which set a record 406 minutes in penalties. The question we ask is inevitable: what is the impact of the violent models of professional hockey on young players?

Nash and Lerner (1981) attempted to assess the impact of professional hockey models on violence that occurs when youth play the game. They conducted their study by gathering two kinds of information. First they wanted to study how professionals, the models, think about fights and other violent aspects of their game; then they set out to learn how youthful players think about these same matters.

To answer the first set of concerns, Lerner observed professional hockey games over a one-month period. He was able to secure a press pass, which allowed him into team locker rooms after the games. While observing the games, he took detailed notes of the circumstances of the fights that inevitably occurred. He jotted down what was happening just before, during, and after the fights; then, after the game, while star players were being interviewed by media representatives, Lerner talked to the men who had been involved in them. He discovered that, by and large the players were willing to discuss what happened. More important, this approach provided a convenient entry to questions about fighting, a subject most players do not frankly discuss with press people. It can be noted that, generally, professional players are quite willing to discuss specific fights, even though they usually do not want to discuss the topic of fighting.

From this data base, the researchers sketched a pro version of the meanings of hockey violence:

1. Players do not regard hockey as a particularly violent game. They play with "force," using such terms as "aggressive," "playing with authority," "hot," or "a run on" to describe the particulars of play. In describing hockey they did not use the word "violent."

2. Players have well-developed conceptions of themselves and their fellow professionals regarding their dispositions to fight or play aggressively. According to their own testimony, there are essentially four types of players: enforcers, whose purpose it is to intimidate and fight; stickers, who use their sticks to intimidate, but who rarely fight; temperamental players, a category that applies to almost all players, indicating that under the "right" circumstances any hockey player will fight; and passive players, who avoid fights at all costs and rely on skill and speed to play the game.

3. Fighting is regarded as a "natural consequence" of a fast and forceful game where collisions are inevitable and clashes of intention are part of the organization of competition. Given this, players are not particularly bothered by the possibility of a "fight" during a game (Nash and Lerner 1981, 231–34).

It seems professional hockey players espouse a version of violence that presupposes a system of knowledge about the game. In short, they regard intimidation as a strategy of play, and this makes fighting unavoidable. Players know fans like to watch fights. Fights add excitement to the game; they punctuate its rhythm and focus attention on the game in a way that even a goal does not. A fight erupts, stops play, and requires the attention of all participants, both on the ice and in the boxes (players' benches). Still, most players consider fighting not to be a part of "good hockey," regarding those who fight habitually to be "bad" players.

Yet there is a resignation about fighting in hockey; though fights are "bad," they are necessary. They must not be eliminated, lest in the void left behind something even more violent, like the increased use of sticks to intimidate, would take their place. Therefore, though they must be controlled, fights themselves act as mechanisms of control and so must be allowed to continue as a part of the game.

From these data, it seems that fighting is for the most part controlled. As one player says, "Fighting is no real problem now, not like it was in the past. The referees pretty much control it now." So, rather than being eliminated fighting has been brought within boundaries through the ritualization of the fight, a ritualized fight being less a life- or body-threatening activity than it is an aggressive display, what Goffman would call a keying. This is not to say that fights are not real or emotions genuine. The hockey fight is not staged in the same sense as is a professional wrestling match. But it is governed by sets of well-understood norms: fighting is with fists, not sticks; fighting generally takes place without gloves, on the ice, in the presence of referees, and as a consequence of something that happened in the course of the game. Players are not vindictive; they do not go out looking for fights, and they don't "fight dirty."

In professional hockey, then, the expression of force to achieve an end is ritualized. Functionally, players' rituals appeal to fans, add excitement and an element of spontaneity to the game, and serve to release tensions that mount during a highly competitive, extremely physical activity.

The interpretation by professional hockey players of violence in general and fighting in particular is complex and can be only partially described here. Nevertheless, it should be clear that the interpretation of violence in professional hockey is built around paradoxical tenets regarding both the undesirability and the necessity of fighting. In the game the role of intimidation is legitimized, with the complex interpretation of violence allowing fine distinctions between "good" and "cheap" play. The ritual of the fight itself acts as an outlet for players' tensions and frustrations by allowing expressions of aggressive displays.

Turning now to the other side of this research, we quote from a father who was heavily involved in a youth hockey program in a northern state and related the following story. The story itself illustrates the particular and even bizarre ways young hockey players have of interpreting their participation in the game.

> After the last game of the regular season, during the thirty-minute ride home, I asked the three boys in my car what they had received penalties for. The first boy replied that he slashed at a boy who punched him. The second said that he had "held" to prevent a "breakaway." I turned to the third boy who had been involved in a fight and I asked him what his penalty was for. "It was for violence," he said.

As Nash and Lerner found through youth hockey observations and interviews comparable to those made with the pros, not only are young hockey players aware of issues of violence, but just as they do in all other aspects of the game, they use their understanding of the pros as a model for interpreting their own participation in fighting. Nevertheless, it is important to note that it is their version of what the pros do that serves them as a guideline. They see the slap shot as "pro," and the boy who can raise the puck in a straight, hard line "on net" enjoys others' esteem. In fact, coaches insist that games are won with the well-aimed, much softer and more deft wrist shot; and they criticize the boy who sets up for a slap. Still, during a game, whenever a player "fires a cannon" the coach and players alike react with approval.

The boys' version of "good" hockey contrasts with the pros'; but the effects of the pro model can be identified. These effects are indirect and are filtered through the vantage points of the youthful hockey player. Nash and Lerner suggest these effects can be appreciated by observing contrasts and similarities between the pro and the youth versions of the game.

First there is a contrast: the boys regard hockey as fun. It is the playing that matters, not the fact of winning or losing. Whenever a coach does not encourage the explicit goal of winning, the talk of the boys focuses on fair distribution of playing time or on requests for "extended ice time." To play and play a lot is the prime objective of the young players. The appeal of hockey is its action. A puck in the corner affords the opportunity to kick, flail, elbow, push, and collide with the other boys. Such legitimate situations are exceedingly rare in the everyday world of the middle-class preadolescent. As boys find themselves closely supervised at school and at home, as adults work systematically to control violence in virtually all aspects of life, there are precious few places where "boys can be boys." As long as a boy "makes an effort" for the puck, he can openly and in a supportive environment exhibit aggressive behavior. For the boy in youth hockey, this is legitimate fun on its grandest scale.

Second, boys do not believe they will be injured while playing or fighting in the game of hockey. Like their pro counterparts, kids, as well as their parents and coaches, espouse the belief that "no one really gets hurt." "Hockey is not like football," a father said, "there are no serious injuries."

Of course—and this is precisely the point—one can question what is a "serious injury." In virtually every game Nash and Lerner observed, at least one boy "went down on the ice"; this means he was injured sufficiently to stop the game. Apparently these "hits" do not count as injuries. In the language of hockey boys "shake it off," "rebound," or "skate it out." Very rarely will a boy down on the ice be out of the game. Instead, he gets his breath back and waits for the pain from a blow to the stomach or a stick to the neck to subside. Going down and rising to the applause of parents and other spectators is part of the game.

Third, the discipline required to play "hard or aggressively" is within the ability range of most boys. This means the rules that referees evoke, and the judgments coaches and parents must make about the appropriateness of "aggression" during the game, take into account the levels of skill and the motivations of the players. Only when sticks get too high, elbows too loose, or checks too late are penalties called. The line between a "great" check and the offense of "charging" is fine indeed, and the player adjudged overly aggressive will receive penalties. Hockey sanctions mistakes, and this aspect of hockey is well understood by the boys who play the game.

The code that players must abide by, as they interpret it, consists of six interrelated tenets:

1. Play hard.
2. Skate fast.
3. Do not complain about ice time or the position the coach wants you to play.
4. Control your emotions and express them appropriately through aggressive play.
5. Do not give "cheap" shots unless in retaliation.
6. Play hockey in kind: clean for clean, cheap for cheap.

In hockey, fighting and getting penalties are not necessarily "bad." Youthful players understand "good" and "bad" hockey by way of a two-dimensional interpretive process. The two dimensions, simplification and accentuation are often used simultaneously. From the broad perspective of social psychology, these processes have been identified as a part of the developmental stages through which our general thinking moves, regardless of the topic (cf. Furth 1980).

Simplification occurs whenever a boy pares down the complexities of adult models into interpretations he can remember. Boys think about hockey in relatively simple terms. The code they use is oriented toward the coach and becomes simple through repetition. In the simplified version the boy uses, mistakes can be made and interpretations of an act may be different from those a pro would make. For example, a boy may confuse "hustle" with "staying in position"—in an effort to please the coach, he may skate too fast and find himself in the wrong section of the rink.

Accentuation entails the purposeful exaggeration and emotive expression of certain themes in the meanings of hockey violence. A team member may come to think of being "ready for a hard check," contrasted with what is really more important, that is, being "in position," as the salient feature of the game. Accentuation seems to function in the management of identity, as in looking "tough" or being "big on the ice." This dimension is emotive and is articulated through personifying, which means establishing a presence on the team through making one's personality visible to others. An example of this would include the custom of "sticks in the air" after each goal a team makes; pros do this as well, but not with the zeal exhibited by the boys.

The game of hockey and a description of how children model their play after the pros tells us that modeling is never a direct imitative process. Boys interpret hockey in accordance with a preadolescent understanding (cf. Furth 1980). They simplify and accentuate themes of available adult models in terms of their own needs and social relationships. The pro model is the model for youth hockey; still, hockey becomes an opportunity for learning an aggressive display. By virtue of the organization of the game itself and through interaction with coaches, parents and, most important, their fellow players, the boys learn the meanings of situational violence, that there is a time, place, and form for aggression. The formal character of hockey equipment, travel, pre- and post-game rituals of handshaking, line changes, and other game procedures allow for the learning of the right time to be aggressive, and, by implication, of the wrong time. Fights and penalties, when they occur, help to define the "proper" channels of aggression by demonstrating to youthful participants the boundaries within which aggression is supposed to take place.

Studies such as this one of how boys learn to play aggressive hockey highlight an important point about aggression and violence in general. Situational meanings ascribed to an action are of primary social psychological importance. In the light of this, we now shift our attention back to more serious forms of violent acts and develop a view of their meaning that focuses on the socialization and institutionalization of violence.

The Violent Home

We have already suggested that violence and aggression are learned responses that vary greatly from one situation to another. We have seen how people involved in a violent situation can attribute different meanings to it, and we have reviewed how membership in groups and the place of groups in the larger society affect the attribution of an action as violent. Whereas society may actually encourage some types of violence (such as the ritual display of aggression in hockey and other sports), other, perhaps even less physically violent acts are regarded as serious and so are discouraged. Recently public attention has been directed to a particular kind of this behavior, family violence.

Perhaps the most important social psychological research done on violence in the home is the work of Gelles and his associates (Gelles 1974; see also Strauss 1973). These authors used interviews in conjunction with surveys to assess the extent and kind of violence existing in American homes. The most general conclusion drawn from these studies is that violence is a part of the organization of family life. Such a statement does not mean all parents are brutal and insensitive toward their children; instead, as Gelles suggests, there are many methods of violence (slapping, punching, hitting with a hard object) and there are different meanings attached to violent incidents by different family members. What is of primary importance here is how family members account for incidents or sequences of violent acts (Gelles 1974, 57). Some forms of violence are regarded as "normal"; that is, there are cases where the use of force to achieve some end is interpreted as routine, normative, and even necessary. Hence, almost one-fifth of all Americans approve of slapping one's spouse on appropriate occasions.

Gelles uncovered several forms of normal violence, finding that husband-wife violence was sometimes thought of, especially by wives, as somehow deserved. Wives would report that their husbands struck them because of their badgering or nagging. Another form Gelles refers to as "I tried to knock her to her senses," which apparently has to do with helping one's spouse control her emotions, to gain and maintain composure. Hence one husband reported that he slaps his wife on the arm to "help her get a hold of herself." This happens infrequently, he said, like when the children get hurt and his wife "loses control of herself."

Another common form of normal violence is embodied in the remarks of several parents in the study; they are summed up by the phrase "kids need to be hit." This belief seems to be quite widespread in American society. Some of us may know it as the adage "spare the rod and spoil the child." This belief amounts to an institutionalized use of force to achieve control over the behavior of children, with the most common expressions of this violence being slapping, pinching, jerking, and spanking.

Gelles shows how violence is built into the family system. But again, this does not mean all family violence is pathological. Borrowing a concept proposed by Strauss (1973, 115), Gelles refers to situations in which disputes over the proper use of violence create additional or secondary violence. A father might spank his young son. His wife in turn might criticize him for this approach to discipline and an argument ensues that ends in a fight between the parents.

Besides this so-called secondary violence, there is a type that Gelles calls volcanic violence. This occurs when

> the offender has reached the end of the line—has run out of patience as the result of externally caused stress such as losing a job, frustration at being unable to communicate with his spouse, or victim-induced frustration (where the victim badgers the offender until he can take no more). Volcanic violence is illegitimate violence that is explained as rising from the buildup of stress and frustration . . . the offender "erupts" into violence. (Gelles 1974, 174)

Other types of family violence include alcohol-related violence; protective-reactive violence (here one spouse strikes the other to stop an anticipated attack); one-way violence (usually a husband assaulting a passive wife); and sex-related violence (a variety that often accompanies jealousy).

Common themes of meaning for the persons involved run through these violent acts whether the violence is interpreted as legitimate or illegitimate and whether it is expressive (spontaneous and emotional) or instrumental (used to achieve an end). And within either the expressive or the instrumental meanings of violence is the questionwhether the violence was seen as victim precipitated.

Gelles interviewed members of eighty families. He sought out families with reputations for violence, traceable through their contacts with agencies established to help violent families and through records of police calls to their homes because of fights and other domestic problems. He found that the incidents of violence even among these "problem" families included a goodly number of legitimate uses of violence. In other words, many of them (pushing, slapping, etc.) did not differ substantially from what might be found in the "average" American family. Certainly these eighty families are not generally representative of American families, but the meanings that those most intimately involved in violence attribute to these actions help us understand the extent to which violence may be institutionalized as a part of family life. Studying these families and distinguishing between acts that "got them into trouble" and those that did not may help us recognize general rules used by society to draw the line between "ordinary" and "extraordinary" violence.

These families volunteered to tell their stories and were aware that their experiences were at least in part outside the norms governing the expression of force in families. If we can be confident that violence is a normatively governed, framed experience in families, and if we are correct in the importance of situational meanings for violence, then why do the members of some families go outside the boundaries, break the frame of the organization of aggression, and take part in excessive violence?

One conclusion we can draw is that out-of-frame, excessively violent acts are at least partly the result of people's different "levels of competency" at interaction. People who act in ways consistently improper might simply not know what they are doing, or, from another point of view, the competencies they have acquired might be unbalanced in favor of violent means of solving problems.

Gelles offers a comprehensive model of family violence that includes all these factors, stressing that an adequate explanation must account for both the situational and societal meanings of acts. He writes about societal factors (like position in society), the stress one experiences daily (like unemployment and financial problems), the self-identities of people, the actual structure of families, and the ways in which members of the family see themselves as belonging, or not belonging, to society. He also investigates the socialization of the members of families, whether they themselves were victims of violence as children, the vitality of the norms governing both expressive and instrumental uses of violence, and the specific norms and values of the community to which the family belongs. Finally, he studies the interpretations that actual experiences receive in routine life courses (situational factors). Gelles's conclusion is that all these factors interact to result in violence.

Gelles (1974, 188–90) summarizes his model in propositional form:

1. Violence is a response to a particular structural and situational stimulus.
2. Stress is differentially distributed in social structures.

3. Exposure to and experience with violence as a child teaches the child that violence is a response to structural and situational stimuli.

4. Individuals in different social positions are differentially exposed both to learning situations of violence as a child and to structural and situational stimuli for which violence is a response as an adult.

5. Individuals will use violence toward family members differently as a result of learning experience and structural causal factors that lead to violence.

Gelles teaches us that violence is both a part of normal life and an aberration. It becomes an aberration whenever its meanings no longer make sense to the people who are intimately involved in the situation or to others who notice it and call it into question.

Anger: One of the Seven Deadly Sins

Before the development of modern social science, the matters we are discussing in this chapter were often thought of as sins, weaknesses in moral character. Among the seven sins said to be "deadly" is anger. In anger, persons show their base nature. In the defense of their lost sense of self, they may act without the civil constraints which make social order possible.

In a fascinating book titled *The Seven Deadly Sins* (1989), Stanford Lyman reintroduces a way of thinking about aggression (anger and its manifestations) as sin. Although he does not wish to dismantle all the knowledge social scientists have amassed about the violent and base ways in which humans sometimes behave, he does want to recover a sense of freedom and responsibility for people who express themselves in anger. He notes that the way in which social theory commonly explains aggression and anger relieves humans of the responsibility of choosing between good and evil. The very terms "good" and "evil," he notes, have been pushed out of the vocabulary of social science. Whether we anchor aggression in the psychological nature of humans, tie it to the frustrations of living in a complex world of contradictory demands, or draw parallels between the animal world and the human, the effect of this reasoning is to shift the focus away from the individual.

Lyman, however, points to recent developments in theory that once again allow us to address the questions of freedom and choice. Even though structural and situational factors may be said to cause violence, there is still the issue of how much of the burden for anger must be laid at the feet of the violent individual. Lyman argues that the fundamental cause of anger is damage to or loss of self-esteem. He continues:

> Modern societies provide a remarkable number of institutional degradation ceremonies that unintentionally or by design deprive

individuals and groups of their sense of personal and moral worth as well. Sending people to social death while leaving them physically alive is a dangerous move, since, like Achilles, they might strike out in enraged fury. (Lyman 1989, 124)

To address the causes of anger, Lyman develops a meaning around the concept of territory. In modern society, he suggests, life seems to be a continual challenge to the sense people have of their territories, both public and private, and anger seems to be very much a matter of display. Its counterpart, aggression, follows the unsuccessful communication of the integrity of one's self and one's territory. Hence in the modern society figurative anger becomes a matter of drama.

Lyman is saying that complexity and increased problems in everyday life have transformed the arena of defense of territory and self. It is no longer the matter of a straightforward issue like the integrity of the home. From a nonmodern concept of stability within a literal context of territory, the weak character without a sense of worth indeed exists in a life of sin. But in modernity the whole matter of self-worth becomes figurative, a dramatic enactment. In order to survive socially today, one must learn to stake claims and defend them with symbols in interaction. With the increased difficulty of performances comes more and more risk of failure and subsequent loss of self-worth. The tasks to be learned are necessary before anger can be expressed mockingly, as by the professional wrestler, or so that rage can be called out for the purposes at hand, such as by the football player before the big game. When these complex learning tasks have been mastered, then

the mock anger of the professional wrestler that everybody who knows the game takes to be only pretense is a source of fun in a harmless and "fixed" encounter. The contrived anger of the businessman, who has rehearsed his part and knows just when and how to explode in rage, is recognized as a useful and sometimes effective tactic in ongoing commercial relationships. But the spontaneous uncontrolled rage of the truly angry person is often taken as a weakness, a defect in character, and, in the older parlance, a sin. (Lyman 1989, 134)

Lyman contends that in modern society it is no easy task to develop a sense of self-esteem. Great significance placed on the ability to "act" and the career performances of everyday life are given on a constantly changing stage. The irony of explaining aggression, violence, and anger in modern society is that the very society that fosters a sense of loss of freedom and responsibility and thereby creates conditions for the expression of anger and aggression also forces the truly angry person to carry the greatest burden, a sense of worthlessness.

The Most Angry of Us: The Underclass

Our description of anger, violence, and aggression has stressed how these phenomena vary with situation and structure. Now we address a related question: what happens to people in their dealings with others when they are locked into a particular location in society? To be sure, violent and criminal acts are committed by persons located throughout all social strata. In fact, the violence of the privileged classes makes for sensational tabloid news, successful television programs, and best-selling novels.

Nevertheless, we are becoming increasingly aware of the skewed distribution of violence in our society. As Gelles notes in his account of conjugal violence, it appears that most violence takes place among persons who occupy the lower rankings of society, and it has long been accepted that social class is clearly associated with violent crimes. Recently we have come to understand that this relationship is not a simple socioeconomic one, nor is it merely a result of temporary conditions under which some people must live before they are fully assimilated into American society.

In *The Underclass* (1982), a highly provocative work, Ken Auletta identifies what he calls the American underclass. This category of people is made up mostly of persons who are poor, ethnically and racially stereotyped, and outside the mainstream experiences of American society—some students find it surprising that there are ten-, eleven- and twelve-year-old children in our society who have never been to a movie theater, a fast-food restaurant, or a city park. Of course not all members of the underclass are violent; and Auletta is careful to show the diversity of the category. He suggests it consists of four types of people: the passive poor, the hostile street criminal, the hustler, and the traumatized (drunks, drifters, homeless "bag ladies," and released mental health patients).

Two of Auletta's points are pertinent to our treatment of the meanings of aggression. First, evidence is growing to indicate that members of the underclass are responsible for a large amount of the serious, out-of-frame violence—the kind that shocks and leaves the ordinary citizen with a strong sense of puzzlement. Auletta is referring to the senseless crimes that make headlines, like the apparently random beating and raping of elderly women or the child being thrown by its mother's jealous lover off the balcony of a fifth-story apartment.

Auletta cites evidence that indicates the magnitude of the problem. He writes about a study conducted in Philadelphia by Marvin Wolfgang that zeroed in on 1,862 mostly repeat offenders. Wolfgang found that this group constituted 54 percent of those persons considered delinquent in the city and committed 84 percent of Philadelphia's crimes. These chronic offenders included a subgroup of persons who had been arrested five or more times, a relatively small group that, it turns out, was responsible for 52 percent of all offenses and 83 percent of the city's serious crimes, ones listed on the FBI index.

Second, according to Auletta, not only do members of the underclass act violently, they also are becoming a permanent feature of the American social structure. If he is correct, the sketch he offers of the profiles of violence in America is much like that of the novelist Anthony Burgess whose *A Clockwork Orange* (1963) society fostered senseless violence.

Our approach to social psychology forces us to be careful with terms like "senseless." For while the acts we have been discussing appear senseless to most ordinary citizens, from the point of view of those who commit them they have a kind of meaning that does make sense. But actually that meaning is vastly out of frame with conventional realities. Auletta makes a unique contribution to our understanding of the "sinful" violence in society by showing us how to understand the roots of meanings so badly out of alignment with the majority of rules for making sense out of everyday life.

We can debate about what is really learned in youth hockey, or whether the violence on television is a significant factor in causing homicides, but we repeatedly end up with a single observation: what counts as a case of violence involves judgments about the meanings of aggressive acts. Many acts of aggression in everyday life carry institutionalized meaning, and the organization of society seems to reflect human efforts to cope with aggression, not to eliminate it. For the most part, the social control of aggression is accomplished through the teaching of interactional competencies, ways of display, and alternative techniques to reach ends.

As society has become vastly complex, a variety of competencies has developed that people can acquire. Most of these are adaptive, that is, they help people deal with the practical problems of everyday life. For some people, however, the very skills that help them survive within their particular social worlds lead to serious trouble whenever they contact larger, more encompassing social worlds. Hence, although most people are socially competent, the senses in which a person may be "competent" are relative to situations of social life. When we compare the relative competencies people possess, some members of society are in very real ways deficient in socially accepted skills. At first the term "deficiency" was used timidly, but now Auletta uses it with confidence to describe the interactional skills of the members of the underclass. The basic lessons of life in mainstream society, which include the framing of aggressive acts, the keying of anger, and above all the mastery of situational propriety, lie outside the repertoire of members of the underclass. This is not meant here as a criticism; it merely points to a reality of social life. In fact, there are situations in which survival in the underclass depends on the performance of acts totally unacceptable in mainstream society. For example, homeless people may have to urinate in public or gang members establish their status through "packing," carrying a weapon.

The violence underclass citizens manifest does not mean they have no interactional competencies. What it does mean is that their skills for building social relationships serve them as poorly outside as they serve them well within their own social situation. As we have suggested, street survival skills do not transform well into adaptive competencies in the larger society.

Unless one has experienced it, it is difficult to imagine the anger at the loss of self-esteem that comes from realizing that "playing the dozens" well does not mean much to a prospective employer or from learning that the comfort that comes with retreating from a problem home environment into the security of membership in a street culture is of no practical value at school. Both male and female members of the underclass live with constant institutionalized reminders of their lack of worth in the eyes of the larger society. Life at the bottom teaches otherwise useless skills and inappropriate attitudes as necessary for survival in the immediate realities of everyday life. To get through the day in the underclass with or without money one must assume identities at odds with the values and attitudes used more generally to build the social worlds of everyday life. It is this dangerous move of sending people to a social death while leaving them alive that Lyman wrote of as a prescription for anger.

In his highly acclaimed *The Truly Disadvantaged* (1987), William J. Wilson emphasizes that the composition of the underclass cannot be fully appreciated apart from race relations. He further suggests that to speak of the underclass in America without examining the role of race does a disservice both to scholarship and to a thorough understanding of racism. There is little doubt, for instance, that African Americans are disproportionately implicated in violent crimes. They constitute 13 percent of the population in cities, yet they account for over half of all city arrests for violent crimes (Wilson 1987, 22).

To stop here might imply that race alone accounts for the propensity to violence observed among members of the underclass. But such a conclusion misses the social meanings of being disadvantaged and black. As Wilson carefully notes, the history of the residual effects of America's race policies and practices, along with changes and dislocations that have taken place in the inner city since the 1970s have created conditions for the learning of violence among the black underclass.

Specifically, the ways urban blacks have been forced to live, including the conditions of life in high-density housing projects, waves of migrations to cities, changes in the nature and types of employment available in the inner city, and pressures on traditional family structure have promoted the practice of violence as part of everyday life for at least some people of the city. These factors together with historical and contemporary discrimination have created the ghetto underclass. Furthermore, as Wilson suggests, policies designed to help the inner city underclass often do not because they are designed to help "the more advantaged groups of all races and class backgrounds" (Wilson 1987, 155); that is, they are not customized to meet the needs of the most disadvantaged. Programs such as the Job Corps therefore are useful only to those best prepared to manage the tasks necessary to profit from the training. Young people with the greatest needs often do not avail themselves of these programs, or they fail in them. With regard to understanding the spiral of violence among the underclass, this means young people find themselves more and more left to their own interpretations of social life, with a view of the world they inhabit that reflects their frustrations and anger.

When we look more closely at the dynamics of the conditions of violence, it appears that the young of society are responsible for most violent crime (James Wilson 1975); and while there are exceptions to this rule, and blacks' involvement in crime is disproportionate to their relative numbers, most violent crimes such as rape, murder, and assault, are committed by young people. It follows that if a population of an area of a city is dominated by young people, we would expect that the crimes young people commit will be likewise overrepresented in that area. This is generally true, but the "increase in the murder rate during the 1960s was more than ten times greater than what one would have expected from the changing age structure of the population alone" and "only 13.4 percent of the increase in arrests for robbery between 1950 and 1965 could be accounted for by the increase in the numbers of persons between the ages of ten and twenty-four" (James Wilson 1975, 17, 18).

So other factors must be sought to understand the concentration of violence in the underclass. We already have described the conditions of being disadvantaged that have developed in the inner city. These coupled with the development of angry interpretations of the meanings of everyday life result in a volatile situation. Young people learn and practice interactional skills, and the behavior of young male blacks on the street often entails verbal, gestural, and even the physical framing of aggression. What is significant about this is not its uniqueness among African Americans. A visit to any high school boys' locker room will convince the skeptic that insults, put downs and roughhousing seem to be "normal" practices.

Nevertheless, for the African American young man in the inner city there may be a difference. First, young people are relatively numerous and concentrated there. And second, they have concluded from their practical experiences that the liberal policies of lawmakers (school desegregation, for instance) do not serve their interests. Among themselves and according to their interpretations and the skills required for their lives, violence becomes a way of life.

Consider not so much the presence of guns in the inner city but the meanings of having a gun. The mythical ideal of gun ownership, perhaps a truth for an early period of our society, is that a father introduces his son to the responsibility of owning a gun. A young man's first gun, for both whites and blacks, once marked his development as a man. He learned the care and maintenance of a weapon in the context of some sporting activity. The American right to bear arms had a social context that assumed a certain institutional stability, particularly in the family.

But now the conditions of life in the underclass are quite different, and the ownership of a gun takes on meaning within that context. Fathers do not give their sons guns. Guns are procured within youth-dominated social circles and definitions of the proper use of guns are lost or are replaced with meanings of personal control and power in everyday life. We know that guns are not only available in the inner city but that their procurement is part of the social order of being "bad" and generally able to "make it on the streets." This means increasingly guns are in the hands of younger and more angry people who have fewer and fewer institutional guidelines for defining their use. There is little wonder, then, that we now see very young people committing acts of violence with guns. Perhaps this is the interactional dynamic that is at the base of James Wilson's hypothesis that there may be a "critical mass" of young people in a community that, when reached or increased, suddenly and substantially sets off "a self-sustaining chain reaction [that] creates an explosive increase in the amount of crime, addiction and welfare dependency" (1975, 19).

Summary

In this chapter we have discussed aggression and violence as topics of research for social psychology. We discovered that aggression is a ubiquitous feature of everyday life. In some cases, aggression seems to be supported by society. Some very powerful influences on the lives of people in modern society foster aggression and even violence. Sport represents one of these influences, media violence another.

In order to understand the ubiquitous and problematic character of aggression, we stressed the description of the attribution of meanings to acts. There are legitimate and illegitimate instances of aggression and violence in society, and the process of assigning a meaning to an act is complicated. People work with cultural belief systems, but they often modify these to fit their location in society. Furthermore, they learn to frame action so that the impressions given off by an action can be controlled, to a degree, through processes of keying or "playing" with the organization of the experiences of aggression.

Families may be the schools of violence, and the intensity and problematic character of family violence is specific to the interactional patterns that develop within families. Since families may be relatively isolated in American society (there is little direct supervision of what goes on in the home), these patterns can become quite esoteric. Still, studies of violence in sports and in the home show the organized nature of most violence and aggression.

This chapter concluded by following Lyman's version of the cause of violence, the loss of self-esteem. A society that systematically promotes such feelings among a selected grouping of its members (the underclass) may well be creating the very problems it seeks to control. The history of discrimination in America along with the life conditions of the inner city have resulted in a particularly violent segment of society, namely inner-city youth. Skilled interaction is a hallmark of human existence; however, the skills acquired and the ends to which these skills are applied vary with the location people have in society.

Most important, we have tried to demonstrate how the increased complexity of organized social experiences brings about multiple meanings open to varied interpretations. In the final analysis, the successful management of violence and aggression becomes a matter of socialization.

Exercises in the Meaning of Violence

1. Visit a professional wrestling match. It is best actually to attend one of these performances, but if you are pressed for money you can always tune in "All Star Wrestling" on television. Describe what happens and record your reactions to the show. Can you identify frames, keys, or other ways in which the violence of the wrestlers was staged?

2. Work in groups of four for this exercise, and have each person make up three fictional cases of "child abuse." Make the cases so they can be ranked from "obviously" abusive to only mildly so. After each of you has three cases prepared, read your examples to each other. See if you all agree on the ranking of the severity of the cases. What particular acts do all of you agree are abusive? Which acts provoke the most disagreement?

3. Draw a map of your campus and show which areas of it "make you anxious" when you have to walk there. Show areas where you feel safe. You might also think of the campus as composed of areas that are warm and friendly or cold and threatening. Share these maps in a group and see if there are differences in how each of you drew your maps. Be sensitive to male/female differences in the sense of danger, and see if you can identify territories of potential violence.

Suggested Readings

A growing body of literature links gender-specific socialization with violence. The argument presented is that males, responsible for most violence in society, learn to normalize violence through sports and other interpersonal experiences with each other. This means they take-for-granted threats and even the use of physical force as routine devices for constructing the meanings of everyday life. Feminist critiques of male socialization outline how these versions of masculinity often result in violence against women. An excellent introduction to this interpretation of aggression and violence is Michael Messner and Don Sabo's collection of essays in *Sport, Men and the Gender Order: Critical Feminist Perspectives* (Champaign, Ill.: Human Kinetics, 1990).

Rap music contains sometimes graphic images of violence, but so too does country music. While these two types of music are quite distinct as styles and in terms of the audiences to which they appeal, Edward Armstrong, in "The Rhetoric of Violence in Rap and Country Music," *Sociological Inquiry* 63 (1993):64–83, shows the similarities in what he calls the "rhetoric of violence" in rap and country music. The general popularity of both musical forms suggests that issues of violence and aggression are quite important for the meanings of everyday life.

Chapter 10

Life in Public Places

The problem of establishing grounds of trust sufficient to permit minimal social order during short periods of interaction is nowhere more readily observable than in what social psychologists call public behavior. Relations in public are a special case of collective behavior; and although they are not strictly outside the institutional meanings for social life, they are also not completely spontaneous or emergent. We all learn how to navigate city streets, avoid traffic, cross roadways, and recognize danger. Of course the special problems of public relations derive from the short-term nature of interaction between strangers, interaction intended to serve limited functions but that nevertheless exposes its actors to public scrutiny.

Ever since the work of Goffman (1971) began to call attention to it, public life has been recognized as a legitimate subject of social psychological analysis. In fact, Goffman demonstrated how the very foundations of social order in modern, urban social life are revealed in encounters between strangers in public places. As the scope and influence of private life diminishes, public life becomes the arena of importance in matters of social control. Since we all depend on overt appearances in order to know each other's intentions and motivations, we must also rely on our ability to learn a great deal about how people interact just by observing what they do in public. In the light of this, Goffman stresses the importance of describing in detail how appearances are organized and how the accomplishment and management of its organization takes place. In short, any comprehensive understanding of the relationship between society and self must include an understanding of public life.

Drawing on an approach developed earlier, we can begin with the observation that matters of organization can be discussed by using the concept of form. When we discussed group forms, we learned how a set of mutual activities among people results in a relatively coherent set of rules for their conduct. For example, Irwin described the rules for proper dress and behavior among surfers. Homans referred to these shared rules as *norms*. And although norms derive from the stable places where an activity happens, once they have been formed and people learn to practice them, there is a sense in which they travel. As we move about in the territories of everyday life, we bring along with us the norms and rules we regard as appropriate. These rules function to define both the places where the rules apply and the activities which can appropriately occur in them.

Senses of place and the ways in which people attempt to use places are subsumed under the concept of *territoriality*. Lyman and Scott suggest that territory in its social sense can assume several forms. Public, home, interactional, and body—each of these territories is significant to an understanding of how people define and accomplish senses of place either in the presence of strangers or in locations that have varying degrees of freedom.

Public territories are "those areas where individuals have freedom of access, but not necessarily of action" (Lyman and Scott 1970, 91)—a public library is a good example. In these areas, there is general agreement among those who enter that the laws of society apply. Hence, in a public territory one expects to be observed, and one recognizes that there may well be people present who have a legitimate claim to enforce the rules. Also in these territories, perhaps only at specified times, certain categories of persons are accorded limited access and restricted activity. As Lyman and Scott point out, children are not expected to play in the park after midnight.

Contrasted with public territory is home territory, a place of intimate, private life, and there can be a wide range of variation in the usage of such private space. Persons are generally at liberty to arrange this space as they see fit, and they have a sense of freedom and autonomy in it. In some localities some sexual acts, even between husbands and wives, are illegal. Nevertheless, couples engage in them in their home territories without any fear of reprisal.

Other territories are mobile and not associated with physical surroundings but are based on the form and content of the social life that takes place within them. These are called interactional territories, areas where "social gathering may occur." Of course they have implied boundaries, but their boundaries are much more fragile than those of either home or public territories.

Finally, there is the space of and around the body. Goffman has been particularly explicit about the shape and functions of body space. He writes that such space varies across different human cultures. The body may become a vehicle, it may be enclosed within a sheathe, occupy a stall, or be composed of parts that vary in terms of their accessibility to others. For instance, in a crowded elevator we may touch elbows but not stomachs. Sometimes the distance people like to keep between themselves and other people during face-to-face conversations is referred to as *vital space*. This space varies from person to person, as well as from culture to culture, and what some people might feel comfortable with others would think of as "in my face" or "too close for comfort."

Ultimately, questions of the meanings of social life in public become ones of describing how people understand place and space and how they negotiate appropriate uses of them (Oldenberg 1989). People accomplish the locations of social life in terms of all four types of territories; in public, however, there is a tension between the way people have habitually come to think of their power to define territory and the fixity of public places with their markers. Public places are organized into larger or smaller zones that explicitly inform us of appropriate uses (the thirty-minute parking zone is one example), and they are often so thoroughly organized that each portion of the territory has a predefined use. In contrast, by virtue of "normal" socialization, people have a sense of home and privacy. In the public domain, this sense of territory is frequently and easily restricted, intruded on, or violated.

Home in Public Places

> Every night a world was created, complete with furniture, friends made and enemies established. . . . At first the families were timid in the building and tumbling of worlds, but gradually the techniques of building worlds became their technique. Then the leaders emerged, then laws were made, the codes came into being. And as the worlds moved westward, they were more complete and better furnished, for their builders were more experienced in building them. (Steinbeck, *The Grapes of Wrath*)

The sense of home is so well entrenched in our commonsense understanding of the meanings of social life that home and family are often thought of together. Families defend their home territories by enclosing them, erecting fences, and sometimes installing elaborate security systems. But what happens to "home," how is it defined and defended, when the family moves about? As Steinbeck suggests, families migrating from the Dust Bowl states in the 1930s learned to take their homes with them both physically and conceptually.

A kind of migration that gives us information about the definition and defense of temporary territory takes place today during vacations. Every summer, millions of families take camping trips. They prepare themselves to move from site to site, establishing and reestablishing a "home" at each site. Of course modern campers are not poverty stricken and eventually return to their "real" homes; but campers share a common problem, the solution to which gives us some basic insights into how humans define and defend home territory within public domains.

The Marking of Home

The sight of a recreational vehicle, a car towing a trailer, a camper bus or a pickup truck outfitted with a houselike enclosure has become a familiar part of the American landscape. All this equipment has one purpose: camping out. Certainly the phrase "camping out" can mean many kinds of activities, from jockeying for a parking place on a level plot of paved real estate with running water and electrical hookups to backpacking miles into the wilderness. Whether in tent or Winnebago, camping out requires solutions to two interrelated problems: how to transform a public place into home territory and how success-fully to communicate this transformation to others.

The principal device through which any public territory is defined and defended as a home is the "marker" (Goffman 1971, 41–44). A marker is an object that communicates territorial boundary. For campers, a marker may consist of odds and ends, like ropes, tires, or pieces of camping equipment, but the effectiveness of the messages that markers send depend on how the people who set them out use conventional knowledge and commonsense about the meanings of "home."

Nash (1982) once conducted a study to observe marking phenomena when he camped out in five western states in national and state forests over two summers, limiting himself to areas officially designated for camping—with facilities such as toilets and sometimes electricity. He gathered observations by walking or driving through the campgrounds, noting cases in which people temporarily left their sites, and on occasion interviewing them about the ways they saved (marked) their places.

Obviously, when a recreational vehicle fills a numbered site where white boundary posts stake out the corners of the lot, there is little trouble in getting the message across that the site is taken. And with tents or trailers left in place, the campers are free to drive around, since the camping equipment automatically marks the site. But the more completely outfitted the "rig," the more self-contained the vehicle used for overnight sleeping, the more difficult becomes the problem of marking the site when temporarily vacating it. When a family driving a camper leaves their campsite to fish a local lake or simply to see the countryside, they take their home with them. Therefore, if they intend to return to the site for the night they must make a conscious effort to mark it.

Types of Markers

Seemingly any object can serve as a marker. A list of such items actually used includes children's toys, a spare tire, sack signs, garbage bags and cans, empty and full six-packs of beer, and a set of longhorns from a steer (used by a couple from Texas to save a spot). But a simple listing of objects does not reveal how these items function as markers; instead, the common meanings they possess must be discovered. For instance, a spare tire (complete with rim) left behind in the middle of the parking space for a site relates a strong message: "We're comin' back!" Whereas a garbage bag and an empty six-pack left in the middle of the site's parking space function as weak markers, seeming to say, "We may have found another place; if you need it, you might get away with taking this one."

The messages markers can convey derive from the relationship between the items themselves and the generally understood knowledge of camping. Any item can serve as a marker if it can enter into an interpretable relationship with features of camper knowledge. The first task to understanding the message, therefore, is to describe the "camper's knowledge" of sites and their features.

Nash describes seven components of meaning which function as the background for marker messages; Table 10.1 presents the components and their dimensions. The first component, scarcity, refers to the perceived difficulty in getting a site, which itself depends on two interrelated situations: whether the sites are managed by attendants who issue sites to campers and whether there is crowding. The second component has to do with the spatial requirements of equipment, and the third with the physical layout of the sites themselves—whether their boundaries are predefined and what their location is relative to other sites. Fourth, what is the camper's commitment to the site or the perceived risk of loss in leaving behind an item; in other words, how worthwhile is the item used as a marker and can it be easily stolen? Included here is a judgment about the personal or impersonal nature of the item: a shovel might be seen as impersonal and a sleeping bag as personal. The fifth component refers to whether a written message, either a sentence like "this site is taken" or a single word, like "taken," is used. (One camper used a paper plate and wrote "taken" on it in four languages.) Number six connotes the identity of the campers: are they a family, a group, a couple or a single? Finally, component seven is the time of day, as that perception relates to access and availability of sites. For example, "early" means before most people try to get a site, and "late," after most have already tried and campgrounds are filling up. Of course this judgment varies greatly from ground to ground; while late can be 7:00 A.M. at a popular location, for some isolated, no-fee areas, one can never be late.

Nash also distinguished five categories of markers: (1) written markers, such as paper platters, sack signs, or ticket displays; (2) equipment markers, such as tents or trailers or smaller items like campstools, stoves, or ice boxes; (3) unit markers, such as children's toys or insignia; (4) personal markers, for instance, clothes on line, food, toilet paper rolls nailed to a tree; and (5) blockages fashioned from rope, tires or trash cans.

Rules of Marker Discourse, or How to Read a Spare Tire

A marker is interpreted by people looking at a campsite in relation to what they know about the various possible combinations of components. An object strategically displayed on a site becomes a message when it is read as such, when the person who placed the marker and the person reading it establish an intersubjective sense regarding the intended message. "This site is taken"; "this site is taken, but you might be able to get it"; "this site is definitely taken"; "No Trespassing!"—obviously, the test of the effectiveness of these messages lies in their practical consequences—whether the message results in the original "taker" finding the site as it was left.

Table 10.1 Components of Meanings for Site Markers

1. Scarcity
    1.1 controlled access
    1.2 open access/little crowding
    1.3 open access/high crowding

2. Equipment Space
    2.1 recreational vehicle (RV)
    2.2 van (Campmobile)
    2.3 pickup camper
    2.4 trailer
    2.5 tent
    2.6 van/tent
    2.7 trailer/tent
    2.8 RV/tent
    2.9 pickup/tent

3. Site
    3.1 isolated/defined
    3.2 with view/defined
    3.3 woodsy/defined
    3.4 level/defined
    3.5 isolated/undefined
    3.6 view/undefined
    3.7 woodsy/undefined
    3.8 level/undefined

4. Commitment
    4.1 strong/impersonal
    4.2 weak/impersonal
    4.3 strong/personal
    4.4 weak/personal

5. Written Form
    5.1 yes
    5.2 no

6. Unit Identity
    6.1 single
    6.2 group
    6.3 couple
    6.4 family

7. Time of Day
    7.1 early
    7.2 late

To see how markers function, we need to look at examples; for instance, the spare tire left in the middle of a parking space for a site is more than a blockage. The tire goes with a vehicle; it is out of place in the space. Since this particular item can be interpreted as an important part of the vehicle (no camper would travel far without a spare) and since special effort was required to remove the tire (oversized spare tires in camper vehicles are often placed in hard-to-access places, like inside a cabinet or under the chassis), such a marker is strong.

Interpretations of the meanings of markers vary according to three rules or conditions. The first is a scarcity condition: the more scarce the sites, the stronger the marker must be to function effectively. The second is the rule of equipment:

different equipment requires different kinds and amounts of space for its use. The third is the rule of commitment: the more risk a sender is willing to take in the display of a marker, the stronger the marker. Obviously an item may be strong under one condition and weak under another.

Early in the day, at a grounds that has open access and little crowding, virtually any item functions as a strong marker if it is for a site that is isolated and defined. For example, an empty six-pack on a table may be sufficient to mark such a site. But late in the day, in an area of controlled access, a family may have to leave a tent and a blockage of bicycles and toys to protect a site with a view but undefined boundaries.

Condition 1: Scarcity

If the scarcity condition is perceived as pertinent, the camper will construct markers carefully. When sites are scarce, competition for them is keen and one camper can count on another being ready to take a site if there is any inkling that it might be vacant. Hence each marker must be selected to form a configuration of the components appropriate to the condition. A child's toy, for example, may function under this condition as either a strong or a weak marker. It would be a strong message sentence if it were used in a controlled-access site (Table 10.1, 1.1) that was isolated and defined (3.1). It would show a weak but personal commitment to the site (4.4) communicated in an unwritten form (5.2) connoting a family unit identity (6.4) early in the day (7.1).

Two components function to give this use of a toy strength as a message. First, the message was left in a controlled-access grounds in which sites have been assigned, and although there may be problems in knowing how long a person, group, or family intends to camp there, at least if they are on the site, they are assumed to have priority. If it is early, the receiver reads the message with no sense of urgency; there is still time for the sender to decide to stay another night. In this circumstance, all that is necessary to mark is an item that displays occupancy: the family is in a van and they have driven off. The toy shows that they will be back. Hence the site is taken.

The same marker, still under condition 1, becomes weak late in the day (7.2) or in the case of more free competition for sites (1.3)—in such cases, seekers are more likely to jump to the conclusion that whoever left the toy probably forgot it when they "pulled up stakes" and therefore aren't coming back.

Condition 2: Equipment

Equipment defines it own environmental requirements. A large RV must have a level site, and a trailer requires a long one. So when campers vacate a site, but leave behind equipment large and complicated enough, it functions as a strong marker regardless of other conditions. This is, of course, the advantage of a tent or trailer over a van or RV. An equipment marker is like a zero-sum game. When present on the site, an RV is overbearing; when gone, no traces remain to serve as markers. Hence, RV owners develop markers to use under conditions 1 and 3. A typical equipment marker would be this: a tent (2.5) left pitched on an open access-site with little crowding (1.2) with isolated and defined boundaries (3.1). The tent connotes a strong and impersonal commitment to the site (4.1) in unwritten form (5.2) for at least a group of people (6.2) late in the camping day (7.2).

A tent is expensive and it is difficult to "pitch and break down." Since it is assumed by campers that all other campers know this about tents, the tent can function as a strong marker. Smaller equipment or less expensive pieces must be used together with markers that operate under conditions 1 and 3. A campstool, for instance, could have been forgotten, does not require much effort to move, and thus carries low potential as an equipment marker.

Condition 3: Commitment

Under this condition, a marker demonstrates a camper's strong commitment to the site. The site might have sentimental importance to a family. It may afford a picturesque view, be the place where they always camp, or simply be "the place we want!" Commitment markers require that a sender display risk, that he or she purposefully become vulnerable to intrusion. This is accomplished by the display of an expensive-looking yet light and uncomplicated movable item.

A shiny, new fluorescent camplight placed on the cement table of a site would function as a strong marker, even under background features that would render a less expensive piece of equipment weak. Since this item is easily stolen, it conveys a strong commitment to the site. Lights, however, are not very personal. Bedrolls are, and so are pieces of clothing, such as underwear or bathing suits hanging on a rope tied between two trees. Although not expensive and not as vulnerable to theft, such items are regarded as highly personal and therefore function as strong personal markers. Thus we see that risk can be both personal and impersonal. To lose an icebox sets back the camper's budget, but to lose one's favorite sweatshirt is an affront. The strength of the marker is in proportion to the risk.

Conditions 1, 2, and 3 work together, but any given marker gets its meaning from the dominance of one or the other of the conditions. Scarcity demands the use of equipment and personal markers of high commitment value, and equipment markers may be personal or impersonal. We say that a marker is successful whenever it effectively conveys the intended meaning of the person who left it; in other words, whenever it is honored.

Unsuccessful Markers

There are three kinds of unsuccessful markers: (1) false markers, (2) weak markers, and (3) markers that result in misunderstanding and/or conflict.

False Markers

False markers are items taken to be markers but not intended as such; they are merely left behind, inadvertently forgotten, or perhaps discarded, but in any event they are wrongly perceived by site seekers. A site cluttered with garbage can be mistaken as a marked site, or a piece of forgotten equipment may preserve a site for days before someone decides the item is not a marker. Generally, false markers are honored as "true" ones under conditions of low scarcity. When high scarcity requires careful marking, an item not obviously displayed will rarely be recognized as a marker. For example, a campstool by a tree near the back of the campsite will not be regarded as a marker under such conditions. In one case at a little-frequented area, however, a child's forgotten toy kept four site-searching families off a site for a full day. At the other extreme, in a very popular campground campers have been known to ignore the presence of a small tent and set up camp around that piece of equipment.

The Problem of the Weak Marker

Often a camper will intentionally leave behind a weak marker. Since campers are itinerant, the certainty of the next night's site is often in doubt. Thus they may hedge on the competition by leaving a weak marker at last night's site, while looking for a better one elsewhere in the campground or even farther down the road. An expendable item may be worth the risk of loss; so if after arriving at a new campground they find too much competition for sites, the campers can return to the weakly marked site in the hope that the marker reserved their place. Using a weak marker allows the camper to think of this practice as "fair." After all, if sites become scarce everybody knows a weak marker will be insufficient to hold a site. But if it works, the rationale is that there were plenty of places to go around anyhow. Because this kind of understanding prevails about the meanings of a weak marker, open conflict over a site rarely surfaces when a marker has been violated. The sender assumes the attitude, "Well, I knew I was taking a chance, but it was worth the try."

In leaving items as contingency markers, the sender has to come to grips with such burning questions as "how many miles is a skillet worth?" It depends on the skillet, of course. Grandma's old skillet, the one she used for those Sunday morning breakfasts on the farm, might be worth hundreds of miles of "backtracking." The $2 skillet from the Coast-to-Coast store in Kearney, Nebraska, does not warrant a ten-mile setback in the day's travel. Since idiosyncratic values cannot be easily conveyed (to the camper who doesn't own it, one old skillet looks like any other) cheap items are used as weak markers. One might fight over Grandma's skillet, but the loss of the $2 item simply does not matter that much.

Conflict and Misunderstanding

Flagrant intrusions on marked sites are rare among campers, but they do occur on occasion, especially under conditions of high scarcity late in the day. Sometimes novice campers or picnickers will disregard markers. This can be a matter of ignorance, or it can show a lack of consideration or even defiance. For instance, a family in an RV goes into town to wash clothes and buy groceries. They mark their site with a tent. On returning, they find an elderly couple eating at the table on the site, their car backed into the parking space with the trunk lid up. The couple looks puzzled when they see the family peering out of their RV. The father at the wheel leans out the window and shouts, "There must be some mistake here—this is our place!" Without a word, the couple pack their food, put it into the trunk, close the lid, and drive off, with a slight nod from the old man. The RV pulls into the site and the family recaptures its "home."

Or, a family drives their Volkswagen camper-bus into town for the afternoon. They are in a controlled-access area where they have paid for two nights and still have one to go. To mark the site they leave on the table a small cheap backpacker's tent and some cooking equipment, including a stove. On returning, they find an RV in their parking space. No one is around; the tent and other items are still in place. The eight-year-old son cries, "Someone took our place."

The mother of the family is cooler and more composed than the father, who keeps muttering something about "knocking blocks off"; she proposes a discussion with the people who must be in the RV. Cooling, the irate father insists on avoiding a confrontation and wants to begin looking for another site. "It's not worth a fight—even if it does have the best view of the mountains." Finally the mother wins. She approaches the RV with caution, gently knocking on the door. Another mother appears:

> *Mother 1:* You have our site.
> *Mother 2:* But it looked abandoned . . . and the attendant just gave us this number.
> *Mother 1:* Wait, here's the ticket, we paid for this for tonight—didn't you see our things?
> *Mother 2:* We're tired—my husband's asleep.

Mother 1: Well, what'll we do?
Mother 2: Go talk to the attendant.
Mother 1: OK, we'll be back. Get ready to move.

Leaving their markers in place, the first family returns to the attendant's booth far down the road. There they produce the receipt and explain the situation.

Attendant: Well, we had a new girl here helping out yesterday. Looks like she forgot to write you down for a second night. It's OK. We have a vacancy, site Thirteen.
Father: The sign says full.
Attendant: Well, we keep a few sites available to handle situations like this. You decide with the other family who gets Thirteen.

Back at the site the mothers resolve the problem—first come, first choice. After all, the site was marked. So the markers function again, the second family moves to site 13.

This conflict demonstrates three facts: (1) scarcity at this ground had resulted in formalized site distribution; (2) markers are still necessary to ward off picnickers and others who might "run the gate" to find an overlooked or extra site; and (3) conflicts and misunderstandings are anticipated by officials who in turn rely on the informal marking system to aid in the mediation of conflict. Precisely because of situations like the one described, campers may be turned away as being "too late," even though in reality some sites remain vacant. The safety valve function of the extra site is apparently worth it to deal with disgruntled would-be campers, and its successful application involves use of the marking system itself.

In the above case the markers were varied and strong, but scarcity of sites overrode their communicative power. When the condition of extreme scarcity was lifted,however, the markers functioned normally. They warranted caution by the second family—who made no effort to move the things, for instance—and they were communicating even during the intrusion, finally helping to settle the question of who would have to move.

Studies of such mundane practices as the marking of campsites reveal how people establish territory in public places. Probably studies could also be done of similar kinds of markings, for example, of students marking places at desks or tables in classrooms, libraries, or cafeterias, or "regulars" at coffee shops and bars marking their spots. Such work can show how humans use available items in association with general and widely distributed knowledge to claim space temporarily. With campsite markers, the general knowledge system has to do with home and family, where privacy and sanctity are seen as rights and where familylike activities may take place. To violate a marker and trespass onto the campers' site is like entering their house without an invitation; even in the absence of walls, a roof, and foundation, the failure of the family to be present physically does not mean the abandonment of the home.

Interactional Territories in Public

Although generally the use of public space is fixed, there is still a considerable amount of freedom within the boundaries of interactional territories and for individual variations in the meanings of usage. Goffman, Scott, Lyman, and others who have led the way in the analysis of relations in public show that a dynamic exists between the official intentions for the use of space and actual uses of it. The accomplishment of the usage of territory varies not only with the physical aspects of urban settings but also with intentions and the competency of people who occupy the space.

Two studies graphically illustrate how the quality of interactional territory varies even in highly urbanized and presumably fixed public space. First, we cite Melbin's (1987), work which ingeniously demonstrates the extent to which a frontier spirit characterizes public night life in the city, and then Nash's (1981), which shows how people's interpretations of weather translate into novel and fresh methods of interacting in an urban environment. We discuss each of these in turn.

Night as Frontier

In a fascinating book, Melbin documents how through technological advantages in lighting, human beings have become active creatures of the night. He suggests that especially in America nighttime is becoming a temporal frontier during which human activity is expanding. He defines a frontier as "a pattern of sparse settlement in space or time, located between a more densely settled and practically empty region" (Melbin 1987, 6). He sees the nighttime as such a frontier and reasons that there should be similarities between the frontiers of space and time.

Melbin begins to build his case by citing data that show how the nighttime populations in the public territories of American cities are more sparse and more homogeneous than those during the the the day. In the night, he argues, there are fewer social constraints and less persecution; these and other conditions that provide an openness not otherwise available convince him that night is a frontier.

Given the openness of a frontier, new styles of behavior emerge there. And while it is true there is more lawlessness and violence in public at night, helpfulness and friendliness can also be found in abundance then. In fact, each of these characteristics depicts both land frontiers as described by historians and time frontiers apparent in the data Melbin gathered.

Melbin set out cleverly to test whether night is a new frontier. His first test involved asking for directions from people on the street. In the second, he requested that strangers consent to brief interviews. The third test involved color-coding keys (so they could be traced to locations where they were left) and placing them at various times in conspicuous spots around Boston; each key had a tag on it listing both the name and address of someone in a city several miles away and the request "Please return." In this test approximate measures of who returned the keys (a day- or nighttime person), from where, and from what possible discovery time could be constructed. The final test involved being sociable in the supermarket, where researchers frequented twenty-four-hour stores in Boston at different times of the day and night and in different areas of the city.

Melbin analyzed the results of these tests and discovered that friendliness in giving directions, willingness to be interviewed and sociability in supermarkets were all significantly higher at night than at any other time. The "key" test, however, revealed that people were much less likely to return the keys that were "lost" at night. Although it may appear that the results of the key test are not consistent with the hypothesis that nighttime behavior is more frontierlike, Melbin explains this finding in the following way:

> If someone finds a key and does not know the owner, he would guess that everyone who passed that way is equally likely to have lost it. Nighttimers, knowing they [themselves] are few, assume on the weight of numbers that the person who lost the key is a daytimer . . . [the data suggest] that the feelings of nighttimers toward daytimers resembles the attitudes of westerners toward easterners a century ago. They perceive they are different and resent the neglect shown by the day people toward them. . . . Whereas frontier people readily help others whom they meet on the frontier, their sense of difference from unknown daytimers leaves them less concerned about the others' plights and they do not return many lost keys. (Melbin 1987, 20)

Melbin conducted his research in public places and discovered that the character of a place can change with those who inhabit it at different times. The lesson is clear: the quality of interaction varies with the interpretations people make of their involvement with others. Nighttime is a frontier, a time zone yet to be as fully routinized and rationalized as daytime. In it, people feel adventuresome, banding together to help each other and coping with the consequences of "relaxed" or absent rules of behavior. In the nighttime, certain kinds of people are encouraged to occupy city spaces, and they form associations not unlike "interest groups."

Melbin concludes his study by pointing out the role expansion has played in the social changes in American society. He refers to the western frontier and its impact on American society and to the questions of policy that might emerge from an increased understanding of the nature of time as a resource. Given the lack of constraints in it, any frontier is subject to exploitation; so if it is governed and regulated more closely, will it lose its distinctive character? By conceiving of time as a social frontier, we can see how interactional territories emerge from the sense people make of the situations in which they find themselves. Working nights, finding a location in the city one can claim, and seeking retreat from the routines of daytime city life are all attractions of the new nighttime frontier.

Relations in Frozen Places

Not only do people create new territories out of old ones in the opportunities that time affords, but they may also discover that other variations brought on by such natural occurrences as changes in the weather provide the raw materials for the construction, or reconstruction, of the social order. One of the reasons social psychologists have focused on public territories is because such places have a fragile and temporary character. Since public places are essentially open to all, what happens in them demonstrates graphically the conflicts that can occur among people due to the different senses of "space" they bring to their interpersonal encounters there. Besides revealing the underlying assumptions that support a general sense of social organization, tensions and changes in the public order help people gauge the amount and nature of work occurring in public. Frontiers are spaces in which an array of human activities takes place, and the concept of frontier applies to space and time, but it may also apply to any change that affords people opportunities to work with and within a social order to achieve their own ends.

In studying behavior in public we realize that even the most routine aspects of everyday life, like walking past a stranger on the street or waiting at a bus stop, are tightly organized into social connections that together constitute the public order. Most researchers who look carefully at this order are interested in its effects on those it influences. For example, Goffman formulates a hypothesis that the more fixed the features of public order are, the greater will be people's sense of alarm when it is disturbed. Others have been interested in the affects of crowding and of the intermingling of strangers on helping behavior. Accordingly, they have even staged scenes in which a person seems to be in distress, to see if passersby will stop to give aid. This "Good Samaritan" research generally shows that people tend to depend on the routines they normally follow to get through the public domain and that they are reluctant to modify those routines to help others. Helping others, they fear, may inconvenience them (by disturbing their established sense of order and the sense of protection it gives them) or could be seen as an intrusion into and violation of someone else's territory.

When news stories began to appear some years ago about the brutal murders and assaults that took place within the hearing and sight of passersby and residents, none of whom even called the police, people began to question the human costs of maintaining a sense of public order. The impact on our awareness of these problems has provided a more formal response mechanism for emergencies in large cities. Not only does the emergency 911 number allow quick response for city services, it also offers people the opportunity to report incidents in convenient and anonymous ways. Thus the public order is being rearranged to allow intrusion and helping behaviors consistent with the general character of public life, in other words, to allow public ways to help.

But the question remains: How much opportunity does public life afford individuals for their "definitions of situations"? Melbin's research on night life shifts the focus of our perspective from the impact of public life on people to people's impact on public life. In this vein, Nash (1981) set out to show that even changes in the order brought on by seasonal fluctuations in the weather provide opportunities for the emergence of new versions of public order.

To document the effects of weather on public order, Nash focused on the sense people make of being out-of-doors in extreme winter weather. To gather materials, teams of researchers were organized and altogether invested some 350 hours in observing those aspects of public life most obviously exposed to winter conditions. The study was conducted in the twin cities of Minneapolis and St. Paul, Minnesota, which are justifiably known as winter cities. Teams of observers concentrated on four settings: parks, streets, ski resorts (within the cities proper), and recreational centers (principally, outdoor skating rinks).

From the myriad observations gathered, there emerged several themes that can be thought of as organizing patterns of meaning addressing the question "What are we doing here?" The first deals with the communication of intention; Goffman calls nonverbal techniques that people employ to signal their intentions and motives for being in a public place "officious displays." The second theme relates to the reduced numbers of people in public during winter. The third emerges from attitudes of festivity and celebration. The fourth theme addresses the adaptability of those who frequently use public territories. Finally, an important general theme emerged concerning the suspension during the winter of the norms that usually govern social order.

Officious Displays Goffman (1971, 130–32) writes of the "orientation gloss," which consists of gestures designed to communicate "official" purposes of behavior. Nash's winter city study found that in winter such gestures became exaggerated. While waiting for a bus, people stand on benches, crane to look for the bus every few minutes, and pace up and down and across the territory of the bus stop. They jump up and down and blow on their mittens or gloves as if to warm their hands.

Phone booths located near a stop may be used as stages for a ritual dance of warmth. By standing in the booth and jumping up and down, one can communicate waiting behavior and engage in "strange" movements within the semiprivacy of the booth. Such devices relate official messages about what the person is doing outdoors in such conditions, and most important they show disdain for a public predicament.

A central theme of public behavior is active disregard for winter by "going about business as usual." Some people communicate this theme by underdressing. A businessman will walk from building to building downtown in a "deliberate normal posture," upright slow gate with arms relaxed at his sides, but without a hat or topcoat. A schoolboy will wait for a bus, down vest unsnapped, in zero-degree weather. One observer waiting for a downtown bus when the temperature hovered near zero reported being "flashed" by an undaunted deviant.

Where Have All the People Gone? Observers recorded definite fluctuations in numbers of people outside according to weather conditions. "Weather conditions" refers not simply to temperature but also to the sensation of being outdoors. In order to assess the relationship between weather and the numbers of people in public territories, the observers used an indicator frankly based on subjective judgment. A sunny zero-degree day with a low wind-chill factor could be judged as "nice" if it came after a week of cloudy, snowy, ten-degree days. Although "nice" days did bring out more people, it is important to note both that people were out even in the bitterest weather and that the peak days yielded numbers of people still far below the summer averages.

The Festive Attitude Sometimes during or after a particularly heavy snowfall, people in public often display a festive attitude. It is as if the weather itself is cause for celebration. As one observer reported on behavior at a sledding hill after a heavy snow:

> The routine for parents is to stand around at the top of the hill, intervening on behalf of the smaller children, or to sit in an idling car with the heater on. Today it was different. Old ladies were laughing like crazy. Distinguished-looking, middle-aged men were guffawing in the snow. The sight of a grandma careening down the hill on a blue, plastic, space-age rocket sled was indeed extraordinary.

Another park observer noted the same phenomenon. After several weeks of bitter cold, the sun came out and the temperature rose into the teens. Gradually the park filled with people. They were sledding, cross-country skiing and even picnicking in the snow. Families and groups of young people spread blankets, buried six packs in the snow, and got out the food. It was like the Fourth of July.

The Big Country Complex The question arose: do those who routinely use public space adapt well under winter conditions? It seems many do. Runners, for example, reported their preference for wintertime training because of the openness of the roads. The outdoor skating rink is deserted on the really bitter cold days, a time that hockey enthusiasts like because "you can practice slap shots" without fear of injury or reprimand. As another observer wrote:

> I was standing on a hilltop watching a lonely cross-country skier, silhouetted against the city skyline, cut across the frozen golf course. I could sense a mastery over the environment. For the moment, the numbness of my fingers was a reminder that I had taken this expanse for my own. If I were tough, brave, reckless enough, this city turf was mine.

This intuitive relationship with the cityscape was reported by several other observers. The streets became personalized; walking down the middle of a traffic lane normally crowded bumper to bumper with automobiles produced, for a fleeting moment, a sense of reclaiming that space. Using the ski areas when others dared not enhanced the experience of doing something special. (Skiers who refused to use headgear—one observer called them "hatless wonders"—somehow demonstrated their mastery of the elements in admirable style).

The Democratization of Winter Space Public territories with fixed equipment and uses in the warm months often yield to a variety of uses in winter. It is as if democracy prevails out of season when there are questions of how to put the space to use. Bus stops offer more ready access to conversation. Benches may be stomped on. Phone booths may be occupied with no intent of making a call. A private country club opens its grounds to sledders and cross-country skiers and hence "goes public" in the winter.

People are allowed many such norm violations. Some readily observable ones include the following:

1. Allowing bus-waiters to stand inside buildings (often blocking doorways).

2. Relaxation of the enforcement of the "no alcoholic beverages" law in parks.

3. Late-night practices of driving cars in such open spaces as parks, golf courses, and schoolyards.

4. A tolerance of the flagrant use of culs-de-sac and parking lots by couples seeking "in city" places to park.

5. Uncharacteristic leniency of the police in their use of crowd-control techniques. (One observer noted an officer on duty at the heavily attended funeral of a prominent politician, "If they choose to be out in this cold, they deserve to get a close look.")

Nash's evidence points not just to single events or isolated occurrences of increased freedom but to a general pattern. The wintertime order appears to operate on assumptions of temporariness, so that when winter conditions prevail over long periods, a kind of anomie occurs while the police and private citizens alike wait for the "thaw."

From the data of this study, we can draw three general implications. First, human attempts to deny nature, however unsuccessful, are distinguished by both the symbolic and literal withdrawal of the majority and the exploitation of this withdrawal by an active minority. Second, both space usage and social policies directed at wintertime utilization should allow for increased individual freedom in definitions of territoriality. In short, planners should take advantage of the "cooling" of the sense of alarm persons feel when using urban space during the winter. Finally, the winter city no doubt exhibits different organizational structures from other types of cities. Similarly, the consequent problems of transferring street layouts, architectural designs, and other features of city planning from warm- to cold-weather cities need to be understood more fully.

Public Life and the Malling of America

As a result of the rebuilding of city centers and the relocation of urban populations into suburbs, public life in America is moving inside. We see this in the great expansion of the American mall. Both shopping and simply going where people are have become for more and more people a matter of going to the mall or shopping center.

In one sense, malls and skyways are simply systems of indoor sidewalks found in some version in many American cities. Atlanta, Chicago, Dallas, Spokane and Cincinnati, for example, all have extensive systems of tunnels that connect hotels, shopping areas and buildings. In the Twin Cities, second-level skyways are a major feature of downtown life. In St. Paul, for instance, most banks, department stores, and places of business are connected by passageways, with separate buildings linked together via enclosed bridges over the street, hence the name "skyways." Architect Bernard Jacob describes St. Paul's skyways themselves as more like "buildings inserted between existing buildings" (1985, 9), and in fact, particularly in the older parts of St. Paul's system, the skyway segments may feel more like buildings than airy bridges. The system itself is so extensive that it is possible to park one's car in a multistory garage, enter any building linked to the system and then travel nearly seven miles throughout St. Paul without ever going outside. The passageways are often narrow corridors similar to those found at airports; in some sections the corridors may actually be walled. The message there is clear—move through with great purpose and at an appropriate pace.

As one moves from building to building across the skyway bridges, there are many doors to be opened and closed. There are points of entry at the street and second levels, at parking ramps, and through department stores, banks and government buildings. At some entry points, "You are Here" maps are posted to orient the walker to the system. While the system is referred to as "the skyways," in fact, the hundred or so bridges connecting buildings at their second floors in the two cities are a small portion of the entire indoor space. The skyway bridges do play a major role in creating the downtown environment, though, because they join otherwise separate buildings into an elaborate system of passageways.

In the newer sections of the Minneapolis and St. Paul systems, the passageways themselves spread out into enclosed plazas with fountains, a park, and a place to stop and look out at the street below. These expansions are responses to the criticisms of architects, designers, and sociologists that skyways have no activity opportunities. The broader passageways and open vistas encourage a more leisurely approach to skyway travel and give novices more landmarks with which to orient themselves. Groups seem to walk together with more ease; people stop to watch other people. These newer sections of the system have become, in look and in atmosphere, very similar to suburban malls.

So extensive is the system and so profound its effects on the downtown areas of the Twin Cities that William H. Whyte, referring to the vacant character of the first level and sidewalks of the city and the transfer of all visual interest to the second, declared St. Paul to be "the blank wall capital of the world" (1988, 156). While Minneapolis has attempted to preserve some street-level commercial and social life, both cities are committed to skyways.

Skyways are also legal entities. In St. Paul, the actual bridges are publicly owned, while in Minneapolis they are part of the buildings they connect. The systems are governed by boards of directors, or bureaucratic bodies (in St. Paul, for example, it is the "Skyway Governance Committee") charged with overseeing public use, expanding service, and integrating the system into the life of the downtown. In many ways skyways seem more like private entities than public ones because they are governed by an extensive set of ordinances to prohibit many behaviors commonly engaged in outdoors. For example, inside the skyway one may not sit, kneel, lounge, lie, or otherwise recline on floors or stairs. One may not stand upon any radiator, seat or other fixture, or commit any act that tends to create or incite an immediate breach of the peace. Prohibited conduct also includes running, obscene language, and noisy or boisterous behavior that might be construed as abusive, offensive, disgusting,or insulting. Furthermore, one may not "stand, stop or otherwise linger in such a manner as to obstruct or impede or tend to obstruct or impede the free passage of pedestrians through the area" (Skyway Ordinance 140.02). Nor may one "play a radio or tape player so as to permit the sound from the radio or tape player to be audible to other persons, except that peace officers may play radios tuned to official police frequencies" (Ordinance 140.02).

According to the Skyway Ordinance (of St. Paul), any of these listed behaviors are misdemeanor violations. A peace officer observing "a person committing any of the acts enumerated in Section 140.02, or shall have probable cause to believe that a person has committed any of the said acts" may "order that person to refrain from doing the proscribed conduct." And, "any person who shall refuse to refrain from such acts or conduct after being ordered to do so shall be guilty of a misdemeanor." There are further prohibitions against animals, littering, sales and unauthorized performances. Thus:

> No group, entity or person shall . . . engage in or cause to be presented any type of exhibition, show, performance or entertainment in the pedestrian skyway system or other pedestrian mall . . . unless such person, entity or group shall first have received a permit from the skyway governance committee. . . . Only non-profit civic, educational, charitable, religious or patriotic organizations shall be eligible for such permits. (Skyway Ordinance 140.6)

The policing of the system is accomplished primarily through the cooperation of private security guards hired by downtown businesses. Some municipal police officers do walk a beat through the system, but most supervision is by way of cameras and private police. The system is also regulated in terms of hours of access. In St. Paul, the entire system is open from 6:00 A.M. (except Sundays) until 2:00 A.M.; in Minneapolis parts close at the end of the regular business hours of the buildings they connect. While both systems are open most of the time, businesses, restaurants, and shops within them may not be. Hence late at night and during early morning weekend hours, there are vacant stretches and the corridors (or "bare tube" sections) become lonely hallways.

The Dimensions of Vitality in Public Space

The relative amount, intensity, and content of social interaction in a particular setting obviously vary. A setting may be said to be vital if it offers opportunities for interaction or "participation" to a wide range of different people who bring to it their particular definitions of participation. That is, participation for its own sake—a sense of the enjoyment of being in the public realm—is a part of the attraction of places. High-vitality public places are more than settings where people are; they are places where people are doing things regarded by those present as interesting (Whyte 1988; Wright 1978). High-vitality places are potential action scenes, places where something unexpected and amusing might take place.

Our observational data (also gathered by Nash and his student researchers, Nash 1981) suggested three dimensions of or conditions for vitality: population diversity (or the presence of various types of people), environmental mastery (or participants' sense of control of a place), and participatory activity (or participant contributions to place activity). We coded field notes collected by our participant researchers for instances of "vital" social interaction. (Of course, styles of reporting differed greatly across the field notes, and the more colorful descriptions of some researchers may have misled us in some cases.) The following illustrate instances of "low" and "high" vitality.

A case of "low vitality" is reported by an observer who sat in a restaurant in the skyway. The establishment was a fast-food restaurant (but not a national chain—franchised names are sometimes banned from newer sections to retain a "hometown" feeling in the downtown) that specialized in self-service ethnic food, sold from a cafeteria-style facility fronting the skyway passage. Customers sat in metal chairs at metal tables centrally arranged in the middle of a wide portion of the skyway passage a few steps from the store.

> First, I noted that most people were eating alone or with just one other person. Most of the tables had one person sitting at them during the day. At the busy lunch hour, people would be forced to share a table. I noticed that most people did not speak to each other, even if they were sharing a table. And, I observed many people eating standing up to avoid intruding on someone who had a table. There was a regularity or standard appearance of the people who eat here. Most men did not wear their suit coats but were wearing dress shirts with ties and trousers. They looked as if they "left their coats back at the office." Women were dressed for the business day and came to eat without outside garments. Almost everyone hurried through lunch, perhaps joking with a friend, rarely ever simply sitting and watching the pedestrians. Only a few people carried anything with them. I saw little marking of territory and was very impressed with how fast lunch was consumed. It is interesting that this establishment closes at 3:00 PM, and that people carrying things usually just walked right by. In fact, you could tell that people eating here worked nearby and that people walking past them with packages did not seem to belong at the restaurant. (field notes 1987)

A specimen of "high vitality" comes from the notes of a student observing a street musician in a downtown park.

> Mango, as the street musician calls himself, has had several run-ins with the police. In fact, he is quite a celebrity. The people who eat their lunches in the park on a nice day know of him, and some like to listen to his music. On this day, people would stop for a while, listen and then move on. At most, about fifty people would be listening to the music. There was a flow of people going by, some would not stop, but just slow down, others would stay a few minutes and a very few would linger for several minutes. Mostly, I would characterize the audience as a mobile one. What seemed to happen is that the crowds were transformed into a kind of audience, but an audience composed of many different kinds of people. They would not be together were it not for the music. (field notes, 1987)

Conditions conducive to vitality vary both within the skyway system and between the out-of-doors and the enclosed skyway spaces. A plaza, for example, may attract different types of people and locate them relative to one another differently than a fast-food area. In each location senses of mastery and participation will vary. Let us now try to specify more carefully how the enclosure of public spaces affects their vitality.

Population Diversity or Categories of Public People

High vitality depends in part on the presence of different kinds of people. The skyways are designed to be used primarily by those who work and shop in the downtown. Because of its mazelike character and the location of entry points (e.g., through a parking ramp used by commuters or at street level through places of business such as banks), the system functions to sort and limit the types of people who use it. Nonetheless, the downtown is public, and the population using the skyways is by no means homogeneous.

In the skyway system, distinctiveness of appearance is largely a matter of dress. The major differences observers noted were between those dressed in occupationally appropriate fashion (business attire, service uniforms, etc.) and shoppers in blue jeans or sports attire. Students' field notes contain numerous references to the tendency of skyways and corridors to group people into similarly dressed clusters. People linked by "tie signs" (holding hands, walking close together—"withs" in Goffman's terms) are easily identified in skyway traffic patterns. One interpretation of these observations is that skyway design contributes to the visibility of categorical identities.

One category of people mentioned frequently by both skyway retailers and visitors is the "undesirables," a term usually used to refer to street or homeless people. Like the outside street, the system does have its local "characters." Business people complain, for instance, about having to "step over" the sleeping street person when on their way to buy breakfast coffee and doughnuts, and pimps are known for their recruiting of young girls who "hang out" late at night. Yet despite such frequent complaints and although they are an everyday part of the outdoor humanscape, undesirables are in fact discouraged from entering the skyway by the very nature of the system itself. One "bag lady" said she goes inside only when she is about to "freeze to death" and researchers documented that "street people" are more often seen at the entrances to the system than in it.

Heterogeneity and the tensions engendered by it enter the system as well in racial categories. As low-vitality spaces, skyways provide a context for officially prescribed activities. That is, high vitality by definition entails uses that, however modestly, contrast and even clash with official prescriptions. If certain categories of people have reputations as high-vitality participants, their presence in low-vitality spaces will be viewed as problematic. In the skyway system, high school youths—particularly black youths—are so viewed.

While the tensions between official and participant definitions of the appropriate character of public life are replete in our data, they are nowhere more obvious than in certain incidents in the St. Paul skyway system and in community reactions to them. The 1986 city task force on the skyway system reported that the skyways were relatively safe places that did not differ significantly from suburban malls in terms of arrests and police calls. But during the winter of 1990–91 a number of incidents in the system called this conclusion into question.

Headlines in the local paper read, "Troublemakers to Be Booted from Skyways" and "St. Paul Begins New Crackdown in the Skyways." These reactions appeared to be in response to the complaints of shop owners and visitors to what they saw as an invasion of "undesirables." One local newspaper ran a series of stories about "groups of youths" who were loud, disruptive, and assaultive. Official police statistics do not clearly indicate discrimination in "the crackdown," but they are suggestive. Of the 571 total arrests during 1990, 261 (46 percent) were of blacks, 242 (43 percent) of whites, 42 (7 percent) of Hispanis, 18 (3 percent) of American Indians and 8 (1 percent) of Asians (*Pioneer Press* 2/17/91).

Personal reports from those expelled do highlight racial categories. For example, one black man who works in the Metro Square Building said a confrontation with security guards over a table led to his being expelled from the system for a year. He said security was called because a cleaning woman told him to move apart two tables placed together in McDonald's. He told her he didn't put the tables together and had just sat down with his girl friend and another friend to eat. He was taking a lunch break late in the day while working a night shift.

He said the woman called security; they came and demanded that all three move. The three refused. The police were called, and he was told he would be arrested if he returned to the skyway. "Because I wasn't in that suit and tie, they thought I was a person here to make trouble," he said. "They're looking to eliminate as many blacks from this mall as possible" (*Pioneer Press* 2/14/91).

Similar incidents were reported in detail in front-page coverage of problems in the skyways, and unusual public hearings were held at a skyway park to air all sides of the issues. Typically, a wide range of opinions were expressed, with some people claiming that groups of young black people come to "the mall" just to look for trouble, and others suggesting that the problem is not racial; usually, any group of people whose appearance and behavior calls attention to them are "trouble" in the system.

The Nash data do indicate that race may very well be a salient category in determining whether a person is seen as a potential troublemaker. For example, a black physician reported that he was detained and questioned by police because he was wearing a beeper. He suggested, and other black professionals have corroborated, that the police associate any black man carrying a beeper with drug dealing. In addition, the fear of gang violence makes many people anxious and suspicious of any large group of young people. During a public hearing an off-duty police officer reported that while visiting St. Paul Center with his children he was stopped by a group of black kids at an escalator. "They were all wearing Raiders jackets and caps cocked sideways . . . with a 'gang-banger' mentality" (*Pioneer Press* 2/14/91). He did go on to say, however, that he would have felt the same if confronted by any group of young men, even if they were members of a local and presumably highly respected high school football team.

In his interview study of black middle-class experiences in public places in several American cities, Joe Feagin (1991) suggests that discrimination in public space takes both subtle and obvious forms. Most of his respondents had had dramatic experiences. While his research does not separate sites according to their inside or outside character, we can relate his findings to our data on skyways. Apparently, black visitors to the skyways are aware that they may have to deal with discriminatory practices and that they may encounter more difficulties in performing ordinary acts of shopping or simply walking through the passageways than do people whose appearance conforms to the stereotype of the "desirable" downtown visitor. This was clearly the experience of the physician with a beeper, and would be in less obvious ways of the groups of black youngsters who simply want to "hang out" in the skyways.

Environmental Mastery or Learning the System

A second dimension or condition of vitality is environmental mastery. People who use the skyways frequently and comfortably have developed a sense of mastery over it. They have solved the problems of getting from one place to another and may even take for granted what they know about the system. Vitality depends in part on this sense of having learned the system, but many users seem not to have it. In a number of our interviews, for example, people spoke about feeling disoriented in the skyways and described plazas and parks as more inviting and relaxing. As another example, one field researcher described a couple reading a map of the Minneapolis Skyway System. They stood isolated, certain only of the space in front of the map, as they tried to figure out how to navigate the system.

As a last example, we note that instances of marking territory with coats and personal belongings were observed far more frequently in outdoor plazas and parks than in the skyways (or even on outside pathways). We read these examples as indicating that people feel more able to "move into" more flexible, open spaces. With a "sense of control" comes a kind of being "at home" in the space and expanding personal boundaries.

Goffman (1971, 300–301) has suggested that people using access points—doorways, gates, subway entrances—may feel a sense of impending intrusion, an uneasiness about their loss of freedom of movement. If this is true, one might expect users of skyways to feel uneasy, perhaps even unsafe. And there are some indications that they do. For example, as we have seen, crimes do occur in the system, but rarely. Yet these rare events engender considerable attention. One incident reported in the *St. Paul Pioneer Press* (9/28/89) involved a "gang" of adolescent girls who mugged an elderly woman in a St. Paul skyway. While the crime was not particularly serious (no one was injured), one informant who uses the skyway system regularly told us that "everybody" he knew—at lunch counters, small food shops, and the like—was talking about the incident and speculating on whether it meant the system was becoming a more dangerous place. Generally, however, most "insiders" seemed to regard the incident as "one of those things" that would probably not recur. The apparent anomaly that skyways are simultaneously "scary" and relatively safe places can be explained in part by noting, as we did earlier, that the system functions to separate out perceived dangerous types. Essentially, people in the skyway system are "safe" because the "safe" types tend to be the major users of the second level.

Participatory Activity

The design of the skyways creates a highly individualized use of space that rewards the mastery of the system by businesslike atomistic users. This mastery in turn leads to skills and styles of participation in the system. Whenever people are in public, they bring resources—appearance, activity, or representation as a certain category of person—that shape and create meanings. This participation in meaning making in public offers an alternative to the "boredom" of private life. In public one may have surprising encounters. The more "characters" one sees and the more "unusual" their antics, the more people can sense "adventure" from simply going where other people are. Our data indicate that the distribution of "sense of adventure" ranges from little or none in the skyway—or even a negative version, alarm at confronting "characters" there—to more festive attitudes toward the action in plazas and parks. Such interpretations of place seem to be on a continuum associated with more and less restriction in the space. Enclosing public spaces seems to enhance "control" of public behavior by officials who may not have succeeded in controlling the older "out-of-doors" variety of public life. Additionally, it allows "commercial interests" to channel public space more easily into a single form, namely, shopping. The architecture itself functions to enhance, ensure and encourage consumption (see, e.g., Crawford 1992 on shopping malls).

Despite all these "structural" contributions to the "one-dimensional" character of skyway life, some "hearty" urbanites seem able to define for themselves their uses of the system. One long-time resident of the downtown explained to us the pride he takes in negotiating his daily routine through the skyways without wearing an overcoat or in opening and closing the doors of the bridges while judging the "appropriate" distance within which he feels obligated to "hold the doors" for others. In an interesting coda to his description of the detailed knowledge required to use the skyway in this way, he commented that sometimes it is simply not worth the effort. One can, after all, go outside and walk a more direct route to any destination. And as a matter of fact, researchers observed that even on the coldest days, the ratio of people outside to inside is much more nearly even than one might expect.

On several occasions, when the outside street seems to move inside the skyways, students observed more inventive uses of usually controlled spaces. Too much use of the system, as happened when masses of people came into the downtowns for the Twins World Series in 1987 and 1991, sets retailers, business people and security guards on edge. But downtowners take advantage of special events, holidays, and celebrations as opportunities to broaden and individualize the experience of public space. In spite of the elaborate rules, at times like these individuals impose their unofficial uses upon the official system. For example, during the Twins' celebrations, groups of people displaced or transferred social identities from a favorite bar to the second level of a parking ramp to watch the victory parade. The street or a public location therefore became defined by the identity of the "guys from work," or the "exercise gang at the Y."

Still, the range of action and meanings one encounters in an enclosed space differs from that discovered outside on a public street. Consider, for example, the contrast between an employee of a photography studio dressed as the Easter bunny whose job is to draw people into the studio on the mall (Hickey, Thompson and Foster 1988) and a street musician playing in a public plaza. Both are involved in "commercialized" activities; that is, they are motivated by a desire to earn money. But the bunny follows a commercial script written by a business and affording the player little latitude in performance. The musician follows an individualized script. It might not always be very spontaneous, or even very creative, but because it is the performer's own it allows him or her more control over what happens. In the mall or skyway commercial and standardized scripts predominate. In outside spaces one may find street musicians and others for whom participation in public life seems the primary goal and commercial success the secondary.

Vitality and the American Urban Landscape

The skyway system stands for the hopes of developers and urban planners and communicates the message that if "the right people" come downtown they will be insulated from the negative aspects of being in public, of being vulnerable "on the street." The original impetus for skyway construction was not protection from the Minnesota winters, though that feature has been highlighted to allay the concerns of potential tourists and conventioners about the weather. The most important consideration was "convenience" for people who wanted to engage in commercial exchange. Hence, from the beginning, the skyway stood as a symbol of the degree to which politicians and business people would attempt to manage environments they regarded as critical in attracting consumers and employers.

The elaborate skyway systems of the Twin Cities have certainly succeeded in duplicating some of the qualities of outdoor spaces. Courts, parks and plazas do attract somewhat diverse participants who contribute their creativity to the use of space, though mostly in ways congruent with the intentions of designers and owners. At the same time skyways are the antithesis of W.H. Whyte's notion of a vital city street (1978, 1980). For example, the narrow conduits of the connecting links in the systems foster single-file, quiet pedestrian movement. Even the hustle and bustle of the inside plaza is muted compared to New York's Washington Square (Harrison 1984) or the outside public life remaining in the Twin Cities.

As we just noted, the hope of city developers was that the skyways would contribute to the commercial life of the downtowns of Minneapolis and St. Paul. And at least some kinds of retail and entertainment activities—upscale clothing shops, restaurants, novelty stores, and nightclubs—do thrive along the system. But that only a limited range of commerce seems adaptable to the new cityscape simply attests to the emergence of new meanings for downtown spaces.

Public life "inside," just like public life "outside," embodies tensions between private and official purposes (Lofland 1985). But our observations in the Twin Cities indicate that tensions increase in enclosed spaces. As skyways become pieces of an elaborate and interconnected shopping system, they generate legal battles over First Amendment rights and struggles over racial categories and discrimination in rule enforcement. Whatever the specific outcomes of these, we suggest that the new enclosed city will be fundamentally different from the old. Although Michael Sorkin is referring to the "creative geography" of Disneyland and Disney World in his essay on the "copyrighted urban environment," his analysis has parallels to our study of enclosed downtowns. "Disneyzone," he comments, produces "urbanism without producing a city. . . . Physicalized yet conceptual, it's the utopia of transience, a place where everyone is just passing through. This is its message for the city to be a place everywhere and nowhere, assembled only through constant motion" (Sorkin 1992, 231).

The skyway system produces the means for traveling through the enclosed "downtown," but as Sorkin concludes about Disneyzone, creating such spaces only hastens the demise of the public realm. An enclosed downtown turns city life inside out, replacing diversity with homogeneity, substituting insider savvy for street knowledge and underscoring the difference between those who belong inside and those who do not.

Alienation and Opportunity

Examinations of night life, winter behavior, and enclosed public places reveal a remarkable variety of unofficial usage, suggesting that people construct social environments as overlays for physical ones. Of course, making sense of public life involves a certain amount of preconditioning by the larger cultural meanings in society. But still, people's sense of appropriate usage of the environment depends on how they define their place in it. Earlier, when we learned how people cope in different ways with their feelings of estrangement, we identified alienation as one consequence of mixing social forms. In fact, the entire question of fit, from integration to alienation, between formal and informal group structure can be seen as the power of the interpretations people offer to each other.

The study of public life requires focusing on a place of preeminent estrangement where the very essence of social life involves using places and things that carry official, ready-made definitions of appropriate use. To contrast different types of territories one must ask, "Who can define meanings?" In interactional, home and body spaces, people feel they can define the meanings themselves. Public meanings, in contrast, are perceived as prefabricated structures put in place by others. In public, then, people generally feel "out of place." Hence they hurry, avoid eye contact, and protect their bodies as vehicles they can maneuver through "unfriendly" territory. Although there are many meanings of alienation in the social science literature, this one is clearly a part of what is intended by those who use the concept.

Nevertheless, what we see when we look closely at actual interaction in public space only partially supports its depiction as alienating. While it is true that strangers do not readily help each other, that night is a dangerous time in big cities, and that northern city streets are barren in the middle of January, there is also evidence that public life in these places offers opportunities for innovation. Nighttimers invent their own sense of belonging, and wintertimers take advantage of suspended norms of public life to enjoy freedom in the streets.

The tension we depict between alienation and opportunity has been documented in an exotic way by Douglas, Rasmussen, and Flanagan in their study of nude beaches (1977). While the authors discovered that the extremely private act of nudity in public did represent a novel use of the beaches, they also found many aspects of the nude beach scene to resemble and illustrate the tension between alienation and opportunity.

For example, Douglas and his colleagues found that many people were motivated to visit and become members of the "bareass" beach because they found the act of public nudity to be a "turn-on." The authors studied the use of the territories of the beach, how people exhibited themselves before one another, how sex acts were accomplished on the beach and the patterns of interaction located there. Generally, they discovered that people attempt to cover up interactionally in ways that enhance the tension between public and private. They do this by categorizing other members of the beach scene, by developing routine practices, and particularly in the case of females, by protecting themselves in small groups. In fact, the authors even suggest that the tension, which in this case derives from a novel use of public territory, was a basic attraction for the "bareass" beach phenomenon. They write that most people who frequented the beach did so to escape the routineness and boredom of everyday life. Nude bathers were in search of excitement and adventure, and while what they found was often exciting, it was so in a slightly different way from what they had expected. Not only did beachgoers have to learn to deal with a variety of people who had quite different ideas about the purposes of nude beaches, they also encountered the values of the larger society, especially when they had to learn to cope with police and property owners. In a section on politics and the future of the nude beach, Douglas et al. conclude that the nude scene depends on contact with and influence on the public world. Even in this extreme effort creatively to redefine the appropriate use of beaches, we see the tension between the need for order among strangers and the opportunities for excitement and adventure that being in the presence of strangers provides.

Summary

This chapter explores the social meanings people attribute to life in public places. We develop a conception of territoriality that appreciates the constructed, changeable, and situational character of human senses of place. There are home, interactional, public, and body territories. Each functions to establish a sense of location around the person's sense of himself or herself.

All of these territories are mobile. We describe how the home territory is marked, and we expand this notion to understand the marking of temporary homes in the form of campsites. We discover that markers, both as physical things and as symbolic messages, communicate the intentions and motives of those who wish to establish a territorial claim.

We see how the ideas of space and time come together in the frontier phenomenon. When we understand how certain features of space yield identifiable meanings, we can look for these meanings in places we might otherwise overlook. The night, according to Melbin, is a time frontier. Although overlooked as a territory because of our narrow definition of territory as space, time territories are concrete in the consequences they have for those who inhabit them. Nighttimers are friendly, willing to engage in conversation, and protective of their identities against the outsiders of the daylight.

The winter city also has a distinctive public life, one characterized by bold officious display, decreases in the number of participants, festive attitudes, and increased freedom in usage for those who persist in the frozen order. And finally, the study of enclosed public spaces shows the relationship between vitality and design and the ways that people bring competencies in dealing with strangers into these built environments, sometimes with unexpected consequences.

The tension between individual or informal senses of territories and collective or official senses of them results in oppressive environments that alienate people, not always functioning as they are officially supposed to. The alienation these tensions produce may provide the grounds for the protection of informal senses of territory or the incentive for novel adaptations.

Exercises in Observing Public Life

1. Next time you are in a public place, start making a list of all the ways you see people marking territory. Keep this up for about a week. You should generate a fairly long list. Then sort the list into categories according to how you think the markers are similar or dissimilar. If you have done a sufficient job at observing this aspect of public life, you should have described several distinctive marking behaviors. Make up names for the ways of marking.

2. Select one of Melbin's four tests for the hypothesis that night is a frontier. Repeat it at different times during the day in your city. You might want to work in groups on this project. Of course your city or town will have its own form of night life. We recommend that you stay as close as possible to Melbin's tests. It would be easy, for example, to repeat his key test on a small scale, or to visit "all-night" supermarkets and ask people for directions or to consent to an interview. Be sure to record the time periods for your observations. The idea of this exercise is to see if your observations confirm Melbin's strong assertion that night is a frontier. You may wish to consult Melbin's article for details of the various tests.

3. Life in public places is rarely examined according to variations in weather. We have seen, however, that the sense people make out of the weather is an important background feature for the way they act toward and judge the intentions of others. Although you may not experience the winter extremes of Minnesota, most parts of the country have some distinctive weather phenomena—high winds, heat, thunderstorms, and so on. Recall your own experiences with such extreme weather and see if you can describe some unusual things you might have done at the time. For example, you may recall playing in the warm summer rain or the special sense of community engendered by "special" weather. Do not use disasters for this exercise. Limit your examples to more or less ordinary weather but weather that also distinguishes your part of the country. Is there some association between territorial usage and weather variation?

Suggested Readings

Probably the most readable and still quite contemporary book on public life is Lyn Lofland's *World of Strangers* (Prospect Heights, Ill.:Waveland Press, 1985). She introduces the study of public life through a delightful depiction of what typically happened in the preindustrial city. She captures the reality of the city by telling about the smells, sounds, and to our modern sensibilities bewildering array of sensual experiences in the preindustrial city. She goes on to describe the modern city with its locational segregation, and relates the skills necessary to deal with strangers in the city.

Murray Melbin's book, *Night as Frontier* (Chicago: University of Chicago Press, 1987), on how time is a social force in public life is important for a complete understanding of the implication of the construction of reality perspectives on public life. Finally, Spencer Cahill and Lyn Lofland have recently edited a selection of essays on *The Community of the Streets* (Greenwich, Conn.: JAI Press, 1993) that documents, interprets, and explains the changes that have occurred in the nature of public life in modern cities.

Chapter 11

Collective Behavior and Social Movements

Social psychologists have long had an interest in collective behavior because they learned early on that the nature and amount of collective behavior in it tell us a great deal about a society. Sometimes called social action, collective behavior usually involves relatively large numbers of people engaged in interactions that have elements of spontaneity and significance, appear novel and innovative, and have meanings not directly addressed by the usual institutions of society. Fads and fashions are examples of collective behavior, but so too are such crowd actions as protests and riots, and even the actions of large groups of people during disasters. The greatest potential of collective behavior is manifest in social movements, the "great stirrings that rattle and threaten the institutional order, attracting adherents whose motivations are diverse and producing manifold effects in society" (Turner 1983, 175).

John Lofland (1981) offers a scheme for bringing coherence to the study of this vast array of "extrainstitutional" behavior by suggesting a sense in which, like any typical social organization, every collective behavior represents a form. According to Lofland, collective behaviors vary along dimensions defined by dominant emotions and organizational forms. In fact, a great many emotions may be expressed within a social movement, but in most cases there is a primary feeling associated with it, "the publicly expressed feeling perceived by the participants and observers as most prominent" (Lofland 1981, 414).

Lofland stresses the variation and gradation present in any instance of collective behavior. In addition, he feels it is important to identify both the definitive sentiments of people caught up in it and the means by which they organize their actions. We have chosen to illustrate Lofland's classification of forms of collective behavior, but in no way do our examples depict all forms of such action. And though we do not cover all the possibilities in Lofland's scheme, the examples we have elected to present are themselves both representative and dramatic.

Crowds

Everyone has at one time or other been a part of a crowd. Most of the time this amounts to an inconvenient or at worst mildly irritating experience. Significantly, this experience is usually ordinary, routine, and perhaps even boring. On occasion, however, something happens to send fear throughout a crowd and rumors that something has happened travel among those present. The most dramatic illustrations of this kind of collective behavior are the several tragic cases of people in nightclubs or at theaters who have learned that a fire has broken out near them. People who had been enjoying themselves moments before in an atmosphere of relaxation and entertainment instantly shift to behaviors they believe will assure their survival. Of course such collective action taken in fear usually has the opposite effect as people rush the doors, disregarding the elemental rules of turn taking that would make orderly escape possible.

Panic is a fear-based response to a situation perceived of as beyond hope, a collective expression of extreme fear. On the social psychological level it means a loss of trust in the routine, a sense that something so extraordinary is going on that the problem-solving methods of everyday life simply do not apply. As Lofland points out, little contemporary research exists on panic; but he does suggest some guidelines that can be drawn for an understanding of the significance of the concept.

Panic may well follow different patterns, developing in sequences from feelings of frustration and excitement to actual expressions of panic. There can, however, be great variation in these expressions; for instance, escape panic, the terror of people afraid of being trapped in a burning building, is quite different in its expression from the acquisitive panic of a crowd trying to gain something, as in attempts to take over a building, secure a territory, or obtain a Cabbage Patch Doll for a Christmas toy.

Panic is also complicated by reactions to the breakdown of social organization. Crowds are minimally organized social groups where no one is in charge and there is no taken-for-granted routine. Though crowds may be described as orderly, we usually mean by this that the people who make up the crowd behave without evil intent and in accordance with certain internalized standards of "good public conduct." The design of a public space, a baseball or football stadium, for example, compensates for the lack of internal social organization in crowds by imposing physical restraints, such as turnstiles to control fans at entranceways or railings to keep them off the playing field (cf. Goffman 1971).

Terror is a gripping expression of crowd fear. Movie makers have long been aware of ways to evoke a sense of terror in an audience by first showing an ordinary scene, a setting everyone takes for granted (a kitchen, a suburban living room, the seaside at a summer resort) and then suddenly violating audience assumptions by showing something totally unexpected. The result evokes the shock of sheer terror.

One scene from the first *Friday the Thirteenth* movie illustrates well what we mean. A young woman casually goes to the refrigerator and opens the door, only to discover the head of her mother poised inside like leftover meatloaf. As she stands shrieking, immobilized by terror, she is knifed in the temple. In another scene, a crisis seems to pass after the killer appears to have been "done away with." As the actors rest relaxed in an ordinary living room, a grotesque figure crashes through the picture window.

Terror is called forth in an audience by a shocking interruption of everyday life; but films like *Friday the Thirteenth*, however effectively, only fabricate terror. Some sociologists (Goffman 1971; Lefebrve 1971) though, have related real-life experiences of it to the particular organization of public life in modern society and the overbearing need to impose order on a disorderly public.

Henri Lefebrve (1971) shows how the overall organization of society operates against the achievement of clarity about one's location in it. To him, routine life is constantly challenged by the sometimes confounding but nevertheless planned changes required by our modern economy. One consequence of the contradictions built into modern society is a social organization divided into vastly different classes, with many citizens feeling they have little chance to move up in the system. Because of the differences literally created by society and the failure of social leaders to fulfill promises of improvement for the lower classes, large numbers of people feel they have nothing to lose by resorting to deviance and disorder, to the point that repression is the only remaining effective means of control.

A repressive society maintains order through both persuasion and compulsion, with the first mode being primarily informal and communicative and the second legal. According to Lefebrve, "over-repressiveness" produces a terrorist society where threats of violence are ever present. In modern society, however, we witness not just overt threats or actual violence against specific individuals or groups; just as important are the threats and violence intruding on all of our everyday lives.

There is irony to life in modern society, says Lefebrve. Whereas everyday life may be devoid of festival, style, and art, and though its linguistic forms seem hollow, a "zero point of language," people are still preoccupied with communication and meaning. Terrorist society, he notes, "is obsessed with dialogue, communication, participation, integration and coherence, all the things it misses" (Lefebrve 1971, 185).

We conclude, finally, that as citizens in modern society we learn to assume a cynical attitude about others and about any hope we may have for a permanently valid interpretation of the nature of our social existence. As a result, we work to establish order in the small worlds over which we believe we do have some control (Luckmann 1974). But these small worlds are built on networks of interaction that, if not stretched thin over relatively large numbers of people of disparate backgrounds (as in the case of crowds), consist of a few friends bound together in close-knit, emotional associations. In either instance, the breadth of change and depth of uncertainty in the larger social world render our small worlds very fragile and leave us vulnerable to modern forms of collective behavior.

Angry Crowds

Whereas many instances of collective behavior in modern society derive from terror, many others develop from a sense of violated distributive justice. With this in mind we can focus on insights gained from our understanding of the social psychological consequences of inequality. For instance, as in the aftermath of the April 1992 Rodney King decision, a riot may be a relatively organized, collective way of expressing hostility. In addition, Wright's (1978) study of the riots in the Watts area of Los Angeles in the late 1960s refutes the impression many lay people have of riots, namely that they are unorganized, irrational, and uncontrolled expressions of hostility.

Instead, Wright discovered that the Los Angeles rioters used rather systematic means to identify what they regarded as proper targets for hostility, and as we read his notes we can imagine a similar account for the beating of the truck driver during the April 1992 Los Angeles riots, captured on videotape and seen by a national television audience. Wright's field notes read:

> As I was making a right turn on the street where the action was centered, several Negro youths ran up to my car. They said, "Turn your inside lights on, Blood, so we can see who it is." . . . Large numbers of men and women and children were gathered on both sides of the street with bricks and other objects in their hands. Just up the street was a car which had been upturned and set afire . . . . A car came roaring down the street. The crowd yelled: "Whitey! Get him!" . . . Bricks, stones and pipes, hurled from both sides of the street, dented both sides of the car. The front windshield was smashed. The car speeded up and kept going until it was out of the area. . . . The people around, watching the man being beaten, kept yelling: "Beat the ___. Teach him to keep his ass out of Watts." (Wright 1978, 47)

Wright's point is that regardless of how we evaluate this kind of behavior, it is based on forethought and judgments and it does involve symbolically significant meaning. Wright suggests that we view these types of "irrational" actions as "situationally rational."

Recalling what we learned from the perspective of Dollard, Miller and Sears (1939), we can note how frustration may well fire crowd hostility. The black citizens of Watts who were residing in undesirable living conditions expressed their hostility toward whites who, according to the blacks' interpretation of the social world, were responsible for those conditions. In 1992, the assailants of the white truck driver in Los Angeles also saw him as a target with symbolic significance for their view of what precipitated those riots. Sometimes an angry crowd can be quite organized and purposive, as seems to be true of the soccer hooligans in England. Some regard themselves as "hard core" hooligans and anticipate matches as opportunities to engage in gang violence, which they call "aggro." Their aggressive and violent crowd behavior revolves around defining their group over against the enemy, the fans of other teams whom they see as "foreigners." Frank, a twenty-six-year-old lorry (truck) driver and self-confessed "football" hooligan, explains his motives for participating in an angry crowd.

> I go to a match for one reason only: the aggro. It's an obsession, I can't give up. I get so much pleasure when I'm having aggro that I nearly wet my pants. . . . I go all over the country looking for trouble. Before a match we go around looking respectable. . . . then if we see someone who looks like the enemy we ask him the time; if he answers in a foreign accent, we do him over; and, if he's got money on him we'll roll him as well. (Dunning, Murphy and Williams 1988, 19–20)

As this example reveals, the nasty side of collective behavior is related to both individual and social experiences, and neither experience can be appreciated without the other.

Joyful Crowds

The literature on collective behavior generally focuses on the darker side of social life, but some reports are far from gloomy. These include a range of phenomena from the sacred to the profane, from fairly routine, annual festivals to excited spontaneous crowds. In one article, Lofland (1982) outlines the important considerations in the understanding of the joyous crowds, instructing the reader to think of them in terms of five dimensions:

1. The level of psychobiological arousal of crowd members.
2. The proportion of minority to majority members displaying this level of involvement.
3. The social definition of the nature, meaning, and import of the arousal.
4. The degree to which joy crowds are institutionalized.
5. The duration of the arousal (Lofland 1982, 357–58)

Among Lofland's examples of joyous crowds are sacred ones, including "ecstatic upheavals," such as the Vailala Madness reported by Goodman (1974, 232). This famous event occurred in 1919, in the then British territory of Papua (New Guinea), where the members of some villages in the territory began to behave "hysterically." Their heads were even said to "go around," as they "twisted" their bodies, fell to the ground and spoke "unintelligible exclamations." These manifestations of extreme joy were interpreted as meaning that the ancestors of the village were about to return in cargo-laden ships. There were several phases to the excitement, generally following a pattern of arousal, climax, plateau, and resumption of routine life.

Lofland continues to demonstrate the variation among sacred joy crowds by discussing ecstatic conventions, which refer to the practice in some societies of "harnessing" crowd energy into regularized occasions. Certain devices in the organization of crowds that can stir up such religious "effervescence" include singing, the swaying of bodies, and the utterance of piercing cries and chants. Such manifestations are typically short-lived, but they may give rise to more enduring forms.

The ecstatic congregation exists in American society among many fundamentalist religious groups. Hardly anyone who attends such a service, even outsiders who may be there only because they heard the group has a good choir, can avoid the feelings of emotional arousal. Of course there are degrees of permanency to these crowds. The most permanent form is the stable congregation, one that meets at least weekly, while a temporary one is exemplified by the euphoric mood that might briefly overtake a crowd in the gospel tent of a jazz and heritage festival during a performance by the Mighty Clouds of Joy. Among some groups there are regular conventions for arousing excitement. Some preachers travel circuits on a regular basis conducting revivals to effect salvation and evoke high levels of joy in congregations. Finally, Lofland identifies "reverent congregations," which can be observed at sacred sites where vast numbers of believers crowd together to celebrate some occasion, like a miracle.

Such crowds contrast with the profane. These latter can be reveling crowds, like those typical of a New Orleans Mardi Gras, or even the wildly excited "Rocky Horror Picture Show" audiences. Of course, celebrations of World Series or Super Bowl victories can result in reveling crowds, ones that sometimes change spontaneously from joy to anger. And most of us have at one time or another been part of an excited group of people, one anticipating the arrival of some celebrity, such as a movie or rock star, or as is often the custom on campuses of northern colleges, one mounted by the gathering of students for a snowball fight after the year's first big storm.

Lofland offers us a program for thinking about the rich and wide-ranging variations accompanying the collective expression of joy. Some leaders of social movements are indeed masters of arousal, using their rhetoric to play to the joy potential in a crowd. By utilizing familiar cultural beliefs, they can, even in the midst of modern society, create occasions of collective celebration. Nevertheless, the meanings we attribute to these occasions are fluid. As we have already suggested, a joy crowd can transform into a hostile crowd with astonishing suddenness. The president of a major university once commended the crowd behavior of football fans after an important game. He said it was true the coach of his team was pelted with eggs and several football players were drenched with liquor by excited fans, but he added, "This was the best-behaved crowd we have had in several years."

Mass CollectiveBehavior

William Kornhauser (1959) distinguished several meanings associated with the word *mass*, differentiating theoretically between people who lead them and have power (elites) and those in them who react or follow (nonelites). He character- ized masses in terms of their accessibility, the degree to which people in control of a given occasion can be influenced by those they control, and their availability, the degree to which people in control can influence those they control. To illustrate, he defines a mass society as typified by both high availability and high accessibility. This distinction can be thought of in terms of the flow of informa- tion: in a mass society information flows from a highly accessible elite to a highly available audience.

Kornhauser's (1959) model helps us appreciate the exchanges that take place between leaders and followers. Since such exchanges often favor the elite they may not be balanced, but neither are they completely one-sided. Consider a typical fall afternoon at a football game. The people in the stadium, physically present and occupying space, are elites; the audience at home listening to or watching the game through the media of radio and television are nonelites. If the game reaches a crucial point, say where time is running out for the home team and a short field goal would ensure a tie but a more risky attempt at a touchdown could win it, the deafening cries of the hometown crowd might, in fact, influence a coach's decision. The nonelites at home, however, have no real effect, even though they can be described as having a symbolic territory and as being a social reality.

Zurcher (1983) details how football games can be seen as elaborate and skillful productions designed to evoke appropriate emotions in both participants and spectators. If a game does not succeed as "staged emotions," if, for instance, it is interpreted as "boring" by the mass audience, then television ratings are low and a network or station may cancel future broadcasts of football games, or at least of games between particular teams. Witness how in a short time "Monday Night Football" (MNF) has reached almost legendary proportions—the match- ups of teams that will appear on MNF involve perhaps the most critical network decisions of the regular season. With the stakes so high, we can easily see how the audience can affect production, and likewise we can grasp the necessity for the production of an exciting event (games that elicit the emotions of fans). At least insofar as televised games are concerned, football at both the professional and college levels can be accurately described as the deliberate staging of a performance, complete with audience warmups, props, costumes, and well- rehearsed performers.

Mass Fear

Floods along the Mississippi, firestorms in California, the resignation of the President of the United States—our memory of these well-televised events returns us to the dark side of collective behavior and fear as a mass phenomenon. Mass fears may be connected to possibilities of environmental and social disasters or to widely publicized trends that people believe will change their lives irrevocably. In a media-dependent society such as ours where the flow of information is from a highly accessible elite to a highly available public, the study of the content and style of news and other information is of vital importance to our understanding of mass fear (Lofland 1981, 421–27).

People's reactions to information they receive about tragic events outside their personal social worlds suggest two kinds of mass fear. First, there is an immediate and often short-lived fear associated with the occurrence. When members of a community first hear of a disaster, such as the explosion at the Texas City Oil Refinery in the 1950s, a sense of fear rapidly spreads over the entire community and beyond. The fear is more intense, of course, among those closest to the site of the disaster either physically or through social ties. Relatives of the men who worked in the Texas refinery reported the eerie feelings they experienced when they heard of the disaster. But events of this type directly affect only relatively small numbers of people. Most of us simply hear about such a disaster, and the fear evoked by the news of it fades in immediacy as it is filtered through media follow-ups and personal discussions. Ironically, our everyday routines tend to transform the really terrifying news that has become a common part of our knowledge of world and community events into impersonal, even taken-for-granted information. Mass fear begins from mass sources—radio, television, and newspapers—but it is absorbed into existing social structures. For example, the report of a disaster becomes something to be fearful of according to how people interpret the relevance of the tragedy to their everyday lives. If the event is relevant, it may be because it involved them in personal tragedy; if they are involved only indirectly or just see it on television, it is seen as irrelevant, giving people simply more information about the tragic nature of life in society.

In a natural disaster, mass fear reaction is a transitional stage leading to redefinitions of ordinary life. The first redefinition involves formulating "rescue" operations into routines. Rescue work may mean actually clearing debris and helping people relocate after a violent storm; or it may consist of emotional and social rescue, as in giving comfort and performing other remedial tasks necessary if victims are to "pick-up the pieces" of their personal and public lives.

In his study of the Texas City disaster, and especially in his account of how persons experience extreme role conflict in connection with such events, Killian (1952) showed the significance of multiple group memberships in the handling of fear. For example, foremen who were home at the time they heard about the explosion at the refinery were caught between feeling they should stay with their families and sense of obligation to be at the refinery with their friends who might need help. Generally, the resolution of this dilemma paralleled the ordering of perceived role obligations. Although this ordering could vary from person to person, it seemed to reflect an internal organization; that is, the reactions of people to the disaster were ordered in ways consistent with their self-concepts. Thus most men looked after their families first and then proceeded with obligations associated with their jobs. The first concern of those who were at the refinery at the time of the blast was to inform family members of their safety. Those who were "off duty" somewhere else first "ordered" their family affairs (located and informed their offspring and spouses) and then headed for the refinery.

Again following Lofland, we note how vast the variations of mass fear can be. Some disasters can be prepared for, as in the case of hurricanes, and more recently with the advent of sophisticated radar equipment, even of tornadoes. Earthquakes are still random from the perspective of everyday life. When we look at the meanings of mass fear, we discover that disasters that seem random yet are perceived as immediate elicit the strongest fears. Rarely occurring phenomena such as major earthquakes can be pushed from our everyday consciousness, as can remote disasters like terrorism in the Middle East.

But actual disasters call for the mobilization of what people know about solving problems and the activation of links between their home territory and larger societal domains. A good way to think about the process that underlies how people make sense of disasters is to remember a generalization: action driven by fear reinforces the existing and potential symbolic links between victims and their larger social environments; but fear without action increases the distance between what people think they know and what they actually know and thereby heightens the vulnerability of social structure.

Several studies illustrate this principle. Truly "massive" disasters such as tornadoes and floods may have far-reaching effects on the social lives of victims. Erickson (1979) studied a flood at Buffalo Creek, West Virginia, and concluded that the disaster damaged the physical community and destroyed the social networks within it. He characterized the residents of the town as apathetic and powerless. As they began to react to their loss, however, they transformed the tragedy into a symbolic starting point for a new sense of community, one that emerged through a process of storytelling about the meanings of the flood for the community.

In contrast, fears for which no corresponding courses of action are available often reach proportions out of scale with the probability or reality of actual disaster. Lofland (1981) refers to such fears as "false," with a good illustration being the reaction to Orson Welles's famous 1938 radio broadcast, "War of the Worlds." When dramatically performed as a newscast, this story of the invasion of the earth by Martians evoked mass fear in the audience. Audiences tuning in late and hearing only parts of the broadcast believed the space invasion to be real. Many people were in their cars "evacuating" the area before they realized the report was fictional.

Of course there is a sense in which false fears reflect real ones. In 1938, people were fearful of an invasion stemming from a war in Europe that might eventually involve the United States. Sometimes fear is based on some actual threat not fully articulated by the persons who are circulating a rumor about it; or it may be fostered by those experiencing a "phantom" or imagined physical symptom, as was ttrue when workers at a clothing factory "suffered what were purported to be insect bites" in the summer of 1962. Subsequent analyses of the "bites" were unable to locate either actual insects or real bites on workers. Still, the fear of the bites increased both complaints and sick time (Kerckhoff and Back 1968).

Studies of false fears provide a model for describing how people deal with information they do not fully understand. Some treat it as an immediate personal threat and may experience an imagined physical symptom. Extreme reactions of this kind of audience, as in the case of the invasion from Mars, include actual preparation for the dreaded event (we might include survivalists in this category). But it is more usual for listeners or witnesses simply to become confused and alarmed, gradually realizing the true nature of the event as they continue to obtain more information about it. But while most of us have learned to distinguish the everyday or the imaginative from the newsworthy, this is not always an easy task.

Mass Hostility

Crowd hostility has been studied extensively, but such is not the case for mass hostility, as it is more difficult to study. Since they are primarily merely audiences, masses cannot act in concert. Whereas crowds act, masses react. But though there are few empirical studies of the distribution of feelings of mass hostility, we can cite observations and experiences that indicate how powerful this form of collective behavior can be.

Anyone who has driven the freeways of a large metropolis is probably familiar with one manifestation of mass hostility. Several years ago, Walt Disney produced a cartoon about the average American driver. The cartoon began with a tranquil scene showing a well-mannered Goofy preparing for an automobile trip. He is the picture of patience and forbearance as he copes with the frustrations of bags that do not close and children who do not cooperate. As soon as he gets behind the wheel of the car, however, he transforms into a hideous monster. His face contorts into a hog's as he battles other drivers for dominion of the roadway; flames roar from his nostrils as his hostility emotes onto the screen.

Because there is something isolating about the vehicular shell that surrounds a driver, it is easier to honk a horn at another car than it is to insult a person face-to-face. The metal and glass seem to insulate one driver from another in the same way rituals of exchange, little niceties of greetings and turn taking smooth out differences of backgrounds and intentions in face-to-face interactions. But the objects of traffic are not people, and to many of us it is easy to treat a car as a proper target of hostility.

The mass hostility that leads people to treat each other as objects may well be associated with specific features of modern life. For example, Phillips's (1983) research indicates that suicide rates are tied to reports of certain media events, like presidential elections, prizefights, and suicides of prominent people. This association might well be linked to increased or decreased levels of mass hostility. Likewise the studies by Smelser (1963) and Spilerman (1976) indicate how dramatic events of disorder in black ghettos are clustered following equally dramatic mass events. Of course the riots and much of the individual violence that followed the assassination of Dr. Martin Luther King, Jr., illustrate this kind of phenomenon.

Although it is difficult to measure, and is usually benign in its effects, mass hostility can still be felt. In the American cities that have National Football League teams, fans whose hometown team has suffered a particularly disappointing loss on Sunday may bring hostility to work with them on Monday morning. This hostility is typically channeled into productive activities, but it may become a negative factor in a person's mode of dealing with the world. Some fans report being depressed or feeling "out of sorts" after a particularly difficult loss. In contrast, they may be "high" on a "sweet victory" for several days. A mass experience such as extreme disappointment with a professional sports team can effect a pervasive mood among members of a community.

Such pervasive moods play a part in the statistical relationships Phillips and others report. In their most malignant forms these moods can target groups for vilification and even punishment. Irwin (1980) documents "swastika epidemics" in American prisons where mass hostility erupts into individual acts of anti-Semitism and vandalism. And as Spilerman asserts, "there is considerable evidence that skyjackings, prison riots, bomb threats and aggressive crimes of other sorts have been spread by television and other mass media" (Spilerman 1976, 790).

Hostility is a concept that usually refers to individual emotion, but it can also be expressed in collective form; and when this occurs it does so in varying degrees of organization. It can be tightly packaged into personalities, it may be the bond of solidarity that holds a crowd together, or it can be a generally distributed feeling collectively experienced but not expressed. Mass hostility is typically diffused through a thousand horn honks and angry verbal exchanges. It flows without focus and without symbolic import in the "keyed" playing of the roles of everyday life. Still, on occasion, it can reach highly organized levels of mass expression.

Mass Joy

At some point in our lives, especially as children, virtually all of us experience mass joy, the most common forms of which are crazes, fashion, and fads. A craze evokes in its participants high arousal levels, but it does not often sustain them. A good example of this was the Hula Hoop craze; for a while, it seemed that the whole nation was twirling circles of plastic, sometimes several simultaneously, around their waists in frenzied but for the most part apparently pointless activity.

At times a craze can grasp the attention of large numbers of people, and in some markets last a relatively long time. One illustration of a fairly long-lasting craze is the rather systematic and energetic "yearning for yesterday" we call nostalgia (Davis 1979). It seems to be everywhere: art deco candle holders, the rediscovery of artists of the 1930s, nostalgia clothing shops, and movies like *Raiders of the Lost Ark* and the ever-popular mobster films that evoke "tones" and "feelings" of bygone days. From "puttin' on the Ritz" to a yearning for a return to the days when some street gangs were noble, citizens of modern society consume versions of the past in ways designed to comfort them and impart meaning to the present.

Davis shows us how as a social phenomenon nostalgia serves collective ends. By reconstructing what the past was like, we can sharpen and define meanings that we want to make important in the present. And although we may know the simplicity of yesterday is lost, through nostalgic enterprises we can express an appreciation of the values and lifestyle of the past and a wish for their return.

Everyday life in modern society is full of problems associated with continuous change and the business of interacting with strangers. So instead of being able to rely on tradition to locate us in society, we must negotiate our own sense of belonging. No wonder, as Davis suggests, nostalgia has its greatest appeal during times of transition both in the society and in the life cycle of the individual. The strong nostalgia craze we witnessed during the 1970s was due in part to a convergence of real changes in our society and the coming of age of millions of Americans. When a yearning for the past takes on the proportions of a national craze, it represents the efforts of a generation of people to reconcile and make sense out of the past and present during times when the continuity between them is difficult to see.

Although most of this yearning is put into practice in acts of consuming tickets to movies, records, clothing and the like, it also serves wider social ends. Davis defines the phenomenon of "generational nostalgia" as the construction of a version of the past by persons who collectively experience rapid social change at critical junctures in their life cycles. Seen in this light, nostalgic sentiment partakes of one of the great dialectical processes of Western civilization: the ceaseless tension of change vs. stability, innovation vs. reaffirmation, new vs. old, utopia vs. golden age. Its role in this dialectic is that of a brake, to be sure, since little in contemporary life seems capable of arresting the march of modern technology and rational organization. Nonetheless it is, perhaps, enough of a break to cause some individuals and peoples to look before they knowingly leap. (Davis 1979, 116)

Fashions and Fads

A fashion is a "pleasurable mass involvement which participants define as important but not critical and in which people are variously engaged depending on the particular fashion" (Lofland 1981, 442). Fashions influence the meanings we give to objects and activities that run the gamut of diversity from apparently trivial things, like the shape of collars on a dress shirt to entire lifestyles. Fashion is clearly influenced by the institutions of society, as the fashion "industry," for example, makes available to consumers the "latest" in clothing design. Certainly there is a mutual influence between the spontaneous emergence of fashion and the institutional production of it. Styles of clothing once thought of as exclusively "hippie" are now part of the standard apparel of the "well-dressed" urbanite. Blue jeans are the best example of this. Since the advent of designer jeans we have exchanged the conscious rebellion of blue-jeans-clad teenagers in the mid-1960s for the designer label across the derriere.

We can appreciate the social psychological significance of fads and fashions by tracing their origins. If we can locate in a social context the fashions of dress, like Ocean Pacific clothes, pierced ears, blue jeans, or long or short hair, then we have yet another way to describe how society and self interrelate at the collective level.

The Scene as an Activity System

John Irwin has developed concepts for understanding some specific types of collective behavior. His ideas also have added greatly to our appreciation of how some seemingly trivial fads and crazes can influence the very normative structures of society. His idea, though simple, is profound in its implication.

He begins by noting the major changes that have taken place in society, the most significant for collective behavior being that individuals now have both increased leisure time and more expendable income. Whereas the workplace used to be the primary arena in which persons established their adult identities, in contemporary society more and more people find themselves employed in jobs that they regard as boring, routine, and most important, unfulfilling. Although a strong case can be made that work in industrial society has always been mostly menial, what is different now, Irwin contends, is the relative pay people receive—they have more money left over after purchasing basics—and the fact that they simply spend fewer hours at the job. The arena in which people derive a sense of self has shifted from work to play, and along with the shift have come several other changes.

According to Irwin, people are self-consciously aware of the degree to which they are "on stage" in everyday life, and they have learned how to participate in small activity systems in ways that allow them to think of themselves as doing important things. Even if the systems of activity they operate in are purely recreational, the people in them have learned to interpret their activities as relevant to their self-concepts. Irwin calls these systems *scenes*.

The scenes Irwin focuses on are urban, leisure oriented, and youthful. They are the territories within which action is sought and which operate to provide people with opportunities for excitement and a sense of doing something out of the ordinary. The picture of scenes Irwin portrays shows loosely organized bands of people coming together around shared interests to engage in "finding where the action is." He discusses how people learn to "plug into" scenes, how they establish levels of involvement in scenes, and how they move from scene to scene in search of new action. He stresses how all this activity is conducted self-consciously, and how even participating in criminal scenes can be transitory, staged, and essentially for fun.

Irwin offers a theory of scenes that gives us insights into the nature of life in modern society. Contemporary lifestyles, crazes, and fads must be understood, he suggests, neither as temporary, passing deviations from normal life nor as revolutionary social movements. Rather, our view of youthful actors playing in their chosen arenas takes into account both the transitory and the genuinely influential aspects of modern scenes.

A scene activity represents learning how to make and maintain contacts and mutual interests, and how to behave in ways that serve individual and social ends simultaneously. Irwin traces the emergence of the scene to pre-World War II California. In a sense, scenes began out of the efforts of large numbers of idled young men to find things to do in the beach towns of southern California. Just as the economic recovery from the Great Depression was moving forward, beach bums began to inhabit the California shores. They simply "hung out," talked, and combed the beaches in search of action and shells. Some of the more athletic men began to surf on heavy redwood boards. World War II broke up these aggregates; but after the war, some of the men returned to the beach. This time some of them had skills in aircraft technologies that they put to work in the design of lighter and better surfboards. After the war there were gradually more and more people on the beach. California boomed, and by the late 1940s and early 1950s, a large enough number of people were interested in and had the skills for a single activity that the first "grand scene" emerged, what we now know as the "surfin' scene."

By carefully describing the history of surfing, we can understand the life phases of any scene, for, according to Irwin, scenes pass through a number of separate stages. First is the articulation stage, where relatively small numbers of people come together around a single activity. For the most active participants, the scene is almost an obsession. They spend hours on end talking about and acting out the scene, one outcome of which is the emergence of norms and values for scene conduct. These often include beliefs about the worth of the action (usually defined in contrast to what are imagined as mainstream values) and strong ideas about the "proper" conduct of it. The norms of a scene are formulated during the articulation phase, and people who may later become heroes and leaders of the scene find they are in the center of a new world.

The second phase in the "natural history" of scenes is the golden age. During this phase, most of the basic norms governing proper activities have been formulated. Leaders emerge, usually charismatic types who happen to have been involved in the original formation of the scene. Finding themselves in the center of the action, they serve new members as references for the mastery of norms and appropriate action.

Third is the period of expansion. Though it is not inevitable in the growth of scenes, expansion usually does occur, especially whenever a scene begins to attract national attention. Surfing, hippie, running and a variety of other scenes have gone through such periods of expansion that the informal character of the norms of these scenes have been stretched to the breaking point. When expansion reaches a certain level there are simply too many people participating in the activity for the old ways to function.

At such times a related problem of control appears. In the articulation and golden age stages of a scene, leaders can oversee the core action. They can literally be in the territories of action, with their presence helping to reinforce the particular versions of meanings for what is going on. Drug "trips" can be managed; the ultimate wave can be discussed in terms of the latest experiences of core members, and the "best" run ever can be judged by those who know and respect each other's competencies at running. When strangers, such as first-timers and the generally uninitiated—gremlins, teeny-boppers and wanna-bes— flood the territory (the beaches, the Haight-Ashbury district of San Francisco, and the roadways of city parks), scenes change and insiders confront squarely the mainstream values of society, eventually having to accommodate themselves to pressures from within and outside their ranks.

From the vantage of scene members, expansion means a corruption of both the normative structure and the purity of action. An almost inevitable consequence of expansion, then, is the spoiling of the scene. This happens as the direct result of institutional social controls, like the narcotics police breaking up hippie "crash pads," the enforcing of no trespassing laws so that surfers are driven off the best beaches, and of course the clashes between runners and motorists in which attempts by communities are made to license runners and restrict them to certain roadways.

Corruption by outsiders forces the scene to be more conventional, "to clean up its act." And though a scene may well survive corruption, when it does it enters stagnation, a stage in which there are remnants of the old norms (a flavor of the "good old days"), but where the scene itself has come under the direction of the more widely distributed control mechanisms of society. Here, what is gained in respectability is lost in distinctiveness; and the scene that used to be a source for the derivation of self-esteem and a sense of uniqueness now becomes routine and businesslike. Although many "diehards," and even latecomers, may sustain a scene for a long period of time, the magic of the stages of articulation and the golden age is lost. Irwin suggests that by the time a scene stagnates most of the original members are into something else.

Irwin substantiates his model with detailed documentation of surfing and hippies. Although the relative length and intensity of the phases varies, each of these two scenes went through the full cycle of the natural history. Irwin calls these two scenes "grand" ones. By this he means they reached a level of popularity in which they involved literally hundreds of thousands of people. The label "grand scenes" suggests they have "special dimensions and unique histories," and that at one time they were exciting and appealing in ways that reached far beyond the actual people participating in surfing or living as hippies. According to Irwin, these scenes not only elicited attention from society but also altered convention. Surfing as a scene continues to be a major influence in clothing styles and musical tastes in America. Likewise, many attitudes toward leisure, work, and the search for meaning in personal life are "hip" in origin.

To appreciate how pervasive the values and norms of surfing have become, we need only watch television, where surfing can still appear as a theme in a beer commercial. A well-known surfer, speaking from a beach bar, beer in hand, expresses the opinion that he might get a job and quit all this "beach life." His friends cease their reveling and in a hush turn their attention to him. There is a long pause. Then he replies, "Naw!" to the joyous relief of his friends.

Irwin's thesis that the workplace has lost much of its power for imparting self-meanings seems quite plausible, as does his idea that profound social changes beyond those of clothing and hairstyles can derive from essentially leisure-time activities. Irwin teaches us how seemingly trivial items of collective behavior can be a part of a process of change affecting even the core values and attitudes of members of society.

From Scene to Social Movement

Irwin's theory of scenes pertains to particular kinds of societies, those with relatively high degrees of affluence for large numbers of their members. Under such conditions, a popular scene becomes a modern social movement. The study of social movements addresses situations in which varied collective responses to some conditions or needs become organized toward specific goals. Social movements, then, are goal-directed actions composed of people, sometimes from disparate backgrounds, who have banded together around a common cause.

Social movements can be focused on a remarkable range of topics, concerns, and real or perceived problems. Currently we are familiar with various ecological movements, some designed to save the American eagle, others, the whales, and still others, the whole world (ecosystem). Of course antiabortion and prochoice movements can be quite strong, as can causes like freedom for political prisoners. It is apparent that movement topics and political persuasions know no limits. But even though movements can encompass an amazingly wide array of issues, they all do have a typical form.

We can discuss two social movements to illustrate this form: First, we examine how people bound together by religious beliefs about the necessity to save the world became a significant social force in the life of many American young people. Second, we look at a particularly contemporary movement, animal rights.

From the late 1950s through the middle 1960s, John Lofland studied what was then an obscure religious cult. It happened that this cult later gained national attention because of the extreme techniques members used to assure conformity among its members and because of the conflicts it had with the conventional culture.

During the course of his study, Lofland, first with Stark and then alone, worked on a model of the conversion process, eventually offering a detailed description of the conditions, both psychological and social, necessary for an individual to experience a conversion (a radical alteration of worldview and social being). The people Lofland observed were not only "joining a cult"; they were also being transformed in what appeared to be a rather fundamental way. People who had been functioning as typical graduate students in a state university suddenly, or so it seemed, expressed a belief in the impending end of the world. Their whole lives were absorbed in the belief and they became members of (and in some cases proselytizers for) the Divine Precepts, also known as "A Complete New Age Revelation." Such dramatic transformations are not very common, thus Lofland sought a thorough understanding of how such a collective movement as the Divine Precepts cult appealed to, recruited, and transformed people living apparently ordinary lives.

He explored the backgrounds of people who had become cult members and in some cases actually observed their conversion to the Divine Precepts. After years of documenting these transformations, he advanced a model to explain the conversion process. Lofland offers this model to account for his observations of the DP (Divine Precepts) cult, but clearly it has implications for understanding how certain beliefs and emotional dispositions already existent among people can be organized to effect significant changes both in their lives and in the lives of those close to them who must deal with their conversion.

Primarily, before a person becomes a candidate for conversion, he or she must have first experienced "enduring acutely felt tensions." These tensions are usually felt in personal ways, perhaps entailing the death of a loved one or a tragic event in one's own life or the life of a close friend. Second, without exception, converts to the DP cult experienced these tensions within a religious, problem-solving perspective. Although not all DP members had been devoutly religious before converting, as is typical of most eventual converts across all such movements, many were living outside any conventional church; and all did tend to evaluate their problems religiously. Hence they saw their problems as resulting from past "sins," and they saw God as either punishing or rewarding their "earthly" deeds.

The third dynamic in the conversion process required a shift in self-concept. Instead of feeling they were suffering at the hands of fate, DP cult members saw themselves as seeking the truth about their own predicaments. As Lofland puts it, they became "religious seekers." Still not full cult converts at this point, typically this is when they first became aware of the Divine Precepts. Generally in quest of religious insights, they now were exposed to the beliefs of the cult, sometimes by chance (they just happened across a pamphlet) or when they ran into a cult member who explained DP to them.

Fourth, the encounter with DP beliefs and believers became a turning point in the converts' lives. Soon the bulk of their waking hours was devoted to thoughts and conversations focused exclusively on the Divine Precepts. This process can be thought of as an immersion in the social world of believers. Although at this stage converts are still not full cult members, they are undergoing what we referred to in an earlier chapter as extreme secondary socialization.

Simply talking and thinking in DP terms, however, is not sufficient for complete conversion. At this penultimate stage the crucial experience seems to be an emotional one as sentiments, or in Lofland's words "affective bonds," emerged, usually after hours of interaction with cult members. In some instances this kind of bonding preexisted in the potential convert, that is, it was established as a style previously, perhaps even in a secular context. But now the emotional ties were fresh and strong. Since the topic of talk and thought at this point was almost exclusively the Divine Precepts and related matters, cult ties began to supplant extracult friendships and social relationships. Lofland refers to this stage as one in which "extra-cult attachments are low or neutralized" (Lofland 1980, 8).

Finally, the indication that full conversion had been accomplished occurred when a person became a "deployable agent," trustworthy enough to go into the world of unbelievers and represent the Divine Precepts. This stage entailed intensive interaction among "true believers," "agents" who served as symbols for the cult. Ultimate incorporation into the cult was apparent when a new believer became a proselytizer for Divine Precepts.

Lofland's work tells us that collective behaviors can become all encompassing for some people. As we know, such movements can on occasion generate considerable interest among the representatives of the conventional culture. Nevertheless, it is important to understand that Lofland is depicting a funneling process of recruitment. At the first stage the criteria are minimal, applying to many, perhaps all members of society. From time to time, all of us feel tension from the problems in our everyday lives; so we all experience some of the preconditions necessary to make us susceptible, as it were, to conversion. But though everyone can be poured into the funnel, most are siphoned off and only a few pass through to the next stage, where the opening narrows. Now the movement draws only from those who see these ordinary problems in an extraordinary way (sacred meanings for secular events). In like manner, each successive stage narrows the opening even more, until only a select minority are chosen as converts.

Social movements often recruit in such a funneling process; hence they build on as broad a base as possible to groom a few core members. Although a social movement may involve relatively few core members, if it uses themes of common experience it can exert a disproportionate influence on society. This is exactly what the DP cult members were able to accomplish, until the formal institutions of social control (courts, churches and families) operated to conventionalize the cult. Faced with the overwhelming power of the institutions of society, most social movements, including the DP cult, adapt.

Adaptation itself is achieved in several ways. Primarily, a movement can retreat from confrontation. When this happens the core goals of a movement may be redefined. For the members of a millennial cult like the Divine Precepts, this may mean changing their beliefs about the necessity of saving the world. They may have to be content with maintaining themselves within more modest goals (like personally being ready for the end or for the second coming of Christ). Cult members may also become more conventional themselves, or as is often the case, a cult may simply fade away when its techniques to neutralize extramovement contact weaken and its members drift back into the mainstream of social life.

Adaptations reflect the ultimate power of convention. Most movements, even grand scenes, fall short of their expressed ends and society remains secular, in spite of literally thousands of hours of human effort on the part of believers to transform it into something more Godlike. Ironically, scenes that are not true movements may have much more lasting effects on society than true movements which have explicitly defined goals for social change. For example, today anyone visiting the University of California at Berkeley, the scene of the 1964 Free Speech Movement, and of the tremendous anti-Vietnam war activity that followed on the heels of it, would find that in ways the students now look and act much more hip than their 1960s counterparts. But this is more of a gloss than anything else; for in fact today's students are much more conservative and probably would not be so ready to support the kinds of movements fostered by students in the past.

The Animal Rights Movement

A contemporary social movement that has reached major proportions in American society is the animal rights movement. It differs from the DP movement because it has as its goal redefining some of the central conceptions of life that have grounded the conventional institutions of Western society.

In the traditional cosmology of Western society, humans have the right to use animals for the benefit of humans: "And God said, Let us make man in our image, after our likeness; and let him have dominion over the fish of the sea, and over the fowl of the air, and over the cattle, and over all the Earth and over every creeping thing that creepeth upon the earth" (Genesis 1:26). Even though within the conventions of Judeo-Christian religion dominion may include a human obligation toward animals, animal rightists as a group generally reject the idea of human dominion as "speciesist." In fact, they reject the traditional Christian God and religion. One survey of animal rights activists indicated that 70 percent are atheists or agnostics, a startling contrast to the 80 to 90 percent of the American population who express a belief in God (Jasper and Nelkin 1992, 38; General Social Survey 1990).

Animal rightists have issued a serious challenge to the prevailing cosmology that gives humans dominion over nature and animals (Singer 1971; Regan 1983). In addition to arguing against speciesism (the tendency to see the world through the interests of our species), they elevate animals to a higher moral position than humans (Nash and Sutherland 1991). In doing this, their movement calls into question the assumptions that allow us to use animals for scientific experiments, food, comfort, work, and recreation and offers to its participants a new kind of moral engagement and commitment in a secular society (Jasper and Nelkin 1992, 175). These features of the movement, we suggest, can be understood as reactions to changes in the institutional structure of society.

First, let consider the goal of animal rights—to formulate a new cosmology. Among other things, a cosmology provides clear beliefs about differences between humans and animals. Most cultures have relatively stable ways for their members to understand what is human and what is animal, and these beliefs function to legitimate their actions. For example, Tapper (1988) has argued that in societies where hunting and gathering is the economic base, different species of animals may be viewed as models for differences between human groups, such as in totemic systems. In pastoral societies, in contrast, where herd animals are in ecological symbiosis with humans, animals may be both identified with humans at one level and differentiated from them at another (Tapper 1988). Whatever the relationship between animals and humans, in most societies the differences are clearly defined by their cultures, economic systems and religious institutions.

As a society like ours shifts to increasingly differentiated production systems, the close connection between culture and nature found in traditional societies diminishes. At the same time, members' consciousness of social processes, their awareness of how society actually works, increases, and the self rather than membership in the group becomes important. In this context, individuals redefine their relationships with animals in terms of the self. Animals, their meanings and uses are then understood as part of the productive and rational structures of society. Understandings about animals in industrial society become instrumental in nature, and animals are often used for research, food, sport and recreation, or people are simply neutral or negative toward them.

As society continues to modernize, both the organization of food production and the specialization of the work people do function to separate them from animals in their everyday lives. Finally, in the postmodern or postindustrial society, only a very small percentage of the activities people get paid for involve any contact at all with animals. According to the General Social Survey data for 1990, less than 2 percent of the American labor force works with animals directly or indirectly. Yet, here and in other Western societies people may go to a great lengths to have animals living in their homes.

Animals, then, have become less important for their place in production and their meanings in institutional contexts are more understandable in specific interpretive schemes of the self, such that they may take on emotional and symbolic value in highly variable fashion. According to animal rightists, people can no longer justify killing animals to produce food. Society should focus instead on the emotions surrounding the act of killing. To citizens of the urban, artificial society, animals become companions, they are treated as family members, and they are reminders of the indirect emotional relationships people have with nature (Nash 1989).

Animal rights as a social movement not only redefines the reality of animals in relation to humans but it also creates a new worldview or cosmology for many of its adherents. To appreciate this thesis, we must look at the features of religion and cosmology animal rights movement participants are in the process of redefining.

Geertz has defined religion as a system of sacred symbols that constitutes a worldview, or cosmology. A world view is a perspective on the way things should be, a comprehensive idea of order (Geertz 1973, 89–91). In any religion there will be some congruence between the way things should be and the way they are. Religion provides both a model of reality (a way to conceptualize the way things are) and a model for reality (a guide to current belief and future behavior). A religious worldview also carries with it an ethos, that is, a moral, emotional, and aesthetic quality (Geertz 1973, 94–97). Besides being emotionally convincing, a religion must provide a general sense of order for existence. A religion includes explanations of phenomena, such as order (the quest for meaning in life), suffering (not only how to avoid suffering but how to suffer), evil (how to recognize good and evil), and justice (how to make sound moral judgments) (Geertz 1973, 100–106).

When religious beliefs are modified and adjusted to the shifts in contemporary society, the religious ethos proceeds systematically to individualize emotions, impulses and feelings. When this happens, the charismatic appeal of social movements such as animal rights can embody the essence of religion without its institutional form. The fragmented self is then free to construct specific narrative versions of the phenomena of everyday life (Wexler 1990, 171–72).

A new social movement may take on the functions of a religious system of belief in what appears to be a secular context, but which in practice deals with and reflects the fragmentation of the institutional systems themselves. The way people understand their society, the stories of the self they tell, their accounts of what happens to them and why, may become eccentric and blur the fundamental boundaries of beliefs.

The animal rights movement in the context of current social change may take on religious or cosmological significance. At the individual level, for instance, people learn attitudes, motives and feelings about the importance of animals; at the social level they create new organizational forms; and at the cultural level they interpret the cosmos. Furthermore, each of the levels addresses questions about human experience that once were within the purview of religion.

The animal rights movement has been building in the United States, Great Britain, and Canada since the publication of *Animal Liberation* by Peter Singer. The animal rights philosophy, as espoused by Singer (1975), Regan (1983), and others, provides a worldview that gives meaning to personal lives, deals with the meaning of suffering and death, defines evil and good, provides conceptions of right and wrong, justice and morality, and gives a sense of identity and belonging to its believers. Let us look at each of these cosmological questions from the animal rights perspective.

Bewilderment

A major concern of animal rightists is, "What meaning does life have for me if I participate in the suffering of animals? All 'sentient' beings are of value, and I can only make sense of life if I include animals in my repertory of meanings." Animal rights' literature makes the treatment of animals a moral issue, often quoting the great religious leader Mohandas Gandhi, "The greatness of a nation and its moral progress can be judged by the way its animals are treated " (Rowan 1988).

An example of the bewilderment animal rights activists confront and resolve through the animal rights philosophy is the question of euthanasia for dogs and cats, which many activists consider to be members of their family. The American Veterinary Medicine Association national estimates are that 100 million dogs and cats are put to death each year in the United States. Twenty million are euthanized by the American Humane Society. The rest are killed by disease or trauma or are "put to sleep" in veterinary hospitals. It is estimated that ten to 25 million are killed because they have no homes. Yet veterinary medicine can do anything for animals that we are capable of doing for humans. So why do we have this "problem"?

According to Dr. Patricia Olsen, a veterinarian who specializes in small animal reproduction, it is due to our neglect of animals. In her research she found the following to be the major causes of owners relinquishing pets to the Humane Society: the owner cannot control the pet, inconvenience to the owner, cost, and inappropriate defecation and urination. But the problem is not only "irresponsible" owners. According to Al Robinson of the Anoka County Humane Society in Minnesota, 141 dogs and cats are born for every American child. Clearly we have a massive overpopulation of pets. Veterinarians have tried both to promote sterilization of pets and to educate the public on the control of pet reproduction. But some veterinarians argue that even a 90 percent effective education program will not be enough. Humane societies and small-animal veterinarians believe that what we now have is chaos. The animal rightists' solution to this is to create a ban on the reproduction of dogs and cats. Their first landmark attempt was the passage of a law in San Mateo County, California, making it an offense ($500 fine) for a dog to have puppies. To get this law passed the San Mateo Humane Society showed on television pictures of a dog being euthanized, thus horrifying millions of viewers.

For participants in the animal rights movement, euthanasia for animals is part of a larger moral dilemma about who lives and who dies, who reproduces and who does not, and how humans and animals should live together. From them there is a call for a new sense of order in which animals have rights to a place on earth without having to subordinate their interests to the interests of humans.

Suffering

The meaning of suffering has been a major focus of the animal rights movement since the 1824 founding of the SPCA (Society for the Prevention of Cruelty to Animals) in Great Britain (Ryder 1989, 89). Animal suffering in biomedical research, hunting and trapping, and in the production of meat and fur have been the main targets of the movement. Currently the stockyards in many cities of the

United States are being targeted by animal rights groups to protest the suffering of "downed" animals before their slaughter. Ironically, the long history of the suffering of the slaughterhouse worker was not considered relevant to these groups.

Many of the assumptions in the animal rights movement about suffering are anthropomorphic, that is, based on human notions of suffering, and "ethnopomorphic," or based on notions of suffering in our society as opposed to other societies. This latter concept is consistent with the rightists' belief that animals in the United States should be treated like people in the United States and not like people in other countries who may have fewer "rights" than animals already have here. For example, experiments have shown that pet food eaten by America's dogs and cats contains more riboflavin, niacin, vitamin A, and iron than the same quantity of the typical rations that relief workers give refugees (*New York Times,* August 10,1992).

So with respect to suffering, the new cosmology redefines the concept to include not just physical pain but also the emotional and psychological suffering of animals. Just what constitutes emotional pain in an animal can be determined by how a human in our own culture would feel. Participants in the animal rights movement "feel" the pain of animals because they can identify their "self" with the "self" of an animal. This gives animals a kind of self and identity previously allocated only to humans.

Good and Evil

A basic premise of the animal rights movement is that humans are the source of all evil (as opposed to the traditional Christian idea that Satan is). In the new cosmology, animals are essentially and intrinsically good. Eschewing the explicit manifesto in Genesis delivering animals into the hands of man after the flood, and the later Christian emphasis on the importance of the soul in humans, thus separating them from animals, which have no souls, animal rightists elevate animals to a moral position higher than humans because animals are pure and innocent, unlike humans who wilfully commit evil acts (Nash and Sutherland 1991).

According to Ingrid Newkirk, the founder of People for the Ethical Treatment of Animals (PETA), "Humans have grown like a cancer. We're the biggest blight on the face of the earth" (*Reader's Digest,* June 1990). A prevailing belief is that animals are not just good, they are better than humans. According to the British philosopher Patrick Corbett, "Animals are in many respects superior to ourselves" (*Intellectual Activist,* September 14, 1983).

This belief is not restricted to the United States. A recent article in the New York Times entitled "French Animal Love: Has It Gone Too Far?" bemoans the fact that in Paris dogs are often given preference over humans. A French anthropologist, Jean-Pierre Digart, has written, "It is a serious problem . . . when we get to the point where we place some animals above men" (*New York Times*, February 2, 1990).

It appears that some animal rights adherents are using the category "species" to determine membership in our moral community. If all species are included in the same moral community with humans, then biomedical research will be viewed as an atrocity. A leaflet recently put out to protest research at the University of Minnesota contains the following:

> Every day of the year, at the hands of white-robed individuals bent on getting recognition, or a degree, or at least a lucrative job, millions of animals are slowly blinded by acids, poisoned, disemboweled, submitted to repeated shocks, frozen to be revived and refrozen, starved or left to die of thirst, in many cases after various glands have been extirpated or the spinal cord has been cut.

The language of this text is reminiscent of horrific tales of Nazi atrocities, and it clearly represents humans as evil and animals as innocent victims. It is followed by a prayer:

> I am
> The voice of the voiceless
> through me the dumb shall speak
> 'til the deaf world's ear
> be made to hear
> the wrongs of the wordless weak
> And I am
> My brother's Keeper
> And I will fight his fight
> and Speak the word
> for beast and bird
> 'til the world shall set things right . . .

Justice

Words such as cruelty, torture, and suffering have very specific meanings to animal rights groups, meanings that may not be shared by the general population. The Animal Rights Coalition (ARC), like many other animal rights groups, believes that any experiment with animals is cruel by definition, even when animals are killed humanely to be used for research. This is because animals should be treated as humans in every way. According to Ingrid Newkirk, "You cannot find a relevant attribute in human beings that doesn't exist in animals as well . . . [and] . . . if you ground any concept of human rights in a particular attribute, then animals have to be included. Animals have rights" (*Harpers,* August 1988, 47). If animals have rights equal to humans, including the ability to decide on issues of justice and morality, then any use of animals in experiments without their consent is immoral and unjust.

For those in the animal rights movement, the principle of equality between animals and humans, and of justice for all, is a clear issue of right and wrong. Rightists have focused their activities around questions of how to deal with injustice to animals and so confront the discrepancy between what is occurring now and what ought to be. They feel personally alienated from a society that is "cruel" to animals, and they work toward a sense of morality and responsibility toward all "sentient" beings.

Social Connectedness

Part of the cosmological importance of the animal rights movement is that it appears to bring together a community of people who have lost a sense of identity with and belonging to the wider society but who come together to save animals from a cruel and unjust world. Profiles of animal rights movement participants (Jamison and Lunch 1990) indicate that they are young (average age thirty), educated (40 percent with at least a B.A. degree), white (93 percent), middle class (44 percent identified themselves as professionals), female (68 percent), and urban (52 percent live in towns of over 100,000 population and 43 percent grew up in such urban places).

Their common idea of morality is reinforced by their protests and the work they do for the movement. For them, no other social or political cause justifies such zeal and emotion. The Animal Rights Coalition hotline in St. Paul is a phone message that announces daily several minutes worth of news about strategy meetings, writing and legal campaigns, pet store watches, speakers, and regular protests and demonstrations. In any one day, the hotline provides enough activities for a person to become fully immersed in the movement. These concrete acts of individual and group action provide a meaningful way for people to be part of a community of concerned individuals. They provide a social connectedness to what might otherwise be alienated lives.

Other practices promoting social connectedness include pet grief therapy for people who need emotional support for the loss of their pets, burial rites at pet cemeteries, dog shows and events, volunteer zoo activity, annual Humane Society blessings of the animals, fund-raising projects, and myriad other activities related to pets. These activities provide links between animal rights activists and welfarists concerned about animals.

A social movement provides support, consolation and reconciliation for its believers. In the face of uncertainty, particularly in a rapidly changing society, believers may not only find support among like-minded believers but they also may be reassured that the version of the world they have is shared by others. Furthermore, failures in one's personal life, losses resulting from the experience of alienation in society, or even "sinful" acts can be forgiven as participants are reconciled in the knowledge that their beliefs not only justify their actions but also make those actions understandable, even if they fall outside the proscribed and desirable range of behaviors.

The moral beliefs of animal rightists also offer a new security and firmer identity to believers. Especially in times of challenges to religion by secular interpretations of experiences, it seems that belonging to a group of similar believers defines identity in an unambiguous fashion for the believer.

For many people, the animal rights movement makes sense because it provides answers to many of the fundamental questions they believe are not addressed in a satisfying way by the core institutions of society. Only with the weakening of institutions like religion and the emergence of impulse and self as core foci of social meaning can a movement such as animal rights begin to have an impact on individuals in society. In this social context, animal rights beliefs provide hope for society through the redefinition of animals as the center of the moral universe. Any hope for society, therefore, is inextricably linked to the salvation of animals. How people treat animals is, furthermore, a statement about the general moral worth of society at large. In terms of symbolic value, the animal rights movement elevates animals to a position of moral superiority as the sacrificial victims of society. The religious significance of animals as symbols is perhaps encapsulated in a bumper sticker seen recently on the car of one animal rights activist: "Learn the Language of Animals; Hear the Voice of God."

Summary

Sociologically, collective behavior refers to the extraordinary, nonroutine occurrences of everyday life. We have related the importance of collective behaviors by placing them within the larger context of social organization, and we have concluded by stressing how describing an organization underscores the concept of group forms.

Wright expresses the reasoning embodied in this concept. Group forms are "the collective configurations or patterns which emerge out of crowd members' distribution in space" (Wright 1978, 12). These patterns in turn result primarily from the nonverbal interactive mechanism for coordinating and carrying out collective activities. The identification of forms is easier the smaller and more contained the collective phenomenon is. As Lofland's scheme demonstrates however, the idea of form generalizes to all collective behavior. Crowds can be angry or joyful; mass collective behavior involves fear, hostility, and elation; and fashions and fads reflect the emergent meanings of groups trying to find some pleasurable mass involvement in society. Whether we are studying a riot, a fad, or the creation of a political party, we are examining how people organize their communications and then communicate them collectively.

When we study collective behaviors we are, in a dramatic way, studying social change. Consistent with our view of modern society as encouraging a complex, multiple social self, we see how collective behaviors in modern society are likewise apt to be complex and multiple. This means not that a single collective phenomenon is necessarily less important in modern society but that it is less likely to alter basic societal trends. This is demonstrated well in Irwin's work on the scene. In contrast, the collective behaviors of citizens of modern society turn out to be very rich and colorful, involving all the fundamental skills of interaction. Everyday life has become, according to Irwin, more scenelike. This means, among other things, that participation in collective behaviors may become routine through the staging of excitement. In short, as is true with many configurations of social meanings in modern society, the distinctions between meanings become blurred. An accurate description of the attitudes of many people in modern society may well be that they routinely expect "to find out where the action is."

A particularly modern social movement involves animal rights, and in it some people have found a way to define their membership in society and engage in meaningful action. As a movement, animal rights challenges the traditional ideas of social life regulating the relationship between animals and humans.

Exercises in Seeing Collective Behaviors

1. Go to your school library or to the local city or county library. Select a month at least ten years in the past and ask the librarian to help you find the newspapers for that month. You will probably work with microfilm or some facsimile. Go through the daily papers for each day of the month, reading only the front pages. Record all events that you believe are instances of collective behavior. Classify all the instances according to Lofland's scheme. Look for dominant emotions and see if there is enough information in the account to guess at the organizational form of the instances.

2. The next time you are at an event where several hundred people are present, like a sports contest or a rock concert, take notes on the mood of the crowd. Describe the seating or gathering arrangements of the people, how they get in and out of the building or grounds and other details of the occurrence. After you return home, read your notes and see if you can detect mood changes throughout the course of the event. If you can, tie these emotional cycles to what the crowd was doing. You should have an interesting data basis from which to discuss the

emergent forms of collective behavior for this particular event. For this exercise, crowds are better than more organized gatherings like audiences at a theater.

3. Recall your junior high school days. List the fads and fashions which were important for you and your group. These should include such details as the kinds of clothes you wore, the labels you wanted (or the way you showed you didn't care about labels), hair styles and shoes. Which of these fashions do you still follow? Can you think of reasons why some of these behaviors have persisted and others have not? Look for "extra-institutional" practices which have become more institutionalized with time. Use Irwin's model of the natural history of a scene as a guide.

Suggested Readings

In a 1991 article by S.B. Kaiser, R.H. Nagasawa and S.S. Hutton entitled "Fashion, Postmodernity and Personal Appearance: A Symbolic Interactionist Formulation," published in *Symbolic Interaction*, the authors suggest that fashion changes, specifically clothing styles, reflect the conditions of life in a society characterized by ambivalence and consumerism. They argue that a plethora of clothing styles are available to us so that we may define and produce a sense of who we are. Who we are, defined by how we dress, must be collectively negotiated through daily interaction, they contend. But the senses of self so based fail because they too become culturally ambivalent, and the result is an ongoing clash of fashion changes.

In a thorough and readable fashion, J.M. Jasper and D. Nelkin in *The Animal Rights Crusade: The Growth of a Moral Movement* (New York: Free Press, 1992), treat animal rights as what they call a "moral movement." They conducted their study in New York, but offer a complete description of the beliefs of the movement, the profiles of its participants and the place of the movement within a larger societal context.

Chapter 12

Emotions and the Social Self

According to our cultural knowledge, feelings are rooted in biology in a way that thinking is not, and we regard thinking as somehow less permanent than feelings. When we want to discover a person's true self, we inquire of them how they feel rather than what they think; we assume a person can easily change his or her mind, but emotions are less easily feigned and presumably genuine.

In our approach, how people understand things is derived from their experiences, with the important question for us being, "How do people experience their relationships with each other?" We can find our answer with some confidence by simply asking people, observing and participating with them in social relationships, and exploring the meanings of our own experiences. And we discover that people believe their feelings are not amenable to control. These beliefs are consistent in both the attitude of everyday life and that of scientific or expert knowledge.

In order to uncover some of the social meanings of emotions, our analysis begins with a vernacular expression: "Trust your feelings!" But which feelings should we trust? We have already analyzed the role of some emotions common in social relations. We learned to appreciate love as a way of seeing relationships (Katz 1971); and anger we found to be associated with aggression, though we also saw how people learn to control and even stage anger (Lyman 1980). And from Homans's theory of group processes, we know that sentiments are linked systematically to the emergence of norms—indeed, sentiments are the reason or condition for the emergence of norms, for uncontrolled they can undercut the assumptions on which social interaction rests. Finally, the treatment of collective behavior emphasized the role emotions play in the emergence and maintenance of collective social forms (Lofland 1981).

When placed in a social context, emotions can be analyzed as one part of the overall meaning of interaction. For example, just as we understood the cognitive basis of interaction in terms of a reciprocity of perspectives, so can we see the emotional aspects of interaction as grounded in reciprocal states. In everyday living, just as we guess about what another person is thinking, we also guess about what he or she is feeling; and these guesses and the various forms they assume are part of the social context characterizing interaction.

As Sue Shott (1979) points out, a person's experiences of emotion generally are composed of two elements: physiological and cognitive. The experience of emotion is both universal in the sense that people across different cultures and social contexts are emotional, and relative since society and culture shape the meanings and expression of emotions. Symbolic interactionism can bring out the "interplay of impulse, definition, and socialization that is central to construction of feeling" (Shott 1979, 1323).

Sentiments in Social Context

Every society is organized so its members may learn about the "proper" communication of feelings. For example, Americans typically are troubled by the outpouring of emotion, such as the explicit expression of sorrow seen occasionally on the television coverage of a tragedy in the Middle East. Indeed, emotional conduct at burial ceremonies is a good indicator of the range of the management and expression of emotions fostered by various societies. In some societies a funeral is almost a festive event; in others the expression of grief and sorrow is highly ritualized, formal, and reserved. Even the preparation of the body and a time and place for crying and loud wails of remorse can be specifically defined and widely understood. In middle-class American society the expression of emotion is controlled with almost stoic resolve, and the outlet for emotions is highly ritualized in song and eulogy. Members of the immediate family are often seated in a special section of the chapel so they cannot be directly observed by others at the service. Anyone who cries must do so discreetly so as not to "interrupt" the service. Even the viewing of the body is seen as a time for the control and suppression of emotion.

Since each world of feelings—such as the world of grief—is a part of a larger social reality, all of them can be analyzed both in terms of the rules governing emotional expression and according to the consequences of emotions staged for subsequent interaction (cf. Kemper 1987). In short, we can address these questions: "How do people learn to recognize situations that have emotional import?" and "How do they move into and out of such situations?"

Routine Feelings

Here, and again, we turn to an old friend and founder, because more than any other sociologist it was Max Weber who first characterized the essential mood of modern society. And many, like Weigert (1981), have since taken up his charge and offered sketches of the way modern society controls and channels the expression of emotions. All these scholars, past and present, see modern society as a place where people are confronted with overwhelming complexity and diversity, a virtual galaxy of choices and decisions, and yet the way this complicated place confronts individuals results in a certain irony: routinely, life in modern society becomes boring. As Brissett and Snow (1993) point out certain features of contemporary American life seem to facilitate boredom, namely a loss of a sense of going somewhere (they refer to this as *cultural arrhythmia*).

Indeed, one can contend that boredom is one consequence of modern life. The argument: The simple pressures of population and the diversity of people require that those things we all have to do must be quite simple. For example, the rules governing traffic and safe driving call for minimal skills. Indeed, most traffic accidents occur not because drivers do not know what to do, but perhaps unconsciously they seek some break from the boredom of driving. Hence speeding, reckless driving and inattention are all derived from the same condition, namely, the boring state of ordinary driving. When the conditions of boredom break down, say when the freeway system becomes overloaded, feelings of frustration may even result in aggression, as has apparently been the case in many freeway shootings. People are encouraged by law and persuasion to be patient and withhold emotional expression as they wait in gridlock for the routines of traffic flow to resume.

With this in mind we can formulate a general principle: the greater the number of people performing some specific act, and the more diverse their backgrounds, the more likely that act will be organized in obvious and simple ways. Crowd-control techniques illustrate this principle, and the continual struggle between the technical requirements of legal language and the necessity to "keep it simple" on forms such as our income tax returns also embody it.

The processes underlying this "simplicity" principle are simplification and ritualization, ideas we have discussed before but in a different context. Now we can imagine how the drive to find a common denominator among a diverse population with a general need (simplification) along with the need to repeat the same solution or response to a problem (ritualization) can be causes of boredom. Weber used the phrase "disenchanted world" to refer to the consequences of these processes of social organization in everyday life. Officially, the modern society is a world without magic, where explanations are scientific and rational for virtually all human states of affairs. This is not to say that people are literally trapped in boring lifestyles, but that their understanding of the world around them (physical and social) is generally rational. Of course people can be excited by legal, scientific or practical explanations, but such excitation is itself rationally understood (a scientist can be obsessed with finding a cure for AIDS, for instance). The problem of sustaining the rational view of the world is essentially one of coping with boredom; that is, as even the most complex of worlds becomes more understandable it becomes more predictable and hence less surprising and enchanting.

John Haiman (1990) has shown convincingly how repetition and the link between language use and practice ritualizes speech. When a word or phrase has been ritualized, figuratively it becomes the meaning of the act and thereby the act itself with which it was once associated. Thus a ritual prayer takes the place of a creative response to emotional situations, such as sorrow, thanksgiving, or remorse. Greetings are ritualized, as is the language of religion, the sales pitch, or the recitation. If fact, Haiman suggests, modern society with its alienating effects on sentiments has had the consequence of ritualizing a great deal of everyday talk. People repeat the same phrases and words in the course of daily life, and these words become hollow and devoid of meaning and even take on a characteristic sing-song enunciation. While he links the conditions of social life to a particular pattern of speech, his idea has implications for our concept of boredom.

As we carry out the routines of daily life, greeting and dealing with people at the supermarket or bookstore, repeating our problem to each department of the city utilities company as we attempt to discover why our water bill seems inordinately high, we find ourselves repeating virtually the same words to only slightly different audiences. And while initially we may become irritated and even given to emotional outbursts, we quickly learn that such displays are not generally effective, and we develop a monotonic, recitational style of talking with each other. As Haiman would say, our talk transforms into a task; after a while we master it, but in the process we become bored with our own efforts, our own lack of originality. Later, when we discuss how people transform ritual talk into sarcasm in an attempt to restore some sense of ownership to what they say, we see how the routine organization of life in modern society can turn our own talk into boredom.

Task differentiation and specialization also contribute to the problem of boredom. As work and play become more complicated, people receive more direct and specific instructions about how to conduct their affairs. Most people do tedious and repetitious work, and even their leisure-time activities can become stale and staid.

In her book *The Managed Heart* (1983), Hochschild demonstrated that in American society people experience feelings dictated by social norms for given situations. And as Shott (1979), Kemper (1987) and Denzin (1984) have shown, different emotions are conditioned by social structure. For example, power relationships are associated with guilt, shame, anxiety, and depression depending on which side of the status and power dynamic a person occupies. So, a given emotion may be understood as having a complicated social context that gives meaning to it and prescribes the appropriate expression of it.

This complex process of interaction Hochschild calls "emotion work." Certain social situations require such work. For example, flight attendants, bill collectors and others who deal routinely with the public experience emotions as a commodity, that is, the way they handle and present their emotions is part of their jobs. Saying "Have a nice day," being friendly and cooperative and "in a good mood" on the job are all governed by "feeling rules" that are essential components of certain kinds of work.

Most of us have elements in our work that are repetitive, and most of us have ways to make this work more palatable. Still our responses, private and rarely articulated to others, may be seen as responses to boredom. As work becomes standardized and as place and time become more situationally defined, boredom is an inevitable consequence. But the extremes to which we will go to escape this boredom and its consequences are remarkable.

Ironically, at the very point at which society becomes complicated people's understandings of it become simple and ritualistic. As we know more about the particulars of our small worlds, we know less about the particulars of those of others. Modern citizens, therefore, are sophisticated about specific subjects but are often naive about general patterns and relationships among the social worlds. "Hip" persons (cf. Zurcher 1972) are tolerant about people "doing their own things," even if they have no idea what those "things" entail. They may believe great diversity exists when in fact it does not; or conversely, that great similarity obtains among people when, from the various standpoints of the people, it really does not. All of this leads to the inescapable conclusion: modern life encourages boredom, and at the same time it is threatened by it.

Adaptations to Boredom

What emotional mechanisms do people have to cope with the boredom that results so paradoxically from the overwhelming complexity of social organization? Put differently, how do people manage the sentiments that arise from having to interact frequently with large numbers of strangers? How do people develop for themselves a formula of functional rationality, and how do they interpret life in the context of their disenchantment with task-specific work and play? These questions are some of the most fundamental to any analysis of life in modern society. Sometimes it seems as if we have become caught up in a social cage, bombarded by stimuli urging us on and eventually forced onto a treadmill we would rather not run, but feel we have no choice. "You gotta go to school," many students say; as if, if they felt they had a choice, they would not be there. Our concern here is how people adapt to the boredom that often accompanies their response to the "barrage" of contemporary life, their doing what they have to do. We begin with one of the most common adaptations, acting as if one has everything under control, or as it is better known, "being cool."

Being Cool

According to the Beach Boys, "good vibrations" bring about "excitations." Long before rock 'n' roll became an idiom for social criticism, Simmel noted that the demands of modern urban life bombard the human senses. Noises and complicated everyday problems contrast with the press toward the routine. In fact, when people follow routines, it is often just to cope with the possibility of sensory overload. When we board a bus, instead of confronting driver and passengers as unique people, we either follow a routine, if we know it, or try to find out what the routine is, if we do not. Usually we have other, more important things on our minds, and the routine of putting coins in the meter box, selecting a seat, and even of sitting and staring out the window insulates us from the impossible task of having to pay attention to every detail in our interactional territory. As long as we remain safe inside our routines, doing-what-everyone-knows-we-should-do, we can retreat from an overwhelming state of excitation. And yet frequently we revert all the way to the other extreme and thus back into boredom.

Boredom, then, is the antithesis of excitation; but often we recognize this only when our routine is disrupted, as when the siren from a passing ambulance alerts us to the excitation of our senses. Because they are stimulating in themselves, and at the same time can momentarily confuse us by forcing us to deal with an "emergency," disruptions of our routines can mean high levels of excitation, and in city life excitation is always close by. Here we refer to excitation as a condition of emotional exaggeration, where sentiments are heightened. These can be positive, like the heightened sense of emotions felt while watching a daring move successfully performed by a circus high-wire act; or perhaps more frequently negative, as the fear of being attacked, the fright from witnessing a crime, or the shudder we feel just after nearly being involved in a serious accident.

> I was driving my car to pick up my four-year-old-son from his day school. I was traveling the same route I use every day. There's part of the three-mile drive where the road I use goes under the freeway. On this day, it was a little cold and there was moisture on the road, nothing really bad, just some puddles on the road under the underpass. I was driving along listening to the radio. I looked in my rearview mirror and saw a car approaching from behind at a high rate of speed. I just continued in my lane. The car cut between me and another car in the outside lane. It passed under the underpass, fishtailing and looking like the driver was really having a "good old time" with some fancy driving. All of the sudden, the car hit the water, went out of control, careened across the median into the path of a compact car. I saw the impact and the look on the face of the driver of the compact car. It was sudden impact, and I felt the crash, and knew there was trouble. I stopped, got out of the car, stood motionless a few seconds in the middle of this busy city street. I didn't want to see what happened. Another driver had stopped, he

approached me. We walked together to the wrecked cars. By this time, the driver of the bigger car was out of his car. He was young and, then, his passengers got out, all but one whose legs were pinned under the dash. He was conscious and everybody else seemed OK. Then, we walked to the other smaller car. Inside, slumped over on her side, was a young woman, no more that twenty-five years of age. She looked peaceful, no visible cuts. But she was dead, the impact had severed her aortic artery. Within minutes the paramedics were on the scene. They could do nothing. I got back in my car as the police worked quickly to get traffic moving again. I drove on to the day school to get my son. I can't really describe how I felt inside, it was like everything inside me was revved up. (Eyewitness Account from Accident Report)

This description of an accident illustrates how excitation can suddenly overtake us just when we least expect it; and while we may seek excitement in a scene of our choice, other kinds of excitement, like the "accidental," are often less welcome. Lyman and Scott (1989) offer a way to understand the relationship between boredom and excitation, stressing how people manage threats of danger and risk while maintaining a sense of being in control. Writing of "Coolness in Everyday Life," they encourage us to think of the cool stance, or "being cool," as a transformed state of boredom, a version of emotional readiness and an attitude toward one's surroundings in which the routines one has learned are doggedly performed. Lyman and Scott define coolness as "the capacity to execute physical acts, including conversation, in a concerted, smooth and self-controlled fashion in risky situations, or to maintain affective detachment during the course of encounters involving considerable emotion" (Scott and Lyman 1989, 145).

According to the authors, risk is any threat to the way persons want to present themselves to others, and they distinguish three kinds—physical, financial, and social. And just as when a routine is disrupted, when people "lose their cool," they show their emotions; thus a political candidate cries in public, a mother curses at her child while standing in line at the grocery store, or a student displays a "case of the nerves" during an oral report to a senior seminar class.

Scott and Lyman believe the essence of coolness is giving off the impression that one is "in control," with a hallmark of coolness being the smooth performance. In our example of the routine interrupted by the witnessing of an accident, the driver maintained his cool by acting according to what he thought was an appropriate response: he simply looked at what happened and obeyed the authorities who requested that he "go about his business." Although he reports how emotionally he was anything but cool, outwardly he was able to give off the appearance of being under control. The metaphor of "stage fright" can be used to depict feelings associated with uncertainty regarding impressions given off, that is, our concern about how those around us will interpret who we are (Scott and Lyman 1989).

For social psychological purposes, we consider coolness as an interpretation of emotions. It is the result of judgments made by others about a person's identity and status. When coolness is lost, performances are marred, as when a "prop" fails. We have all "felt" for a speaker when he or she must deal with feedback noise in a public address system or when a heckler intrudes on a performance. Embarrassment is perhaps the chief nemesis of coolness. When someone is embarrassed, an interpretation of identity not desired or one inconsistent with the performance at hand is made by one's audience. Hence a speaker is embarrassed by a word improperly used, as when a professor who wishes to give off the impression of being erudite and urbane inadvertently reveals a lesser refinement by using an adjective as a noun, saying "a myriad of problems," rather than the correct "myriad problems."

If we can become aware of a routine when it is disrupted, one way to understand coolness as the management of emotion is to examine its loss. As Scott and Lyman write:

> A failure to maintain cool, a giving way to emotionality, flooding out, paleness, sweatiness, weeping or violent expression of anger or fear are definite signs of loss of cool. On the other hand, displays of savoir faire, aplomb, sangfroid and especially displays of stylized affective neutrality in hazardous situations are likely to gain one the plaudits associated with coolness. (1989, 149)

One cannot really test for coolness in the routine situations of everyday life, for it is only under stress or in new or confusing circumstances that a person must work to maintain coolness. It is precisely when a person is most likely to become emotional that he or she is supposed to remain in control; thus one way to develop and thereby learn to display coolness is to seek out and even create social situations that entail risk to body, pocketbook, or identity.

People do lose their cool; but this does not necessarily mean emotions are beyond control. In fact, we discover that many popular if not dramatically successful approaches to group therapy rest on the assumption of the manageability of emotions. A common example used in such approaches goes like this: Remember when you were at the fevered pitch of an argument with a "significant other," and the phone rang. What happened? In most cases people report that they simply answered the phone in a normal tone of voice. The phone call is a summons, often from a stranger and certainly from someone who does not know "what's going on" at the other end of the line. It requires a response and the response must fit a formula, what some sociologists (Mehan and Wood 1974) refer to as the answer's "greeting slot." Filling this slot requires a simple "Hello!" Such a greeting triggers a sequence of routine conversational responses, thoroughly a part of what everybody knows about appropriate ways to speak on the phone. Almost never does one start a phone conversation with a high level of expressivity.

The fact that most people are capable of suspending or socially "bracketing" their feelings when the occasion requires it illustrates the essentially constructed character of emotions. Surely the rituals of society help us to control our emotions, but the manipulation of feelings sometimes is coded to enhance the accomplishment of an emotional display. For example, Barely (1983) describes in detail how, as part of their occupation of dealing with emotional situations, funeral directors prepare bodies to achieve a posed and restful expression. The management of emotions shows at the least how the practical consequences of the expression of emotions create fabricated worlds.

As therapists rightly contend, the ways in which we express emotions sometimes become so habitual we come to think of them as inevitable, simply the way things are. Nevertheless, the most powerful feature of any approach to the management of emotions involves first changing situations to expose the constructed and artificial nature of the expression of emotion. In this fashion, one can learn to maintain cool.

We understand that emotions are inseparable from the context in which they are expressed. Given this, we can note how the relationship between being excited and being cool has been explored by Buckholdt and Gubrium (1979) in their fascinating study of emotionally disturbed children. They entitle their study *The Caretakers*, stressing how the behaviors of children labeled "emotionally disturbed" can be fully understood only if considered in social context.

In the home for children with behavior problems that they researched, an index for children's emotional instability was their display of inappropriate behavior. Objectively, this behavior consisted of yelling, thrashing about, punching, and kicking. When careful observations were made of the kinds of incidents that got children into trouble, however, Buckholdt and Gubrium discovered that children and staff alike used a gloss to cover a wide range of emotional states that, taken together, evidenced the state know as "emotionally disturbed." The gloss was blowing up. Whenever children "blew up," they showed the reasons they were in the home. Invariably, blowing up got the children into trouble with the staff; conversely, a child's ability not to "blow up" was a positive sign which the staff interpreted as meaning progress was being made toward solving the child's problem.

The Caretakers covers in detail the methods staff and children used to make complicated decisions about progress, or the lack of it, in the care of emotionally disturbed children. What is of primary importance to us is the way this research documents how losing coolness can have negative consequences for adults as well as children. Adults are assumed to have more control over their emotions, however, and even in anger seem to have a measure of mastery over their feelings. Children, in contrast, are allotted a degree of latitude because of their alleged "inability" to be cool. Also, they can be seen as victims of environments largely outside their power to manage. Sociologically, the problem faced by a child who blows up is that he or she has no reputation of coolness to fall back on. Adults in the everyday world who give off impressions of being normal are generally judged by those with whom they interact as being in control. Children, then, are at the mercy of those who decide the meanings of their behavior. A "blow up" is equated with the lack of control, not only by parents but even by professional psychologists. Thus, from *The Caretakers*:

> Consider an afternoon in cottage four as the boys are watching TV shortly after returning from class. James Brown and Lester Moceri furtively exchange derogatory names across the room when the cottage worker is not looking. Lester apparently intensified the exchange when he called James' mother a "whore." James crosses the room, stands briefly in front of Lester who is cowering, and warns him "not to say that again." As James returns to his seat, Lester whispers, "Black whore." James quickly turns around and runs toward Lester who buried himself beneath some pillows. James delivers several swift kicks to Lester's exposed legs. Lester begins screeching loudly, even before he is kicked, and calls for Jim Boyko, the cottage chief. Boyko emerges from the office where he was talking on the phone and asks Lester what is happening. Lester points to James who is still hovering over him and tells Boyko that James was kicking him and that it really hurt. As he walks back toward the office, Boyko commands James to return to his seat "right now." Lester again whispers, "Black whore" and James leaps on top of him, kicking and hitting any accessible part of Lester's body. Boyko races across the room, grabs James, and restrains him. James struggles to get free from Boyko and return to Lester, who is peering from beneath his pillows, mouthing the same words that have so angered James. Boyko now calls for Amy Langley, the day worker in the cottage. When she arrives, Boyko asks her to sit on James so that he can remove James' shoes and belt. A Cedarview rule requires that these two items be removed before a child is placed in the control room. James kicks and screams as his shoes and belt come off. He cries, "Get your fucking hands off of me! Nobody touches me!" Boyko then carries the still kicking James to the control room and locks him inside. When he returns, Amy asks him, "What happened?" Boyko replies, "He really blew. This is about the worst I've

seen. He's so damn strong he could really hurt someone when he gets like this. Wild, man, wild!" (Buckholdt and Gubrium 1979, 95–96).

Buckholdt and Gubrium report how children learn both to recognize and even to exert a measure of control over the "blow up." For example, every boy knows that the staff regard the "blow up" as an indicator of emotional instability and that he will experience directly the consequences of his outburst, even if at first he is not sure just what constitutes "blowing up." Beyond this, children may protest the staff's judgment about what they did, saying their behavior was not "blowing up," but in the process of so saying, providing the evidence that they did, in fact, go off. Or they may generalize behavioral outbursts and stretch the meaning of "blowing up" to include a wide range of behaviors that cover routinely normal expressions of emotions.

Even though children's versions of inappropriate expressivity may differ from adult staff's, this does not mean the children either don't understand or are totally out of control. Some children, it turns out, learn to "stage" emotional displays. This is not particularly surprising given the ability of children, especially these children, historically to get what they want through the display of emotion. But in this home children had learned to get even with each other through the management of blowing up. One would, then, in order to get even with another child, mess up his bed, knowing that when he saw his covers in disarray he would yell and protest. They knew further that this behavior would result in the staff "isolating" the child for a "cooling down" period (which was seen as punishment for the children). In this fashion, children were managing not only their own emotions but to a degree those of their peers. They were manipulating emotional displays for each other in efforts to establish their variety of social order under a situation of constrained and close social control.

On the basis of the descriptive work we have reviewed and considering how closely tied emotional displays are to the quality of the social relationships from which they derive, we conclude that expressivity, the communication of emotions, is merely another part of the whole of social situations constituting everyday life. Emotions are best understood as aspects of the meanings of everyday life, and some authors suggest there are occasions on which these aspects can override all other meanings in a social encounter.

Being Erotic

In *Smut: Erotic Reality, Obscene Ideology* (1983), Murray S. Davis extends the conceptualization of the layered meanings of social life to include his assertion that there is a socially constructed reality that is erotic in nature. Accordingly, participants in any social interaction have among the options open to them the possibility of transforming their relationship into a sexual experience. As most readers already recognize, of course, such an experience can be highly emotional.

Davis treats the transformation to this reality as accomplished, dependent in a way on the interactional work through which partners to the experience "lasciviously" shift from ordinary meanings or even from special ones, like the medical or artistic, to the erotic. The lascivious shift functions to ready partners for the "sensual slide into erotic reality"; and through the sex act itself, they finally generate that reality, with separate experiences of time and space and, most important, of self. As soap operas and many contemporary movies illustrate dramatically, potential partners have ways to communicate to each other their social arousal or readiness to begin a sexual experience. In some humorous passages, Davis depicts how this arousal often fosters problems in leaving ordinary meanings and entering into the separate reality of the erotic.

Just as a couple "slides into" erotic reality, they may be "blown out" of this precarious state by several "factors": "low status" behaviors from everyday life (farting); idiosyncratic behaviors (chewing gum during intercourse); "prop failures" (the bed falls down); the intrusion of others (the phone rings, a family member walks into the bedroom); the intrusion of the environment (earthquakes, warning sirens); or a sudden transformation of one of the copulators themselves (one has a heart attack or stroke and perhaps even dies). Davis's analysis clearly shows how the most emotional state of all (making love) is dependent on individual competencies at moving from one reality to another, as well as on the support, or lack of it, from society. Over time, people learn to enter erotic reality; and in places like "singles bars" and other well-known "pick-up" spots, different in different cities, they actively set out to put what they've learned into practice. And beyond this, in thinking of the transformation to erotic reality in ways that make sense to them in terms of what they know about themselves and others, people use metaphors of everyday life to understand it.

Some people humorously refer to various sexual perversions in terms of upper-class Madison Avenue corporate abbreviations ("S and M," "B and D," "AC-DC," "69") or lower-class service industry shop talk ("blow jobs" and "hand jobs"). And in some subcultures even normal sex is referred to as "taking care of business." Such business metaphors for sex often provoke laughter because they describe the human activities of an erotic reality, one supposed to be an emotional refuge and expressive escape from the workaday world, in the most instrumental terms of everyday reality. Although such instrumentality has no real place there, frequently it is required to accomplish the difficult task of transporting both parties from everyday to erotic reality. Thus humor can be used to relieve the tension created by the discrepancy between the mundane means of seduction and the unearthly ends of eroticism. Both the incongruity and the instrumentality of sex were nicely captured in the 1957 movie The Fuzzy Pink

Nightgown when Jane Russell attempted to ward off a would-be seducer by exclaiming, "None of that 'funny business'!" (Davis 1983, 227–228).

This is not to suggest that the management of emotions during the shift and slide into erotic reality is ever easy, or even that virtually anyone can successfully negotiate the transformation. Davis simply amplifies the fact that all of us must manage multiple realities in social life by showing the stark contrasts between two of them, the everyday and the erotic. In many ways, the starkness of such a contrast depends on the control and expression of emotions during intimate forms of interactive encounters.

Adaptations to Modern Existence

Everyday life seems to be so potentially exciting, perhaps "agitating" is a better word, that we cope by organizing our experiences into routine habits that produce the emotional effect of boredom—when we are excited, we try to appear bored or cool. Beyond this, as Davis says, "one of the melancholy aspects of human existence is that there are not enough lovables to go around" (Davis 1983, 28). Continuously, then, we deal with a dynamic dilemma between how we would like to live and what we imagine we could do; so there is little wonder that our worlds of feelings include fantasy.

Fantasy can function as a survival mechanism, a safety value for managing the tensions that have become part of daily life. We use our "fantastic" imaginations to attempt escapes from the everyday; and when we do, these attempts become an integral part of the organization of what we have come to understand as modern society, and particularly modern experience.

We can begin to understand the nature of imaginative and emotional escapes from everyday life by analyzing contemporary experience and what gives it its distinctiveness. Given the electronic world in which we all now live, one way of doing this is by examining the video experience, that is, by studying how the monitor is used as an information medium and so becomes a mechanism in our repertoire of experiences. Obviously the passive experience of watching the screen, as in viewing a television program, is part of the video experience, but so are the more active and interactive experiences of playing games at a video arcade or playing video poker at a casino, or even getting money from a cash machine.

Throughout this book we have sketched a characterization of modern society, noting how the dynamic between self and others changes as a society becomes complex and diversified. In a sense, every chapter has contained a part of the total picture of modern life. But before we consider the video experience as embodying some essentially modern features and hence as a reflection of the meanings of societal expressivity, we must have a clear definition of the global concept of modernity.

Global concepts usually are provocative and controversial and modernity is no exception. It is defined in many ways in the literature and more often than not its definition embodies an ideology. Some writers use the concept to discuss a new social order that they hope will "correct" the injustices of an older one, while others refer to an amorphous dark cloud of social change threatening the cherished values of the past. Because the video experience symbolizes modern society so thoroughly, it provokes a similarly wide range of reactions and interpretations. In an attempt to synthesize a working definition of it for our purposes, we draw on three characterizations: 1) modernity can be seen as a distinctive style and organization of consciousness (cf. Schutz 1971; Berger, Berger and Kellner 1973; Weigert 1981); 2) it can be depicted as the management of appearances (Goffman 1974, 1981; Deegan 1989); and 3) it implies a certain range and type of social control (MacCannell 1976; Faberman 1980).

Berger and his colleagues highlight the impact of modern society on the thought and feelings of individuals. By tracing the effects of industrial capitalism and the bureaucratic state on consciousness both in terms of content (packages) and processes (carries), they sketch the "worldview" modern society fosters. Their sketch follows indirectly the demands of technology and bureaucracy, listing rationality, componentiality, multirelationality, makeability, plurality, and progressivity as features of modern consciousness. The authors identify forms of thinking where society itself becomes "reality," that is, where there are formal organizational principles, public and private spheres are allocated and human rights are considered to be bureaucratically identifiable. Given its tendency to omit the more human and humane aspects of social life, this characterization forces our consideration of the "discontents" of modernity:

> These discontents can be subsumed under the headings of "homelessness." The pluralized structures of modern society have made the lives of more and more individuals migratory, ever-changing, mobile . . . the individual migrates through a succession of widely divergent social worlds. Not only are an increasing number of individuals . . . uprooted from their original social milieu, but . . . no succeeding milieu succeeds in becoming truly home. . . . A world in which everything is constant motion is a world in which certainties are hard to come by. (Berger, Berger, and Kellner 1973, 184)

In the second characterization, the management of appearances, our focus shifts to interactive phenomena and how these are said to be differentiated (Parsons 1971; Cuddihy 1974, 10). Progressive differentiation has the effect of hollowing out any substance of interaction and reducing our social lives to matters of appearance.

As Goffman made clear in increasingly eloquent statements, there are precise ways in which appearances are formulated and presented. He theorized that one's place in society imparts meaning to one's social interaction, and this meaning determines the details of how people present themselves to each other in differentiated situations. Finally for Goffman, in a thoroughly differentiated society appearance is reduced to mere "forms of talk." So although speakers have the freedom to work, sometimes ingeniously within the confines of ritualized, participation frameworks and the identities embedded in the minds of their audience, the essence of talk is its ability to absorb and in a sense neutralize these matters into an organization for social exchange. As Williams writes of Goffman's conceptions of talk: "It is the accommodative feature of conversational interaction that is one of its distinguishing features, this feature being brought about through the concatenation (sequencing) of ritual and communicative elements" (Williams 1980, 230).

The final portion of our sketch portrays the ways in which modern society exerts control over its members. From Weber's metaphor of the iron cage to recent accounts of the role of fantasy, analysts stress how individuated and pluralized life worlds do not necessarily mean individual autonomy. In fact, the weakening of traditional social controls may bring out new and more tyrannical means of constraint, with any new modes being perhaps more subtle but nevertheless just as effective as the older symbols of order.

Farberman (1980) observes that everyday life is typically thought of as a "drag," with the prospect of real action residing "elsewhere." He and others, notably Gouldner (1975), use the concept of everyday life in connection with the consequences of modernity. Hence, a result of having adopted the modern worldview is a dualism between the ordinary and the extraordinary, the authentic and the unauthentic. Individuals in such a state of mind can be moved with relative ease into social arrangements that promise to provide the bright side of the dialectic; but these arrangements more often than not carry a price tag. They are in the final analysis modalities of rational exchange that embody the symbols of effective social control for society in general, that is, the very state from which escape was sought: "So, the circle closes, people escape the drag of everyday life by retreating episodically into moral regions where they live out their dreams and fantasies which, like bait on a hook, land them in someone else's net. The dreams and fantasies that they use tend to transcend the world view not reinforce it" (Farberman 1980, 20).

Modernity, then, means styles of thinking, ways of interacting, and modes of social control that typify societies highly differentiated according to rational criteria that have technologically sophisticated modes of production and that value individuated experiences. It is out of such societies that the experience we now examine emerges. The video experience—enjoyed and fussed over daily, day in and day out, by millions of Americans—stands for modern meanings of interaction.

A Study of Video Phenomena

Nash and several student colleagues studied the social world of video game playing by first visiting video arcades and then playing the games. They wanted to understand the nature of the experience of playing video games and the emotions associated with playing.

As they observed and played, their initial reactions were frustration, confusion, and embarrassment at not being able to stay on a game, stay "alive" on an activated screen, for more than a few seconds. As they picked up on the sounds of the arcade environs, though, the character of their research notes and observations began to change. Before they had tried to play, the place seemed merely loud, the noise serving as a background to cover conversations and provide the appropriate ambience for teenage interaction. Soon after beginning play, however, they noticed subdued rock music and became more sensitive to the emotions of the scene.

Now they were ready for their first "video experience," which came while one of them was playing Zaxxon, and it marked the beginning of their discoveries of the symbolic meanings of the games.

Zaxxon cannot be played with any degree of expertise until the player learns to perceive depth through its graphics. Of course, lucky reactions to obstacles might carry the player up to the first guarded opening, which is a niche in a brick wall blocked on the top by a force field. At this juncture, the player must see the hole and maneuver his shuttle craft through the opening. Quite suddenly, after playing the game several times, one of the researchers reported seeing the opening; and although this player did not successfully fly through it, at least he knew it was there.

The basic task of the video experience became clear, namely, to ascertain order from apparent chaos. The problem was one of finding a frame that might serve as the base portion of the organization of the world of video experiences. This problem is distinctively modern in that it requires a mentality of cool detachment and the ability to function coherently against a strangely superfluous background. The experience is modern in a profound way because it is composed almost totally of appearance; that is, experience itself is the commodity.

A player must both learn and cultivate the video experience, and this entails emotional work associated with five interrelated tasks: seeing the game, learning to play, controlling emotions, beating the game, and renewing the challenge.

Some players, especially youngsters, seem to see the game almost immediately. But actual playing is learned. Several player-researchers actually learned to play a "respectable" game and used the account of their progress to reveal the elements of seeing a game. In each case, in the beginning the players were unable to sustain play for more than a few moments. But they continued to observe other players, became engrossed in the images on the screens while others played, and from this experience formulated vague ideas about how to play; this provided for them a sufficient motive to play again. Specifically, their attitude allowed the learning of a few moves.

The image a game presents must, of course, be relevant to potential players. Games, therefore, reflect popular themes in the media (including stereotypical understandings of city life). The space game dates from the beginning of video games and remains a staple of today's arcade. Some games still reflect the images of popular science fiction movies or fantasy games, Varth, for example, and new sophisticated holographic adventures. Other games are sports relevant, like boxing, basketball, and motorcycle and automobile racing, with some of them promoting current figures from the world of professional sports. Still another category of games builds from images of urban life. These games are usually fighting games, such as, Undercover Cops, Street Fighter, and other games that invariably involve martial arts images. There are also very clever games based on everyday life and building on the success of earlier games, like Pac Man, Dig Dug, and Frogger. These games may parody a routine activity, like shopping or delivering newspapers, and the rise and fall in the popularity of games depends on what is "in or out" of favor with groups of players.

Learning to play is a matter of hands-on experience, as well as watching others play. Hands-on experience consists of being able to keep the game going long enough to get the feel of it. Players have difficulty articulating exactly how they learn to play, sometimes saying it is a matter of "getting inside the game"; according to one aficionado:

> I like the graphics on Varth, the sounds are great too. After I started playing, I got the feel of the controls. It's a question of anticipating the opponents and timing your attack just right. You can't wait to react like on some games, and I like that. You have to see the patterns, choose a place on the field and plan your moves. Finally, I guess, I really got hooked when I was able to make plays and anticipate the program's next move. (field notes, 1992)

"Anticipating moves" refers to a player's method of watching the figures on the screen enter and disappear and preparing to attack in anticipation of a figure's appearance. The area of play in many games is not a traditional closed space like a football field but an interconnected universe most of which appears only as the figures on the screen move into it, and players learn to set up moves by using what they learn about the properties of the universe as part of their strategy of playing.

There are many ways to learn to play the games, and we have documented a few to show that idiosyncratic methods still have in common an element of symbolic interaction. Ultimately they depend on a player's ability to take on the attitude of both the game and its program and of the other players whose skills are continuously made public through their play. In a strict sense, the player is interacting with the programmers of any particular game, attempting to figure out strategic moves and ways to anticipate the behavior of the characters in the game. Learning how to play, then, is a matter of learning how to interact, not so much with the machine, although that is a part of the process, but with the human elements of the games.

Our description of how players relate to video games parallels Goffman's (1974) notion of keying. Keying involves interacting at levels of "as if" experience—treating a serious remark as if it were a joke, or an error of speech as if it were intended. In order to play well, one must be able to treat the images on the screen as if they were alive, and so the player keys the game.

Since the programs for the games have become so sophisticated, learning to play can be a frustrating affair. The games create the illusion of fresh movements, essentially through a multiplication of possible reactions to player moves. For example, opponents in martial arts games may appear on the screen in various locations and with various levels of strength that determine the number of hits required to make them disappear. In racing games, course patterns appear as curves, straightaways and the like, and just as a player masters a part of the course, the task changes with the appearance of other cars or vehicles.

Freshness of moves is also achieved through a bombardment of the senses. Simmel (1971) noted that the modern city amounted to an environment in which the typical inhabitant experiences an assault on the senses; and playing video games, especially in crowded arcades, overloads the senses. In an episode of a 1970s television show, "Taxi," which can still be seen in reruns, Iggy, a burned-out refugee from the hippie movement, gets hooked on Pac Man. He is engrossed in the noises, the chase, and the obstacles of the chase. Bells, flashing lights, and unanticipated impediments capture his attention and he proclaims his first Pac Man game to be "the greatest experience of my life." Iggy's unflappability typifies coolness, but it also makes him vulnerable to a form of exploitation. He is "hooked" by the video experience and cultivates his habit through repeated play. The next payday, his boss—who is also proprietor of the video game machine —pays him with bags of quarters.

Coolness is important to the video experience. Certainly there are players who lose their cool, but our researchers noticed patterns in the control and expression of emotions that could be understood only in terms of the symbolic context of the arcade. Players' reactions range from facial expressions to the use of expletives to physical retaliation against the machine. The first reactions are clearly the coolest. A grimace, a facial contortion, a barely audible groan—these allow a young man to communicate to his audience that he is aware of having been momentarily taken by the machine, but that he still maintains his detached involvement with it. If he continues to play and ultimately amasses an impressive score, he will have achieved the highest state possible of the video experience.

This state is the interactive outcome of learning to play and controlling one's emotions within the context of the arcade. (And with some luck, such impressive winners will achieve high enough scores to enshrine themselves, as it were, in the game itself. Usually a top player has the opportunity of entering his or her initials or other three-letter "tag" on a screen that periodically appears when the game is idle.)

The use of expletives is widespread among young arcade players, with such words usually indexing emotionality. And although such outcries are not particularly cool, they are more often than not subdued and audible only to those close by. Of course the background noise of the machine and the music of the arcade help mute the cries of the players and thereby enhance the accomplishment of coolness.

Finally, one can lose coolness altogether and strike the machine. Even here the notion of coolness helps us understand these outbursts. "Totally uncool" is "blowing up" which is acting out of control and doing physical damage to a machine. Hence one youth once broke a joystick and another bent the steering wheel on a racing game. Although such feats are among the folklore of players, they are negative incidents; they get you kicked out of the arcade, or worse, you may get the reputation of being a hotheaded player. Everybody sympathizes with "blowing up" at the machine on a particularly frustrating occasion. But most players, when really frustrated by the game, strike the machine a glancing blow, usually on the controls (joystick or buttons) with an open hand and under an attitude of control; thus there are cool ways to lose your cool. Mastering the range of ways to keep cool, from supercool stances to the controlled blow-up, constitutes a major learning task in the experience of playing video games.

Next in the learning and cultivating of the video experience is beating the game, which is both a triumph and a defeat. In fact, the modern condition of ambivalence is clearly exemplified in the phenomenon. At the very moment when the game is figured out, or when a quirk in the program allows the player to amass points in an easy way, the image of freshness disappears and the mechanical nature of the game becomes apparent. Players refer to this experience as "playing a pattern."

At this point, the final phase of cultivating the experience begins— coping with boredom. To combat boredom a player must learn to renew the challenge of the game, and this is accomplished essentially by trying games that provide a new twist on the experience or by playing old games in a new way. Specific games clearly have a playing life, and return visits to arcades at shopping malls show that within a five-year period virtually all games are new or are modified versions of old ones.

Given the similarities of most games, it is not surprising that certain aspects of playing are transferable from game to game; for example, all video games require hand-eye coordination. Perhaps more important though, one's attitude about the emotional conditions necessary for play is transferable. Having learned not to blow up, the player is able to approach a new game coolly. Thus a young man can be confident that although he may not do well first time out, he will not commit a faux pas. His emotional display and his attitude toward it is best described as "controlled panic." When the game overwhelms him, as he knows it surely will, he is comfortable in the knowledge that he can rely upon a display of coolness to maintain his image of being a player and to serve him as a taking-off point for learning the new game.

The player who has mastered a blasé attitude toward the game and who knows how to search for patterns can renew the challenge of the video experience by moving to new games or by altering play between patterned and spontaneous strategies. In patterned play, one tries to ignore impending danger and "trust" the pattern. Hence in the classic Pac Man game, although Winkie may be about to kill you, with experience you know that at a certain spot on the board, "he" will change directions and you will be able to follow your route. Learning a new pattern can be very exciting. Learning a new game likewise reconstitutes the challenge of play.

Environments of Feelings: Observations at the Arcade

A major contention of the sociology of emotion is that feelings derive from a social context, and the study of video game playing illustrates how this experience evokes distinctive feelings. To appreciate the accomplishments of these feelings fully, the researchers recorded observations over a six-month period at seven different arcades. These observations are summarized here.

An arcade is first of all a location, a business location. It has the features of a "hangout," providing youngsters and all players with access to the games, but it is also a place where video experiences occur. The setting itself constitutes the social context for the characterization of arcade games as symbols of modernity.

At arcades, players talk to the games and to each other in front of and around the machines. Critics of video games have remarked that the machines have the effect of social isolation; to an extent this is true, as we pointed out in our discussion of how the games can be engrossing. But it is blatantly false if isolation is taken to mean the lack or absence of social interaction. Players accuse the machines of unfair moves, of playing cheap, and of taking advantage of unusual playing circumstances. On the offensive side, players may warn the machine or the characters within the game of their impending defeat, or they may talk to the joysticks or otherwise attribute human qualities to the parts of the machine.

This practice of talking to the machine is recognized by game manufacturers, and they have put games on the market that not only make sounds but that "talk back" to players as well. An advertisement for a home video game extols the fun of communicating with the games through the voice synthesizer: "Hear cheers, strategy, and taunting." A few games capitalize on the taunting and actually call the players names, deriding their skills whenever they fail. A Western fast-draw game takes the player through "shootouts," with laser disc narration.

Furthermore, players make gestures at the machine. Most of these are in response to an unexpected termination of play. They communicate to others in the arcade, or perhaps just for self-satisfaction, their defiance and frustration. The symbolic value of such gestures is to inform others participating in the video experience about the emotive states of the player.

A surprising amount of interaction takes place among the player and those spectators attracted to his or her performance. The principle forms of sociaton taking place in front of the games are observing play, admiring and congratulating, and remedial remarks such as "nice game," "nothing you can do about that," and "not bad." While it is true that much of this interaction is nonverbal, or consists of only short verbal utterances, the communication system is nevertheless effective. When a young player displays unusual skill at a game, older more accomplished players will recognize the player's potential. This is done either through direct remarks or by comparisons. For instance, the older players may remark, "Wow, this kid's goin' t' better my score," or "Man, I never thought a little kid could play like that."

Much of this interaction functions to enhance the effects of play (excitation) and to establish status among the players. The effects of play are further amplified by spectators, who could readily embarrass the player with deriding remarks. The status system at the arcade is primarily informal, but there is a formal dimension to it as well. As we noted earlier, most machines allow high-scoring players to record their initials or "tags" on the machine display. These initials appear regularly on the screen of the game between plays. Arcade goers know the initials of top-notch players and struggle to beat, or at least get close to these scores. Through word of mouth, direct observation, and informal networks of peers, one's reputation as a player is established. All serious video players can quote their high scores on their favorite games, and there seems to be a surprising amount of veracity in these self-reports. Even youngsters seven and eight years old remember five- and six-digit scores.

Much of the interaction in and about the arcade is focused on financing play and transportation to and from the arcade. Among others, there is the practice of marking one's turn at the game with a quarter or token. Perhaps it is a universally accepted practice (observed at least in Europe as well as throughout the United States) to mark one's turn by "putting a quarter up," meaning simply putting a quarter (or token) on the face of the game. When arcades are busy, at popular games there may be as many as ten quarters lined up. Players not only honor this system but keep close account of whose quarter is up next. A boy who wishes to play more than one game will put several quarters up, and when he has played these he usually has the option of "one last game." Other normative courtesies, such as players skipping over a quarter because they knew its owner was playing at a different game, then honoring that player's place when he or she returned or even calling to them from across the room were observed.

Such complex interaction takes place within all arcades; nevertheless, each one takes on distinctive features depending on its social environs. Kenen (1982) documented how laundromats have ethnic, racial and class identities. The same may be said for arcades. In the arcade study there were three arcades owned and operated by the same franchise. In interviews with their attendants, each was depicted according to its clientele. Number one was located in an upper-class neighborhood and was regarded by the attendant as a "kid's place." In fact, he noted that the arcade had become a hangout. On Friday and Saturday nights the arcade became a place to meet friends and members of the opposite sex, and no serious video playing was done by regulars at this arcade on these nights. The arcade was so crowded on "social" nights that most people simply stood in the middle of the floor between the rows of games and engaged in conversation. (It is interesting to note how mechanical games, like table hockey, have been introduced to the arcade. They are placed in the middle of the room and are the kinds of games that allow more talk and socializing to take place.) On social nights, the atmosphere was partylike, and the location became secondary to the flow of sociability. Attempts for high scores were made mostly by those not fully integrated into the peer culture or by those insiders wanting to display their skills.

Another arcade was located in a semiresidential neighborhood of mixed classes, light industry and businesses. This location was characterized as appealing to more mature players who were often serious about their scores; indeed, a quick check of the displays on the games showed that the scores here were significantly higher than those at the number-one location. It was also not uncommon to find families with very small children in this arcade, the children watching or tottering around as their fathers played the games.

The third arcade was located in an area with a disproportionately black and transitory population. Here seven- to nine-year-old unsupervised kids could be seen just hanging out. It is also interesting to note that this arcade was the first in this franchise to change to token-operated games, in which every player must deal with the change machine. In this fashion, management thought it could control the arcade more effectively. Apparently the need for this close supervision was not perceived as existing at the other arcades.

This arcade study was conducted in the 1980s. Since then, arcades have been attacked by neighbors objecting to the crowds they attract; others have closed because of competition from sophisticated and low-cost home video games, and the remaining arcades have retreated to amusement parks and shopping malls where sociability comes under the control of large agents such as mall or park security. Still although arcades seem to take on the character of the mall in which they are located, they remain places very similar to those originally studied.

Finally, one interesting development has occurred with the games themselves. Originally, one quarter bought one play at most games, and though limited time extensions were possible—by a player continuing to score well—eventually the game ended and that was that; a new coin had to be inserted for a new game. Now many games, as soon as play has ended, offer the player a ten-second "window" with the opportunity to deposit another coin and begin another play where he or she left off. The two main consequences of this are interrelated. First, it encourages players to continue at a game once begun, and they are likely to exercise their option here if they are playing games they particularly like or ones they "really want to beat." Some players will pump quarters almost indefinitely into a single game—recently one player "dropped" five dollars into one game at one sitting—or will play until boredom sets in. The second consequence is that continuous play leads to the artificial inflation of scores. Thus when one sees "R.A.T." as number one on the Highest Scores screen, it might represent a great player or it could be a good one who had a dozen quarters to spend before quitting.

As symbols of contemporary society, video games embody meanings that parallel features of modernity, especially with regard to the display of emotions in public places. The styles of thinking necessary to play well, the modes of interaction observed at arcades, the technology itself, and most important the nature of the experience encompass both the content and the form of modernity.

The games require interactions of a complex nature, often with strangers. Sets of rules have been developed by players to maintain and enhance excitement and coolness, and these rules, though rational, promote a sense of membership and feelings of belonging. Arcades are essentially "hangouts" that absorb locally constructed social identities. The accomplishment of play is ephemeral and understandable only in terms of the situated context of video occasions. Finally, the order that emerges from the experience represents at least a nascent mode of control.

The video phenomenon amounts to a framing practice in Goffman's sense of the concept (Goffman 1974). The player keys appearances and learns to master acting "as if." In this process, the technology of the computer is demystified, the routine and boring aspects of everyday life are temporarily escaped, and avenues for constructing social relationships are cultivated and practiced. What makes video games both attractive and repulsive to large numbers of people is the degree to which the games symbolize modern ways of experiencing life, a chief component of which is the framing of emotions.

The "Poor Dear" Hierarchy or Making Emotional Sense of Life

We have tried to show that young people learn to make emotional sense of their experiences according to how they understand their place in society, at least in the delimited context of playing video games. At the other end of the age continuum, Hochschild (1979) documents "emotional work" that residents in an old-age community do to interpret who they are.

In her study of Merrill Court, a senior citizens' community, Hochschild discovered an "unexpected community" complete with an informal status hierarchy based on the distribution of "honor" and "luck." While she carefully points out that this system may not be typical of the experiences of most elderly people in our society, it does provide insights into how we, as symbolic creatures, make emotional sense out of the major life events we have experienced.

The widows of Merrill Court whom Hochschild studied saw differences among themselves, even though most were from the same social-class background, as matters of luck. In this shared system of ranking, she who had good health won honor. "She who lost the fewest loved ones through death won honor and she who was close to her children won honor. Those who fell short on any of these criteria were often referred to as 'poor dears'" (Hochschild 1979, 58).

The "poor dear" system established a sense of superiority among the residents. Someone who was called a "poor dear" seldom called those who called her a "poor dear" a "poor dear." But whenever a resident was labeled a "poor dear," they would turn to someone they felt was less fortunate and refer to them as "poor dear." The hierarchy honored residents at the top and pitied "poor dears" at the bottom, and this system established distinctions that would not have been recognized by outside society.

What is important about this "poor dear" hierarchy is that it allowed residents to experience deeply felt emotions about what life has brought them in a way that is both reasonable in the context of larger society and within their particular life situation. One simply cannot control the death of a husband or whether children write or visit. An elderly woman cannot always manage her health so that vitality is maintained into the later years, but she can interpret her feelings, and even manage them in terms of an association of luck and honor. As long as "poor dears" can be found, one can manage a sense of being "lucky" in life.

As Hochschild (1979, 63) suggests, perhaps there is a premium on finishing life off with the feeling of being a "have." Just as "luck" plays a role in playing video games, just as the young player must learn to feel that he is at least able to deal emotionally with "failure" in front of the video screen, so the elderly in their "isolated" lives apart from work and family learn to think about what has happened to them with a sense of "honor". They have a systematic way of thinking and feeling about what life has brought them. There are winners and losers, and their feelings are associated with the distribution of luck.

We know that "luck" is partially conditioned by privilege in society, but the point of this analysis is to show that people adapt their emotions. They adapt by constructing meanings that interpret their particular life circumstances. For us to understand that emotions are social, we must see them as occurring in a context of thinking people.

Sarcasm

Some of the social conditions that shape emotions are widely distributed in patterned ways in our society. John Haiman (1990) has recently explored sarcasm, which he regards as a particularly contemporary way to frame emotion. Sarcasm has many meanings in everyday talk—contempt, derision, irony, mockery, or ridicule. And surely people of all cultures experience these emotions; but Haiman suggests that modern society, with its voracious consumption of communication, tends to foster a disproportionate amount of sarcasm in the speech of its citizens, especially those who feel most alienated from membership in society. Young people, especially middle-class white men and women, seem particularly skilled at and sometimes even become engrossed in sarcasm. Haiman uses the metaphor of the "stage" to understand sarcasm and so documents the mechanics of being sarcastic.

Sarcasm is first of all a "metamessage"—those who produce sarcastic messages intend the opposite of what their message would normally mean. Accompanying their behavior (which need not be verbal) and "keying" it as fictive is a metamessage that may be paraphrased as "I'm not serious" (Haiman 1990, 181). The effect of oppositional meaning is achieved through three means, all of which are ironically motivated:

1. Formal indices of direct quotation or repetition—one may use a quotation mark (He said, and I quote, "Well, she is very attractive."), adjectives like "so-called" (And that's the so-called "Student Service Center"), and inappropriate repetition of full phrases in lieu of anaphora or shifters (That's just fine, just fine.)

2. Incongruity between segmental and suprasegmental texts (incongruous suprasegmentals include the phonetic reflexes of sneers and laughter, deadpan monotone, caricatured exaggeration of the appropriate melody, and stylized or singsong intonation). Hence one might express her dislike of a girl friend's new hairstyle with "Well, that's just beautiful (with 'beautiful' sung)" or, "Aren't we just sexy with that hair, girl?" Perhaps due to the popularity of television's "Saturday Night Live," another widely used device to produce the effect of sarcasm is "not!" So, "This is a really great book . . . not!"

3. Hyperformality includes both high register and the substitution of linguistic signs for paralinguistic symptoms. Most languages have a variation of address that signifies importance or formality. In American parlance, we use titles—Mr.,

Ms., Doctor, Your Honor. In many European languages, high register is grammatically marked by the use of officially different forms of address. In addition, a speaker may be sarcastic by using titles inappropriately or generally matching the reference of the meaning with its opposite formal meaning. For example, if a banker friend of yours suggests that you take an herbal remedy for your stomachache and you wish to reply sarcastically, you can say, "Thank you for that advice, Doctor." Or in German a speaker can refer sarcastically to one of lower status than oneself by using "*Sie*," the high form of the pronoun for "you," which is used to show respect, usually to someone of higher status.

Following Goffman's lead, Haiman makes us aware of the theatrical character of sarcasm. To be sarcastic, one must consciously recognize the social organization of sentiments; then he or she may "break frame," step out of character, or play roles in such a way that the message "this is not serious" is communicated. Now all this takes on added significance within a theory of emotions in modern society where we are constantly exposed to our own and others' emotions. If we are both fascinated and threatened by the expression of true feelings, and if in the course of daily life we are compelled to play roles to which we feel no emotional attachment, sarcasm can allow us not only to play these roles but at the same time to convey our feelings about our loss of authenticity.

The Development of the Emotional Self

The interactive and linguistic skills required to be sarcastic presuppose the development of what Cathryn Johnson (1992) calls the "emotional self." More generally, understanding emotions as part of the context of social life forces us to consider emotional experience as a social phenomenon. In other words, emotions are another dimension of constructed social meaning. Just as we showed how the development of a kind of thinking is necessary to practice social life, so different experiences of emotion may be placed within a developmental framework.

We have learned that the social self emerges through certain stages. G.H. Mead (1934) described the specific stages of development through which an individual moves on the way to acquiring a social self, passing from simple learned responses to stimuli, through the acquisition of gestures and symbols, and on to a consciousness of self and the maintenance of social relationships. Corresponding to the ability to imagine the thinking of others is the possibility of complex interaction, including joking, engaging in conversation, and even sarcasm. Mead's model, however, does not consider the role of emotions in this formula.

Johnson (1992), working extensively with small children, observed what she regards as seven stages of emotional development, beginning with responses to external or internal stimuli experiences as sensations and expressive cues (crying, cooing, smiling). Emotions such as joy, fear, anger, and surprise now emerge in conjunction with mutually affective reciprocity, that is, with emotions being directed at one another. Next these emotions are shared, then identified as others' emotions, and then as awareness of one's own emotions. At this point, a child can recognize that Mommy is angry or happy or sad. Further development brings the child to role-taking in which emotions are directed toward oneself, and such emotions as embarrassment and shame are felt. Here a child begins to develop consciousness of relationships and can experience second order, reflexive emotions (can feel guilty about feeling guilty or can be proud of the other's accomplishment). Finally, the seventh stage involves the management of emotions.

In this last stage, which requires the mastery of the interactional skills of the earlier stages, "children learn ways of changing their inappropriate feelings" (Johnson 1992, 197), acquiring, for example, the ability to suppress or mask feelings. As Haiman, Goffman and others would say, this "emotional work" is at the heart of interaction in the modern world, or at least of that part of our lives where we must deal with strangers whose "true intents and feelings" are not available to us. Johnson(1992) points out that the management of emotion creates complex emotional selves, complex because we learn different ways of experiencing emotional interactions: "We learn to identify and interpret emotions, direct emotions toward others and ourselves, and even try to change our emotions to fit the situational feeling rules. Given the complexity of our emotional selves, one can see why it is so easy to misidentify or misinterpret our own or another's feelings" (p. 198).

We add that one can see why sarcasm and other "keyed" modes of interaction are important devices for the practice of social life. When one is conscious of emotions and sees that the expression of emotions is integral to a desired interactive outcome, tools that allow one to gain control over any aspect of the interactive setting are useful. While alienation may stimulate the use of management skills, some of these very skills, such as sarcasm, may further the separation of people from one another and from their own feelings.

Summary

This chapter began by building a rationale for looking at emotions, a subject only recently considered part of sociological social psychology. Emotions can be understood within the same general analytic framework that appreciates the constructed nature of social meanings. In order to apply this framework it was first demonstrated that emotions are a part of the interactive problems making up everyday life.

At the heart of this demonstration is the thesis that feelings are at least partially bound in social context. Coolness as an emotive state, for instance, is best understood as a synthesis or neutralization of two polar states, excitation and boredom. Since both boredom and excitation are intrinsic consequences of modern social organization, coolness represents an emotional adaptation.

Even erotic experiences, typically understood from either a medical or a moral stance, can be analyzed as the result of interactive work to establish a reality separate and distinctive from everyday life.

A participant observation study of video games and arcades made the point that the experience of video games and occasions are best seen in the relief of modernity. They foster forms of interaction that are essentially cool emotively. We learned that among elderly people, emotions about what life has brought on are conditioned by the social settings in which they live. And sarcasm was introduced as a wide-spread way to frame emotions and as perhaps becoming a dominant form at least for individuals who feel alienated from the mainstream of participation in society.

Framed or keyed emotions require that a person have an emotional self, and this self, while a natural consequence of development, may play a role in fostering confusion about sentiments or even alienation. As one develops the ability to manage social life, to practice interaction, consciousness of one's own and others' self (cognitive and emotive) allows for layered and fragmented experiences. Emotions are therefore woven into the social fabric not so much as a natural fiber but as a synthetic. Furthermore, the ability to manage, repress, frame and express emotions takes place within both developmental and social contexts.

Exercises in Understanding Emotions

1. Watch a "daytime drama" (soap opera) on television. Videotape it if possible. Watch it several times and list the range of emotions displayed by the actors and the situations in which they displayed these emotions. Describe the facial and verbal expressions that carry the display for each scene. Are props or other aids such as background music or scenery used to enhance the effect? After you have a rather full descriptive account of several emotions, try to make generalizations about the relationship between emotions and the social contexts in which they are displayed for this form of drama.

2. Visit a video arcade—they are easily found in shopping malls. Take notes on what you see (you might want to do this mentally to avoid attracting attention to

yourself. You can always write down ideas and observations after you leave the arcade). Compare your data with the observations offered by this chapter's study of the video experience. Did you see "cool" displayed? Did you see turn-taking rules at work? How about the relationship between players and machines? If you find you have quite different observations, why do you think this happened? Many observations reported in this chapter were gathered in the mid 1980s. Are 1990s arcades different? Does the arcade change when it becomes part of a shopping mall? Think about changing social contexts and the essentially modern character of the video experience.

3. Write down all the things that bore you, what you do to avoid being bored, and how you escape boredom when you find yourself "trapped" in a boring routine. Organized into groups of three, you should be able to generate a list of "boring practices" and a variety of different escape attempts. Have the list for the entire class typed up and duplicated so it can be distributed to each group. Then in group sessions see if you can figure out what attributes "boring things" have in common, and in what ways escape attempts are similar and different.

Suggested Readings

Marvin Scott and Stanford Lyman's article "Coolness in Everyday Life" (in Lyman and Scott, *A Sociology of the Absurd* [Dix Hills, N.Y.: General Hall, 1989]) has become a classic. In it the authors develop in detail an hypothesis about the relationships among potential danger, its management, and the control of it. We recommend reading the original to reinforce one's understanding of this important insight into modern life.

In a provocative article entitled "Sarcasm as Theater," *Cognitive Linguistics* 1–2 (1990), John Haiman, a linguist, identifies the theatric character of sarcasm and sets up the idea that alienation in society may contribute to the emergence of sarcastic talk. Noreen Sugrue, in "Emotions as Property and Context for Negotiation," *Urban Life* 11 (1982), instructs her readers on the conception of emotion as property that can become an important "commodity" for negotiation. She relates a fascinating instance of a patient named Kathy who struggles with doctors over the proper treatment and her emotional states.

Chapter 13

Conclusions and Directions

No single theoretical bent can capture a social psychology seeking to describe the nature and variety of social experiences. What we are calling social psychology actually is rooted in differing perspectives: phenomenology, symbolic interaction, ethnomethodology, and dramaturgy to name the major ones. Even these groupings are not clearly separated from each other, though, as each may deal with contemporary issues, such as feminist concerns, race relations, and unemployment, from a similar perspective. To complicate matters further, within each of these perspectives there may be divisions such as existential theory within phenomenology or labeling theory within symbolic interactionism. Still, these perspectives, taken together, form a "sociological orientation concerned with the experiencing, observing, understanding, describing, analyzing and communicating about people interacting in concrete situations" (Douglas et al. 1980, 1). In short, they are all social psychological.

Still, a specific study, say of emotions, may draw on different perspectives, and a student should appreciate the range of social psychological thinking in order to see how the power of a perspective allows for a distinctive understanding of a problem. To help gain such an appreciation, in this chapter we provide a brief and selective introduction to some branches of "subjectivist" social psychology.

Ours is not the first to attempt to demonstrate the unity of social psychology. For example, Morris (1977) refers to the enterprise as *Creative Sociology*, Douglas et al. use the title *The Sociologies of Everyday Life* and Reynolds (1993) suggests *Interactionism* as a covering term for all varieties of analysis. Some proponents of ethnomethodology and phenomenology prefer to establish their domains of inquiry outside the boundaries of "conventional" sociology (cf. Handel 1982; Psathas 1973), and still others prefer to develop special versions of study, such as Dorothy Smith's (1987) feminist, or standpoint epistemology, which seeks to recover and present the experiences of everyday day life for women.

With the awareness of the importance and diversity of social psychological thinking, however, has come an attitude of reconciliation among those who practice the analysis, and efforts to articulate the pivotal concerns of social psychology have increased as well. Douglas, et al. (1980) have made such an effort, as has Weigert (1981), with work emphasizing both the importance of the concept of everyday life and similarities of analytic and methodological proce-

310

dures in doing social psychology. Perhaps most important, Hilbert (1992) has shown that the subjectivist sociology of Harold Garfinkel is centered in socio-logical concerns with social and normative order. We begin with a consideration of phenomenological sociology and move on to review the other varieties of social psychology with the purpose of uncovering points of convergence and core concerns that, taken together, make up the essentials of social psychology.

Phenomenological Sociology

In all its various manifestations, sociology has close ties with philosophy, but phenomenological sociology is the area of inquiry in which the tie is most obvious and integral. Primarily, the goals of a social psychology informed by a phenomenological attitude are close to those of philosophical analysis: (1) to describe social realities, (2) to discover the social essence of each of those realities, and (3) to investigate the meaningful relationships among the essences.

Phenomenological thinking depends on a philosophy that takes conscious-ness as the prime ingredient of human existence (Dickens 1979). The process by which people come to know what they know, along with the content of what they know—their consciousness of things, each other, and themselves—constitute the fundamental realities of existence. Our world, the phenomenologist therefore contends, consists of many different phenomena understood according to the nature of consciousness. In the modern world, scientific consciousness tends to dominate all other forms, its principal rival being the attitude of everyday life or common sense.

In attending to the phenomenological variation of the social world, one must first describe what phenomena really are—what makes them different from one another. For example, what are the essences of scientific thinking, or commonsense knowledge, of religious belief, loving, aggression, or gender. Phenomenological sociology is the result of the application of a philosophy to primarily social psychological topics. Although phenomenological sociology can deal with societal experiences (most of Peter Berger's work exemplifies this), it is always connected with the task of appreciating the nature of human consciousness.

Such studies begin with consciousness as it is discovered by the analyst, in other words, as it is given. In order to conduct inquiry, we must suspend as best we can our own knowledge of the social world, holding in abeyance any preconceived notions we might have. Although we can never fully accomplish this, we can use our imagination to doubt our knowledge about a given thing. This often radical shift frees us from our accustomed ways of thinking, thus allowing us to look freshly even at the mundane world around us and to see or understand the world through the eyes of others. Such methodological procedures are referred to as *bracketing*.

Phenomenologists want to know what forms of consciousness or knowledge are taken for granted by actors in the context of their social lives. Their interest is in how knowledge is used (by those actors) in an unreflective fashion to serve as a basis for a sense of existence. Schutz (1971) illustrates this task by analyzing Cervantes' classic story of Don Quixote.

Quixote lived in a fantasy world of knights, a world of history book chivalry that he resurrected several hundred years later. Quixote has a sidekick named Sancho Panza, his loyal manservant. Sancho was never fully converted to Quixote's way of seeing the world, but he dutifully followed, served, and conversed with his master.

The story of one of Quixote's adventures shows clashes among three separate universes or phenomenological ways of experiencing existence: chivalry, common sense, and science. Quixote and Sancho, while riding along a river, come upon a boat. To Quixote, the boat is special, capable of rapid travel to transport the knight to some noble person in distress. To Sancho the boat is ordinary. They tie up the donkey they have been riding and get into the boat. Shortly, Sancho hears the donkey braying and concludes that they have traveled but a short distance down the river. Quixote thinks they have traveled at least two thousand miles. They debate the question of distance traveled. To resolve the dispute, Quixote refers to the scientific knowledge of his time. Without proper measuring instruments, he does the next best thing; he evokes an empirical law. According to the Spaniards and others who traveled over the sea to India, when crossing the equatorial line, lice die on everybody aboard ship. Quixote reckons they have traveled past the Equator. To test this, he wants Sancho to pass "his hand over his head and see if he catches anything." Sancho objects. He can see and hear the donkey and therefore believes such a "test" to be unnecessary.

To this Quixote replies that as an unlearned man Sancho could not possibly have the knowledge of a scientist. He goes on to remark that if Sancho were to possess this knowledge, he would know they had traveled a great distance. Quixote says, "Once more I ask you, feel and fish!" To this Sancho obeys, he raises his head, looks at his master and says, "Either the test is false or we haven't got where your Worship says" (Schutz 1971, 151–52).

This example shows how three separate realities can operate within the same "objective" set of circumstances. Quixote thinks he is a knight and the boat is his enchanted transportation. Sancho is a common man. He knows only what he senses and must rely on what his previous experiences tell him. Quixote shifts realities, becoming a scientist and reasoning "scientifically." Sancho understands neither the world of knights or scientists, but knows when he has caught lice.

A phenomenological study usually investigates thinking, both its nature and its social consequences. According to Schutz, the paramount reality is the reality of everyday life; in the final analysis, it overrides, all others. To understand the meanings of social life fully, however, one must still describe in detail and with fidelity, the coherence and sense (essences) of all the various experiences people have.

Every phenomenologically informed inquiry focuses on the deep structures of social life, structures lived in and known about by virtually everyone, but understood only by those able to stand outside experience and observe it. There is a philosophical flavor to this type of inquiry, for its goal is neither the codification of knowledge nor the production of research techniques. Instead, it seeks to pare forms of understanding down to elemental and irreducible components and to offer extraordinary and nonobvious understandings of obvious and ordinary occurrences.

Symbolic Interaction

The phrase "symbolic interaction" was coined by Herbert Blumer because he thought the terms of Mead's social psychology, known for years as a form of "behaviorism," were too easily misunderstood. Concerned that its distinctiveness was not being properly reflected, Blumer intended only to name, not to change Mead's conception of social psychology.

Of the four branches of subjectivism we discuss, this is probably the most difficult to depict. Authors and researchers identifying themselves as symbolic interactionists range from those who rely on abstract phenomenological reasoning to ones seeking empirically grounded generalizations about the organization and causality of self-concepts. Nevertheless, two considerations consistently set off the work of symbolic interactionists from that of phenomenologists. Primarily, and without exception, symbolic interactionist studies are connected in an explicit way to the works of Mead, Cooley and Thomas, or others who stress the symbolic or communicative quality of interaction. In addition, virtually all symbolic interactionists place a strong emphasis on research or data-based theorizing. A symbolic interactionist will write of "data" and of "generalizations" about them, while a phenomenologist will write of "bracketing procedures to arrive at essences."

Beyond such idiomatic differences as these, the symbolic interactionist is as clearly indebted to Mead as the phenomenologist is to Schutz. This means both that a symbolic interactionist's work concerns the self as a focal concept and that, among symbolic interactionists, language and communication are understood in general and less technical ways. In fact, symbolic interactionist studies are often based on questions raised by Mead himself, with their task being to develop a version of social life that not only appreciates Mead's self-theory but even expands it in ways acceptable to, or at least conversant with, the concerns of sociology proper.

For some interactionists, the primary difference between their work and that of psychological social psychology is in the kinds of data they examine. Symbolic interactionists insist that data convey a "direct sense of what people are about" (Lofland 1971, 1). Others in the fold have expressed this same idea through the proclamation that theory must be grounded (Glaser and Strauss 1968), meaning that it is derived and developed through the researcher's total immersion in the experiences of others. And such grounding is accomplished through various techniques. Life histories and other autobiographical materials provide data with a valid perspective, as do interviews that require repeated and increasingly intimate exchanges between the researcher and the "subject"; and, of course, there is participant observation, a delicate technique involving both subjective involvement in and objective observation of a research setting.

Each approach has its advantages and disadvantages. In the first, the autobiographical, the observer can be certain of the "stance" of the data, but there are always doubts about the veracity of self-reports and the completeness of the life accounts. In a recent work, McCall (1990) developed techniques that provoke people to write "life histories." These techniques allow the researcher a measure of control over the subject matter of life histories, something often lacking in historical and other incidental life accounts.

McCall and her colleagues have also experimented with the performance of their data—having actors (often those who conducted the interviews or collected the life histories) speak the interviews to an audience of sociologists. Such innovative staging of data not only preserves the "stances" and perspectives of those studied but figuratively gives voices to them. Some symbolic interactionists, especially those with feminist convictions such as McCall (1990) and Smith (1987), have carried the charge of fidelity to those they study to a moral principle. They believe the techniques of research they employ have the potential to empower the subjects involved in the study, giving them a way to be understood in their own right.

As these contemporary scholars have shown, interviewing can be effective and efficient; but there is always the danger of the researcher imposing personal interests on those being queried, or, as the feminists' critics have demonstrated, of their even ignoring or misrepresenting the experiences of subjects. Because of this, researchers who have worked diligently to develop skills of interviewing are able to offer guidelines designed to avoid such problems. Lofland and Lofland (1987) suggest what they call "intensive interviewing," which amounts to a cross between interviewing in a formal sense and simply conversing with a subject. In contrast, some feminist researchers have proposed using the techniques of data gathering and analysis to further programs that give voice to women's experiences and so help achieve the end of equality or even of feminizing society (Fergurson 1985).

Participating in what one researches can assure the natural character of observations, but field studies are quite time-consuming, perhaps inefficient, and on occasion involve serious ethical problems. For example, how much, if anything, should researchers tell their subjects about what they are interested in, and to what degree should they become involved in the ongoing activities of the people studied, especially if these activities are illicit (see George and Jones 1980). Surely, there are limits to researcher-subject relationships. In her recent study of intimacy among Hassidic Jews, El-Or (1992) recounts how she worked to ingratiate herself with her informant, Hanna. After two years of field work, El-Or had learned a great many intimate details about the private life of this ultraorthodox woman, but finally she faced the predicament of breaking off the research or of herself becoming part of her subject's intimate world. But while she did gain Hanna's confidence and was able to participate in rituals of cleaning in the *mikva* room, in the end her role as gatherer of information conflicted with her role of friend. As El-Or writes,

> Wishing to preserve the sociological endeavor through ethnographic methods, not via force or fallacy, puts a heavy burden on the depth and endurance of intimate and reciprocal relations. "Do you still see Hanna a lot?" people ask me. "Do you keep in touch?" they wonder. "We only talk on the phone, I visited her when she had her new baby, we talked during the Gulf war," I answer. "We can't be friends because she was my object and we both know it." (El-Or 1992, 71)

We do not want to leave the impression that symbolic interactionists who immerse themselves in their studies face an irreconcilable predicament between either becoming an advocate to those they study or doing scientific work. We merely want to convey a sense of the kind of enterprise going on under each branch of sociological social psychology. The phenomenologists devote their efforts to analysis with a decidedly philosophical, even detached, tone, whereas the symbolic interactionists more likely begin, and perhaps end, with a "research project." These differences are not mere matters of taste; they derive from differences in what each regards as the pressing intellectual task of understanding.

Ethnomethodology

This style of social psychology dates from the publication of *Studies in Ethnomethodology* (Garfinkel 1967) and is a method that mixes several influences. Phenomenological in origin, it shares with symbolic interactionism a concern for research; but born as a reaction to the professional sociology of the 1960s and 1970s, ethnomethodology has a distinctively critical and confrontational bent. While the work of contemporary ethnomethodologists has taken a linguistic and technically objective turn (see Handel 1982), the original intent of this branch of inquiry must be considered. Many sociologists were attracted to it because they saw it as an alternative to traditional survey research and experimental social psychology. In idiom and purpose, its audience is the graduate student and the practicing sociologist; hence, much of the material associated with it is difficult for the beginning student to synthesize. In fact, the members of the ethnomethodological "group" have been called cultists (see Mehan 1976 for a reply to this charge).

Two themes run through most ethnomethodological studies: (1) a conception of multirealities, that is, an extreme form of relativistic thinking; and, (2) an inherent criticism of "normal" empirical social science. These themes led early researchers to look at esoteric and unconventional topics, for they felt ordinary, everyday life assumptions were readily observable through contrasts. Recently, however, ethnomethodological techniques, particularly those employed to analyze conversational data, have been applied to a remarkable array of topics such as the congressional Watergate Hearings (Molotich and Boden 1985) and even scientific breakthroughs and discoveries (Garfinkel 1989).

Ethnomethodologists expand the systems-of-knowledge conceptualization into a position stating that all social reality is constructed, fragile, dependent on constant work for its maintenance, and readily open to influence. And more than the other schools, ethnomethodology draws out the implications of the notion of reflexivity.

Mehan and Wood (1974) contend all social realities are essentially "faithful," that is, they require that people believe in them. The authors refer to the articles of faith as incorrigible propositions, or beliefs necessary to the existence of a particular social reality. Now, while it is true that the knowledge derived from such propositions is not necessarily testable in a scientific sense, the concept of incorrigible propositions is not meant to suggest social realities are essentially matters of opinions, but instead that every system has a way of accounting for its version of reality. Knowledge systems may be far from "functional," complete, or even practical, but they operate to explain away anomalies in the struggle between their own and alternative ways of thinking and being.

In the struggle to uphold and live by a particular perspective, each system provides its own account of its existence and its own means of evaluating how it is doing. This is why socially constructed realities are referred to as being *reflexive*—"reflexive" meaning "to denote an action reflected back upon an agent or subject," such as do reflexive pronouns: he hurt himself, she helped herself, and so forth. Social realities consist of systems of knowledge that continuously define and redefine themselves through the interaction of persons who believe in them. Proponents of this view maintain that all social life, and ultimately all human life, has a reflexive quality, a point evident in Merton's self-fulfilling prophesy and Thomas's notion that real ideas, though perhaps only mental aberrations, produce real consequences in the social world.

Ethnomethodologists, however, take this point to far-reaching conclusions. They suggest that talk itself is reflexive, by which they mean every utterance we make, every word or sentence we speak, says something about us and is heard not only by the person to whom we speak but by ourselves as well. In listening to ourselves, and through our imaginations of how "others" must understand, we develop our own understanding of how the social world is organized. Although other methodologists share this idea, only the ethnomethodologists turn their conceptual framework back upon themselves in a rigorous way, insisting that they, too, must be subjects in the same sense as are those whom they study.

In *Ways of the Hand*, David Sudnow (1980) examines the meaning, subtleties, and organization of the act of moving one's hand. Offering a technical but readable account, largely of his own hand movements, his data consist mainly of his musings over the appearance of his hands at tasks such as typing and playing the piano. But any social occurrence has a double quality: what is intended by the action, as well as the actors' judgments of each other's intention. Given this, all action is said to "fold back upon itself." Thus, ethnomethodologists can attend to the ways in which hands appear, or how a conversation unfolds. Invariably, they discover that social acts have several layers of meanings, layers that take on different practical consequences, depending on the contexts of interaction. Mehan and Wood illustrate how reflexivity operates in a simple greeting:

> To say "hello" both creates and sustains a world in which persons acknowledge that (1) they sometimes can see one another; (2) a world in which it is possible for persons to signal to each other, and (3) expect to be signaled back by (4) some other but only all of them. . . . When we say "hello" and the other replies with the expected counter greeting, the reflexive work of our initial utterance is masked. If the other scowls and walks on, then we are reminded that we were attempting to create a scene of greeting and that we failed. Rather than treat this as evidence that greetings are not "real," however, the rejected greeter ordinarily turns it into an occasion for affirming the reality of greeting . . . [for example] "he didn't hear me." (Mehan and Wood 1975, 13–14)

Such a theory highlights the importance of the researcher in the act of research and makes possible the use of "personal experience" (the other's or the researcher's) as primary data.

Ethnomethodological criticisms of "conventional" research methods have opened new vistas for inquiry, and, along with them, new ways of doing research. Although ethnomethodological literature is strong on critique, it is generally weak on clarity about how research is to be conducted. But, at least in part, this is the result of the nature of the inquiry; for, actually, much attention has been directed to the question of how sociologists do research. And this question itself is framed by a broader consideration, namely, "How is social reality accomplished?" for as its practitioners agree, ethnomethodology itself is a social reality, and hence can be described in terms of how it is established.

Look for mistakes, misfires, and breaks in the social order, or, idiomatically, "breaches" in the routine!—this proclamation is the methodological maxim of ethnomethodology; for it is essentially a methodology of confrontation. It is easy to be "blind to the obvious"; the trick is to learn to look at the obvious and see it from a fresh perspective, one of readiness for surprise or discovery. The techniques those who follow Garfinkel have used are ingenious. Some have resorted to mechanical devices, such as prisms worn as glasses to "invert" the world; others have developed breaching devices, such as displaying inappropriate manners in rather formal settings. Some of Garfinkel's students talked to an award-winning scientist at a university dining hall as if he were the maitre d'; others acted as if they were strangers in their own homes. Purposive violations such as these of established, routine social realities provoke reactions in others. In turn, the meanings of people's reactions reveal the essential features of the original reality. Generally, studies of this type use equipment breaches and contrived breaches, or they focus on settings of everyday life where there is some built-in ambiguity (these situations are sometimes referred to as strategic interactive settings). Examples of the latter are evident in the studies of bus riding (Nash 1975), transsexuals (Garfinkel 1967), and door ceremonies (Walum 1974). Since these kinds of studies pioneer new ways of conceiving of and gathering data, they are often controversial and are not well codified. They may, however, prove to be quite useful in a variety of research endeavors.

Mehan and Wood (1975) give a brief account of several innovative ways to "understand" everyday life. They cite the methods of zatocoding, and enjambing. In zatocoding, one records observations of the scene of interest on cards or slips of paper, one observation per card. These cards are simply stored without any particular schedule or prearranged organization for a long period of time (the length varies with the nature and intensity of the social interaction being studied). After collecting many hundreds of seemingly disjointed pieces of information, one then tries to organize them according to how one believes a person in the scene where they were gathered would do so. Of course, the effect is to test whether the researcher has become competent as a member of the social reality being studied.

Likewise, with enjambing, transcriptions of interviews or conversations are prepared without punctuation or other customary ways of designating who is talking to whom and in what fashion. The researcher must sort out this enjambed language and punctuate it in a manner that a scene member would find socially correct. Again, failure to be able to do so indicates the researcher has not yet "become the phenomenon." Indeed, this technique draws on skills not dissimilar to ones listeners and "singers" of "hip hop" music use when they "bust a rhyme." That is, being able to understand rap requires being able to assume the posture of the rapper and supplying a context—knowledge of the rapper himself or herself and of the general "hip hop" scene. Busting a rhyme is a sign that the listener and the musician are one with each other; likewise, to punctuate an enjambed transcript succesfully is to "become the subject," to "understand" the social context as well as the content of the interview or conversation. An underlying maxim for all these techniques is that social realities must be confronted by the researcher before they will reveal their true nature.

As ethnomethodology has become a part of the sociological curriculum and as new generations of students practice it, its major area of influence has become conversational analysis. By developing conventions for transcribing conversation—techniques that preserve the true character of naturally occurring talk—ethnomethodologists have improved the fit between the experience of social life and the means of conveying it. They have also demonstrated how talk is a major device of social interaction, and how, through it, many of the end results, or pragmatics of social life are accomplished. This linguistic turn has moved ethnomethodologists close to pragmatics, the branch of linguistics that studies the use of context to make inferences about meanings (Fasold 1990). By conceiving of talk as a way of acting, it has been possible to understand how people complain (Hanna 1981), are polite (Brown and Levinson 1987), use sarcasm (Haiman 1990), and, perhaps most impressively, to depict the complex logic people use when they engage each other in everyday life.

Ethnomethodology is critical, highly observational, and moored in linguistic and phenomenological inquiry. Phenomenological inquiry supplements the scientific character of ethnomethodological work with connections between empirical investigations and investigations of wider philosophical meanings.

Dramaturgical Sociology

This approach is important not so much because of its distinctiveness from the others but because it illustrates another important aspect of social psychological inquiry: that understanding can be accomplished through the use of metaphor. Metaphorical reasoning involves the use of "a word or phrase literally denoting one kind of object or idea in place of another by way of suggesting a likeness or analogy between them" (Random House 1990). The social psychologist can look at a description of some social setting and then think of it as if it were something else. In this way, he or she can ascertain patterns and regularities that may lead to new insights about the social setting itself.

The name usually associated with the analysis of social phenomena by metaphorical reasoning is Erving Goffman, whose early work suggested that the social world is essentially stagelike. Persons play roles and enact scripts given to them by social organizations. But there can be different purposes and intentions in role playing. Each person has a social mask, a persona, which he or she presents to others. Those others evaluate this mask and make judgments about its appropriateness for the "playing out" or "staging" of the social encounter. For example, in *Stigma: Notes on the Management of Spoiled Identities*, Goffman sets up a scheme for treating the way persons deal with discredited social identities. When a person's appearance communicates some negative meaning, that appearance becomes evidence that the person's persona is not acceptable. As is often the case with so-called handicapped people, the discredited person must cope with a damaged persona.

Goffman related example after example of the various ways in which this coping may develop: Persons acquire stigmatized social identities and think of themselves as outcasts. They may even develop a biography or history as a type of person, a role to play that derives from "standard or starring performances." Goffman calls these patterns "moral careers" (1963, 32–40), and he shows how information about the discredited and the discrediting person, and how the processes of being discredited or having a hidden identity that might be discreditable amounts to a high drama of everyday life, a dramatic enactment of protagonists and antagonists. According to Goffman, normality is the consequence of the management of impressions; in society, we discover the script for acting out what it means to be "stigmatized."

Goffman offered a systematic version of metaphorical social psychology in his classic *The Presentation of Self in Everyday Life* (1959), where he introduced the idea of actors varying in skills and script, of directorship and a supporting cast in the performances they give. In some of his other works Goffman drew on the findings of animal studies and on the abstraction of the form itself for yet other metaphors for social understanding.

Just as animals have territories they defend and claim as their own, humans possess contrived and culturally relative, but nevertheless real, senses of "territories of the self" (cf. Lyman and Scott 1989). In a public place, for instance, a person may claim a "stall" that is the well-bounded space to which individuals can lay temporary claim, possession being on an all or none basis" (Goffman 1971, 32–34). A telephone booth, a table with a view, or a place on the beach can be marked with a designation item—a purse or a phone off the hook for a brief time. Intrusions on claimed stalls often precipitate conflict and renegotiation of the space boundaries and time claimed. Just as wolves mark their territorial boundaries, humans claim areas of public domains for themselves with regard to use, intention, and relationship with other areas.

Goffman continuously updated his metaphors for social understanding. His final efforts dealt with the ways in which formal analyses of language can and cannot enlighten us as to the social functions of human communication. It is important to recognize that Goffman did not use analogical reasoning uncritically; instead, he employed it as a device in much the same way the ethnomethodologists use devices, to further his analytic aims. Hence, on occasion, he found it necessary to specify where analogical understanding distorts or falls short of complete descriptive validity. Hence, in *Frame Analysis*, he devotes a chapter to showing the ways in which theater and everyday life are not alike, and in *Forms of Talk* he makes it clear that formal linguistic analysis alone will not exhaust the meanings of human communicative exchanges.

Goffman's contributions to understanding social life are immense. Nevertheless, the reader should be cautioned about a danger of metaphorical understanding. The analyst, even if he or she is very careful, may become more interested in the model than in the phenomena themselves. Thus, Cicourel (1970), commenting on Goffman's work, writes: "Descriptive statements are prematurely coded, that is, interpreted by the observer, infused with substance that must be taken for granted, and subsumed under abstract categories without telling the reader how all of this was recognized and accomplished" (p. 20).

The metaphorical model can provide entrance into the world of firsthand experience. It can be a handy device for organizing information and a helpful tool for weaving one's way through the maze of detail that constitutes everyday life. If we are interested in achieving a sense of what it is like for other people to be in their social environments, we must avoid mistaking the metaphor for the phenomenon. Goffman's work moves us toward understanding by teaching us the truth of the saying "everything in the social world is significant." Goffman was the master of using *fait divers*. His books are full of the details that others overlook or discard as unimportant; and although he never developed what could be called a program for research, Goffman's contribution to social psychology is virtually immeasurable.

Recent scholars such as Charles Edgley (1990) are keeping the dramaturgical approach vital. Their work usually extends Goffman's metaphor into many aspects of everyday life. For example, Pin and Turndorf (1990) describe how we stage-manage dramatic performances of our ideal selves at social gatherings. Their study is in the classic mold of Goffman's early work, as is Kolb's use of concepts of props, front stage and back, and what actors "give" and what they "give off" to demonstrate "how mediators manage the impression of rapport, intimacy and legitimacy in order to persuade their clients to accept proposals and settlements" (Musolf 1993, 267).

Other contemporary extensions of dramaturgical analysis apply the metaphor to areas not examined by Goffman, such as politics. Welsh (1990, 400), for instance, looks at the role that impression management plays in the legitimation of power. The state becomes a performer, as it exercises power through "mystification." The state, according to Welsh, serves the interest of the privileged few, but it presents itself as existing for the benefit of the total society. Hence the state must perform so as to give off the impression of choice through election rhetoric; the state must define issues so that its "words may be successful even if its policies fail" (cf. Eldeman 1977), it must stage debates to create the impression of "negativity, opposition and choice," and it must perform dramas of crisis such as "bureaucracy versus democracy" to "con" people into believing that "accountability" will solve the crisis and that patriotism is being served.

As the work of Welsh (1990) and others (Denzin 1990) clearly shows, these attempts to extend the social psychological perspective have been accompanied by critical analysis. Denzin (1990) employs the postmodern theme of "reading" text and films and uncovers the meanings of popular culture. Others wish to expand the dramaturgy of Goffman to political and cultural criticism. Indeed, such wide-ranging applications of symbolic interactionism led Gary Alan Fine (1993) to muse about the contributions and future of the movement.

Fine suggests that the approach we have called sociological social psychology is characterized by fragmentation, expansion, incorporation, and adoption. He means by fragmentation that within the approach itself, many have divided the perspective into finer and finer points and insights. Some refine the insights of the masters, others define new areas of study, still others defend the purity of the perspectives. Often, much of what makes up contemporary literature consists of "in-house" debates about the perspective ("What Mead would have said?"), and these may have the effect of breaking the perspective up into fragments of theories. Fine writes about fragmentation, "symbolic interactionism in the 1990s has a diversity that may vitiate its center" (1993, 65).

Also, the perspective has been expanded and linked with many often exotic theories, such as chaos theory. But most prominent among the expansions has been into the political domain and the area of postmodern criticism. Symbolic interactionism has been expanded to address virtually all issues in sociology proper, inequality, class, race and ethnic conflict, and even the development of civilization (Couch 1984). Perhaps because of the successes of expansion, many of the basic tenets of Mead, Thomas, Schutz, and even Garfinkel have been incorporated into sociology and other disciplines. This is what Fine means by incorporation and adoption.

Fine also points out that symbolic interactionism has made important contributions in all areas of sociology, especially to our understanding of social coordination, emotions, how self and identity are formed, how our social worlds are constructed, and how to understand societal meanings. In this sense, symbolic interactionism has been a "glorious triumph." But it has also faded into broader concerns and techniques of analysis. Fine's essay is quite helpful to those of us who practice symbolic interactionism; it makes a point that with success come pitfalls. If our perspective is adopted and incorporated widely, our role must change, since we no longer can claim exclusive rights to our concepts. But this is a triumph. We have formulated a way of seeing the social world, and we can appreciate this by looking toward our points of convergence.

Points of Convergence

The branches of social psychology we have briefly reviewed differ form one another in some significant ways, and the reader is encouraged to pursue the theoretical issues raised by these differences in the many fine volumes devoted to this enterprise. Nevertheles, it is the convergence among them that allows for a vital sociological social psychology. Although no true, unified social psychology exists today, we can examine the common threads of a theory woven into the fabric of inquiry, and close by reiterating and reweaving these threads

The Significance of Subjective Meanings

Thomas wrote that "if situations are perceived as real, they are real in their consequences." And although he did not demonstrate how these consequences and their objective antecedents are similar, he did pave the way for the recognition of "social meaning" as the proper subject matter of social psychology. Psathas (1973) puts it this way:

> The world is not filled with objects that have appearance independent of humans who experience them, nor does subjective experience exist independently of the objects, events, and activities experienced. Subjective awareness of consciousness is consciousness of something. Whether that thing is real or imagined matters little in its impact on human experience. Subjective meanings are not found in psychological mechanisms of perception. They are experienced as being "in the world." Perception, therefore, can not be limited to what is received through the senses, but must include the meaning structures experienced by a knowing subject of that which is being perceived. (p. 14)

In the systems of thought we have reviewed, to say that something is subjective, known intuitively, or part of cultural knowledge in no way detracts from its significance. In fact, the systems all agree that theses aspects comprise the important features of social life. This is not to say that objective considerations such as the number of people living in certain geographical areas or the ratio of males to females in a given population do not enter into the total understanding of individuals in society. But these approaches all point out that every object has meaning that can be attributed in part to human mental acts and that has relevance in the social world.

Everyday Life as Topical

The social meanings we pursue cannot be discovered in the theories of sociology, psychology, or another social science. Of course, each profession possesses a social meaning structure of its own. But sociological social psychology professes to study people and societies to the extent that both experiencing a social world and understanding it become a part of the same meaning structure. Thus, what other sciences take for granted—the world of routine, day-to-day living—becomes the central subject matter. Phenomenologists say we must begin with the world as we find it "given in consciousness." Symbolic interactionists anchor their concepts in the symbolic reality of real people participating in real-life activities. Ethnomethodologists speak of "sense making" in daily living. And all point to the importance of focusing on the organization and content of everyday life.

In modern society, shifts in everyday life take place continuously, and we cannot assume patterns manifest in one historical period will have any relevance for another. To understand how one individual connects with another, and how this connection makes up society, we must begin with contemporary descriptions of everyday life. If we are to understand it, we must start with the integrated whole of society as we find it, and not study merely those things that happen to interest us when they do. The full range of meanings encompassing everyday life must become the object of our inquiry. This frequently means that the social psychologist may be intrigued with topics of everyday life that others might regard as inconsequential or even trivial. But we have learned that profound meanings and the essential structures of society are embodied in the ordinary. In his recent book on fashion, Davis (1992) eloquently dedicates his work to Herbert Blumer, who taught him to "treat seriously topics thought frivolous."

Strategies for Observation

Although each branch of inquiry proposes different modes of research, a common ground for the characterization of these approaches to research can be sketched.

Suspicious Observations As much as possible, social psychologists should rid themselves of any preconceptions they might have about the form and content of the experiences being studied. This includes discarding hypotheses derived from theories invented by sociologists about the nature of the subject. As we pointed out earlier, without the bracketing of our beliefs, without a stance of doubt and suspicion, we have already decided what is important about what we study. A social psychologist overly confident about his or her knowledge of the nature of the social world under investigation may take for granted how the people being studied experience life, or some small portion of it. Such a stance toward research restricts analysts from discovering the answers to a limited range of questions. Specifically, and simply, they can find out only if they are right or wrong about certain things; and their answers, while they may be definitive, will provide little in the way of a narrative description or true social understanding.

We are after an answer to a broader question, "What reality is happening, how is it happening, and what is its nature?" All the branches of inquiry assume the critical importance of a descriptive attitude.

Naturalistic Attitude Researchers with serious interests in the accurate description of social phenomena must work from the perspective of a naturalistic attitude—the mental perspective from which the researcher purposefully seeks to discover the meaning of things as they exist free from any outside influence. Just as other naturalists observe how organisms behave in their natural environments, social psychologists observe people at football games, in offices, running on tracks, eating in restaurants, or drinking at bars.

Most conventional, positivistic forms of social psychology require that subjects know not just that they are being observed but that they also accommodate the researcher in some fashion. The survey researcher requests that people respond to his or her questions, taking time out from their routines to address sets of queries designed by the social scientist. This is also true, but to a lesser extent, in interview methods, where much of the structure and direction of the interview can be left up to the subject. And, of course, the experimenter brings people into the laboratory, in some cases actually paying them to serve as subjects. Some natural biologists might liken this to their gathering data on the behavior of lions by going to a zoo. The varieties of social psychology presented here, in all four branches, turn the conventional research arrangement around. With them, the researcher goes to the people and accommodates himself or herself to them. Matthew Speier (1973) writes: "Generations of students have been trained to talk about the social world without ever taking the trouble to actually look at it. It has become commonplace for students to develop very elaborate and highly abstract ways to talk and write about society . . . without making concrete observations" (p. 3).

Watching and wondering about people engaged in their ordinary affairs, going to them and attempting to understand them in and on their own terms—these are methodological maxims of sociological psychology. Jane Goodall discovered that chimpanzees can be very brutal animals only after she spent months in careful observation of them in their natural habitat. Thus now it is widely known that animals behave quite differently in captivity than they do in nature.

In just living their daily lives, people, on occasion, "capture" each other, and often live in a kind of captivity of their own design. And there is a sense in which we can say laboratory studies, survey questionnaires, and the like are a part of the humanly constructed social world. But Speier refers to the correspondence between the natural reality, or essence, of the setting about which information is gathered and what the researcher concludes it to be. Studying human social life simply requires being there.

Observational Tactics Because the branches of social psychology regard ordinary experiences to be the base portion of analysis, the student of social life faces a unique problem. Linguists describing an exotic, unwritten language do not know that language before they begin to study it; likewise biologists do not assume they know how chimps act. Social psychologists, however, are already a part of the phenomena being studied. They have friends, live with fellow human beings, and have several experiences and membership stances on which to draw; hence, the methodological task of understanding is difficult. The zatocoding of ethnomethodology, the participant observation, interviewing and life-history techniques of symbolic interactionists, the radical description of phenomenologists, and the metaphor of dramaturgy—without these special devices the analyst becomes "blind to the obvious." And even though no guarantees of insight come with any of them, together these devices provide us with an impressive set of tools, some of which we should be able to put to use to further our own descriptive ends.

Finally, all aspects of the study of social meaning deal with one other problem. After the analysis is finished, the researcher may be confronted with the feeling expressed by the song stylist Peggy Lee, when she laments, "Is that all there is?" Indeed, it is very difficult to do a good job belaboring something we presume we already know. We can see that people in other cultures know a great deal, however tacitly, about how to think, feel and act within their own complicated contexts. We are fascinated by descriptions of "exotic" practices partly because they contrast so sharply with our own tacitly known worlds. Throughout, this book employs the tactic of comparison. In the study of everyday life in modern society, this often amounts to focusing on "deviant" or "extraordinary" occasions and happenings. Of course, these social experiences can be designated "normal" or "unusual" only in terms of contrasts among several perspectives. This means that as soon as we succeed in depicting a typical understanding, we discover we have described a setting in which it would be accurate to say that "everybody knew that all along." Icheiser (1970) suggests a paradox, because the more we penetrate into the hidden and obvious features of our existence by uncovering commonsense knowledge, the more we create the impression of saying something which everybody knew all along. But as he also notes, "the point to remember, however, is that the illusory impression arises only after the analysis has been completed and is simply the consequences of taking implicit awareness (immediate experience) to be explicit knowledge" (Icheiser 1970, 11).

The Question of Social Order

While there are several approaches to fundamental theoretical questions of sociology and different sociological theories reflect these approaches, a singular concern often underlies a sociological perspective—the question of social order. We have raised the question of how order is achieved throughout the various chapters of our book and have tried to show that it is a product of the processes of social interaction. This approach is shared by all the varieties of sociological social psychology—all see order as a product of engaging in social life. Still, many students of sociology divide accounts of order between those that see it as imposed from outside the individual (coming from society) and those that see it as integrally subjective. On this issue of order, perhaps more so than any other, a subjectivist social psychology is distinct.

Sociological social psychology, hence, is usually treated as separate from the classic concerns of sociology proper—that is, depictions of the forces of society operating on individuals. In his recent book, Hilbert (1992) attempts to correct what he regards as this misreading of both classical sociology and subjectivist social psychology, namely, ethnomethodology. His thesis is important for us to consider here because it suggests not only that there are points of convergence among the varieties of social psychology but that, especially in the work of the ethnomethologists, there are points of convergence between classical social theory and what we have called social psychology. To put the matter as Hilbert does, there are classical roots in ethnomethodology. This means that the work of Garfinkel and his students may be read as addressing some of the same problems as sociology proper.

To appreciate his thesis, let us consider how he recasts Durkheim's theory of anomie. We discussed Durkheim as a founder of social psychology, and we mentioned how this is somewhat unconventional since Durkheim is usually interpreted as developing a theory of the causes of suicide that is independent of an individual's consciousness. Generally, the logic of this classical explanation goes like this: Society exists as a phenomenon separate from individual consciousness and its components can be measured objectively in terms of the organization of society. Some societies promote a high degree of integration among their members. According to Durkheim, this integration assumes the forms of religion, politics, and family. He showed, through statistical association of rates of suicide with measures of the degree of integration into society, that societies in which people are encouraged to be highly involved with family, religion, or politics are societies with low rates of suicide. The Durkheimian hypothesis that suicide is inversely related to integration is perhaps the best known in sociology. And, it is taken as evidence that society affects everyday life, that is, that society is a real force that influences what people do.

Durkheim reasoned further that under conditions of rapid social change, a society can be temporally without norms, that is, in a state of anomie. The state of anomie, which Hilbert (1992, 92) depicts as one where any rule or account will do, or none will, is associated as well with suicide or more generally with nonconforming behaviors. Now anomie is conventionally taken as a cause of deviance. But Hilbert points out that there are similarities between this state of normlessness and the problem that ethnomethologists address, that is, how members of society sustain a sense of accountability regarding their actions. Hence, Garfinkel's "breaching" experiments create anomie and make it observable in individual consciousness. Through Garfinkel's concern with how members deal with making sense, we see the empirical basis of anomie. Anomie, then, to Durkheim, is the condition to which Garfinkel's subjects respond. They employ, as Hilbert says, "anomie-prevention practices" that consist of ways to make sense out of a "senseless" interactive situation.

The ways that members sustain interaction in these situations is identical to the way Durkheim says they maintain collective consciousness in the absence of any clear example of its fulfillment: ritualized recognition of extreme cases as falling outside proper parameters such that the impression of parameters, as well as "core meaning," can be maintained. Any conversation, for example, could be a locus of such ritual, especially where matters of clarification, repetition, correction, definition and so on are called for. Or, in the case of rules, wherever there is a call for justification in terms of "underlying intent" wherever clarification is sought, and especially wherever violations are determined to have taken place, here also is a Durkheimian event, a ritualized reproduction and reclarification of the transcendent premise, that of core meaning and correct use as conformity with that core meaning (Hilbert 1992, 92).

Part of what it means is, then, that the conventional interpretations of Durkheim as focused on social reality independent of individual consciousness are incorrect, and Durkheim may be read as concerned with meaning in the same way that sociological social psychology is. Deviance, or suicide, or other nonconforming behaviors become results of sense-making procedures found in the practice of members. These may well have a distribution in society, that is, some members may face anomie more often and in more dramatic ways than others, and presumably would therefore act in "deviant" ways.

Hilbert suggest that social psychology was moved by Garfinkel again to the heart of sociological analysis, from which it was removed by Parsons's reading of Weber and Durkheim.

Now the details of Hilbert's thesis require that we have a working knowledge of classic sociological literature, particularly, Weber, Durkheim, and Parsons. We mention it here to point to the convergence that we see between sociology proper and sociological social psychology, that is, that a concept such as "order" may be appreciated as equally forceful in our understanding of social life as reacted meaning as it can from a conventional reading of classic sociological literature.

Directions of Inquiry

Why is understanding so important? Isn't it enough simply to leave well enough alone? Why take tacitly understood experiences and go through the often arduous exercise of rendering them explicit and communicable? Why run the risk of becoming a disenchanted, cynical analyst? We answer these questions by following the same methodological maxims we outlined earlier.

Several scholars have described the nature of scientific inquiry in terms of shared assumptions and tacitly understood knowledge structures that support it. Gouldner referred to the socially constructed support experiences of science itself as domain assumptions (Gouldner 1970). Others, such as Jurgen Habermas (1987), have classified types of inquiry according to the purposes and aims of the inquirer. Each attempt makes clear in its own way that science, including social psychology, is an everyday human activity and as such can, indeed must, be analyzed and understood in the same way other more "mundane" human endeavors are understood. This means one way of making sense out the efforts of social psychological inquiry is to see them as routine social experiences. The problems in analyzing and depicting social psychology as human experience, then, are no different from those entailed in, for example, Lofland's analysis of being a member of the Divine Precepts cult.

Habermas (1987) suggests that inquiry can be classified according to the ends to which its proponents believe it should be put. First, there is the experience of inquiry as strict science, practiced by those whose work is guided by reasons for inquiry stating they seek the explanation of phenomena, by which they mean the ability to predict and control.

Why study human experience? Their answer is quick and to the point: to predict and control it. Sophisticated arguments as to why prediction and control are the criteria for adequate explanation invoke the incorrigible propositions which ground this inquiry and state, essentially, that there are canons of logic which in form alone are valid. Of course, we allude to symbolic logic and specifically deductive logic. If one starts with accurate descriptions, and these materials are arranged according to the formal properties of logic, then the conclusions reached will allow the "errorless" anticipation of similar occurrences; by implication, if one is in the position to prearrange conditions and thereby engender the phenomenon, that phenomenon can be controlled. The version of science we describe here is known generally as positivism, whose advocates experience inquiry as it is reduced to the prediction and control of observable experience.

Second, inquiry can be experienced as leading to understanding. This entire text has been devoted to showing what understanding means. Like Jerzy Kosinski's character, Chance the gardener, we rely on the powers of others to understand what we mean when we say "we understand." In his startling novel *Being There*, Kosinski shows how people read into the experiences of others the meanings they wish to see there. This process, of course, is the essence of social life. Inquiry can have as its purpose the understanding of what it means to understand, but although profound, and even entertaining, this is rarely the sole concern of social analysts.

The third purpose, reflexivity, completes the program of inquiry. Gouldner used the term reflexive sociology to refer to inquiry that studied itself to uncover self-interests and unravel the interconnectedness of interests in order to see who is and who is not benefiting from the inquiry. A return to the origins of social psychology reveals that this aspect of inquiry has always been a crucial component in programs of understanding.

Many members of the Chicago school were concerned with questions of how to establish order from the disarray they saw in their own city from the turn of the twentieth century through the Great Depression. Mead showed how in an expanded "generalized other" there is the possibility of tolerance and goodwill as a basis for a new and broader community. Gouldner admonished his fellow sociologists to express clearly the values they wished to maintain and promote.

But, of course, we always face the question, "Whose values?" A contemporary sociologist, Howard S. Becker, addressed this question in his article "Whose Side Are We On?" We discussed this problem in the chapter on "deviance," where we learned how the defense of values is bound up in the question of perspective. Understanding as the result of methodological and theoretic devices may be "context free," but the action we take on the basis of the understanding is not.

Our inquiry can evoke in us a sense of what it is like to be the other person, but our understanding makes sense only in terms of any ensuing practical results. We can use our own understanding to write a book or an article, thereby serving our own interests as well as those of our readers. Or understanding can become the basis for immediate experience, like political or social action. Our very program of inquiry teaches the impossibility of simply "understanding." We understand something or someone and then do something on the basis of that understanding. This dimension to inquiry is most widely referred to as "critical." Hansen (1976) expressed it well:

> The invitation of critical sociology is an invitation to become an involved, critical explorer of human and societal possibilities . . . In Mead, we find an invitation to self-other awareness. That awareness is seen as the groundwork of our personal freedom and creativity and of our personal responsibility, for neither our freedom nor our responsibility to ourselves can be untangled from the freedom of others and our responsibility to them. (pp. 12–13)

One direction of social psychology is to become critical. Although the current volume cannot treat all the ethical aspects of critical social psychology, two values that seem to be widely distributed among social psychologists can be explicated here: tolerance and autonomy. These two values, taken together, allow for a version of reciprocity sufficient to warrant the conclusion, "I understand what social psychology is really about."

Perhaps better than any other twentieth century thinker, Mead expressed the problem of tolerance. Through increased awareness of self-other relationships, we see how in our differences we share a common humanity. Mead takes us much farther than this. He shows how tolerance is an outcome of understanding the real nature of self and others, It is only in coming together with others that we recognize our unique qualities; yet as we express our unique qualities, we separate ourselves from the group. "Individuality requires order and destroys it" (Hansen 1976, 35).

Social psychology serves in the interest of tolerance—tolerance of differences of opinion, differences of bonds holding groups together, and finally differences of global social structures. But this tolerance must be two-sided, coming from both the self and the other. Mead's legacy to the purpose of social psychology is a challenge to expand self-other awareness, and at the same time find grounds for an overarching bond, a system of solidarity that holds people of dissimilar backgrounds and interests together in a atmosphere of mutual respect. Using Mead's own terms, the ideal society is one in which the individual's *I* can grow and express itself without fracturing the *me*. In this sense, social psychology as developed in this book is an effort to grapple with the fundamental issues of what it means to be human. This book has presented some of the many-sided features of social psychology's responses to that challenge.

David Reisman (1950) raised the question of autonomy within the context of social pressures toward conformity. The way he thinks about the problem serves to illustrate another of the values of social psychology. Much of the content of social psychology is devoted to a demonstration of the forces that impinge on the individual. In understanding self-other relationships, we come to appreciate the necessity of control and the complicated mechanisms of socialization and external forces that result in uniformity of action among members of society. Still, the very act of trying to understand these forces implies the possibility of avoiding, adjusting to, coping with, or manipulating these forces. It is only from the vantage point of understanding them that the possibilities are known. Reisman talks about the forces of modern society in terms of their effects on individuals. He writes that the forces of modernity could result in people who are tuned-in to the signals of approval or disapproval of others, people without inner guidelines for morality and self-worth. These people make up their minds, act and feel disproportionately with reference to what they think others think of them. Of course, this is the famous "other-directed" personality.

Although individualism is deeply ingrained in the American character (Gans 1988), and surely manifested itself in the narcissistic social order of the 1970s and 1980s (Lasch 1978; Bellah et al. 1985), Reisman's analysis still rings true. He focused on the value of inquiry by discussing the ways in which people use their understandings of the social forces that influence them. He suggested the concept of the autonomous person (1950, 239–60), one who is aware of both the possibilities of freedom and the requirements of group membership. In the duality of these stresses is a balanced position; it is not adjusting but is close to what we have called adaptation, or a creative coping with the external and internal requirements of social life that allows persons to use competencies acquired in social interaction to further mutually perceived interests. Of course, a social psychological understanding is a necessary condition of autonomy. As Reisman (1950) writes:

> Autonomy, I think, must always to some degree be relative to the prevailing modes of conformity in a given society; it is never an all-or-nothing affair, but the result of a sometimes dramatic, sometimes imperceptible struggle with those modes. Modern industrial society has driven great numbers of people into anomie, and produced a wan of conformity in others, but the very developments which have done this have also opened up hitherto undreamed-of possibilities for autonomy. As we come to understand our society better, and the alternatives it holds available to us, I think we should be able to find a great many more alternatives, and hence still room for autonomy. (p. 257)

Our social psychology has been conceived of and presented as a descriptive science with the goal of understanding; but it is incomplete without a critical dimension. Each person who travels the path of social inquiry must creatively and intellectually make a critical commitment to become involved in, and to explore the possibilities of human social interaction. And these interests must be recognized. How a person becomes critically involved will vary according to the styles, values, and interests of that person's engagement with the people he or she studies. Having appreciated the layered, multiple, and diverse qualities of social interaction, and having recognized the act of inquiry as a form of social life, it should not be surprising that social psychology does not promise a single theory of human behavior, nor does it aim to establish a body of knowledge of invariant and stable validity. Its purposes are to be found in the meanings it discovers and the consequences of its discoveries.

Exercises in Varieties of Social Psychology

1. Next time you visit home over a school vacation or on holiday, try a zatocoding exercise. Buy a pack of 3 by 5 cards (or use slips of paper) and write down one word or one phrase on each card for the impressions you have as you travel home, enter your home, greet your parents after a long absence, and so on. Continue this recording of words or phrases until you have complied at least one hundred cards or pieces of paper. Wait a few days, maybe until you return to school, and sit down with your cards or pieces of paper and try to sort them into categories that make sense to you. Sort and resort until you have a system. If you have a Macintosh computer, you might try working with these notes in the hypercard system. When you can see an order to the system you have constructed, write a short paper in which you explain your reasoning for the category system. This exercise will uncover many implicit things that you know about your home environment and will generate data for the description of the ethnomethodological accounting of your experience of home.

2. Select a typical day in your life. Write a script instructing another person whom you do not know how to play the part of you in this routine day. Include at least some lines as well as instructions about props, setting, and the life necessary to produce a play about you.

3. Divide up into groups of three. Designate one person as an interpreter in the group. Follow the rule that two people will talk to each other through the interpreter, and that the interpreter cannot simply repeat what has been said but must rephrase and restate what is said. The principal conversationalists cannot talk directly to each other. Try this for a few minutes and then suspend the rules

and discuss what you really meant to say and whether or not the interpreter actually represented what you intended. You should discover that the interpreter is in a strategic position to understand how the attempted communication is organized as social interaction. This may be a frustrating situation, but it should also generate some interesting data.

Suggested Readings

To suggest readings for this chapter is to suggest readings that go beyond the scope of this book. As you know, there is an extensive literature in each of the branches of social psychology we have reviewed. We refer you to a range of sources. Warren Handel's *Ethnomethodology: How People Make Sense* (Englewood Cliffs, N.J.: Prentice Hall, 1982) remains perhaps the most readable and convincing introduction to ethnomethodology. Phenomenological sociology awaits a Handel to articulate its precepts to the uninitiated, but Peter Berger and Thomas Luckmann do the job under the cover of "sociology of knowledge" in their classic *The Social Construction of Reality* (Garden City, N.Y.: Doubleday, 1966). Goffman should be read in the original and his *Stigma: Notes on the Management of Spoiled Identity* (Englewood Cliffs, N.J.: Prentice Hall, 1963) still can capture the reader's attention and, in a timeless fashion, conveys the essentials of a dramaturgical approach to understanding social interaction.

Appendix

Organizing Observations:
The Methodology of Social Psychology—A Brief Review

How do people reason and feel about their experiences? In social psychology we answer this question by observing people, usually in their own natural settings. As observers, we must rely on more than just observing, or even having experiences typical of those whose social lives draw our attention; otherwise we would be satisfied with simply being able to interact with and like those we study. Of course we must insist that our descriptions of the meanings of social life be true to the experiences of others, even though, after all, this interaction itself is based on guesses about what others are thinking. So the task of our social psychology is a peculiar one; not only must it preserve in description the reasonableness of the thinking, feeling and doing of those studied, but it must also communicate this understanding to an audience.

According to Agar (1980), in accomplishing this task social psychologists themselves must become "professional strangers," always a part of the worlds they study and yet also always maintaining a detached attitude toward their own experiences and the relationship between their insights and already existing bodies of knowledge. In sum, accomplishing valid understandings and effectively communicating them are the primary purposes of methodology.

Methodology is the rationale for organizing observations and developing the means for understanding them. In everyday life, all people tacitly concern themselves with methodology. Each of us has to figure out what is happening in the social world so we can act in it. In this "natural" attitude of everyday life, however, we are rarely called on to make explicit to others the basis of our interactional work. Below, then, we present a sketch about how peculiar social psychology is in requiring exactly the opposite of the natural attitude. That is, whereas in everyday life tacit assumptions often work best when they remain hidden, outside the critical eye of our fellows, in social psychology the precise means used to organize observations and the rules evoked to draw conclusions and assertions from these observations must be explicit. Although the way a social psychologist attempts to understand self and society may be painstaking and extraordinary, it is also a necessary condition for any claim of validity for the undertaking itself.

Essentially, there are two ways to learn about the experiences of others: by asking or talking to them and by observing them. Both have elements of indirectness, both have advantages and disadvantages; and together in their various forms they constitute the methodologies of social psychology. We consider each in turn here.

How to Ask People about Their Experiences

In everyday life, as actors with a natural attitude, we simply ask questions. But if we look critically (we might say "scientifically") at the act of inquiry, we see that asking is actually a method of finding out about the experiences of others. To do it well, we must know the other person's language; we must ask questions that tap their motivations; and we must make judgments about their backgrounds and the skills they possess in interaction. Although we do not think about these things, they are the tacit basis of the work we do whenever we ask a question. Of course, in everyday life we get by without having to test each and every tacit aspect of social life, but in the scientific attitude we must explicate all the pertinent aspects of what we do. Social psychologists have developed conventions for communication with each other regarding the ways they go about their research (asking questions). Sometimes they even insist on a rigid way of talking or writing while asking, and this most thoroughly organized and delineated form of asking we call the *survey*.

In the survey, the precise wording of questions is carefully prepared before the researcher asks someone to tell of his or her experience. Social psychologists can do this only when they are very confident of their knowledge about the way people think and the subjects that people think about. Hence a survey question may ask people to respond to a sentence couched in terms the researcher assumes they can understand. Most often the way subjects can respond is restricted to versions of "yes" and "no." Typical survey questions, for example, look like this:

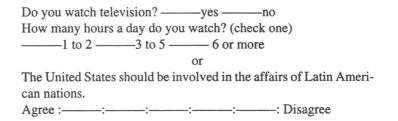

In most cases the responses people make to questions like these are coded and treated as comparable to ones they make about other experiences they may have had, like having a certain kind of job or feeling some way about an ethnic group. The science of survey research has become very precise in recent years. It is possible, for example, to predict purchasing behavior, to anticipate the outcomes of elections, and even to explain shifts in attitudes toward policy and political candidates, all from the use of survey questions.

Nevertheless, in doing a survey one must assume that people's responses mean the same (a "yes" from one person on a particular question means the same as a "yes" from everyone who so responds), that the background differences among respondents are irrelevant, and that experiences are similar enough to allow comparisons without adjustments for qualitative variations among them. Indeed, there are many subjects for which the survey question has provided valuable information for analysis. We have learned a great deal about the experience of social class from surveying how people react to categories of other people, and, for example, about how certain conditions of social life, such as health and even the quality of life are associated with the unitary meanings of gender.

Most social psychologists require some detail before they make assertions about the character and organization of experience. Hence they rely on a more intensive form of questioning than that found in most surveys. As with the survey question, if they already know a great deal about the subject matter (from previous studies or from their own experiences), they may be able to ask questions from a *prepared interview schedule*. Also, if a researcher is interested in questioning large numbers of people, he or she may give up some detail and flexibility in favor of the sheer bulk of information available from asking the same question of many different people. The difference between the survey question and the schedule is one of degrees of freedom in response. In the survey question the respondents are limited to categories of responses as they are defined by the researcher. In the interview schedule respondents may subjectively indicate categories. The researcher may ask the same question of each of those studied, but does not preform or prejudge the response categories. In fact, categories are usually generated from the observed range of responses given to the questions. For example, if we suspect that bigots are both intolerant and impervious to criticism, we may ask people suspected of bigotry to answer a question we think might elicit responses manifesting both these characteristics. Such a scheduled question, if used with a white male, might be formulated as follows: How would you feel if your company assigned you to work under an African-American supervisor?

Here the respondent would be free to shape his response as he wished, and the researcher would have varying degrees of freedom to hear answers in the responses. Therefore, he or she may code what the respondent says as being "tolerant" or "open to criticism" or may simply record responses under decoding procedures indicating that they are a "part of what-everybody-knows-who-knows-the-language"; in other words, the answers may be seen as ordinary instances of talking about hypothetical situations.

Interviewing is a special case of simply asking questions. It can vary from a way of asking organized according to the researcher's interests to one that is virtually the same as conversational exchange. The open-ended interview is often much like ordinary talking, but it usually takes place at a single time in a situation officious and contrived. The problem with such conventional ways of interviewing is that they do not allow time for the questioner and the respondent to get to know each other, even though in many cases the rapport established between the parties involved is important to the validity of the information gathered. Thus Lofland (1971) proposes a technique he calls the *intensive interview*. In this form of talking with the respondent the researcher repeatedly visits the people being studied, using responses from previous interviews to start subsequent sessions. In this way a greater amount of information that is also more accurate can be obtained.

Ethnographers also use a similar approach to talking with people. They insist on repeated sessions in which the person being talked to (they call such a person an "informant") actually teaches the questioner. Informants come to play an active role in shaping the information given to the social scientist. Likewise, ethnographers have developed ingenious ways to elicit responses from informants and, after they have the responses, to categorize them for analysis. For example, Spradley (1979) advises starting the first interview session with a "grand tour" question, one requesting that the informant orient the researcher, show him or her around the domain of knowledge. A study may start with curiosity about some social phenomenon as if it were a puzzle. Say a female student notices men walking around her small suburban community dressed in buckskins. She inquires about the men and discovers they call themselves "muzzle loaders," after their primary interest in building and firing muzzle-loaded flintlock guns. She finds an informant and asks a grand tour question: "Just what is muzzle-loading all about?"

This begins the long and possibly tedious process of depicting the cultural knowledge of this activity. The goal of the ethnographer is to describe in detail the organization of this knowledge activity. The ethnographer however, like the survey questioner, makes assumptions about the nature of this organization. The ethnographer believes the knowledge can be described in categories and that these categories can be contrasted with each other in terms of certain features or components. The enterprise finally results in taxonomies and flow charts that allow the ethnographer to communicate what he or she has learned from the informants in a powerful, precise, and concise manner.

In social psychology, an amazing variety of ways to ask people about their experiences have been developed. In summary, we can list these in terms of how fixed or flexible the language in the questions is and the degree of freedom respondents have to formulate their answers (see Table A.1.).

Table A.1.

Flexibility in Questions and Answers for Ways to Talk to People

	Degree to which questions are fixed	Degree to which answers are fixed
Surveys	High	High
Interview schedules	High	Moderate
Open-ended interviews	Moderate	Low
Ethnographic interviews	Moderate	Moderate
Intensive interviews	Low	Low

Of course, so far we have simply outlined the various forms of talking to people. When we discuss the process of talking, the enacting of talk, we move into another aspect of the methodology of social psychology. And in fact, many excellent sources give advice and counsel about gaining entree into settings, how to get approval for research and then develop relationships with those being studied, and finally, even about the "nuts and bolts" of taking notes and recording field observations (Emerson 1982).

Field research techniques themselves are becoming increasingly complex and sophisticated. Of course video and other recording equipment can be used, and now the microcomputer is increasingly employed to compile, retrieve, and analyze information. Perhaps most important, with increased experience researchers are sharing their knowledge about the problems of qualitative research. For example, from among the many complicated issues entailed in doing any kind of social science inquiry, Douglas (1976) has cited the need for an investigative attitude for research that involves talking to others. He discovered that though people are often willing to discuss even the intimate details of their lives, they have a variety of reasons for doing so, and may shape and distort the information they give.

In his study of a nude beach, for instance, he happened to run across a person he had already been interviewing for another project on sexual practices. This provided him with an opportunity to talk to others in this new setting about this person. In the first instance, the middle-aged man in question had been serving as an informant for several months, often relating detailed and seemingly credible stories about his and others' sexual experiences. But beach members gave accounts about this man that conflicted with his own. He had said his daughter approved of his adventures and that she was even present at "swinging parties." Beach members said the man's daughter was repulsed by her father's practices. And there were many other discrepancies between the man's stories and the accounts of those who knew him. Douglas's point is well taken: the form and content of talking cannot necessarily be trusted, even though they may seem to fit together. Hence he suggests that the role of researcher requires a healthy dose of skepticism and a critical eye able to see beyond the appearance of things; in short, an investigative attitude.

Ways to Watch People

The second major device for discovering the meanings of the experiences of others involves watching them act. This method can provide either direct or indirect evidence of meanings, since we can watch people without necessarily talking to them, or we can join them in the activity while also watching. In a strict science, the model for watching is the experiment itself. And although the literal application of the rationale for experimental research does not aid in the explication of social meaning, we can still adapt our organization of experimental observations to the purposes of social psychology.

In order to do this, however, we have to ask why one might want to experiment on others. Put simply, we would do so to see if they will do something either they might not do in the routine of everyday life or that they might not otherwise allow us to see. In this sense, an experiment is a kind of "setup," a way to "trick" people into doing things. Hence Garfinkel's experiment in which he had students speak into a microphone under the false belief that a counselor would answer their questions is such a device. The results of this setup revealed the ways in which students gave organization and meaning to their school-relevant experiences. We use such a device when we believe we cannot otherwise see the meanings in routine life, or when we do not have the time to go into the field to see them.

The ethnomethodologist often writes of "breaches," meaning breaks in routines, occurrences that call into question the commonsense bases of immediate interaction. Students who act like strangers in their own homes breach the ordinary meanings of family membership. Breaches can be natural or they can be contrived. A natural breach is something so extraordinary that it suspends the taken-for-granted knowledge usually used to make sense out of things. Disasters, such as floods and hurricanes, are natural breaches.

On the other hand, sometimes the social psychologist actually creates breaches. For example, to study conflict resolution Sherif (1961) first organized Boy Scouts at a camp into two distinct groups (Eagles and Snakes) so that they would develop strong but separate senses of group identity. Then he contrived situations, such as the breakdown of a Jeep, that forced the groups to cooperate. He set up the students to see if having to perform a cooperative task would weaken their separate group identities, which it did. This type of observation is sometimes referred to as a *field experiment*.

Of course, all devices for observation require that the researcher somehow be there. Whether he or she sets up the situations of observation or merely goes to the scenes, the researcher must to a degree be involved in the experiences of those studied. The classic example of this is called *field research*, and the most widely used type is *participant observation*. Throughout, this book relies on many such studies. Simply being there does not necessarily imply participation; and on the other hand, we have to be able to be so detached as to be there without really being there. Fishman's (1978) study of taped conversations of married couples illustrates a form of observation where the researcher is not present in person but is there in the form of a tape recorder, for the machine surely takes on meanings in the interaction. Some couples were "observed" saying, "Turn that thing off" or, "Remember, we're being recorded." Further, the use of concealed cameras or even concealed observers, as in the case of one sitting in a warm building while watching people wait for a bus, is a form of detached observation. But we must offer a note of caution. In all these cases, if the observer is detected, either strategies for observation must change or the potential influence of the detection itself must be taken into consideration as part of the analysis.

So we learn that in the ideal, observational devices vary from those requiring us to be complete observers to those in which we are complete participants. As observers we are detached from the experiences of others; as participants we may literally become the phenomenon we study, and our own experiences can be taken as representative of those of other people. As we suggest, in reality these stances, of participant and of observer, are matters of degree; so while we may be more one than the other, we are always at least a little of each.

Several years ago, Junker (1960) worked out a chart illustrating the relationships among the dimensions of participant and observation (see Figure A.1.). From Junker's chart we can see that observational devices involve both the "artificial" attitude of the researcher and the natural attitude of simply living in society. It is apparent then that while researchers have the advantage of their own experiences (cf. Rothman's 1982 book on natural childbirth), at the same time they must be able to separate their attitudes as researchers from those they hold as participants. The conventions of doing research help in the management of this continuing intrinsic problem. The trappings of the laboratory, the white coat of the researcher and the use of equipment—even if this is only a note pad and a tape recorder—enhance the attitude of detachment. Still, in the final analysis, the researcher is always to some degree participating in the experiences of those studied; and a major part of the methodology of social psychology is given over to realizing how this involvement is related to the understandings we have of social life. Techniques of research help us move from observation to participation and back, but they do not solve the problem of the intrinsic, inextricable connections among being there, knowing about it, and communicating it to others.

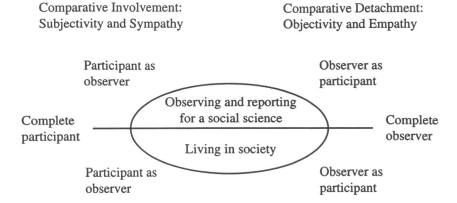

Figure A.1. The relationship of participation and observation. Adapted from Junker, Buford, *Field Work: An Introduction to the Social Sciences* (Chicago: University of Chicago Press, 1960, 146.

Understanding at the Moment and Over Time

Conventionally in the social sciences, a distinction is drawn between "one-shot" studies and studies that focus on a phenomenon over several different observational periods. The first type of study is called *cross-sectional* and the latter *longitudinal*. Although it is necessary to observe over time in order to assess causal links among phenomena, longitudinal studies are very costly and very difficult to manage in societies where people are mobile and generally protective of their private worlds. Hence most social psychological studies are cross-sectional. They define a set of phenomena to be observed and are explicit about the time frame in which the observations take place.

Of course cross-sectional studies can be used to measure changes in phenomena over time as long as the researcher can specify the sense in which the phenomena measured are comparable. For example, the Lynds first studied "Middletown" (Muncie, Indiana) in the 1920s, assessing the organization of the social lives of the residents on matters such as family life, leisure-time pursuits, and work. Then they returned in the 1930s, to assess the impact of the Great Depression on the social fabric of the community; and more recently a team of sociologists visited the town in the 1970s, to see how family life compared then with what the Lynds had observed (Lynd and Lynd 1929, 1937; Caplow et al. 1982).

Not surprisingly, most of the people who participated in the first and second studies were not involved in the third. Although some of the high school students who answered the questions of the most recent researchers were related to the subjects of the original study, this work is not longitudinal in the strictest sense. To be so, it would have had to follow the same people through the decades, asking them questions and observing them at set intervals. Still, taken together, the Middletown studies give us a view of the continuity of family and community life in America. They show, for example, a surprising degree of stability over the decades in the meanings of work and leisure and most importantly in the degree of importance attributed to family life. And they exemplify how much of the descriptive work of sociology can function to document the meanings of social life at particular conjunctions in history.

But as we move beyond description to pursue the goal of social psychology, to see how understanding functions as a basis for action, we find that the ideal of a "hard" science, to portray causal relationships, cannot be directly applied to social phenomena. As Friedrichs (1972) asks, are we to say that Jonah's prophecy was invalid because the people of Nineveh heeded his advice and successfully avoided their prophesied destruction? In fact, people continuously change their interpretations of the meanings of things, and they adapt their behavior accordingly. To deal with the effects of changes in meanings we can modify the ideas of cross-sectional and longitudinal research to fit the nature of social phenomena.

The methodology used by linguists to assess language change helps alleviate the problems of understanding both at the moment and over time. In analyzing the way a language is structured and how it functions both at a given time and over time, linguists are able to show how the meanings of words change and can have quite different meanings at different times in the history of a language. We see this, for example, in contemporary assertions about sexism in the English language that question the use of "chairman" or "he" as generic terms. But linguists take the analysis further; they illustrate how a single word or segment of language can be seen in terms of how it both fits into the organization of contemporary usage and the historical development of the language. The word "Mississippi," for instance, is composed of a single unit of meaning (morpheme) when understood in terms of current usage (it means a specific river). But when the word is examined in terms of origins (its roots in a Native American language), it has three distinct units, Father of Waters.

Linguists call the study of language at a given time *synchronic analysis* and the study of the development of language *diachronic*. This distinction is particularly useful in the study of social phenomena, for when we depict the experiences of others, we must be clear about our analytic point of view. That is, our readers or listeners must be able to distinguish when we are talking about the sense of experience at a particular moment, such as how a group of workers in a bank make sense of dress codes (cf. Jackall 1977), from when we are attempting to put together a picture of minor changes in how people understand their involvements with each other. The shifts from "collective" senses of self to "individual" ones in the transition from traditional to modern society usually represent this latter analytic stance. In the end, the version we give of understanding meaning is inextricably tied not just to how we see people in relationships with each other in particular settings but even to how they, and we, conceive of time in relation to the problem at hand.

The Research Act

A research act is more than "doing a study." It requires that researchers assume, master, and work within a form of consciousness in which they can employ devices for finding out about the experiences of other people. With these devices researchers can imagine the practical consequences of various experiences as they appear in their social contexts; that is, they can "check out," according to some criteria, the extent to which certain experiences have been described and preserved. And finally, they can communicate all this to an audience, which communication itself can be understood as a social phenomenon. The research act is, then, an active commitment to information, perspective, and procedure (Denzin 1978). To commit such an act is to participate in social life as a kind of intellectual reporter, a person who tells stories about the way people think, feel, and act toward one another. The stories, however, are not "natural" because they are not told in a "natural" language. Instead, they require the mastery of specialized idioms and attitudes. Schutz referred to the attitude of the researcher as that of the "expert."

As we discover in this book, it is often not so much what the social psychologist knows that allows the claim of being expert, but the way in which it is known. The researcher's attitude is a heavy burden, requiring the suspension of commonsense perspectives for the purposes of understanding them. Without the grounding that makes the process of sense-making uncritical in the "natural attitude," the researcher is set adrift in ways of thinking that blur distinctions between the obvious and the nonobvious, the commonplace and the extraordinary. Although a project may delimit the focus of this consciousness, the consciousness itself is always critical, calling into question the very foundations of social life.

Certainly the earlier thinkers such as Mead and Thomas appreciated these points. Just as the self and society are two sides of the same coin, so theory and research, observation and concept are binary pairs of the same reality. The kind of thinking we depict as necessary to social psychology has been called *nonlinear* (Curtis 1978). More conventional discussions of methodology leave the reader with versions of relationships which stress how things, though related, are actually separate and measurable, each with identifiable features. This approach calls up images of causality and a straight-line progression of time (linearity). The nonlinear approach, on the other hand, "resolves dichotomies . . . into binary pairs, which interact and each term of which is equally necessary" (Curtis 1978, 22).

Since our work addresses constructed, language-created phenomena, the methodology we employ must be capable of appreciating the layered and interpenetrating character of social phenomena themselves. Research acts are as much matters of consciousness as they are techniques for gathering information through observation. What one sees in the social world is as much a result of how one thinks as it is a reflection of "what's out there."

But in no way should this be construed to mean that such an approach to social psychology lacks rigor or standards in its methodology. Just the opposite is true. Methodology means the pairing of theoretical consciousness with ways to get information, and it requires that the pairing make sense as a unit in and of itself. It also means that no list of ways to ask questions or to observe can be presented for a given topic of study. Methods and theory are binary. The researcher usually discovers that the odyssey from living in society to reporting about it necessitates the use of many different ways to gather information. Further, as has been the case with all breakthroughs in science, new methods always have to be devised for developing pertinent data. But because it is a human endeavor, the continuous search for creative new ways to get information about human experience raises provocative and serious questions of an ethical nature regarding methodologies of social research.

Ethics and Understanding

Since so much of the subject matter of social psychology is simply "ordinary life" and since ordinary life entails a full array of rules to follow and break, it should come as no surprise that certain questions about the ethics of some of the methods of social psychology have arisen. If a researcher observes illicit acts and does not report them, to what degree is he or she an accomplice? When an ethnographer uncovers how workers in a formal organization slack off to cope with rules they regard as "unfair," should that ethnographer tell management? Or on the other side of that question, should the ethnographer teach workers how they might subvert and manipulate the official rules of an organization when they feel they are being treated unfairly? (cf. Van Maanen 1979).

Often these matters boil into bitter conflict. Members of a town that has been the subject of a research project may discover their secrets revealed to the world. Or sociologists may fight among themselves over the proper ethical stance regarding a project. Perhaps the most noteworthy case in recent years took place between a minister-turned-sociologist, Laud Humphreys—who studied homosexuals by observing them in public restrooms (tearooms)—and a prominent sociologist, Alvin Gouldner. Apparently Humphreys would pass himself off as a lookout (watching for the police, say, while the others engaged in sex); and Gouldner, it seems, was critical of such methods employed by sociologists in research on deviant behavior. He suggested that they were more interested in their own professional advancement than in the plight of the deviants they studied. Professor Gouldner was accused of calling Humphreys a "peeping parson," while Gouldner was characterized by graduate students as a "bird that feeds on underdogs" (*New York Times*, June 9, 1968). Although the problem was solved without seriously damaging the career of either man, the incident shows the depth of emotions that research can evoke.

At issue of course is the nature and degree of involvement researchers should properly have in the lives of those they study. Gouldner argued that sociologists must deal with their own values in what he calls "reflexive sociology." Humphreys and others tend to be less judgmental in conducting research, taking a laissez-faire attitude toward what is being observed. In fact, both sides of this debate were concerned with the fate of those studied; and perhaps it is because their commitments were so strong that their disagreements over how to be involved became so embittered.

On another level, the federal government and other institutions that finance or carry out research on human subjects often require that consent forms be filled out by subjects before a research project can begin. Initially such precautions were designed to protect subjects in medical or psychological research. But clearly, even when from a distance we observe children at play, for example, the question arises of how they are our subjects and whether we should receive consent from those responsible for them.

This matter of what has been called *covert research* has also received close attention in the literature. Some claim that studies in which the researcher's intentions and identity are concealed from those whom he or she studies should never be allowed (cf. Erickson 1967), while others argue that research of this kind holds more dangers for the researcher than for subjects (for a thorough discussion, see Blumer 1982).

These questions are indeed serious. They raise issues of the invasion of privacy, the control of official information, and more fundamentally of the interests and freedom of inquiry of both the people being studied and those studying them. We can summarize the positions as they have been articulated as two camps. Some argue that special caution and procedures are necessary to safeguard the rights of subjects. They therefore generally oppose covert research and support the use of consent forms and other legal guarantees for subjects' rights. In the other camp however, are those who maintain that social psychologists who seek understanding (as opposed to those who follow the model of the hard sciences) are actually a part of the ongoing social interactions being studied.

This means, consistent with our nonlinear methodology, that the researchers and their subjects represent a binary pair and that each then affects and influences the other as people studying people.

Two conclusions can be drawn. First, the social psychologist enjoys no special privileges owing to his or her professional commitment. He or she is a citizen of the society as well as an expert in it. The laws of the land govern research in the same way they govern everyday life. This means libel and slander can apply to the social psychological uses of knowledge. But it also means that the obligations a researcher has to those studied are not completely a consequence of legal documents and contracts alone. They grow from the human contact inevitably experienced in acts of research.

Although professional bodies such as the American Sociological Association should and do draft codes of ethics, the practice of these is a matter of interaction and must be understood as such. Lest we forget, our way of understanding as social psychologists contrasts with the natural attitude and hence we may on occasion fail to distinguish among our various stances of consciousness as clearly as we would like, and in the process we may fail to see the legal or organizational implications of our writing and talking about social life. When this happens, the professional may be judged, as occurred when a well-known sociologist received a suspended sentence for tape recording the deliberations of a jury. Or a researcher may be vindicated, as was Humphreys when he won his suit against the university that had fired him for his controversial research. In the end, the larger community and the people who belong to it will be the judge. They represent the practical court of ethical judgments, and one must be aware of their potential reaction at each stage of one's research. Ultimately, the ethics of research are the ethics of everyday life.

References

Allport, Gordon W. 1968. "The Historical Background of Modern Social Psychology." Pp. 1–80 in Gardner Lindzey and Elliot Aronson, eds., *The Handbook of Social Psychology*. Reading, Mass.: Addison-Wesley.

Altheide, David, and John Johnson. 1980. *Bureaucratic Propaganda*. Boston: Allyn and Bacon.

Armstrong, Edward G. 1993. "The Rhetoric of Violence in Rap and Country Music." *Sociological Inquiry* 63 (1): 64–83.

Auletta, Ken. 1982. *The Underclass*. New York: Random House.

Barley, Stephen R. 1983. "The Codes of the Dead: Semiotics of Funeral Work." *Urban Life: A Journal of Ethnographic Research* 12 (August): 3–31.

Bateson, Gregory. 1972. *Steps to Ecology of Mind*. New York: Chandler.

Becker, Gaylene. 1980. *Growing Old in Silence*. Berkeley: University of California Press.

Becker, Howard S. 1963. *Outsiders: Studies in the Sociology of Deviancy*. New York: Free Press.

———. 1967. "Whose Side Are We On?" *Social Problems*. 14: 239247.

Bellah, Robert N., et al. 1985. *Habits of the Heart: Individualism and Commitment in American Life*. Berkeley: University of California Press.

Berger, Peter L. 1979. *The Heretical Imperative*. Garden City, N.Y.: Anchor Books.

Berger, Peter L., Brigitte Berger, and Hansfred Kellner. 1974. *The Homeless Mind: Modernization and Consciousness*. New York: Vintage Books.

Berger, Peter L., and Thomas Luckmann. 1966. *The Social Construction of Reality: A Trestise in the Sociology of Knowledge*. New York: Anchor Books.

Blau, Peter and Marshall W. Meyer. 1987. *Bureaucracy in Modern Society*, 3rd ed. New York: Random House.

Blumer, Herbert. 1969. *Symolic Interaction: Perspective and Method*. Englewood Cliffs, N.J.: Prentice Hall.

Boden, Deirdre. 1990. "People Are Talking: Conversational Analysis and Symbolic Interaction" Pp. 244–74 in Howard S. Becker and Michal M. McCall, eds., *Symbolic Interaction and Cultural Studies*. Chicago: University of Chicago Press.

Bogan, David, and Michael Lynch. 1989. "Taking Account of the Hostile Native: Plausible Deniability and the Production of Conventional History in the Iran-Contra Hearing." *Social Problems* 36 (June): 197–224.

Bonvillain, Nancy. 1993. *Language, Culture and Communication: The Meanings of Messages*. Englewood Cliffs, N.J.: Prentice Hall.

Brissett, Dennis and Charles Edgley, eds. 1990. *Life as Theater: A Dramaturgical Source Book*. New York: Aldine de Gruyer.

Brissett, Dennis and Robert P. Snow. 1993. "Boredom: Where the Future Isn't." *Symbolic Interaction* 16 (Fall): 237–256.

Brown, Penelope, and Stephen Levinson. 1987. *Politeness: Some Universals in Language Usage*. New York: Cambridge University Press.

Brown, Roger. 1954. "Mass Phenomenon." In G. Lindzey, ed. *Handbook of Social Psychology*. Vol. 2. Cambridge, Mass.: Addison-Wesley.

Buckholdt, David, and Jaber F. Gubrium. 1979. *The Caretakers: Treating Emotionally Disturbed Children*. Beverly Hills, Calif.: Sage.

Burgess, Anthony. 1963. *Clockwork Orange*. New York: Norton.

Cahill, Spencer, and Lyn Lofland, eds. 1994. *The Community of the Streets*. Greenwich, Conn.: JAI Press.

Callois, Roger. 1961. *Man, Play and Games*. New York: Free Press.

Cegala, Donald J. 1982. "An examination of the Concept of Interaction Involvement Using Phenomenological and Empirical Methods." In *Interpersonal Communication: Essays in Phenomenology and Hermeneutics*. Washington, D.C.: University Press of America.

Cicourel, Aaron. 1970. "Basic and Normative Rules in Negotiation of Status and Roles." Pp. 445 in Hans Peter Dreitzel, ed., *Recent Sociology*. No. 2. New York: Macmillan.

———. 1974. *Cognitive Sociology: Language and Meaning*. New York: Free Press.

Clark, Colin, and Trevor Pinch. 1992. "The Anatomy of a Deception: Fraud and Finesse in the Mock Auction Sales 'Con'." *Qualitative Sociology* 15: 151–176.

Coates, Jennifer, and Deborah Cameron. 1988. *Women in Their Speech Communities*. New York: Longman.

Collins, Randall and Michael Makowsky. 1993. *The Discovery of Society*. 5th ed. New York: McGraw-Hill.

Comstock, George S. 1977. "Types of Portrayal and Aggressive Behavior." *Journal of Communication* 26: 189–98.

Cook-Gumperz, Jenny. 1975. "The Child as Practical Reasoner." In Mary Sanches and Ben C. Blount, eds., *Sociocultural Dimenisons of Language Use*. New York: Academic Press.

Cooley, Charles H. 1909. *Social Organization*. New York: Scribner's.

———. 1922. *Human Nature and the Social Order*. New York: Scribner's.

Coser, Lewis. 1971. *Masters of Sociological Thought*. New York: Harcourt, Brace.

Crawford, M. 1992. "The World in a Shopping Mall." in Michael Sorkin, ed., *Variation on a Theme Park: The New American City and the End of Public Space*. New York: Hill and Wang.

Cuddihy, John M. 1974. *The Ordeal of Civility*. New York: Dell.

Cuzzort, Ray P., and Edith W. King. 1980. *20th Century Social Thought*. 3rd ed. New York: Holt, Rinehart and Winston.

Dalton, Melville. 1957. *Men Who Manage*. New York: Wiley.

Davis, Fred. 1979. *Yearning for Yesterday: A Sociology of Nostalgia*. New York: Free Press .

———. 1992. *Fashion, Culture and Identity*. Chicago: University of Chicago Press.

Davis, Murray S. 1983. *Smut: Erotic Reality/Obscene Ideology*. Chicago: University of Chicago Press.

Deegan, Mary Jo. 1989. *American Ritual Dramas: Social Rules and Cultural Meanings*. New York: Greenwood Press.

Denzin, Norman K. 1978. *The Research Act: A Theoretical Introduction to Sociological Methods*. New York: McGraw-Hill.

Derber, Charles. 1979. *The Pursuit of Attention: Power and Individualism in Everyday Life*. New York: Oxford University Press.

DeVilliers, Peter, and Jill G. DeVilliers. 1979. *Early Language*. Cambridge: Harvard University Press.

Dickens, Davis R. 1979. "Phenomenology." In *Theoretical Perspectives in Sociology*. New York: St. Martins Press.

Diggory, James C.. 1966. *Self Evaluation: Concepts and Studies*. New York: Wiley.

Dillard, J.L. 1972. *Black English: Its History and Usage in the United States*. New York: Vintage Books.

Dollard, J.D., L.W. Miller, and R.R. Sears. 1939. *Frustration and Aggression*. New Haven: Yale University Press.

Douglas, Jack, and John Johnson, eds. 1977. *Official Deviance: Readings in Malfeasance, Misfeasance and Other Forms of Corruption*. New York: Lippincott.

Douglas, Jack, and Paul Rasmussen, with Carol Ann Flanagan. 1977. *The Nude Beach*. Beverly Hills, Calif.: Sage.

Douglas, Jack, et al. 1980. *Introduction to the Sociologies of Everyday Life*. Boston: Allyn and Bacon.

Dumont, Richard, and William J. Wilson. 1967. "Aspects of Concept Formation, Explication and Theory Construction in Sociology," *American Sociological Review* 32 (December): 985–95.

Dunning, Eric, Patrick Murphy, and John Williams. 1988. *The Roots of Football Hooliganism*. New York: Routledge and Kegan Paul.

Edelman, Murray. 1977. *Political Language: Words That Succeed and Policies That Fail*. New York: Academic Press.

Ellis, Donald, Leonard C. Hawes, and Robert K. Avery. 1981. "Some Pragmatics of Talking on Talk Radio." *Urban Life: A Journal of Ethnographic Research* 10 (July): 155–77.

El-Or, Tamar. 1992. "Do Your Really Know How They Make Love? The Limits of Intimacy with Ethnographic Informants." *Qualitative Sociology* 15 (1): 53–72.

Erickson, Kai. 1976. *Everything in Its Path: Destruction of Community in the Buffalo Creek Flood*. New York: Simon and Schuster.

Faberman, Harvey A. 1980. "Fantasy in Everyday Life: Some Aspects of the Intersection between Social Psychology and Political Economy," *Symbolic Interaction* 3 (Spring): 9–21.

Fabrega, Horacio, and Peter K. Manning. 1973. Pp. 251–304 in George Psathas, ed. *Phenomenological Sociology: Issues and Applications*. New York: Wiley.

Fasold, Ralph. 1990. *Sociolinguistics of Language*. Cambridge, Mass.: Basil Blackwell.

Feagan, Joe R. 1991. "The Continuing Significance of Race: Antiblack Discrimination in Public Places." *American Sociological Review* 56:101–16.

Ferguson, Kathy. 1984. *The Feminist Case Against Bureaucracy*. Philadelphia: Temple University Press.

Fine, Gary Allen. 1983. *Shared Fantasy: Role Playing Games as Social Worlds*. Chicago: University of Chicago Press.

———. 1993. "The Sad Demise, Mysterious Disappearance, and Glorious Triumph of Symbolic Interactionism." *Annual Review of Sociology* 19: 61–87.

Fishman, Pamela. 1978a. "Interaction: The Work Women Do," *Social Problems* 25: 397–406.

———. 1978b. "What Couples Talk about When They're Alone." In D. Butturf and E. L. Epstein, eds. *Women's Language and Style*. Akron, Ohio: University of Akron Press.

Furth, Hans G. 1980. *The World of Grownups: Children's Conceptions of Society*. New York: Elsevier.

Garfinkel, Harold. 1963a. "Common-Sense Knowledge of Social Structure: The Documentary Method of Interpretation." Pp. 689–712 in Jordan M. Scher, ed. *Theories of the Mind*. New York: Free Press.

———. 1963b. "A Conception of, and Experiments with, 'Trust' as a Condition of Stable Concerted Actions." In O.J. Harvey, ed. *Motivation and Social Interaction*. New York: Ronald Press.

———. 1967. *Studies in Ethnomethodology*. Englewood Cliffs, N.J.: Prentice Hall.

Garfinkel, Harold, Michael Lynch and Eric Livingston. 1981. "The Work of Discovering Science Constructed with Materials from the Optically Discovered Pulsar." *Philosophy of the Social Sciences* 11: 131–158.

Garson, Barbara. 1975. *All the Livelong Day: The Meaning and Demeaning of Routine Work*. New York: Penguin Books.

Gecas, Viktor. 1981. "Contexts of Socialization." In Morris Rosenberg and Ralph Turner, eds. *Social Psychology: Sociological Persepctive*. New York: Basic Books.

Geertz, Cliford. 1973. "Religion as a Cultural System." In *The Interpretation of Culture*. New York: Harper and Row.

Gelles, Richard J. 1974. *The Violent Home*. Beverly Hills, Calif.: Sage.

Georges, Robert, and Michael O. Jones. 1980. *People Studying People: The Human Element in Fieldwork*. Berkeley: University of California Press.

Glaser, Barney, and Anselm Strauss. 1968. *The Discovery of Grounded Theory, Strategies for Qualitative Research*. Chicago: Aldine.

Goffman, Erving. 1959. *The Presentation of Self in Everyday Life*. New York: Doubleday.

———. 1963. *Stigma: Notes on the Management of Spolied Identity*. Englewood Cliffs, N.J.: Prentice Hall.

———. 1969. *Strategic Interaction*. Philadelphia: University of Pennsylvania Press.

———. 1971. *Relations in Public: Microstudies of the Public Order*. New York: Basic Books.

———. 1974. *Frame Analysis: An Essay on the Organization of Experience*. Cambridge: Harvard University Press.

———. 1979. *Gender Advertisements*. Cambridge: Harvard University Press.

———. 1981. *Forms of Talk*. Philadelphia: University of Pennsylvania Press.

Gold, Ray. 1952. "Janitors Versus Tenants: A Situation of Income Dilemma." *American Journal of Sociology* 57: 486–93.

Goodman, F. 1974. "Disturbances in the Apostolic Church." In F.D. Goodman, J. Henry, and E. Resel, eds., *Trance, Healing and Hallucination*. New York: Wiley.

Gordon, David. 1974. "The Jesus People: An Identity Synthesis." *Urban Life and Culture* 3: 159–78.

Gordon, David Paul. 1983. "Hospital Slang for Patients: Crocks, Gomers, Gorks and Others." *Language in Society* 12, 2: 173–85.

Gordon. Steven L. 1981. "The Sociology of Sentiments and Emotions." In Morris Rosenberg and Ralph Turner, eds., *Social Psychology: Sociological Persepctive*. New York: Basic Books

Gouldner, Alvin W. 1954. *Wildcate Strike: A Study in Worker-Management Relationships*. New York: Harper and Row.

———. 1970. *The Coming Crisis of Western Sociology*. New York: Avon Books.

Grimshaw, Allen. 1966. "Directions for Research in Sociolinguistics: Suggestions of a Nonlinguist Sociologist." *Sociological Inquiry* 36 (Spring): 191–204.

Habermas, Jurgen. 1987. *The Theory of Communicative Action*, trans. by Thomas McCarthy. New York: Beacon Press.

Haiman, John. 1990. "Sarcasm as Theater." *Cognitive Linguistics* 12: 181–205.

Hall, Edward. 1966. *The Hidden Dimension*. Garden City, N.J.: Doubleday.

Handel, Warren. 1982. *Ethnomethodology: How People Make Sense*. Englewood Cliffs, NJ: Prentice-Hall.

Hansen, Donald. 1976. *An Invitation to Critical Scoiology: Involvement, Crticism and Exploration*. New York: Free Press.

Harrison, S. 1984. "Drawing a Circle in Washington Square Park." *Studies in Visual Communication* 10: 68–83.

Hecht, Michael, Marry Jane Collier, and Sidney A. Ribeau. 1993. *African American Communication: Ethnic Identity and Cultural Interpretation*. Newbury Park, Calif.: Sage.

Herman, Nancy J. 1993. "Return to Sender: Reintegrative Stigma-Management Strategies of Ex-Psyhiatric Patients." *Journal of Contemporary Ethnography* 22 (October): 304–23.

Herman, Nancy J., and Charlene E. Miall. 1990. "The Positive Consequences of Stigma: Two Case Studies in Menal and Physical Disability." *Qualitiative Sociology* 14 (3): 251–69.

Herman, Nancy J., and Larry T. Reynolds. 1994. *Symbolic Interaction: An Introduction to Social Psychology*. Dix Hills, N.Y.: General Hall.

Hewitt, John P., and Randall Stokes. 1975. "Disclaimers." *American Sociological Review* 40 (February): 1–11.

Hickey, K.V., W. E. Thomspon, and D.L. Foster. 1988. "Becoming the Easter Bunny: Socialization into a Fantasy Role." *Journal of Contemporary Ethnography* 17: 67–95.

Higgins, Paul C. 1980. *Outsiders in a Hearing World.* Beverly Hills, Calif.: Sage.

————. 1992. *Making Disability: Exploring the Social Transformation of Human Variation.* Springfield, Ill.: Charles C. Thomas.

Hilbert, Richard A. 1992. *The Classical Roots of Ethnomethodology: Durkheim, Weber and Garfinkel.* Chapel Hill: University of North Carolina Press.

Hochschild, Arlie Russell. 1979. *The Unexpected Community: Portrait of an Old Age Subculture.* Berkeley: University of California Press.

————. 1983. *The Managed Heart: Commercialization of Human Feelings.* Berkeley: University of California Press.

Hoffding, Harold. 1891. *Outline of Psychology.* London: Macmillan.

Homans, George C. 1974. *Social Behavior: Its Elementary Forms.* New York; Harcourt, Brace and World.

————. 1992 (1950). *The Human Group.* New Brunswick, N.J.: Transaction.

Hummel, Ralph P. 1987. *The Bureaucratic Experience,* 3rd ed. New York: St. Martin's Press.

Icheiser, Gustav. 1970. *Appearances and Realities.* San Francisco: Jossey-Bass.

Irwin, John. 1977. *Scenes.* Beverly Hills, Calif.: Sage.

————. 1980. *Prisons in Turmoil.* Boston: Little Brown.

Jackall, Robert. 1977. "The Control of Public Faces in a Commerical Bureaucratic Work Situation." *Urban Life: A Journal of Ethnographic Research* 6 (October): 277–302.

————. 1988. *Moral Mazes: The World of Corporate Managers.* New York: Oxford University Press.

Jacobs, Bruce A. 1992. "Undercover Drug-Use Evasion Tactics: Excuses and Neutralization." *Symbolic Interaction* 15 (4): 435–53.

Jacobs, Leo M. 1989. *A Deaf Adult Speaks Out.* Washington, D.C.: Gallaudet University Press.

James, William. 1890. *Principles of Psychology.* New York: Henry Holt .

Jamison, W., and W. Lunch. 1990. "A Preliminary Report: Results from Demographic, Attitudinal, and Behavioral Analysis of the Animal Rights Movement." Oregon State University.

Jasper. J.M., and D. Nelkin. 1992. *The Animal Rights Crusade: The Growth of a Moral Movement.* New York: Free Press.

Joas, Hans. 1985. *G.H. Mead: A Contemporary Re-examination of His Thought.* Cambridge: Polity.

Johnson, Cathryn. 1992. "The Emergence of the Emotional Self: A Developmental Theory." *Symbolic Interaction* 15 (2): 183–202.

————. 1994. "Gender, Legitimate Authority, and Conversation." *American Sociological Review* 59 (February): 122–35.

Kaiser, S.B., R. H. Nagasawa, and S.S. Hutton. 1991. "Fashion, Postmodernity and Personal Appearance: A Symbolic Interactionist Formulation." *Symbolic Interaction* 14 (2): 16585.

Kaplan, Sidney, and Shirley Kaplan. 1983. "Video Games, Sex and Sex Differences." *Journal of Popular Culture* 17 (Fall): 61–66.

Katcher, A. 1955. "The Discrimination of Sex Differences by Young Children." *Journal of Genetic Psychology* 87: 131–43.

Katz, Judith Milstein. 1976. "How Do You Love Me? Let Me Count the Ways (The Phenomenology of Being Loved)." *Sociological Inquiry* 46: 17–22.

Kemper, Theodore D. 1978. "A Sociology of Emotions: Some Problems and Some Solutions." *American Sociologist* 13 (February): 30–41.

Kenen, Regina. 1982. "Soapsuds, Space and Sociability." *Urban Life: A Journal of Ethnographic Research* 11 (July): 163–84.

Kerckhoff, A.C., and K.W. Back. 1968. *The June Bug: A Study of Hyterical Contagion.* New York: Appelton-Century-Crofts.

Killian, Lewis. 1952. "The Significance of Multiple-Group Membership in Disaster." *American Sociological Review* 57: 309–14.

Klockers, Carl B. 1974. *The Professional Fence*. New York: Free Press.

Kockmann, Thomas, ed. 1972. *Rappin' and Stylin' Out: Communication in Urban Black America.* Urbana: University of Illinois Press.

Kohlberg, Larry. 1969. *Stages in the Development of Moral Thought and Action*. New York: Holt, Rinehart and Winston.

Kolb, Deborah M. 1990. "To Be a Mediator: Expressive Tactics in Mediation." Pp. 317–32 in Dennis Brissett and Charles Edgley, eds. *Life as Theater: A Dramaturgical Source Book*. New York: Aldine de Gruyer.

Kornhauser, William. 1959. *The Politics of Mass Society*. Glencoe, Ill: Free Press of Glencoe.

Labov, William. 1970. "The Logic of Nonstandard English." Pp. 153–89 in Fredick Williams, ed. *Language and Poverty: Persepctives on a Theme*. Chicago: Markham.

———. 1974. The Art of Sounding and Signifying." Pp. 84–116 in William W. Gage, ed. *Language in Its Social Setting*. Washington, D.C.: Anthropological Association of Washington.

Laing, R.D. 1969. *The Politics of the Family*. New York: Harper and Row.

Lane, Harlan. 1976. *The Wild Boy of Averyron*. Cambridge, Mass: Havard University Press.

Lasch, Christopher. 1978. *The Culture of Narcissism*. New York: Norton.

Lefebrve, Henri. 1971. *Everyday Life in the Modern World.* New York: Harper and Row.

LeMasters. E.E. 1975. *Blue-Collar Aristocrats: Life Styles at a Working Class Tavern*. Madsion: University of Wisconsin Press.

Lemert, Charles. 1967. *Human Deviance, Social Problems and Social Control*. Englewood Cliffs, N.J.: Prentice Hall.

Lever, Janet. 1976. "Sex Differences in the Games Children Play." *Social Problems* 23 (April): 479–87.

Levi, Ken. 1981. "Becoming a Hit Man: Neutralization in a Very Deviant Career." *Urban Life: A Journal of Ethnographic Research* 10 (April): 47–63.

Lofland, John. 1980 (1965). *Doomsday Cult: A Study of Conversion, Proselytization and Maintenance of Faith*. Englewood Cliffs, N.J.: Prentice Hall.

———. "Collective Behavior: The Elementary Forms." Pp. 411–46 in Morris Rosenberg and Ralph Turner, eds. *Social Psychology: A Sociological Perspective*. New York: Basic Books.

———. 1982. "Crowd Joy." *Urban Life: A Journal of Ethnographic Research* 10 (January): 355–82.

Lofland, John, and Lyn Lofland. 1987. *Analyzing Social Settings*. Belmont, Calif.: Wadsworth.

Lofland, John, and Rodney Stark. 1965. "Becoming a World Saver: A Theory of Conversion to a Deviant Perspective." *American Sociological Review* 30 (December): 862–74.

Lofland, Lyn, 1985. *World of Strangers: Order and Action in Urban Public Space*. Prospect Heights, Ill.: Waveland Press.

———. 1989. "Social Life in the Public Realm: A Review." *Journal of Contemporary Ethnography* 18: 453–82.

Lorenz, Knorad. 1963. *On Aggression*. New York: Harcourt, Brace and World.

Luckmann, Bentia. 1974. "The Small Life-Worlds of Modern Man." Pp. 275–90 in Thomas Luckmann, ed. *Phenomenology and Sociology*. New York: Penguin Books.

Luker, Kristen. 1984. *Abortion and the Politics of Motherhood*. Berkeley: University of California Press.

Lyman, Stanford M. 1989. *The Seven Deadly Sins: Society and Evil*. Dix Hills, N.Y.: General Hall.

Lyman, Stanford and Marvin Scott. 1989. *A Sociology of the Absurd*. 2nd ed. Dix Hills, N.Y.: General Hall.

McCall, Michal M., and Judith Wittner. 1990. "The Good News about Life History." Pp. 3–89 in Howard S. Becker and Michal M. McCall, eds. *Symbolic Interaction and Cultural Studies*. Chicago: University of Chicago Press.

MacCannel, Dean. 1976. *The Tourist: A New Theory of the Leisure Class*. New York: Schocken Books.

McLuhan, Marshall. 1964. *Understanding Media: The Extensons of Man*. New York: McGraw-Hill.

Mannhein, Karl. 1938. *Ideology and Utopia*. New York: Harcourt, Brace.

Mayo, Elton. 1933. *Human Problems of Industrial Civilization*. New York: Harcourt, Brace.

Mead, George Herbert. 1899. "The Working Hypothesis in Social Reform." *American Journal of Sociology* 5: 367–71.

————. 1936. *Mind, Self and Society*. Chicago: University of Chicago Press.

————. 1964. "The Genesis of the Self and Social Control." Pp. 267–93 in *Selected Writings of George Herbert Mead*. A.J. Reck, ed. New York: Bobbs-Merrill.

Mechanic, David. 1961. "Stress, Illness Behavior and the Sick Role." *American Sociological Review* 28: 51–58.

Meehan, Albert J. 1992. "I Don't Prevent Crime, I Prevent Calls: Policing as a Negotiated Order," *Symbolic Interaction* 15 (4): 455–80.

Mehan, Hugh. 1976. "De-Secting Ethnomethodology." *American Sociologist* 11 (February): 13–21.

Mehan, Hugh, and Houston Wood. 1975. *The Reality of Ethnomethodology*. New York: Academic Press.

Melbin, Murray. 1987. *Night as Frontier: Colonizing the World After Dark*. New York: Free Press.

Merleau-Ponty, Maurice. 1964. "The Child's Relations with Others." In Jame L. Edie, ed. *The Primacy of Perception*. Evanston: Northwestern University Press.

Merton, Robert K. 1963. *Social Theory and Social Structure*. Glencoe, Ill.: Free Press of Glencoe.

Messner, Michael, and Don F. Sabo, eds. 1990. *Sport, Men and The Gender Order: Critical Feminist Perspectives*. Champaign, Ill.: Human Kinetics Book.

Mills, C. Wright. 1940. "Situated Actions and a Vocabulary of Motives." *American Sociological Review* 5: 904–13.

Modigliani, Andre. 1971. "Embarrassment, Facework and Eye Contact." *Journal of Personality and Social Psychology* 17: 15–25.

Morris, Monica B. 1977. *An Excursion Into Creative Sociology*. New York: Columbia University Press.

Musolf, Gil Richard. 1993. "Some Recent Directions in Symbolic Interactionism." Pp. 231–83 in Larry T. Reynolds, ed. *Interactionism: Exposition and Critique*. Dix Hills, N.Y.: General Hall, Inc.

Myiamoto, Frank S., and Sanford M. Dornbusch. 1956. "A Test of Interactionist Hypotheses of Self-Conception." *American Journal of Sociology* 61: 399–403.

Nash, Jeffrey E. 1975. "Bus Riding: Community of Wheels." *Urban Life: A Journal of Ethnographic Research* 4 (April): 99–124.

————. 1976. "The Short and Long of It: Legitimizing Motives for Running." Pp. 16181 in Jeffrey E. Nash and James P. Spradley, eds., *Sociology: A Descriptive Approach*. Chciago: Rand McNally.

————. 1977. "Decoding the Runner's Wardrobe." Pp. 172–85 in James P. Spradley and David W. McCurdy, eds., *Conformity and Conflict*. 3rd ed. Boston: Little Brown.

————. 1981. "Relations in Frozen Places: Observations on Winter Public Order." *Qualitative Sociology* 3 (Fall): 229–43.

————. 1982. "The Family Camps Out: A Study in Nonverbal Communication." *Semiotica* 39 (3/4): 331–41.

————. 1989 "What's in a Face? The Social Character of the English Bulldog." *Qualitative Sociology* 12(4): 357–70.

Nash, Jeffrey E. and Eric Lerner. 1981. "Learning from the Pros: Violence in Youth Hockey." *Youth and Society* 13 (December): 229–44.

Nash, Jeffrey E., and Anedith Nash. 1994 "The Skyway System and Urban Space: Vitality in Enclosed Public Places." In Spencer Cahill and Lyn Lofland, eds. *The Community of the Streets*. Special Supplement to Research in Community Sociology. Greenwich, Conn.: JAI Press.

Nash, Jeffrey. E., and Anne Sutherland. 1991. "The Moral Elevation of Animals: The Case of Gorillas in the Mist." *International Journal of Politics, Culture and Society* 5 (1): 111–26.

Natanson, Maurice. 1956. *The Social Dynamics of George Herbert Mead*. Washington, DC: Public Affairs Press.

Nelson, Margrette L., and Carol L. Jorgenen. 1975. "The Green Bag: The Uses of Ambiguity in Eliciting Covert Cultural Assumptions." *Human Organization* 34 (Spring): 51–61.

Ogles, Richard H. 1980. "Concept Formation in Sociology: The Ordering of Observational Data by Observational Concepts." Pp. 143–74 in Lee Freese, ed. *Theoretical Methods in Sociology: Seven Essays*. Pittsburgh: University of Pittsburgh Press.

Oldenberg, Ray. 1989. *The Great Good Place*. New York: Paragon House.

O'Neill, John. 1973. "Embodiment and Child Development: A Phenomenological Approach." Pp. 65–84. in Hans Peter Dreitzel, ed. *Recent Sociology*. New York: Macmillan.

Ortega y Gasset, José. 1973. *Man and People*. New York: Norton.

Parsons, Talcott. 1971. *The System of Modern Society*. Englewood Cliffs, N.J.: Prentice Hall.

Perinbanayagam. R.S. 1992. *Discursive Acts*. New York: Aldine de Gruyter.

Phillips, Davis P. 1983. "The Impact of Mass Media Violence on U.S. Homicides." *American Sociological Review* 48 (August): 560–68.

Pierce, C.S. 1958. "Questions Concerning Certain Faculties Claimed for Man." *Journal of Speculative Philosophy*, 2: 103–44.

Plutzer, Eric. 1988. "Women's Support for Feminism." *American Sociological Review* 53: 64049.

Psathas, George. 1973. "Introduction." Pp. 1–21 in George Psathas, ed. *Phenomenological Sociology: Issues and Applications*. New York: Wiley.

Regan, Tom. 1983. *The Case for Animal Rights*. Berkeley: The University of California Press.

Reisman, David. 1950. *The Lonely Crowd: A Study of Changing American Character*. New Haven: Yale University Press.

Reynolds, Larry T. 1993. *Interactionism: Exposition and Critique*. Dix Hills, N.Y.: General Hall.

Riemer, Jeffrey W. 1979. "Work Setting and Behavior: An Empirical Examination of Building Construction Work." *Symbolic Interaction* 2 (Fall): 131–51.

Rosenthal, R. 1968. *Experimenter Effects in Behavioral Research*. New York: Appleton-Century-Crofts.

Rosenthal, R., and L. Jacobsen. 1968. *Pygmalion in the Classroom*. New York: Holt, Rinehart and Winston.

Rosow, Irving. 1966. "Forms and Functions of Adult Socialization." *Social Forces* :35–45.

Rothe, J. Peter. 1994. *Beyond Traffic Safety*. New Brunswick, N.J.: Transaction.

Rowan, A.N. 1988. "The Power of Animal Symbols and Its Implications." In *Animals and People Sharing the World*. Hanover and London: University Press of New England.

Ryder, R.D. 1989. *Animal Revolution: Changing Attitudes towards Speciesism*. Oxford: Basil Blackwell.

Sacks, Harvey. 1972a. "An Intial Investigation of the Usability of Conversational Data for Doing Sociology." Pp. 31–74 in David Sudnow, ed., *Studies in Social Interaction*. New York: Free Press.

———. 1972b. "Notes on the Police Assessment of Moral Character." Pp. 28093 in David Sudnow, ed., *Studies in Social Interaction*. New York: Free Press.

———. 1975. "Everybody Has to Lie." Pp. 57–80. In Mary Sanches and Ben C. Blount, eds., *Sociocultural Dimensions of Language Use*. New York: Academic Press.

Schegloff, Emmanuel, and Harvey Sacks. 1973. "Opening up Closing." *Semiotica* 8: 289–327.

Schien, E.H., I. Schneier, and C.H. Barker. 1961. *Coercive Persuasion*. New York: Norton.

Schutz, Alfred. 1971. *Collected Papers II: Studies in Social Theory*. The Hague: Martinus Nijhoff.

Schwartzman, Helen B. 1993. *Ethnography in Organizations*. Newbury Park, Calif.: Sage.

Schwendinger, Herman, and Julia R. Schwendinger. 1974. *The Sociologists of the Chair: A Radical Analysis of the Formative Years of North American Sociology 1883–1922*. New York: Basic Books.

Scott, Marvin, and Stanford Lyman 1968. "Accounts." *American Sociological Review* 33, (1): 46–62.

Scott, Marvin, and Stanford Lyman, 1989. "Coolness in Everyday Life." In Lyman and Scott, *A Sociology of the Absurd*. Dix Hills N.Y.: General Hall.

Shalin, Dimitri N. 1991. "G.H. Mead, Socialism and the Progressive Agenda." Pp. 21–56 in *Philosophy, Social Theory and the Thought of George Herbert Mead*, Mitchell Aboulafia, ed. Albany, N.Y.: SUNY Press.

Shibutani, Tamotsu. 1955. "Reference groups as perspectives." *American Journal of Sociology* 60: 562–69.

Shotland, R. Lance, and Lynne Goodstein. 1983. "Just Because She Doesn't Want to Doesn't Mean It's Rape: An Experimentlly Based Causal Model of Perception of Rape in a Dating Situation." *Social Psychologcial Quarterly* 46 (September): 220–32.

Shott, Sue. 1979. "Emotions and Social Life: A Symbolic Interactionism Analysis." *American Journal of Sociology* 84:317–34.

Simmel, Georg. 1971. *Georg Simmel on Individuality and Social Forms*. Chicago: University of Chicago Press.

Singer, Peter. 1975. *Animal Liberation: A New Ethics for Our Treatment of Animals*. New York: Avon Books.

Smelser, Neil J. 1963. *Theory of Collective Behavior*. New York: Free Press.

Smith, Dorothy E. 1987. *The Everyday World as Problematic: A Feminist Sociology*. Boston: Northeastern University Press.

Snow, David, and Leon Anderson. 1993. *Down on Their Luck: A Study of Homeless Street People*. Berkeley: University of California Press.

Sorkin, Michael, ed. 1992. *Variation on a Theme Park: The New American City and the End of Public Space*. New York: Hill and Wang.

Speier, Matthew. 1973. *How to Observe Face-to-Face Communication: A Sociological Introduction*. Palisades, Calif.: Goodyear.

Spilerman, S. 1976. "Structural Characteristics of Cities and the Severity of Racial Disorder." *American Sociological Review* 35: 627–49.

Spradley, James P. 1988. *You Owe Yourself a Drunk: An Ethnography of Urban Nomads*. New York: University Press of America.

Stebbins, Robert D. 1969. "Studying the Definition of the Situation: Theory and Field Research Strategies." *Canadian Review of Sociology* 6: 193–211.

Stone, Gregory P. 1962. "Appearance and the Self." Pp. 86–118 in Arnold M. Rose, ed., *Human Behavior and Social Processes*. Boston: Houghton Mifflin.

Stouffer, Samuel A., et al. 1949. *The American Solider: Adjustment During Army Life*. New York: Wiley.

Strauss, Murray A. 1973. "A General Systems Theory Appraoch to the Development of a Theory of Violence Between Family Members." *Social Science Information* 12 (June): 105–25.

Stryker, Sheldon. 1979. "The Profession: Comments form an Interactionist's Perspective." *Sociological Focus* 12: 175–86.

Sudnow, David. 1978. *Ways of the Hand: The Organization of Improvised Conduct*. Cambridge: Harvard University Press.

Sugrue, Noreen. 1982. "Emotions as Property and Context for Negotiation." *Urban Life* 11 (October):280–92.

Sutherland, Anne and Jeffrey E. Nash. 1994. "Animals Rights as a New Envirnomental Cosmology." *Qualitative Sociology.*17:171–185.

Sutherland, Edward. 1935. *The Professional Thief.* Chicago: University of Chicago Press.

Suttles, Gerald D. 1968. *The Social Order of the Slum.* Chicago: University of Chicago Press.

Sykes, G., and David Matza. 1959. "Techniques of Neutralization." *American Sociological Review* 22: 664–70.

Szasz, Thomas S. 1961. *The Myth of Mental Illness.* New York: Harper and Row.

Tapper, R. 1988. "Animality, Humanity, Morality, Society." In T. Ingold, ed., *What Is an Animal?* London: Unwin Hyman.

Tester, K. 1991. *Animals and Society: The Humanity of Animal Rights.* New York: Routledge.

Toennies, Ferdinand. 1940. *Fundamental Conceptions of Sociology.* New York: American Book Company.

Turner, Ralph. 1983. "Figure and Ground in the Analysis of Social Movements." *Symbolic Interaction* 6 (Fall): 175–81.

Vaz, Edmund W. 1982. *The Professionalization of Young Hockey Players.* Lincoln: University of Nebraska Press.

Wagner, Helmut R., ed. 1970. *Alfred Schutz: On Phenomenology and Social Relations.* Chicago: University of Chicago Press.

Walum, Laurel Richardson. 1974. "The Changing Door Ceremony: Notes on the Operation of Sex Roles." *Urban Life and Culture* 2: 506–15.

Weber, Max. 1958. *The Protestant Ethic and the Spirit of Capitalism.* New York: Scribner.

Weigert, Andrew J. 1975. "Alfred Schutz on a Theory of Motivation." *Pacific Sociological Review* 18 (January): 183–206.

———. 1981. *Sociology of Everyday Life.* New York: Longman.

———. 1983a. "Identity: Its Emergence within Sociological Psychology." *Symbolic Interaction* 16 (2): 183–206.

———. 1983b. *Social Psychology: A Sociological Appraoch through Interpretive Understanding.* Notre Dame: University of Notre Dame Press.

Welsh, John F. 1990. "Dramaturgy and Political Mystification: Political Life in the United States." Pp. 399–410 in Dennis Brissett and Charles Edgley, eds., *Life as Theater: A Dramaturgical Source Book.* New York: Aldine de Gruyer.

Werthman, Carl. 1969. "Delinquency and Moral Character." In Donald Cressey and David Ward, eds., *Delinquency, Crime and Social Process.* New York: Harper and Row.

West, Candice and Don Zimmerman. 1977. "Women's Place in Everday Talk: Reflections on Parent-Child Interaction." *Social Problems* 24: 144–72.

———. 1983. "Small Insults: A Study of Interruptions in Cross-sex Conversations between Unacquainted Persons." Pp. 103–18 in B. Thorne, et al., eds., *Language, Gender and Society.* Rowely, Mass.: Newbury House.

Wexler, Philip. 1990 "Citizenship in the Semiotic Society." Pp. 164–75 in Bryan S. Turner, ed., *Theories of Modernity and Postmodernity.* Newbury Park, Calif.: Sage.

Wieder, D. Lawrence. 1975. *Language and Social Reality: The Case of Telling the Convict Code.* The Hague: Mouton.

Williams, Robin. 1980. "Goffman's Sociology of Talk." Pp. 210–36 in Jason Ditton, ed., *The View from Goffman.* New York: St. Martin's Press.

Wilson, James Q. 1975. *Thinking About Crime.* New York: Basic Books.

Wilson, William Julius. 1987. *The Truly Disadvantaged: The Inner City, the Underclass, and Public Policy.* Chicago: University of Chicago Press.

Whyte, William. H. 1978. *The Social Life of Small Urban Spaces*. Washington, D.C.: Conservation Foundation.

———. 1980 "The Humble Street." *Historical Preservation* , January/February, 376–81.

———. 1988. *City: Rediscovery of the Center*. New York: Doubleday.

Whyte, William F. 1981. *Street Corner Society*. 3rd ed. Chicago: University of Chicago Press.

Wright, Sam. 1978. *Crowds and Riots: A Study of Social Organization*. Beverly Hills, Calif.: Sage.

Zeitlin, Irving M. 1990. *Ideology and the Development of Sociological Theory*. 4th ed. Englewoods Cliffs, N.J.: Prentice Hall.

Zimbardo, Philip C., C. Haney, and W.C. Banks. 1973. "A Pirandellian Prison." *New York Times Magazine*.

Zurcker, Louis A. 1982. "The Staging of Emotion: A Dramaturgical Analysis." *Symbolic Interaction* 5 (Spring): 1–22.

INDEX

359